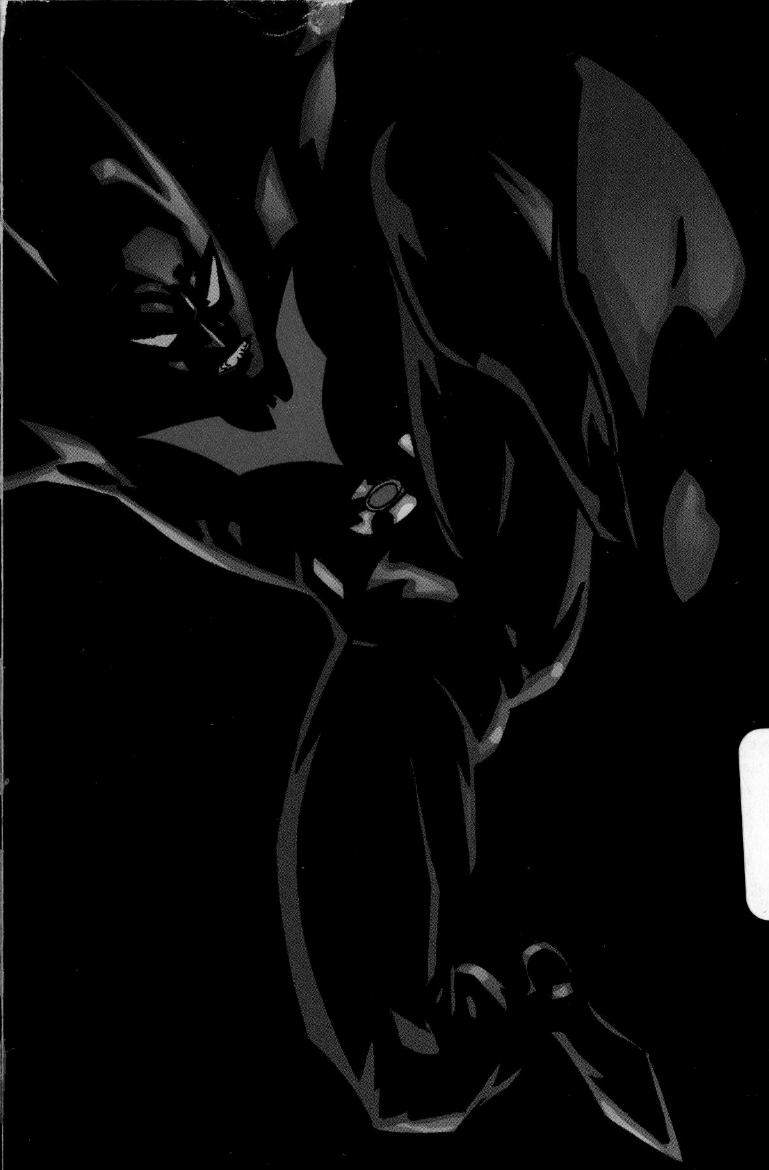

BATMAN
BEYOND
INDUSTRIAL
REVOLUTION

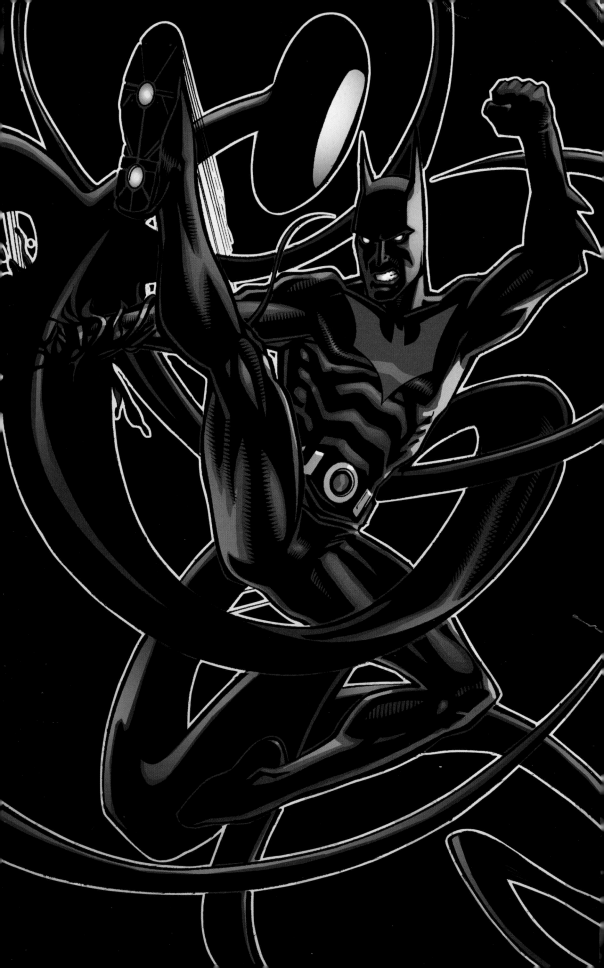

BATMAN BEYOND
INDUSTRIAL REVOLUTION

ADAM BEECHEN WRITER
RYAN BENJAMIN PENCILLER
JOHN STANISCI INKER

"LEGENDS OF THE DARK KNIGHT: MAX"
EDUARDO PANSICA PENCILLER
EBER FERREIRA INKER

"LEGENDS OF THE DARK KNIGHT: INQUE"
CHRIS BATISTA PENCILLER
RICH PERROTTA INKER

DAVID BARON COLORIST
SWANDS TRAVIS LANHAM LETTERERS
DUSTIN NGUYEN ORIGINAL SERIES COVERS
DARWYN COOKE COLLECTION COVER

BATMAN CREATED BY **BOB KANE**

BATMAN BEYOND: INDUSTRIAL REVOLUTION
Published by DC Comics. Cover and compilation Copyright © 2012 DC Comics. All Rights Reserved.

Originally published in single magazine form in BATMAN BEYOND 1-8. Copyright © 2011
DC Comics. All Rights Reserved. All characters, their distinctive likenesses and related elements
featured in this publication are trademarks of DC Comics. The stories, characters and incidents
featured in this publication are entirely fictional. DC Comics does not read or accept unsolicited
ideas, stories or artwork.

DC Comics, 1700 Broadway, New York, NY 10019
A Warner Bros. Entertainment Company.
Printed by RR Donnelley, Salem, VA, USA. 12/23/11. First Printing.
ISBN: 978-1-4012-3374-7

THE HEART OF THE MATTER PART 1: MADNESS, MAYHEM, & MENTACHEM

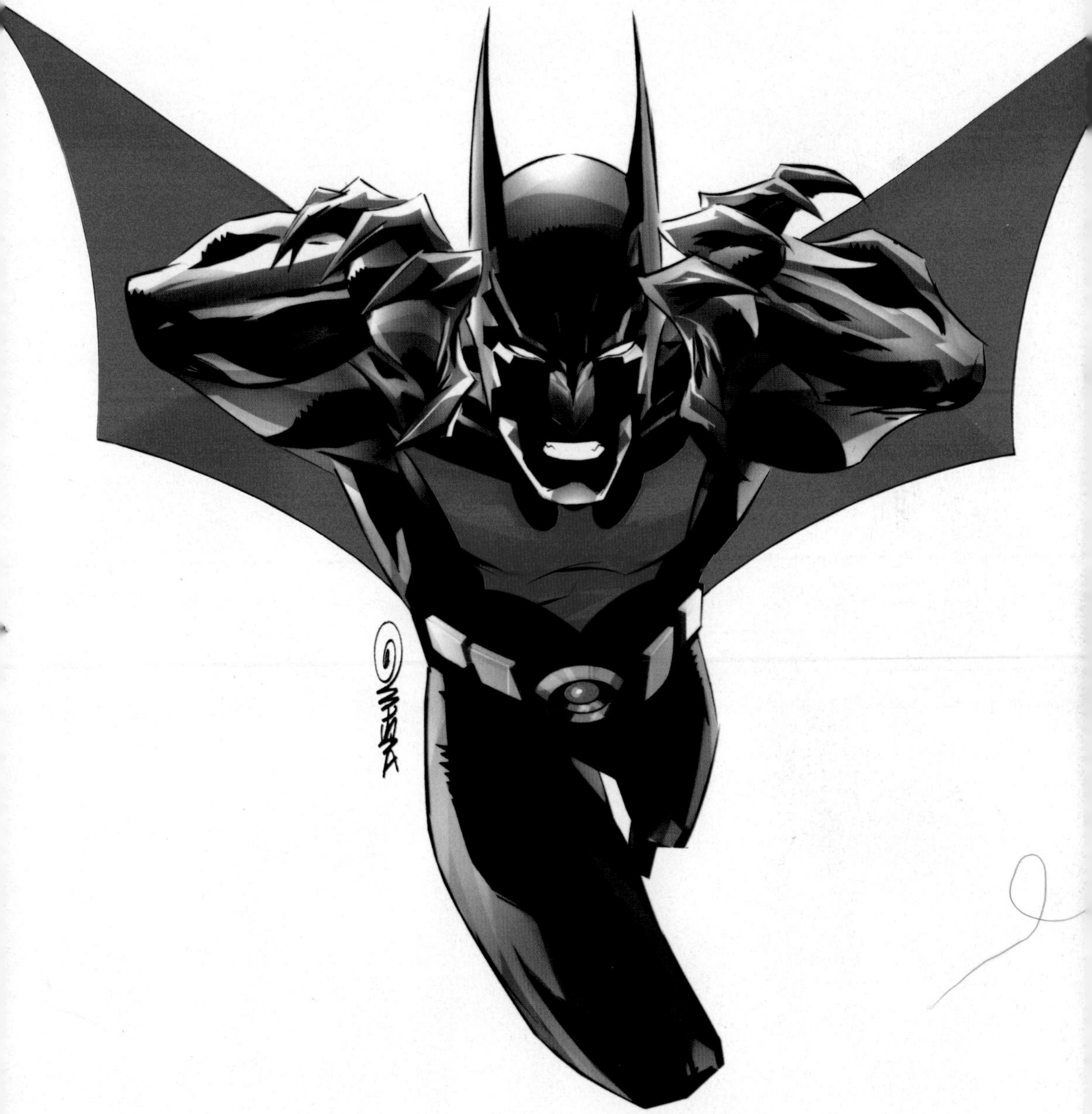

BATMAN BEYOND #1 VARIANT COVER BY DARWYN COOKE

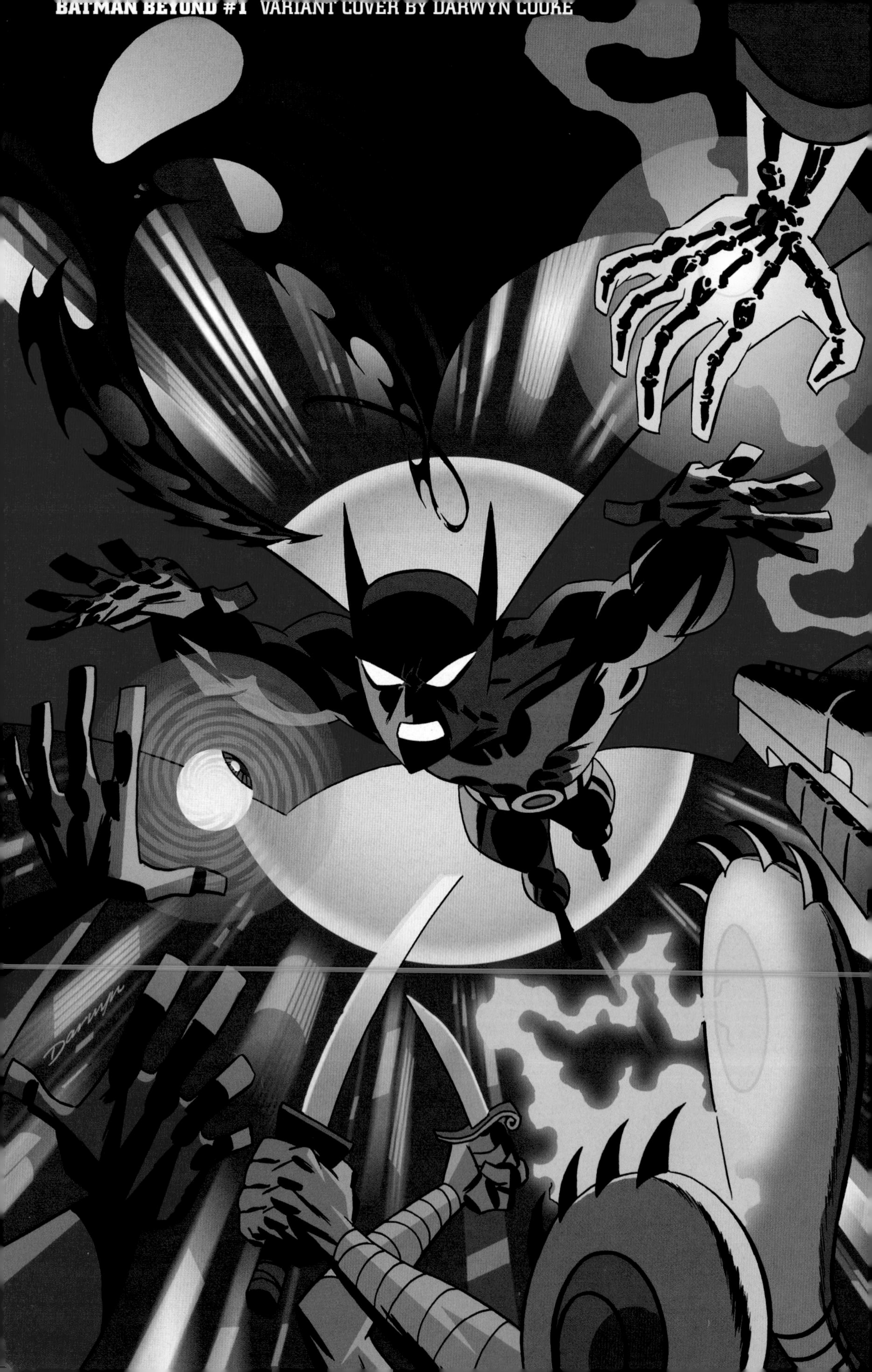
Darwyn

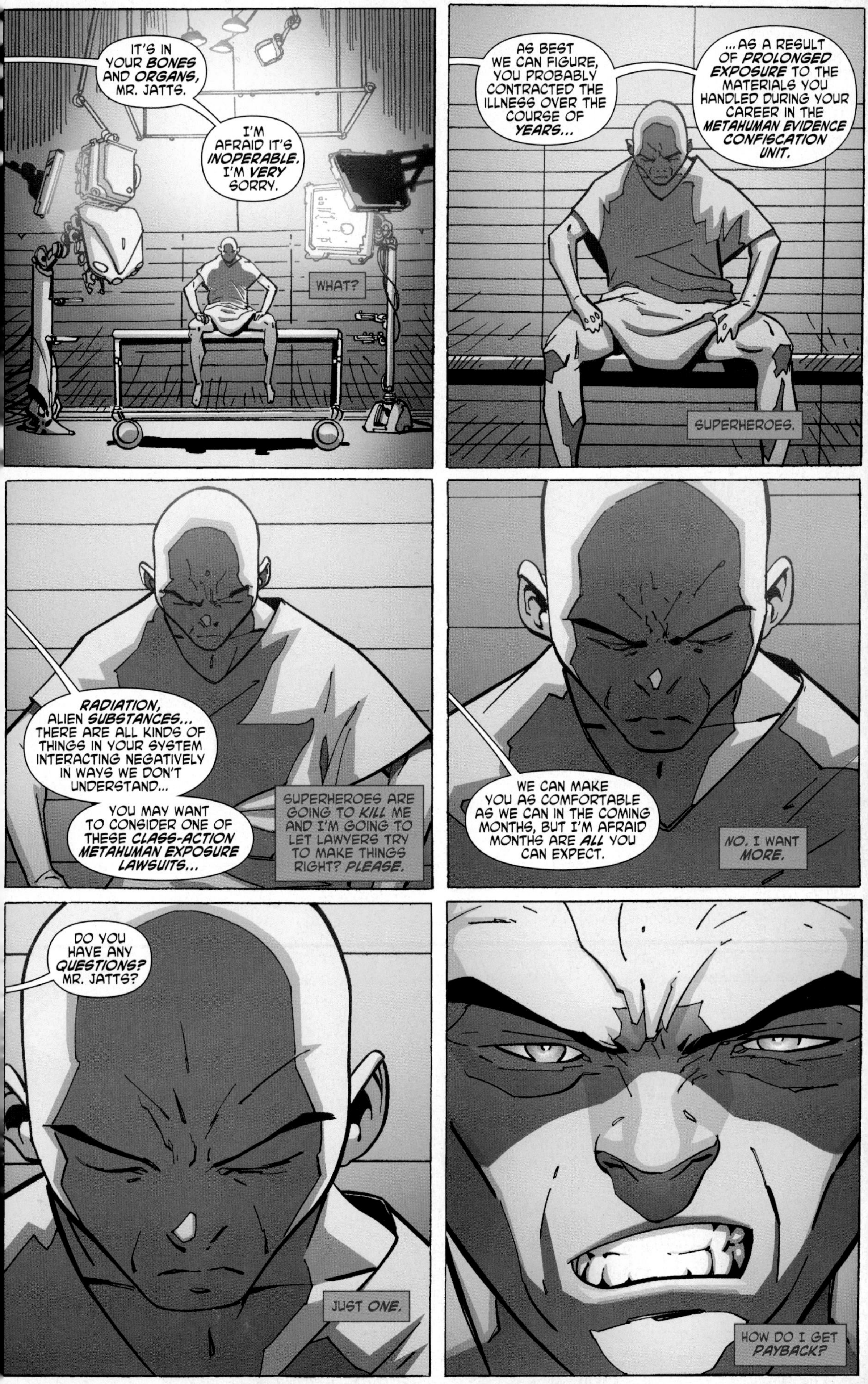
IT'S IN YOUR BONES AND ORGANS, MR. JATTS.
I'M AFRAID IT'S INOPERABLE. I'M VERY SORRY.
WHAT?
AS BEST WE CAN FIGURE, YOU PROBABLY CONTRACTED THE ILLNESS OVER THE COURSE OF YEARS...
...AS A RESULT OF PROLONGED EXPOSURE TO THE MATERIALS YOU HANDLED DURING YOUR CAREER IN THE METAHUMAN EVIDENCE CONFISCATION UNIT.
SUPERHEROES.
RADIATION, ALIEN SUBSTANCES... THERE ARE ALL KINDS OF THINGS IN YOUR SYSTEM INTERACTING NEGATIVELY IN WAYS WE DON'T UNDERSTAND...
YOU MAY WANT TO CONSIDER ONE OF THESE CLASS-ACTION METAHUMAN EXPOSURE LAWSUITS...
SUPERHEROES ARE GOING TO KILL ME AND I'M GOING TO LET LAWYERS TRY TO MAKE THINGS RIGHT? PLEASE.
WE CAN MAKE YOU AS COMFORTABLE AS WE CAN IN THE COMING MONTHS, BUT I'M AFRAID MONTHS ARE ALL YOU CAN EXPECT.
NO. I WANT MORE.
DO YOU HAVE ANY QUESTIONS? MR. JATTS?
JUST ONE.
HOW DO I GET PAYBACK?

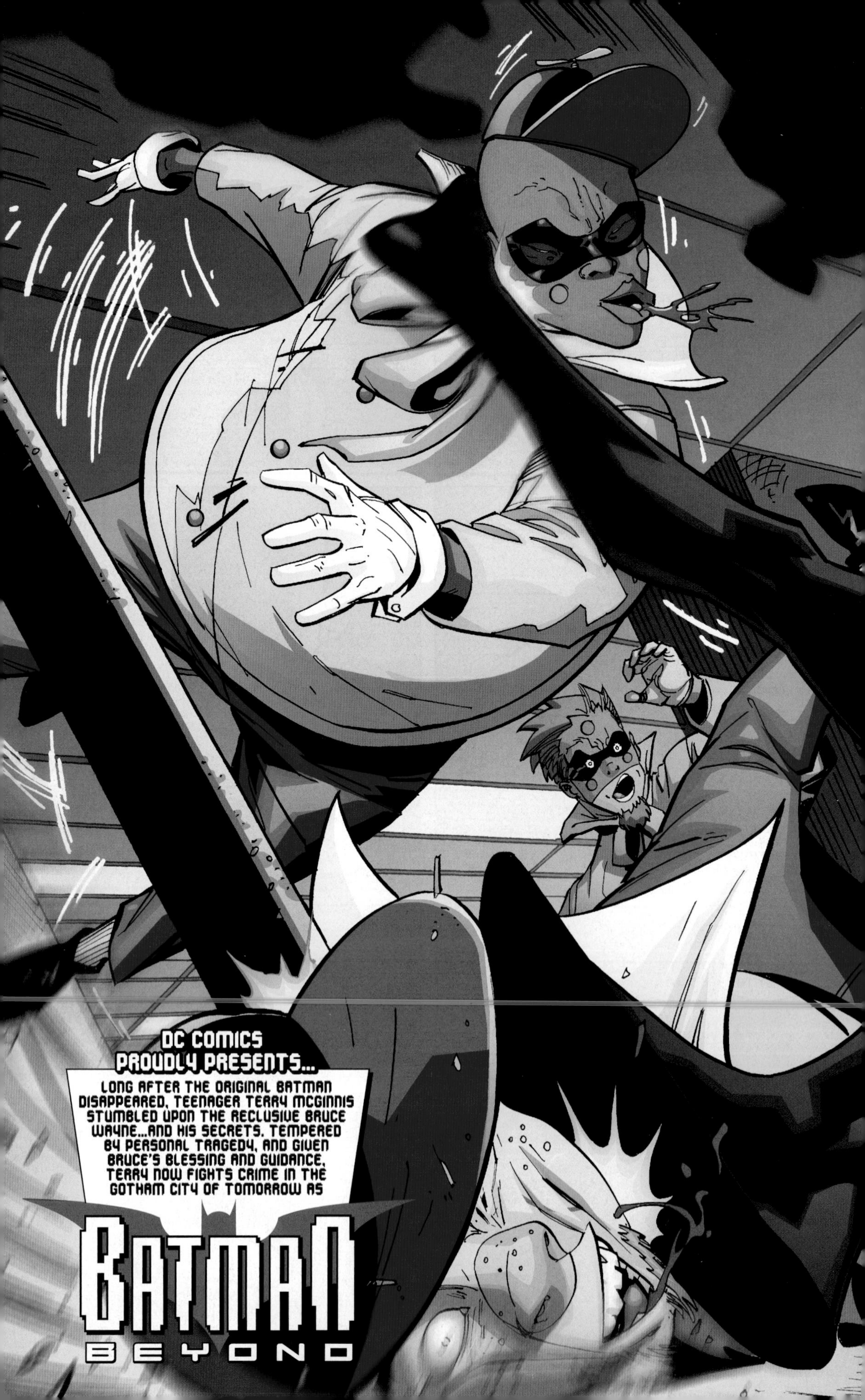
DC COMICS PROUDLY PRESENTS...
LONG AFTER THE ORIGINAL BATMAN DISAPPEARED, TEENAGER TERRY MCGINNIS STUMBLED UPON THE RECLUSIVE BRUCE WAYNE...AND HIS SECRETS. TEMPERED BY PERSONAL TRAGEDY, AND GIVEN BRUCE'S BLESSING AND GUIDANCE, TERRY NOW FIGHTS CRIME IN THE GOTHAM CITY OF TOMORROW AS
BATMAN BEYOND

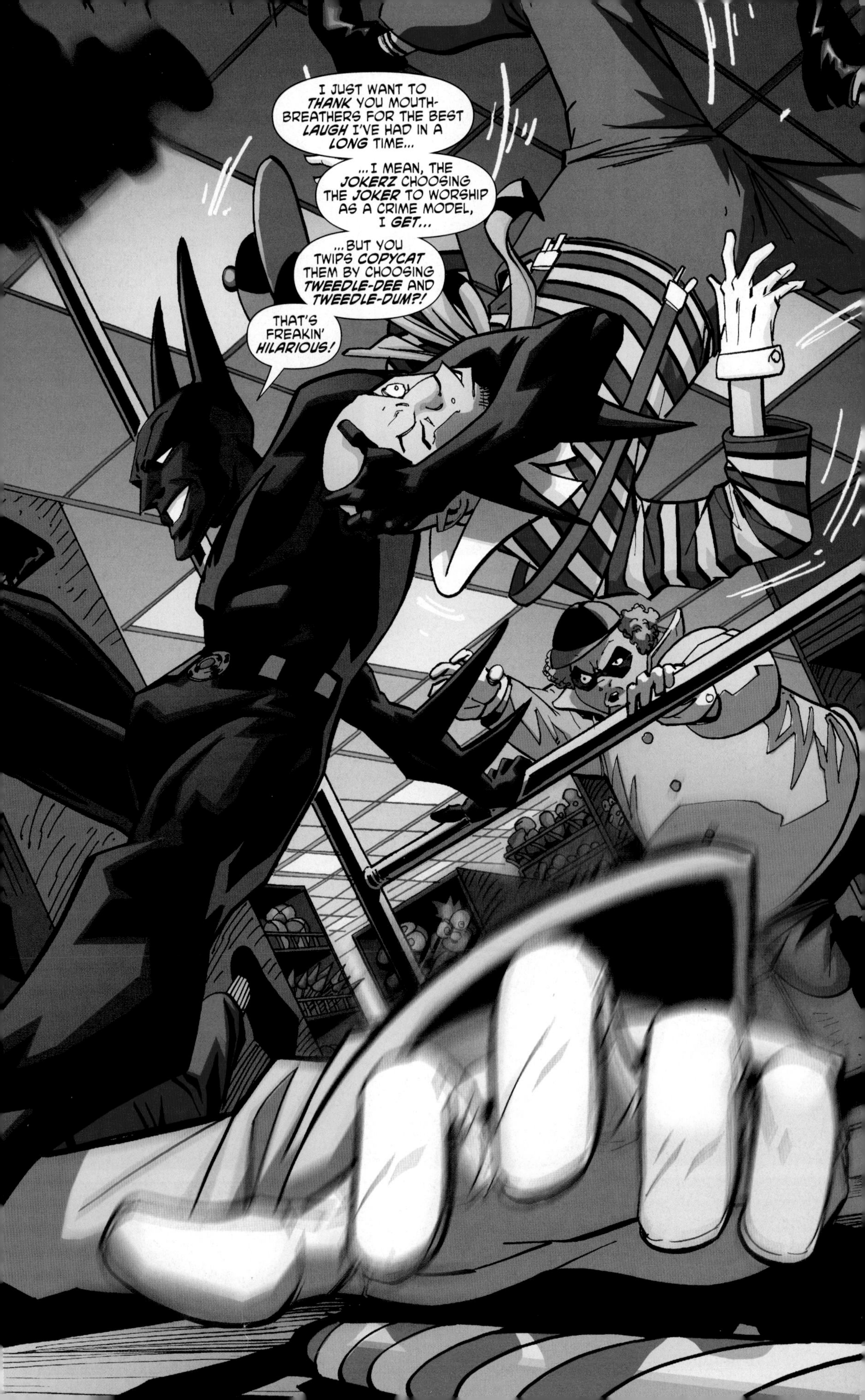
I JUST WANT TO THANK YOU MOUTH-BREATHERS FOR THE BEST LAUGH I'VE HAD IN A LONG TIME...
...I MEAN, THE JOKERZ CHOOSING THE JOKER TO WORSHIP AS A CRIME MODEL, I GET...
...BUT YOU TWIPS COPYCAT THEM BY CHOOSING TWEEDLE-DEE AND TWEEDLE-DUM?!
THAT'S FREAKIN' HILARIOUS!

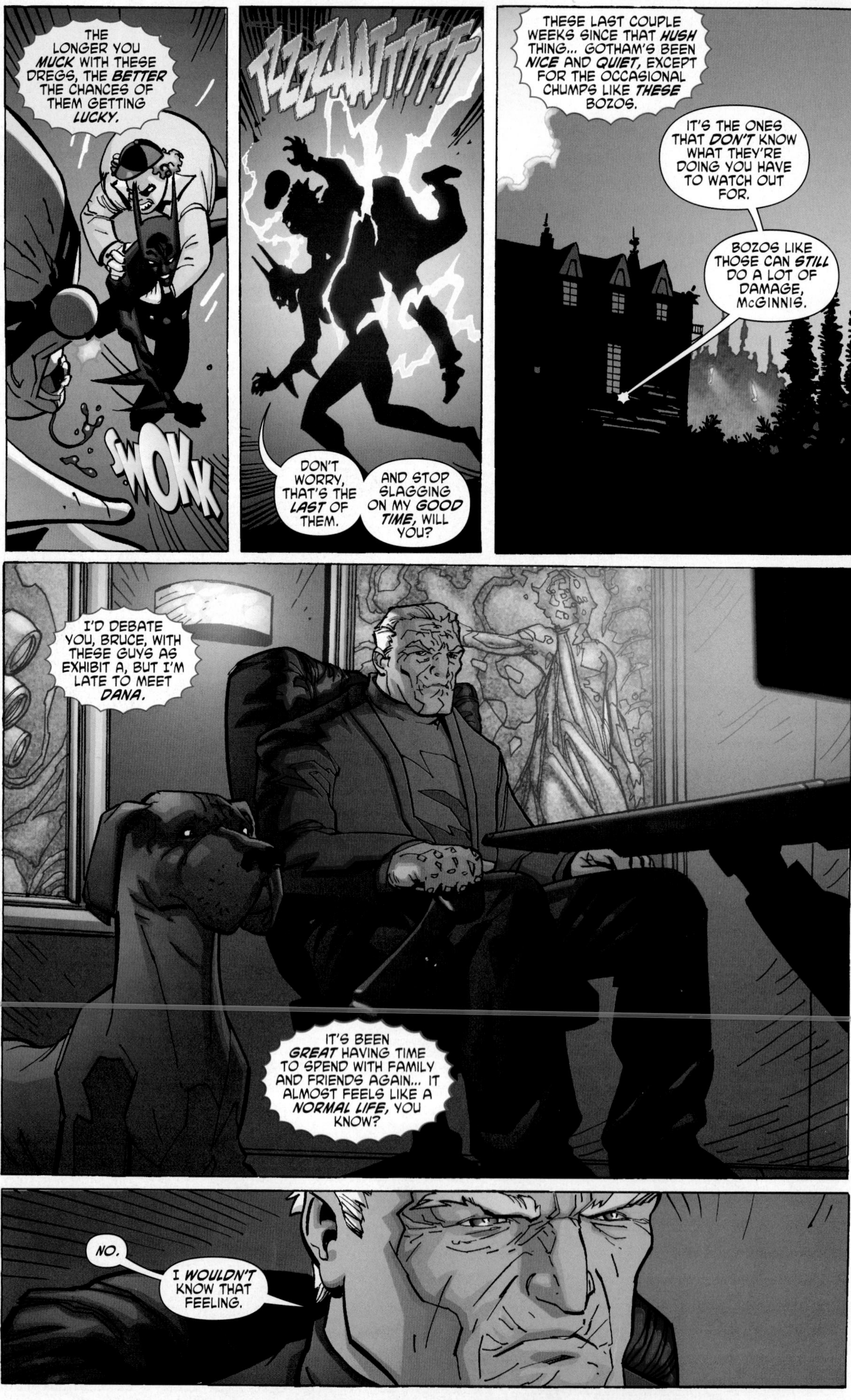
THE LONGER YOU MUCK WITH THESE DREGS, THE BETTER THE CHANCES OF THEM GETTING LUCKY.
SWOKK
TZZZZAAATTTTTT
DON'T WORRY, THAT'S THE LAST OF THEM.
AND STOP SLAGGING ON MY GOOD TIME, WILL YOU?
THESE LAST COUPLE WEEKS SINCE THAT HUSH THING... GOTHAM'S BEEN NICE AND QUIET, EXCEPT FOR THE OCCASIONAL CHUMPS LIKE THESE BOZOS.
IT'S THE ONES THAT DON'T KNOW WHAT THEY'RE DOING YOU HAVE TO WATCH OUT FOR.
BOZOS LIKE THOSE CAN STILL DO A LOT OF DAMAGE, McGINNIS.
I'D DEBATE YOU, BRUCE, WITH THESE GUYS AS EXHIBIT A, BUT I'M LATE TO MEET DANA.
IT'S BEEN GREAT HAVING TIME TO SPEND WITH FAMILY AND FRIENDS AGAIN... IT ALMOST FEELS LIKE A NORMAL LIFE, YOU KNOW?
NO.
I WOULDN'T KNOW THAT FEELING.

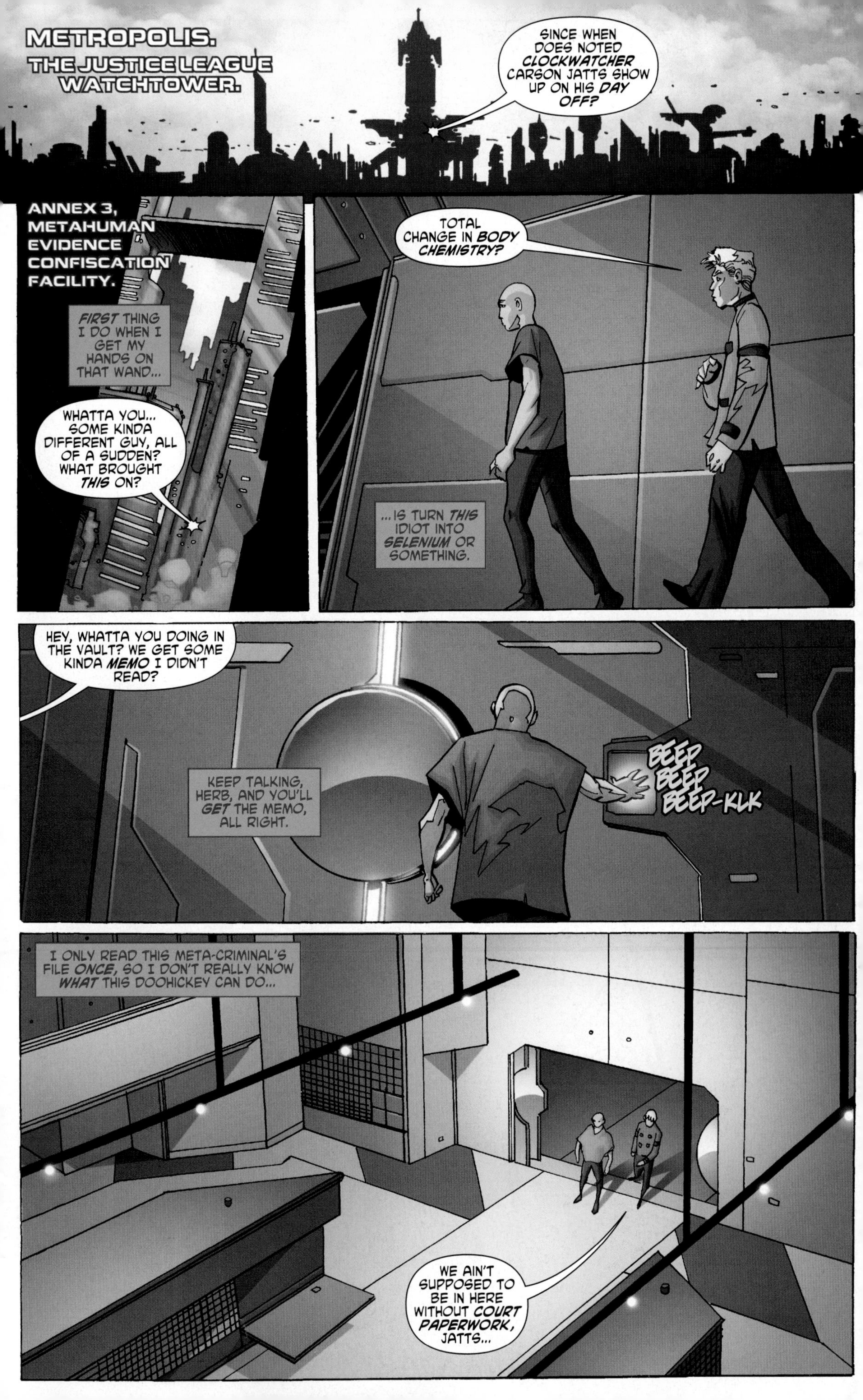
METROPOLIS.
THE JUSTICE LEAGUE WATCHTOWER.
SINCE WHEN DOES NOTED CLOCKWATCHER CARSON JATTS SHOW UP ON HIS DAY OFF?
ANNEX 3, METAHUMAN EVIDENCE CONFISCATION FACILITY.
FIRST THING I DO WHEN I GET MY HANDS ON THAT WAND...
WHATTA YOU... SOME KINDA DIFFERENT GUY, ALL OF A SUDDEN? WHAT BROUGHT THIS ON?
TOTAL CHANGE IN BODY CHEMISTRY?
...IS TURN THIS IDIOT INTO SELENIUM OR SOMETHING.
HEY, WHATTA YOU DOING IN THE VAULT? WE GET SOME KINDA MEMO I DIDN'T READ?
KEEP TALKING, HERB, AND YOU'LL GET THE MEMO, ALL RIGHT.
BEEP BEEP BEEP-KLK
I ONLY READ THIS META-CRIMINAL'S FILE ONCE, SO I DON'T REALLY KNOW WHAT THIS DOOHICKEY CAN DO...
WE AIN'T SUPPOSED TO BE IN HERE WITHOUT COURT PAPERWORK, JATTS...

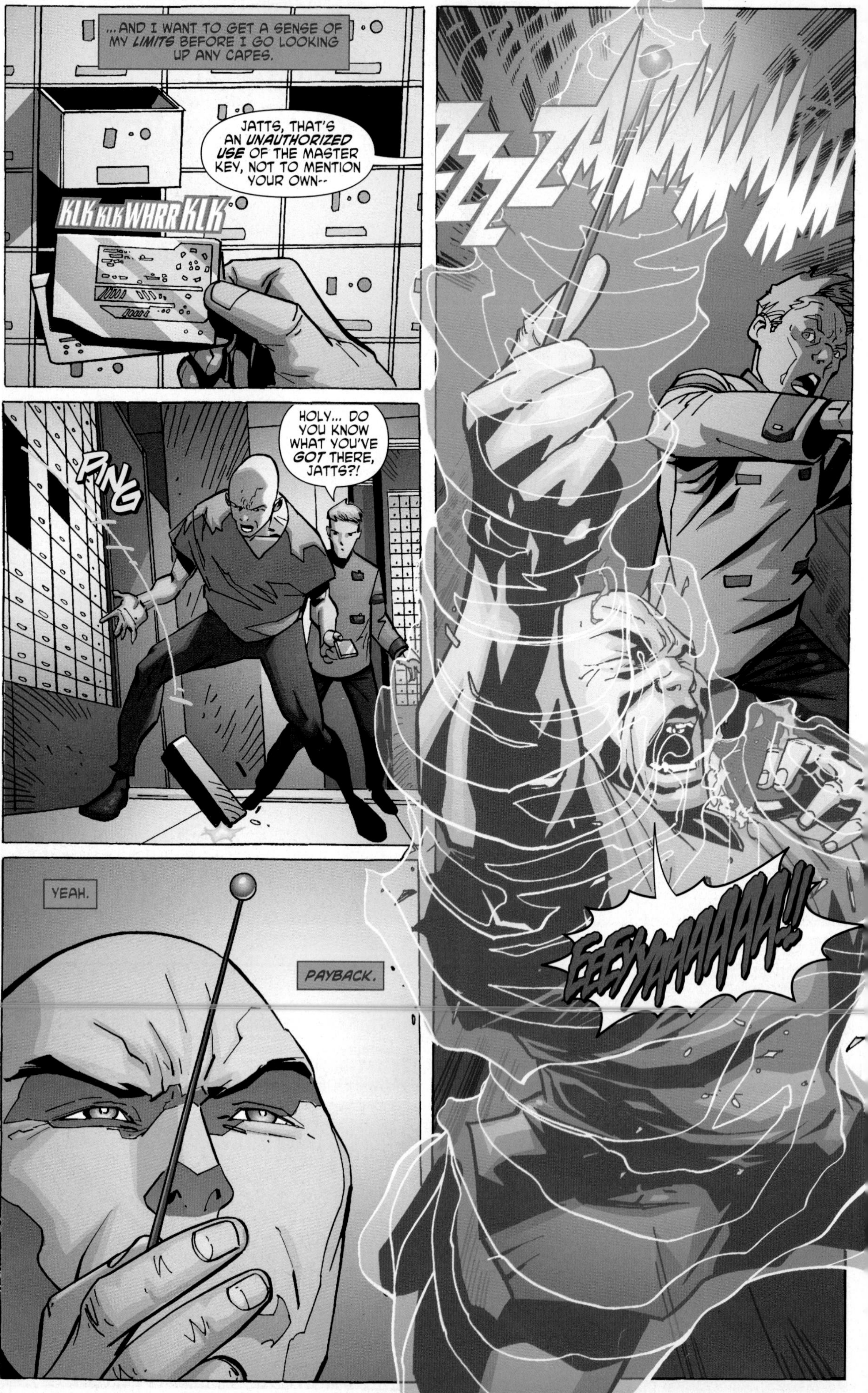
...AND I WANT TO GET A SENSE OF MY LIMITS BEFORE I GO LOOKING UP ANY CAPES.
JATTS, THAT'S AN UNAUTHORIZED USE OF THE MASTER KEY, NOT TO MENTION YOUR OWN--
KLK KLK WHRR KLK
HOLY... DO YOU KNOW WHAT YOU'VE GOT THERE, JATTS?!
PING
YEAH.
PAYBACK.
ZZZZAAMMMM
EEEYYAAAAAAA!!

JATTS...? YOU *OKAY*, MAN?

THE *WAND*... MUST'VE REACTED WITH ALL THE *CRAP* IN MY BODY...

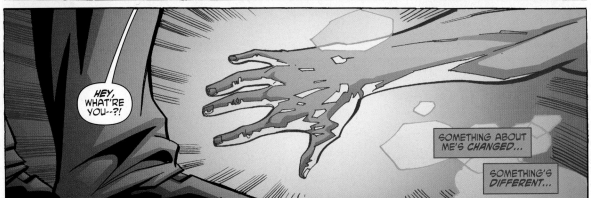

HEY, WHAT'RE YOU--?!

SOMETHING ABOUT ME'S *CHANGED*...

SOMETHING'S *DIFFERENT*...

LEAD.

I TURNED HIM INTO *LEAD*.

THIS... THIS *ISN'T* WHAT I WAS EXPECTING...

GOTTA GET *AWAY*... GOTTA *THINK*...

GOTTA GET *OUT* OF METROPOLIS BEFORE *THEY* COME AFTER ME... BEFORE I'M *READY*...

META HUMAN
EVIDENCE CONFISCATION FACILITY

ERRNT ERRNT ERRNT ERRNT ERRI

SECURITY BREACH

NOW, WHO WOULD BE *DUMB* ENOUGH TO DO SOMETHING LIKE *THIS*?!

DEPENDING ON WHAT'S BEEN *STOLEN*, FOR THE THIEF'S SAKE...

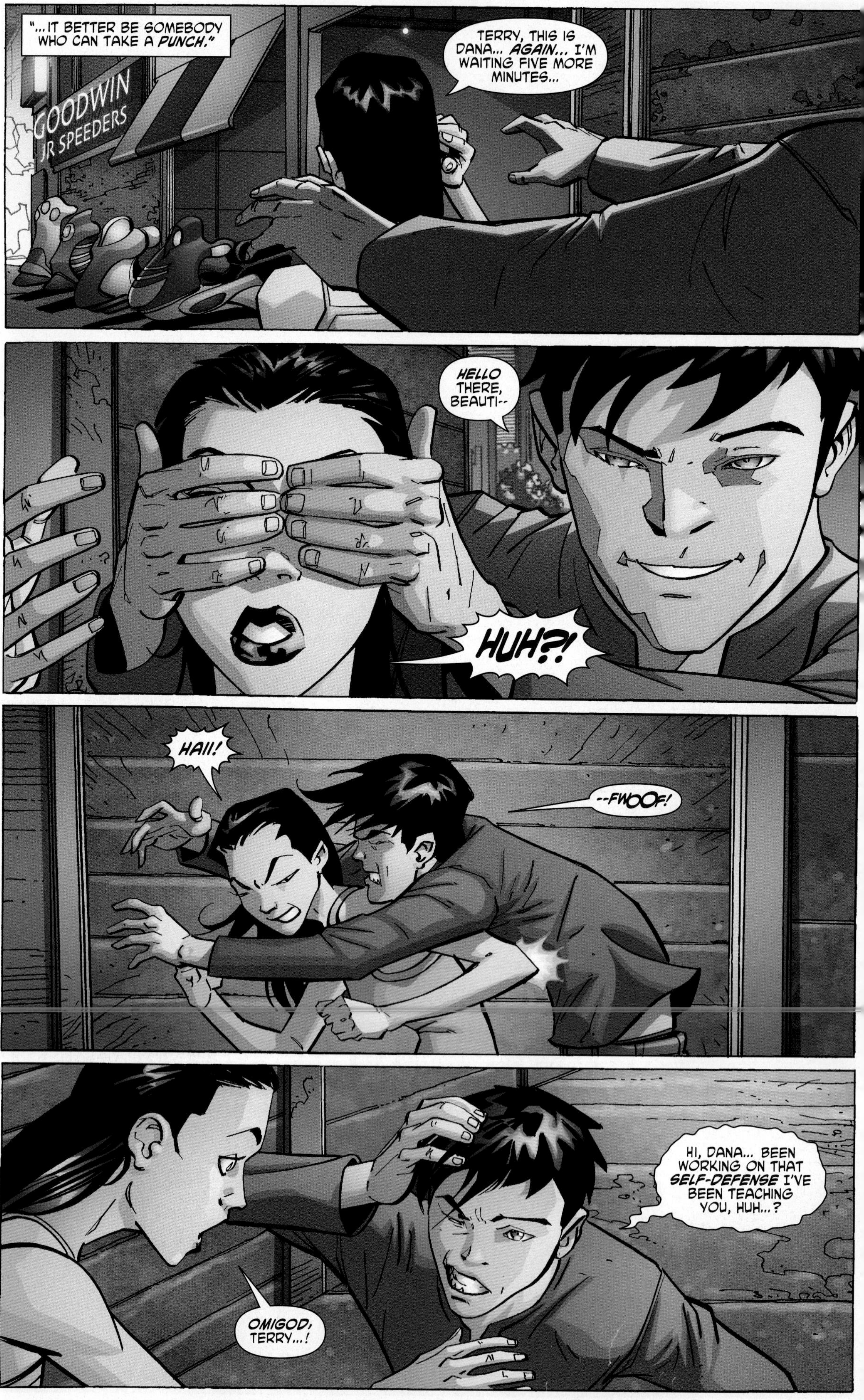
"...IT BETTER BE SOMEBODY WHO CAN TAKE A *PUNCH.*"
GOODWIN JR SPEEDERS
TERRY, THIS IS DANA... *AGAIN...* I'M WAITING FIVE MORE MINUTES...
HELLO THERE, BEAUTI--
HUH?!
HAII!
--FWOOF!
HI, DANA... BEEN WORKING ON THAT *SELF-DEFENSE* I'VE BEEN TEACHING YOU, HUH...?
OMIGOD, TERRY...!

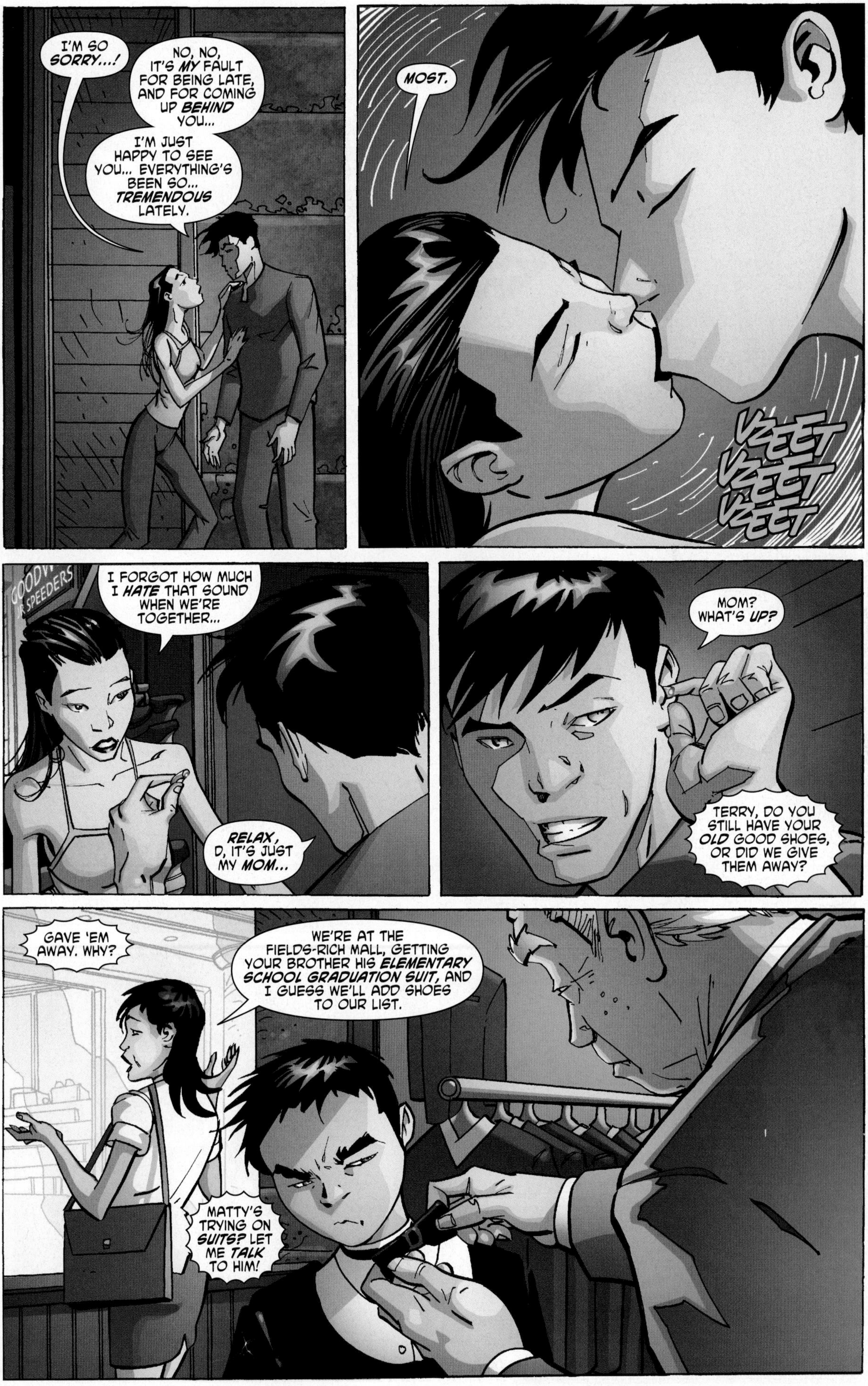
I'M SO SORRY...!
NO, NO, IT'S MY FAULT FOR BEING LATE, AND FOR COMING UP BEHIND YOU...
I'M JUST HAPPY TO SEE YOU... EVERYTHING'S BEEN SO... TREMENDOUS LATELY.
MOST.
VZEET VZEET VZEET
I FORGOT HOW MUCH I HATE THAT SOUND WHEN WE'RE TOGETHER...
RELAX, D, IT'S JUST MY MOM...
MOM? WHAT'S UP?
TERRY, DO YOU STILL HAVE YOUR OLD GOOD SHOES, OR DID WE GIVE THEM AWAY?
GAVE 'EM AWAY. WHY?
WE'RE AT THE FIELDS-RICH MALL, GETTING YOUR BROTHER HIS ELEMENTARY SCHOOL GRADUATION SUIT, AND I GUESS WE'LL ADD SHOES TO OUR LIST.
MATTY'S TRYING ON SUITS? LET ME TALK TO HIM!

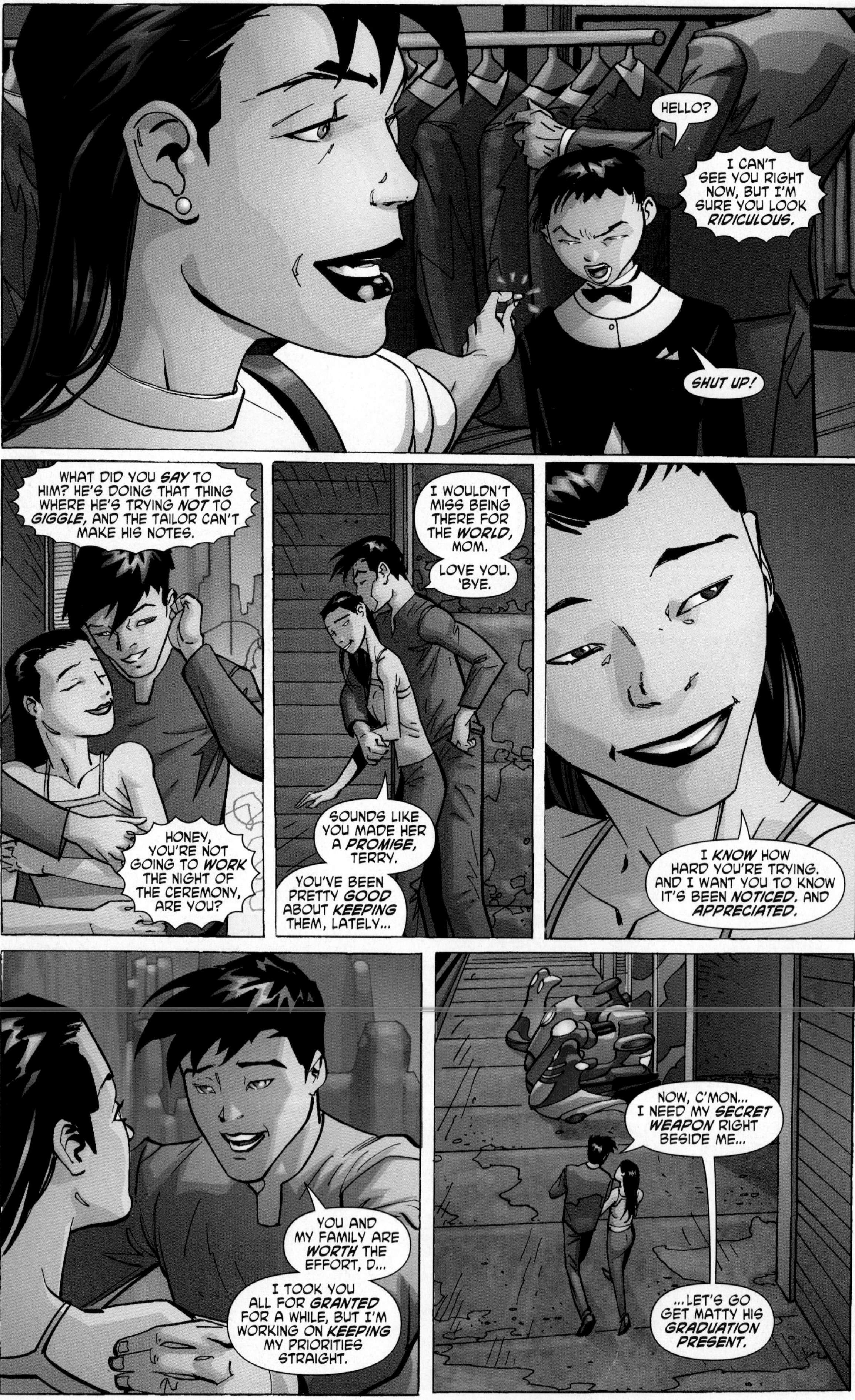
HELLO?
I CAN'T SEE YOU RIGHT NOW, BUT I'M SURE YOU LOOK RIDICULOUS.
SHUT UP!
WHAT DID YOU SAY TO HIM? HE'S DOING THAT THING WHERE HE'S TRYING NOT TO GIGGLE, AND THE TAILOR CAN'T MAKE HIS NOTES.
HONEY, YOU'RE NOT GOING TO WORK THE NIGHT OF THE CEREMONY, ARE YOU?
I WOULDN'T MISS BEING THERE FOR THE WORLD, MOM.
LOVE YOU. 'BYE.
SOUNDS LIKE YOU MADE HER A PROMISE, TERRY.
YOU'VE BEEN PRETTY GOOD ABOUT KEEPING THEM, LATELY...
I KNOW HOW HARD YOU'RE TRYING. AND I WANT YOU TO KNOW IT'S BEEN NOTICED. AND APPRECIATED.
YOU AND MY FAMILY ARE WORTH THE EFFORT, D...
I TOOK YOU ALL FOR GRANTED FOR A WHILE, BUT I'M WORKING ON KEEPING MY PRIORITIES STRAIGHT.
NOW, C'MON... I NEED MY SECRET WEAPON RIGHT BESIDE ME...
...LET'S GO GET MATTY HIS GRADUATION PRESENT.

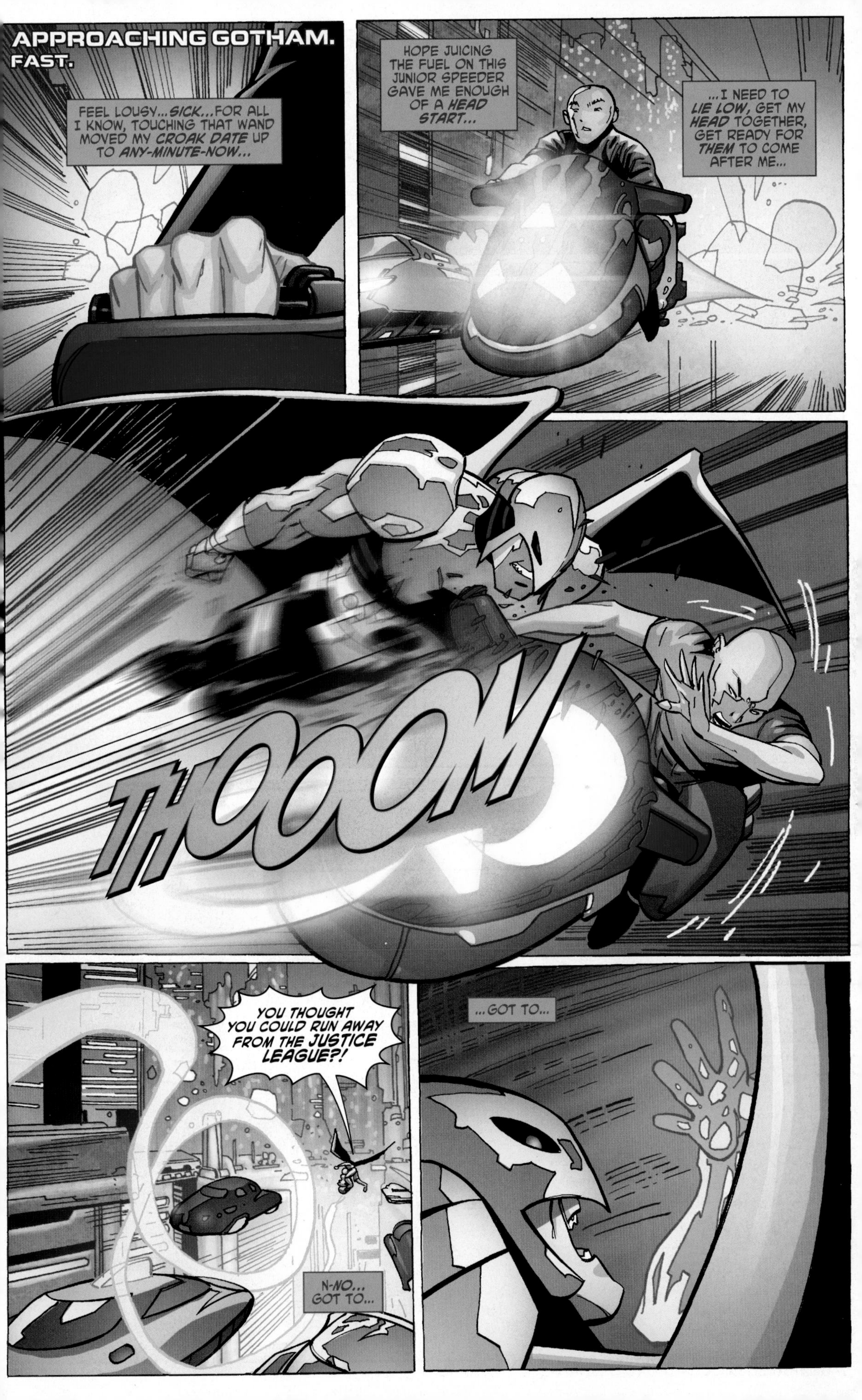
APPROACHING GOTHAM.
FAST.
FEEL LOUSY...SICK...FOR ALL I KNOW, TOUCHING THAT WAND MOVED MY CROAK DATE UP TO ANY-MINUTE-NOW...
HOPE JUICING THE FUEL ON THIS JUNIOR SPEEDER GAVE ME ENOUGH OF A HEAD START...
...I NEED TO LIE LOW, GET MY HEAD TOGETHER, GET READY FOR THEM TO COME AFTER ME...
THOOOM
YOU THOUGHT YOU COULD RUN AWAY FROM THE JUSTICE LEAGUE?!
N-NO... GOT TO...
...GOT TO...

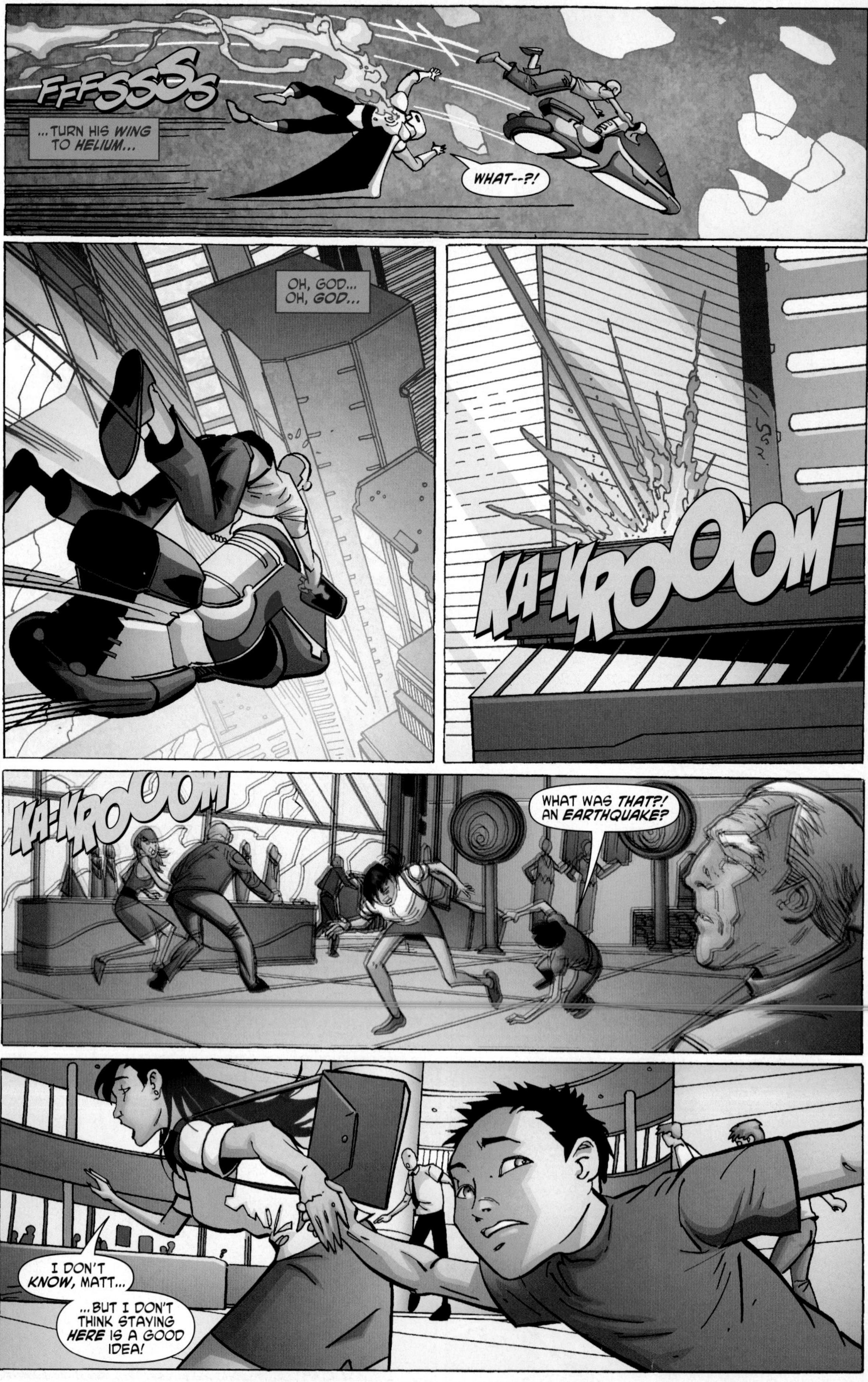
FFFSSSSS
...TURN HIS WING TO HELIUM...
WHAT--?!
OH, GOD... OH, GOD...
KA-KROOOOM
KA-KROOOOM
WHAT WAS THAT?! AN EARTHQUAKE?
I DON'T KNOW, MATT...
...BUT I DON'T THINK STAYING HERE IS A GOOD IDEA!

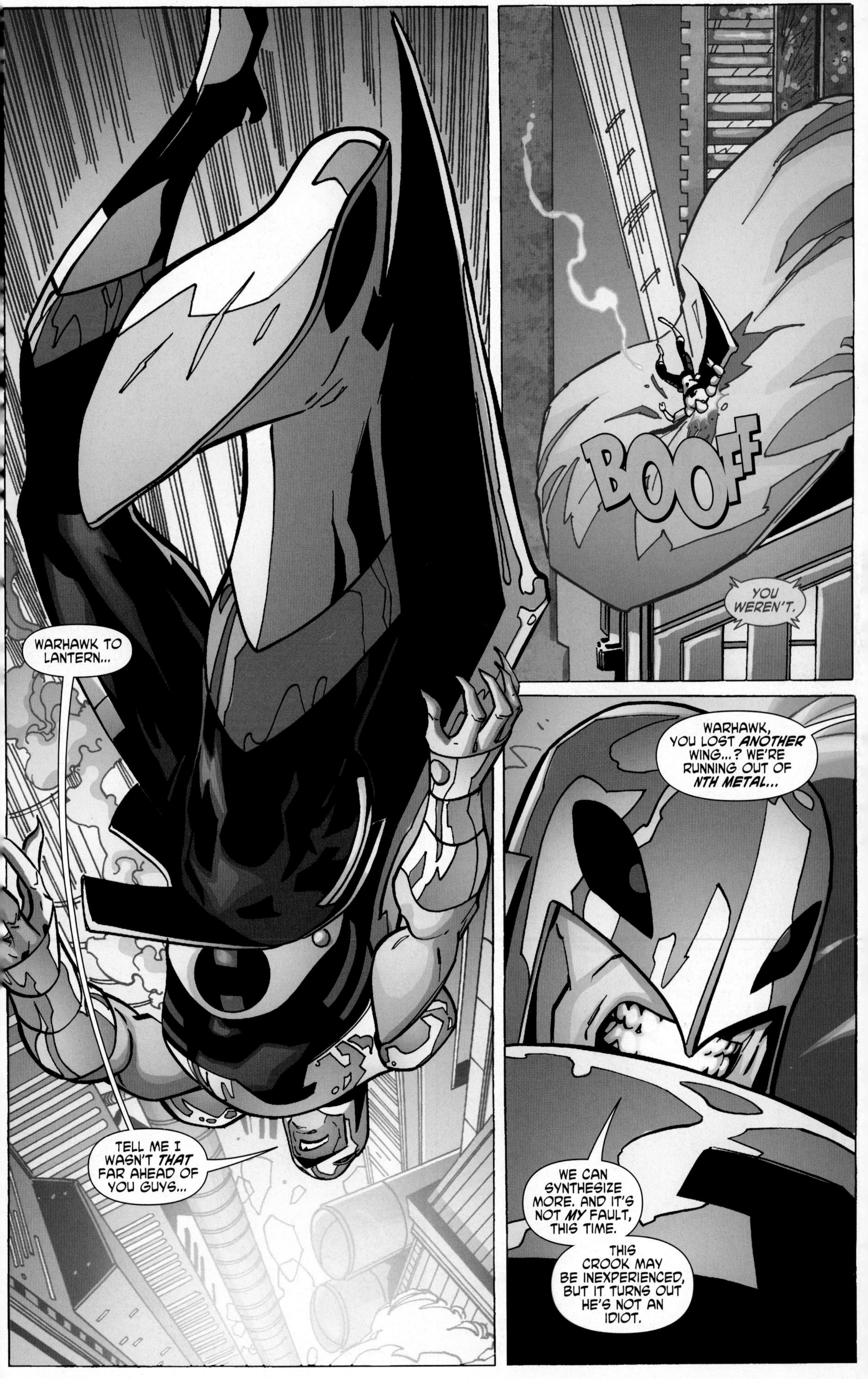
WARHAWK TO LANTERN...
TELL ME I WASN'T *THAT* FAR AHEAD OF YOU GUYS...
BOOFF
YOU WEREN'T.
WARHAWK, YOU LOST *ANOTHER* WING...? WE'RE RUNNING OUT OF *NTH METAL*...
WE CAN SYNTHESIZE MORE. AND IT'S NOT *MY* FAULT, THIS TIME.
THIS CROOK MAY BE INEXPERIENCED, BUT IT TURNS OUT HE'S NOT AN IDIOT.

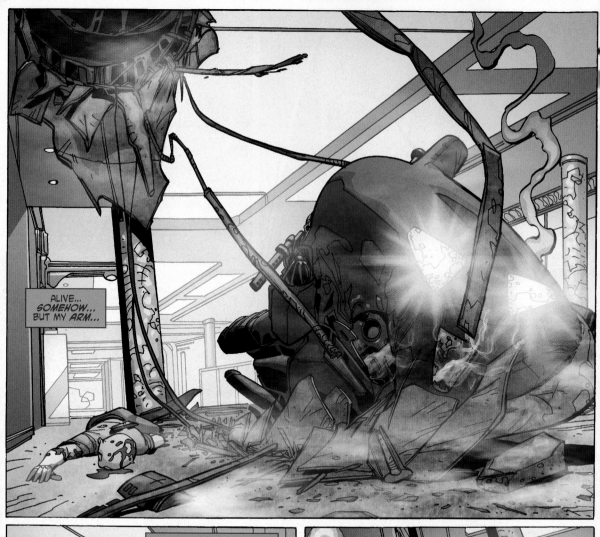

ALIVE... SOMEHOW... BUT MY *ARM*...

AND THE JUSTICE LEAGUE...

...THEY'RE GONNA *FIND* ME...

...SO I GOTTA MAKE IT *HARD* FOR THEM TO GET *TO* ME!

UNLESS YOU WANT ME TO DO TO *YOU* WHAT I DID TO THE *OUTSIDE* OF THIS MALL...

...EVERYBODY *STOP!*

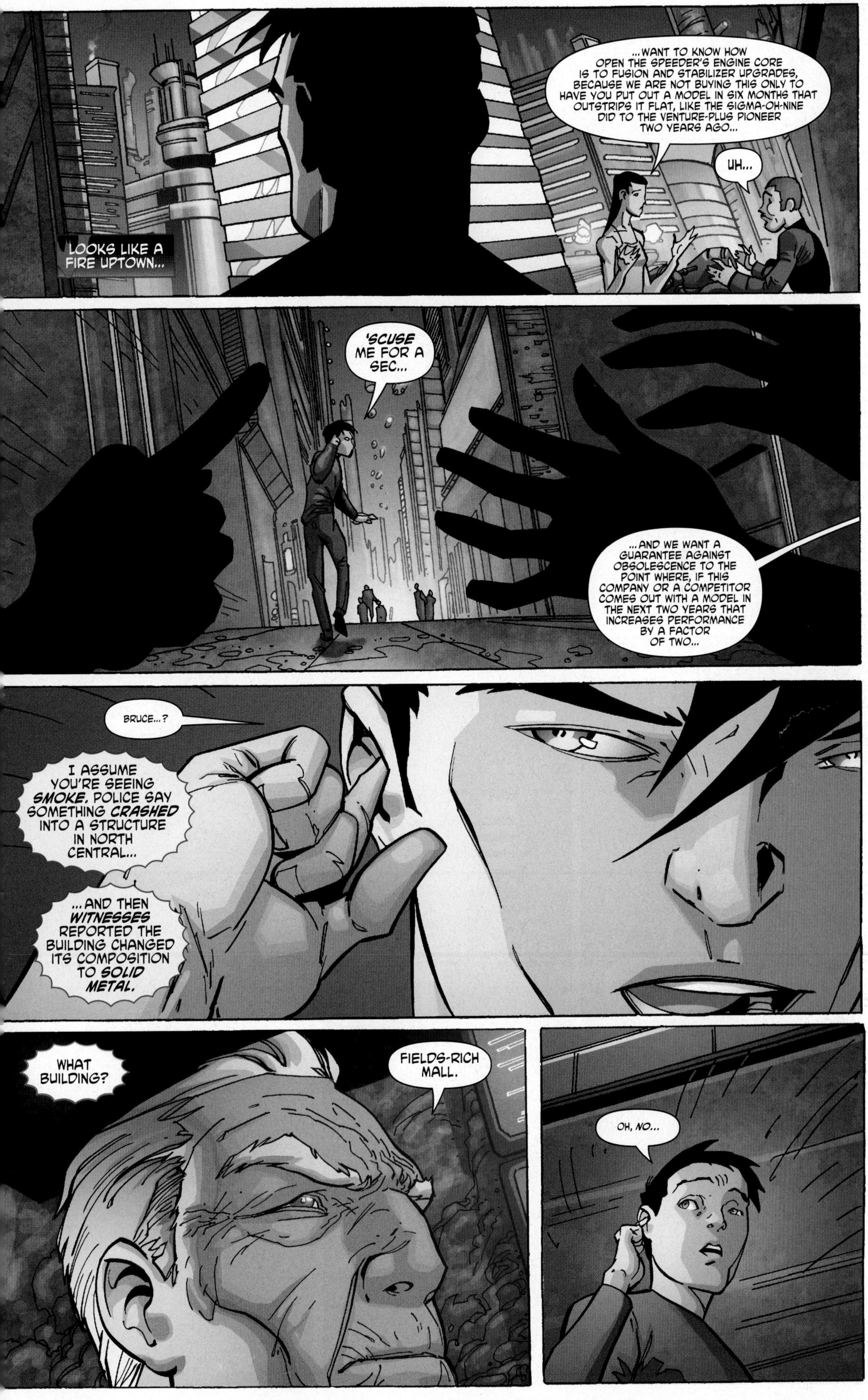
...WANT TO KNOW HOW OPEN THE SPEEDER'S ENGINE CORE IS TO FUSION AND STABILIZER UPGRADES, BECAUSE WE ARE NOT BUYING THIS ONLY TO HAVE YOU PUT OUT A MODEL IN SIX MONTHS THAT OUTSTRIPS IT FLAT, LIKE THE SIGMA-OH-NINE DID TO THE VENTURE-PLUS PIONEER TWO YEARS AGO...
UH...
LOOKS LIKE A FIRE UPTOWN...
'SCUSE ME FOR A SEC...
...AND WE WANT A GUARANTEE AGAINST OBSOLESCENCE TO THE POINT WHERE, IF THIS COMPANY OR A COMPETITOR COMES OUT WITH A MODEL IN THE NEXT TWO YEARS THAT INCREASES PERFORMANCE BY A FACTOR OF TWO...
BRUCE...?
I ASSUME YOU'RE SEEING SMOKE. POLICE SAY SOMETHING CRASHED INTO A STRUCTURE IN NORTH CENTRAL...
...AND THEN WITNESSES REPORTED THE BUILDING CHANGED ITS COMPOSITION TO SOLID METAL.
WHAT BUILDING?
FIELDS-RICH MALL.
OH, NO...

HE'S *COMPLETELY* SEALED IT OFF. IT'S SHAPING UP AS A MASSIVE *HOSTAGE* SITUATION, BUT NO *DEMANDS* HAVE BEEN MADE YET...

DANA! I'M CRAVING *MONGOLIAN* FOR LUNCH... I'LL GO PICK SOME UP. YOU GOT IT UNDER CONTROL HERE?

TOTAL CONTROL. TAKE YOUR TIME.

I *LOVE* MY *SECRET* WEAPON.

IF THE HOSTAGE-TAKER IS A *TRANSMUTER,* WE COULD BE LOOKING AT A *LOT* OF CIVILIAN COLLATERAL DAMAGE BEFORE THIS IS OVER, IF WE'RE NOT *CAREFUL.*

MY *MOTHER* AND *BROTHER* ARE IN THE MALL!

...

DAMN.

TERRY... CAN YOU BE *OBJECTIVE* ABOUT THIS SITUATION, TREAT IT LIKE *ANY OTHER* AND DO *WHATEVER* NEEDS TO BE DONE?

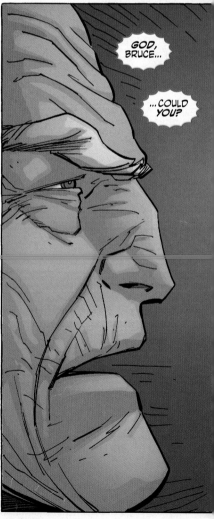

GOD, BRUCE...

...COULD *YOU?*

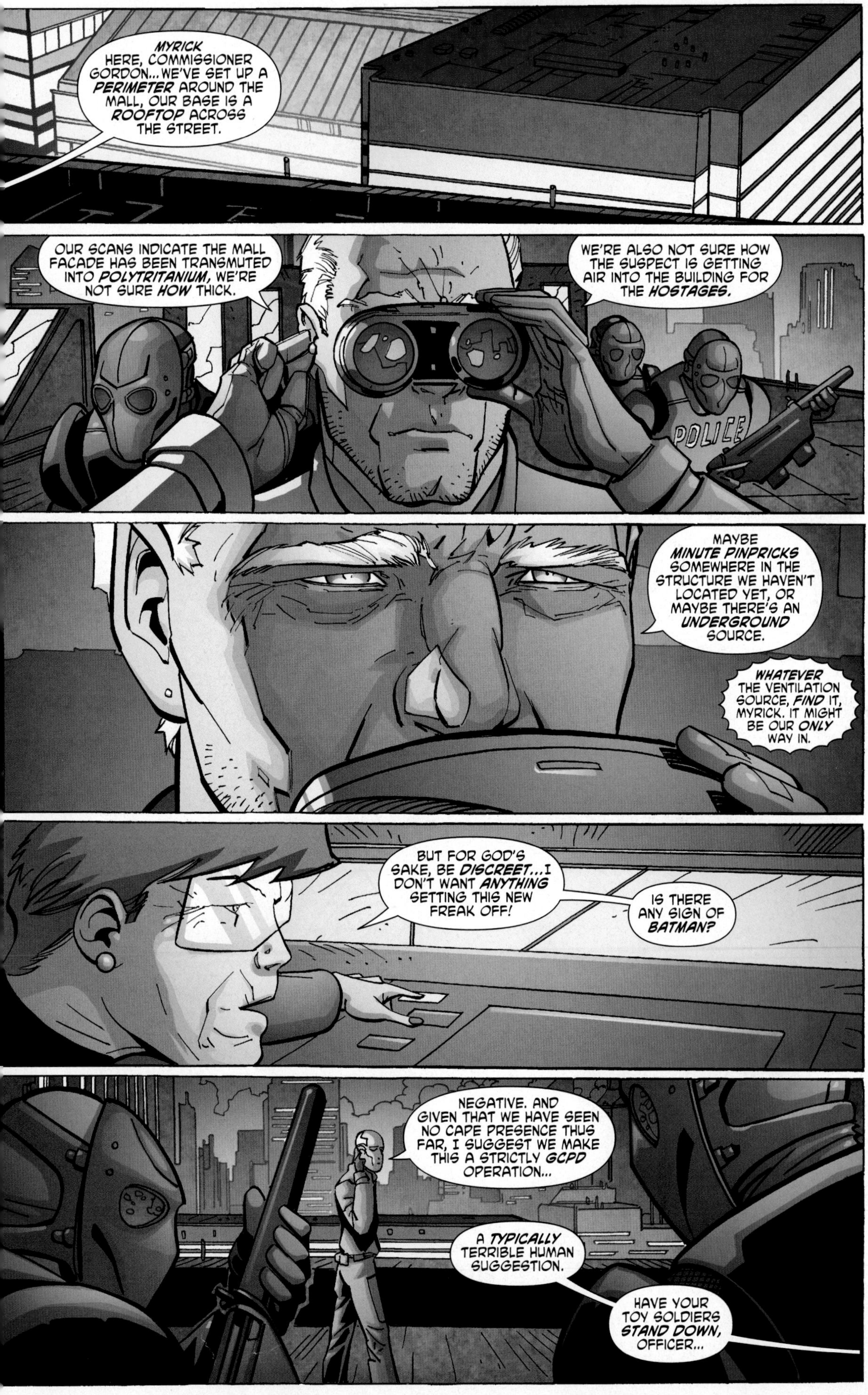
MYRICK HERE, COMMISSIONER GORDON...WE'VE SET UP A PERIMETER AROUND THE MALL, OUR BASE IS A ROOFTOP ACROSS THE STREET.
OUR SCANS INDICATE THE MALL FACADE HAS BEEN TRANSMUTED INTO POLYTRITANIUM, WE'RE NOT SURE HOW THICK.
WE'RE ALSO NOT SURE HOW THE SUSPECT IS GETTING AIR INTO THE BUILDING FOR THE HOSTAGES.
POLICE
MAYBE MINUTE PINPRICKS SOMEWHERE IN THE STRUCTURE WE HAVEN'T LOCATED YET, OR MAYBE THERE'S AN UNDERGROUND SOURCE.
WHATEVER THE VENTILATION SOURCE, FIND IT, MYRICK. IT MIGHT BE OUR ONLY WAY IN.
BUT FOR GOD'S SAKE, BE DISCREET...I DON'T WANT ANYTHING SETTING THIS NEW FREAK OFF!
IS THERE ANY SIGN OF BATMAN?
NEGATIVE. AND GIVEN THAT WE HAVE SEEN NO CAPE PRESENCE THUS FAR, I SUGGEST WE MAKE THIS A STRICTLY GCPD OPERATION...
A TYPICALLY TERRIBLE HUMAN SUGGESTION.
HAVE YOUR TOY SOLDIERS STAND DOWN, OFFICER...

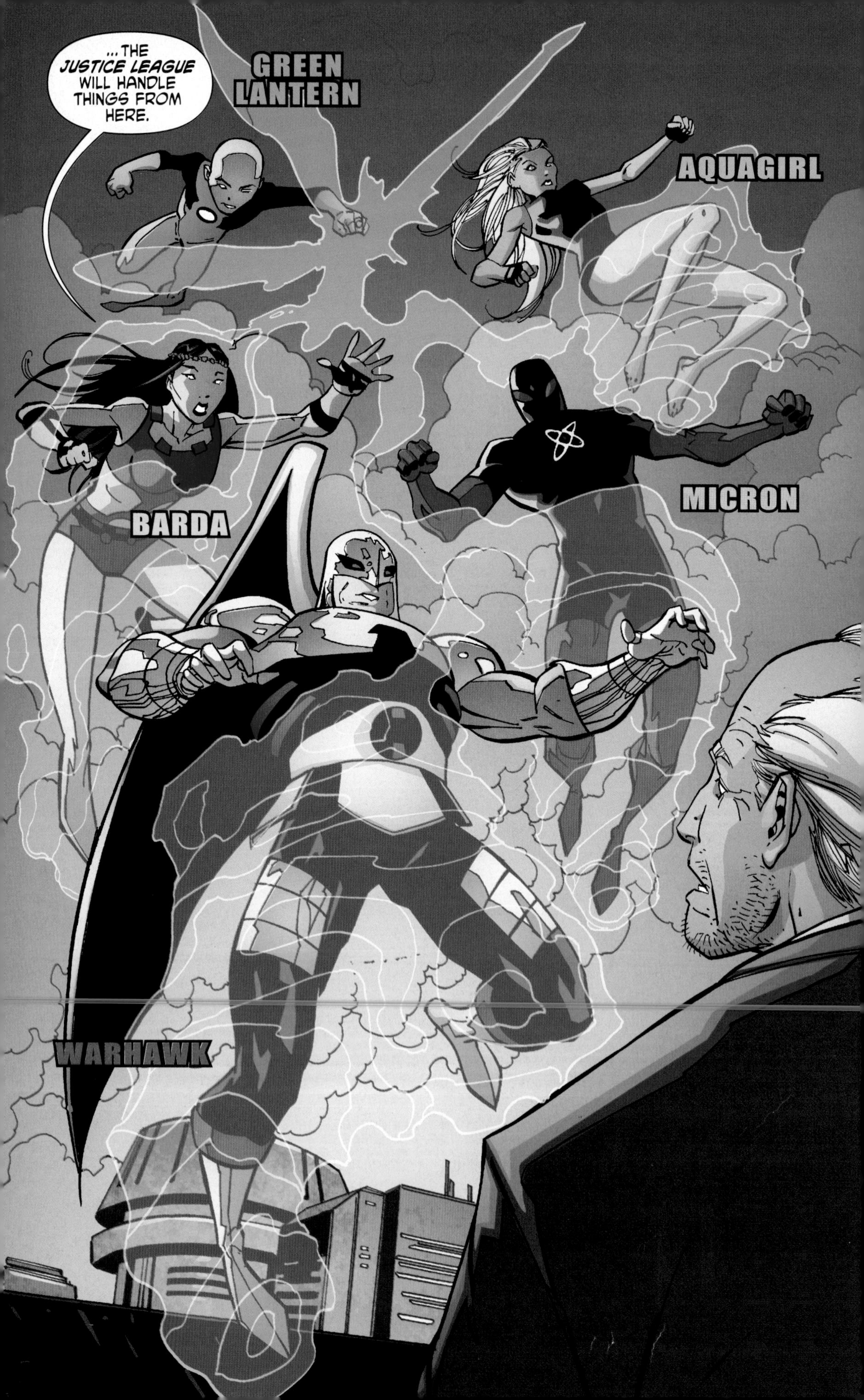
...THE *JUSTICE LEAGUE* WILL HANDLE THINGS FROM HERE.
GREEN LANTERN
AQUAGIRL
BARDA
MICRON
WARHAWK

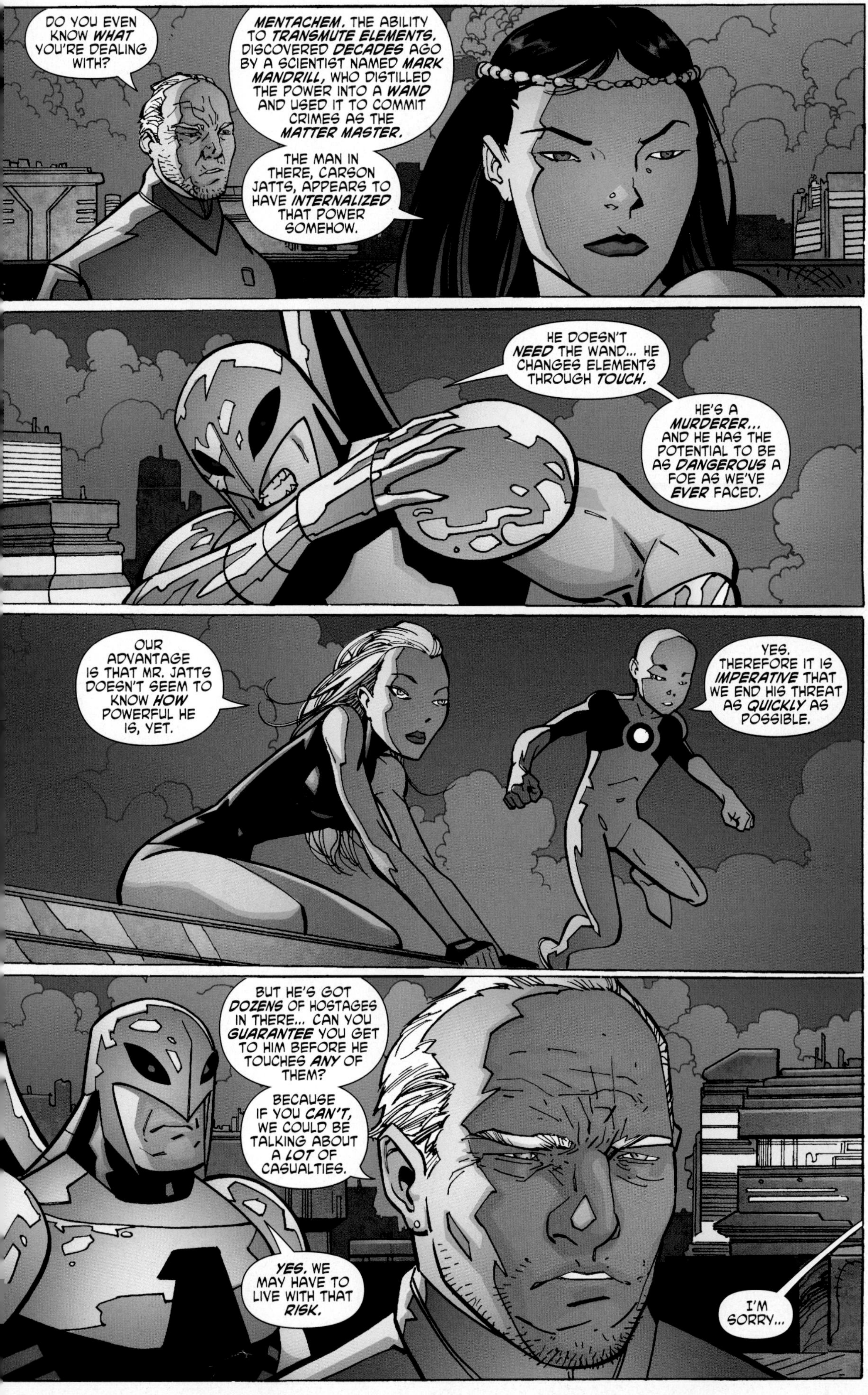
DO YOU EVEN KNOW WHAT YOU'RE DEALING WITH?
MENTACHEM. THE ABILITY TO TRANSMUTE ELEMENTS. DISCOVERED DECADES AGO BY A SCIENTIST NAMED MARK MANDRILL, WHO DISTILLED THE POWER INTO A WAND AND USED IT TO COMMIT CRIMES AS THE MATTER MASTER.
THE MAN IN THERE, CARSON JATTS, APPEARS TO HAVE INTERNALIZED THAT POWER SOMEHOW.
HE DOESN'T NEED THE WAND... HE CHANGES ELEMENTS THROUGH TOUCH.
HE'S A MURDERER... AND HE HAS THE POTENTIAL TO BE AS DANGEROUS A FOE AS WE'VE EVER FACED.
OUR ADVANTAGE IS THAT MR. JATTS DOESN'T SEEM TO KNOW HOW POWERFUL HE IS, YET.
YES. THEREFORE IT IS IMPERATIVE THAT WE END HIS THREAT AS QUICKLY AS POSSIBLE.
BUT HE'S GOT DOZENS OF HOSTAGES IN THERE... CAN YOU GUARANTEE YOU GET TO HIM BEFORE HE TOUCHES ANY OF THEM?
BECAUSE IF YOU CAN'T, WE COULD BE TALKING ABOUT A LOT OF CASUALTIES.
YES. WE MAY HAVE TO LIVE WITH THAT RISK.
I'M SORRY...

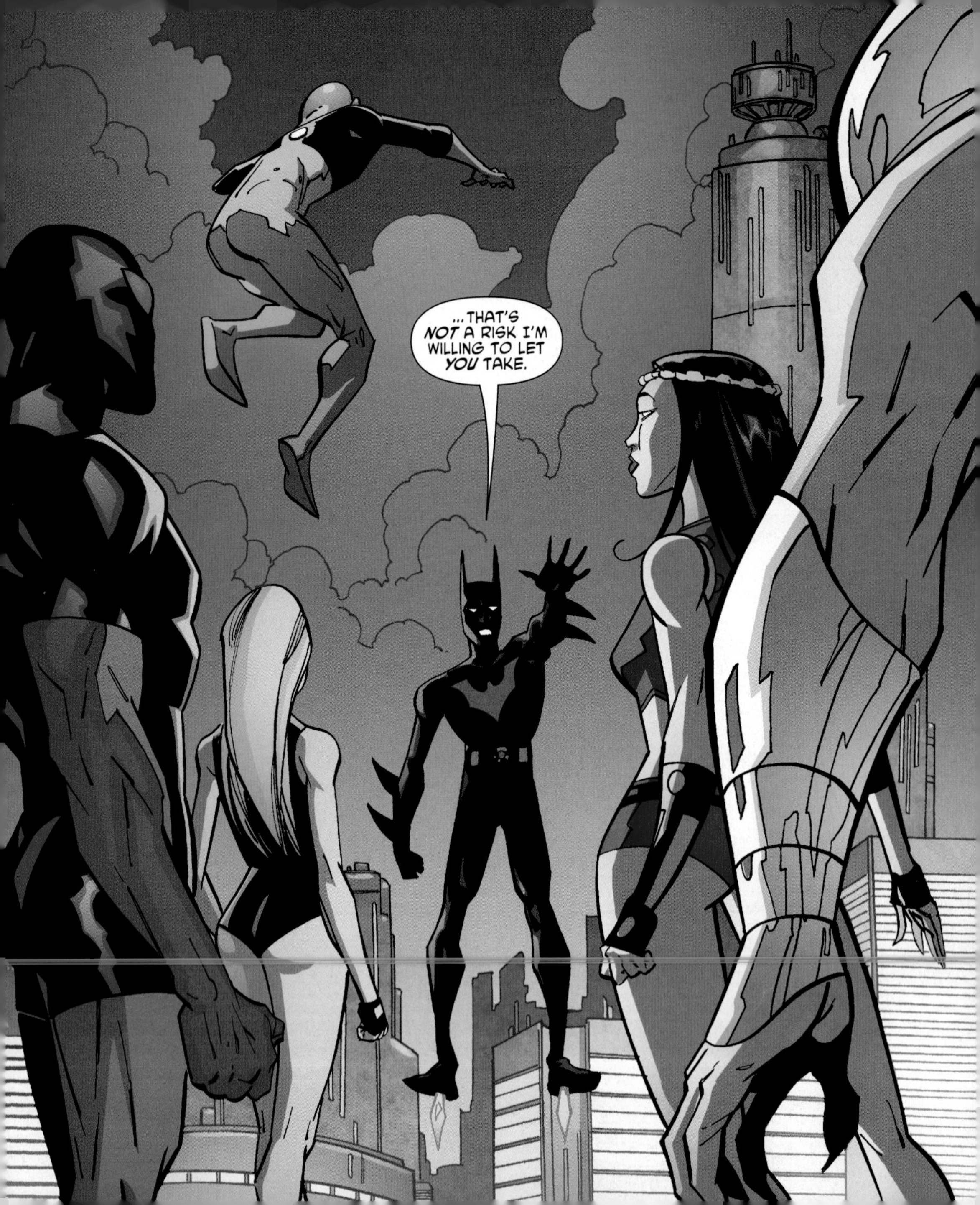
...THAT'S NOT A RISK I'M WILLING TO LET YOU TAKE.

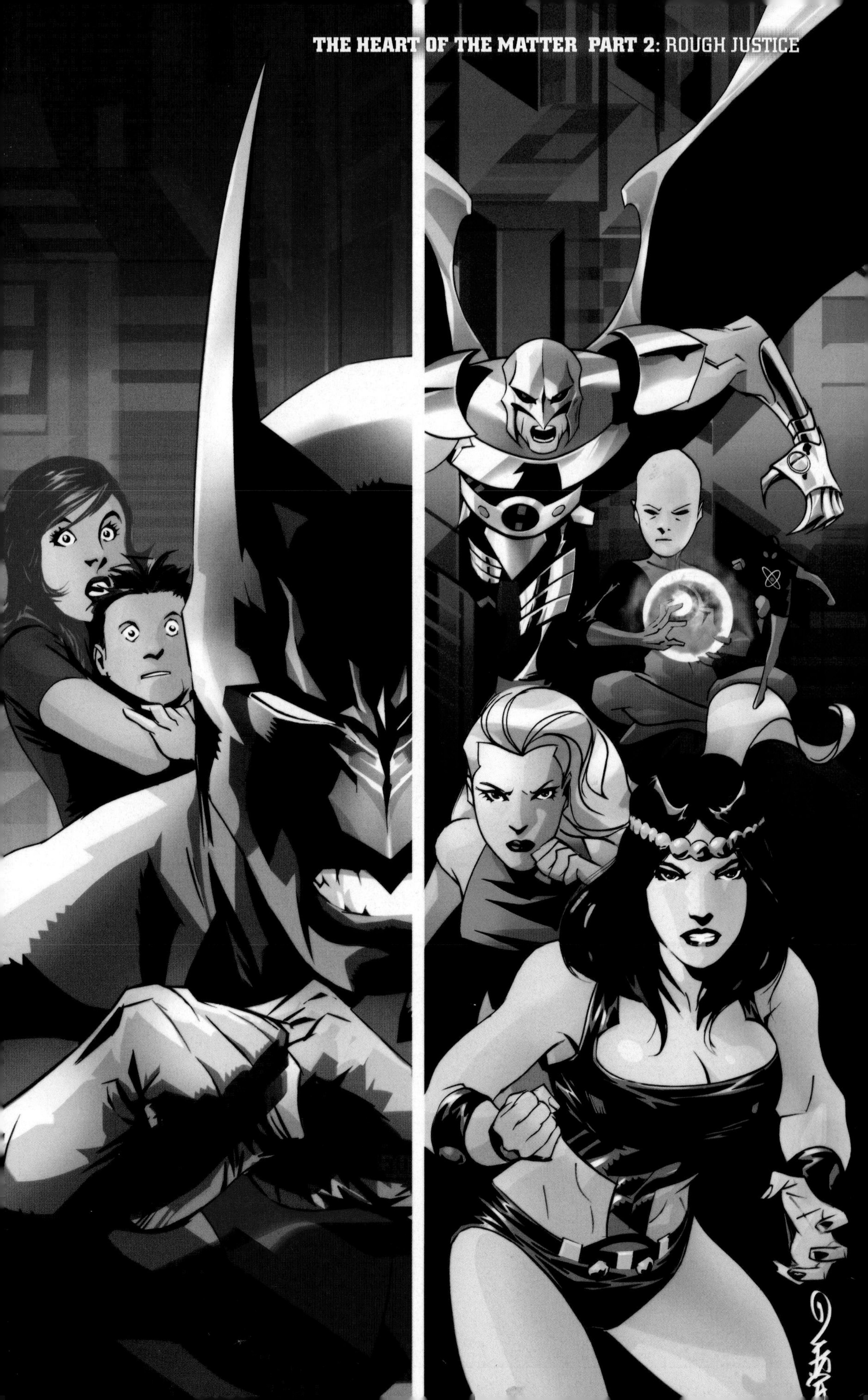
THE HEART OF THE MATTER PART 2: ROUGH JUSTICE

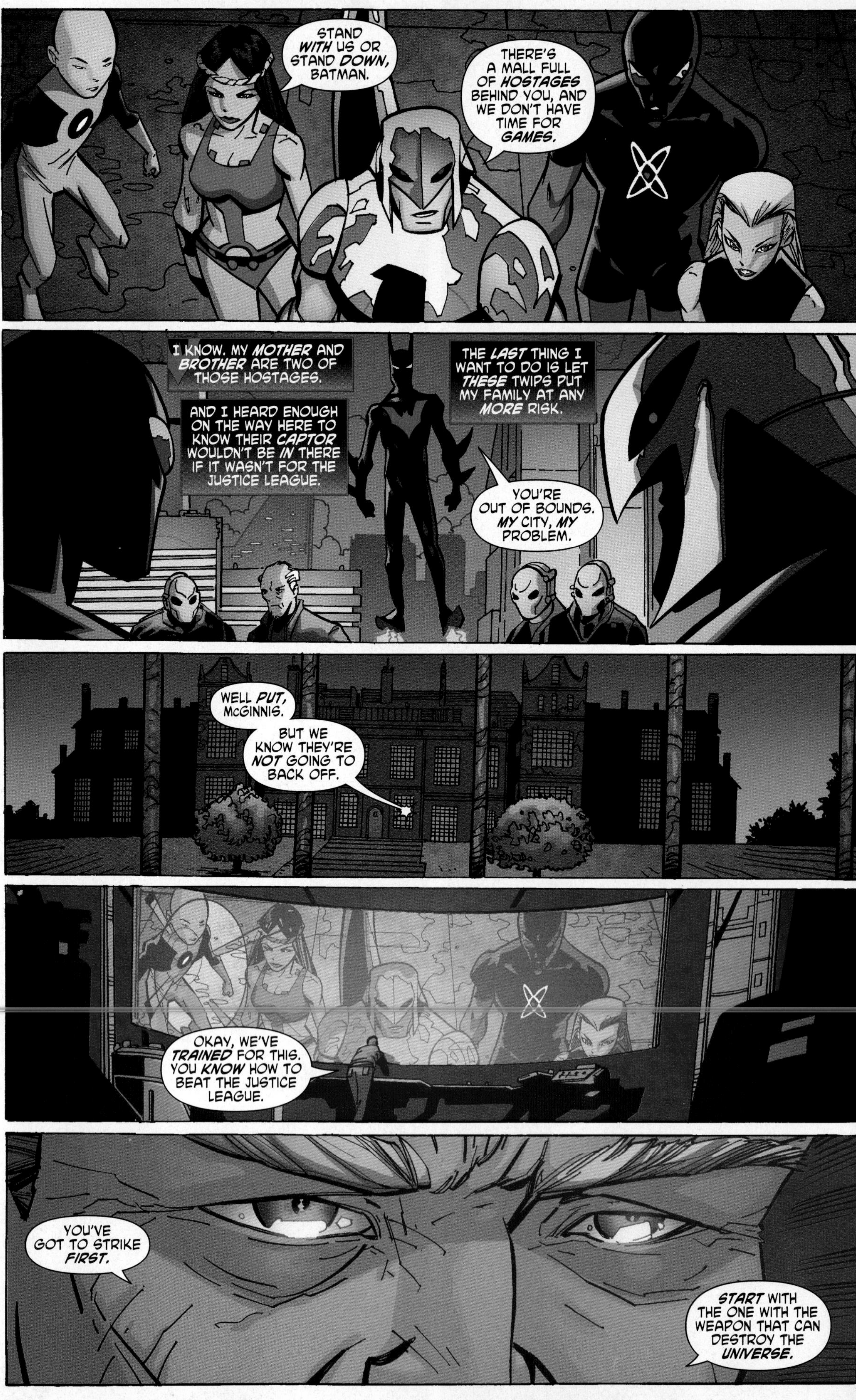
STAND WITH US OR STAND DOWN, BATMAN.
THERE'S A MALL FULL OF HOSTAGES BEHIND YOU, AND WE DON'T HAVE TIME FOR GAMES.
I KNOW. MY MOTHER AND BROTHER ARE TWO OF THOSE HOSTAGES.
AND I HEARD ENOUGH ON THE WAY HERE TO KNOW THEIR CAPTOR WOULDN'T BE IN THERE IF IT WASN'T FOR THE JUSTICE LEAGUE.
THE LAST THING I WANT TO DO IS LET THESE TWIPS PUT MY FAMILY AT ANY MORE RISK.
YOU'RE OUT OF BOUNDS. MY CITY, MY PROBLEM.
WELL PUT, McGINNIS.
BUT WE KNOW THEY'RE NOT GOING TO BACK OFF.
OKAY, WE'VE TRAINED FOR THIS. YOU KNOW HOW TO BEAT THE JUSTICE LEAGUE.
YOU'VE GOT TO STRIKE FIRST.
START WITH THE ONE WITH THE WEAPON THAT CAN DESTROY THE UNIVERSE.

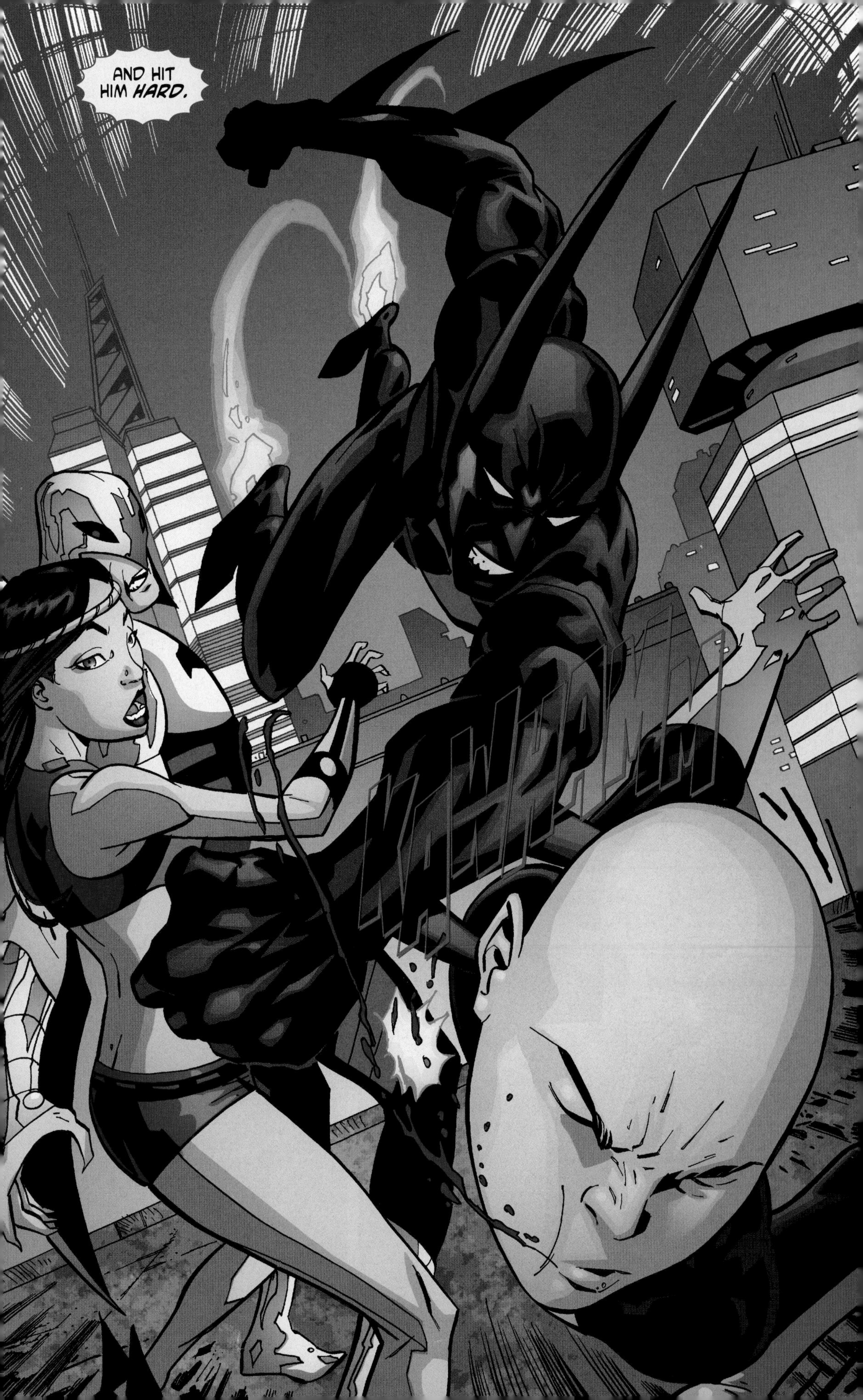
AND HIT HIM *HARD.*

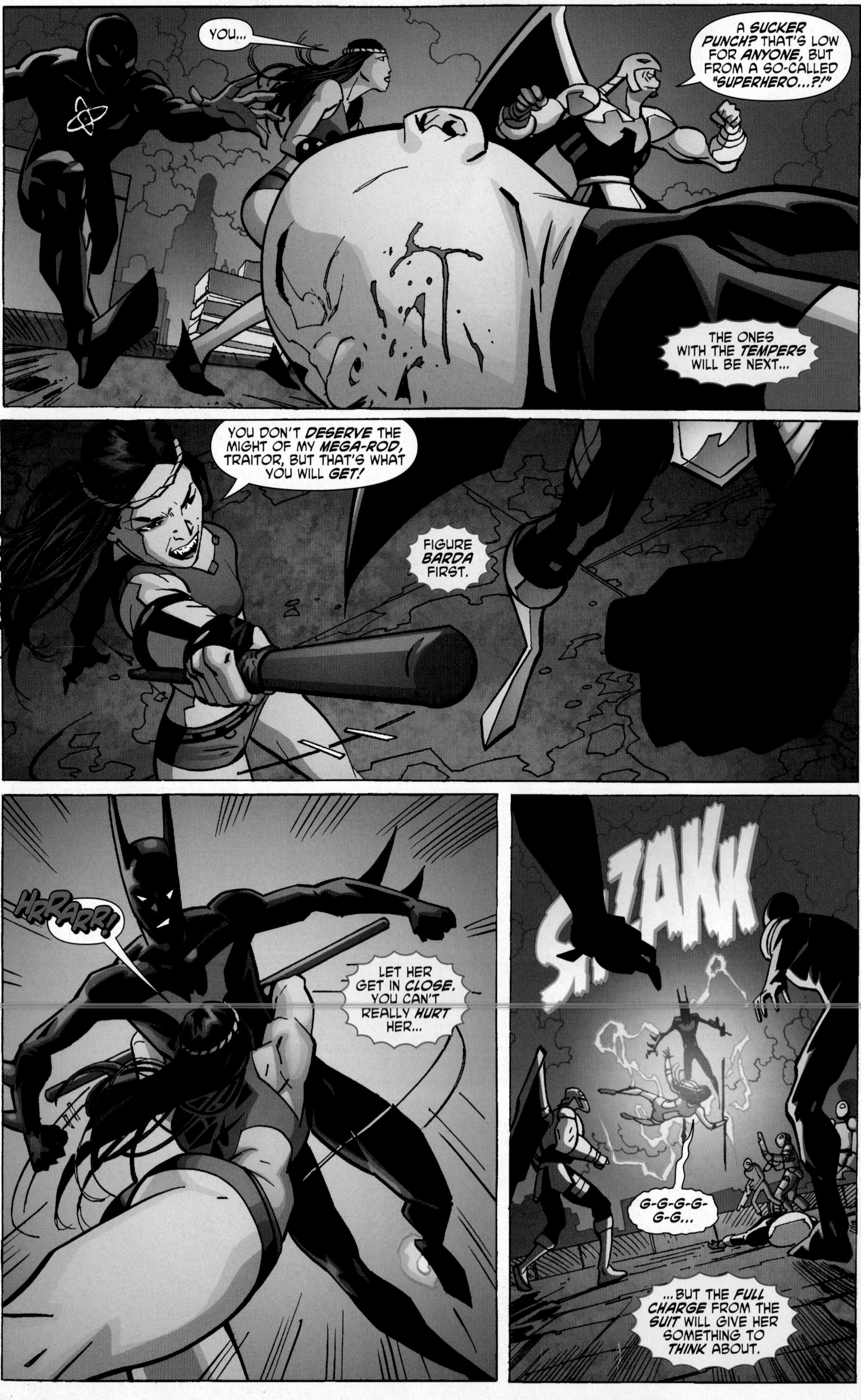
YOU...
A SUCKER PUNCH? THAT'S LOW FOR ANYONE, BUT FROM A SO-CALLED "SUPERHERO...?!"
THE ONES WITH THE TEMPERS WILL BE NEXT...
YOU DON'T DESERVE THE MIGHT OF MY MEGA-ROD, TRAITOR, BUT THAT'S WHAT YOU WILL GET!
FIGURE BARDA FIRST.
HRRARR!
LET HER GET IN CLOSE. YOU CAN'T REALLY HURT HER...
SHZAKK
G-G-G-G-G-G...
...BUT THE FULL CHARGE FROM THE SUIT WILL GIVE HER SOMETHING TO THINK ABOUT.

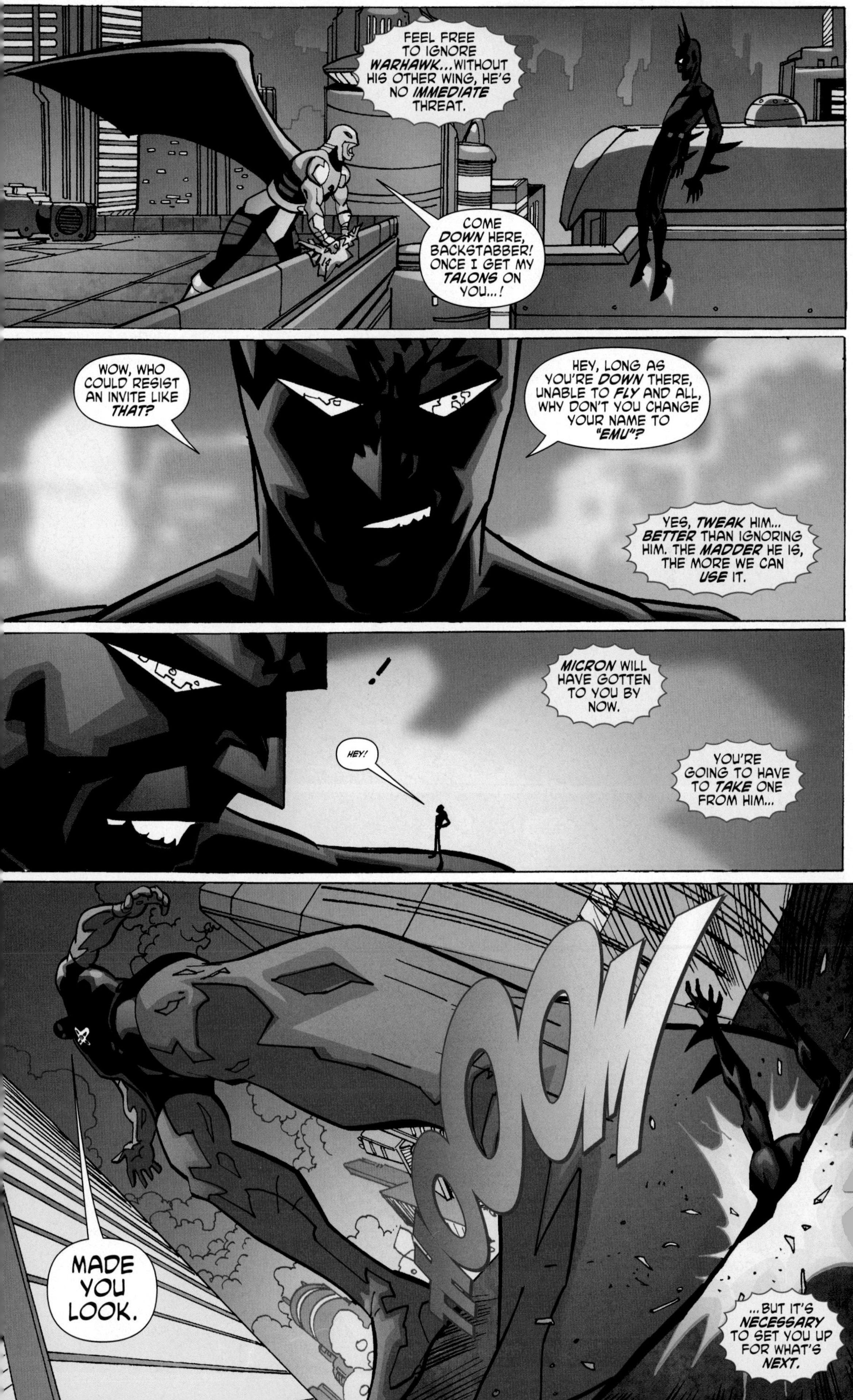
FEEL FREE TO IGNORE WARHAWK...WITHOUT HIS OTHER WING, HE'S NO IMMEDIATE THREAT.
COME DOWN HERE, BACKSTABBER! ONCE I GET MY TALONS ON YOU...!
WOW, WHO COULD RESIST AN INVITE LIKE THAT?
HEY, LONG AS YOU'RE DOWN THERE, UNABLE TO FLY AND ALL, WHY DON'T YOU CHANGE YOUR NAME TO "EMU"?
YES, TWEAK HIM... BETTER THAN IGNORING HIM. THE MADDER HE IS, THE MORE WE CAN USE IT.
!
MICRON WILL HAVE GOTTEN TO YOU BY NOW.
HEY!
YOU'RE GOING TO HAVE TO TAKE ONE FROM HIM...
BOOOM
MADE YOU LOOK.
...BUT IT'S NECESSARY TO SET YOU UP FOR WHAT'S NEXT.

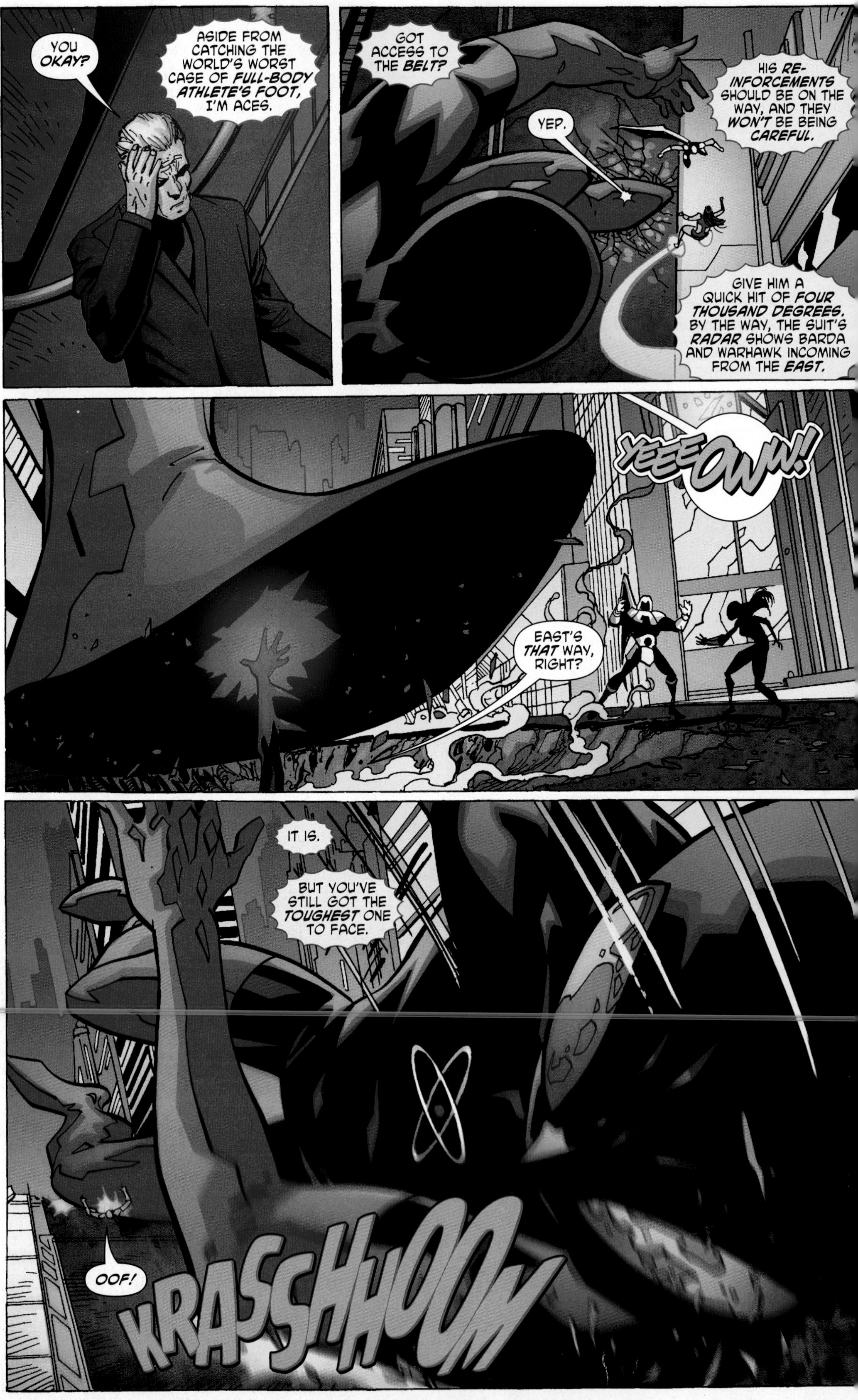
YOU OKAY?
ASIDE FROM CATCHING THE WORLD'S WORST CASE OF FULL-BODY ATHLETE'S FOOT, I'M ACES.
GOT ACCESS TO THE BELT?
YEP.
HIS RE-INFORCEMENTS SHOULD BE ON THE WAY, AND THEY WON'T BE BEING CAREFUL.
GIVE HIM A QUICK HIT OF FOUR THOUSAND DEGREES. BY THE WAY, THE SUIT'S RADAR SHOWS BARDA AND WARHAWK INCOMING FROM THE EAST.
YEEEOWW!!
EAST'S THAT WAY, RIGHT?
IT IS.
BUT YOU'VE STILL GOT THE TOUGHEST ONE TO FACE.
OOF!
KRASSHHOOM

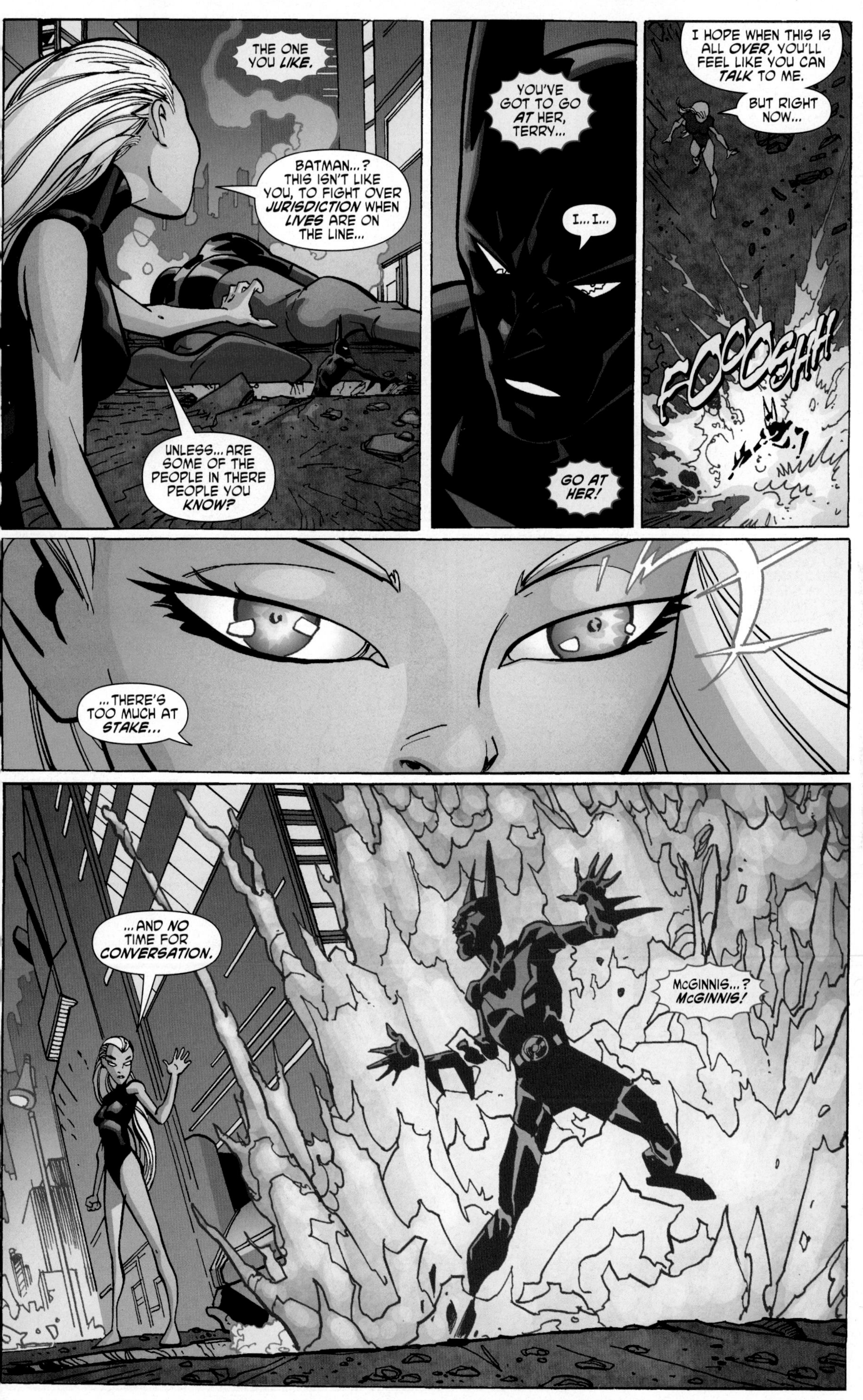
THE ONE YOU LIKE.
BATMAN...? THIS ISN'T LIKE YOU, TO FIGHT OVER JURISDICTION WHEN LIVES ARE ON THE LINE...
UNLESS... ARE SOME OF THE PEOPLE IN THERE PEOPLE YOU KNOW?
YOU'VE GOT TO GO AT HER, TERRY...
I... I...
GO AT HER!
I HOPE WHEN THIS IS ALL OVER, YOU'LL FEEL LIKE YOU CAN TALK TO ME.
BUT RIGHT NOW...
FOOOSHH
...THERE'S TOO MUCH AT STAKE...
...AND NO TIME FOR CONVERSATION.
McGINNIS...? McGINNIS!

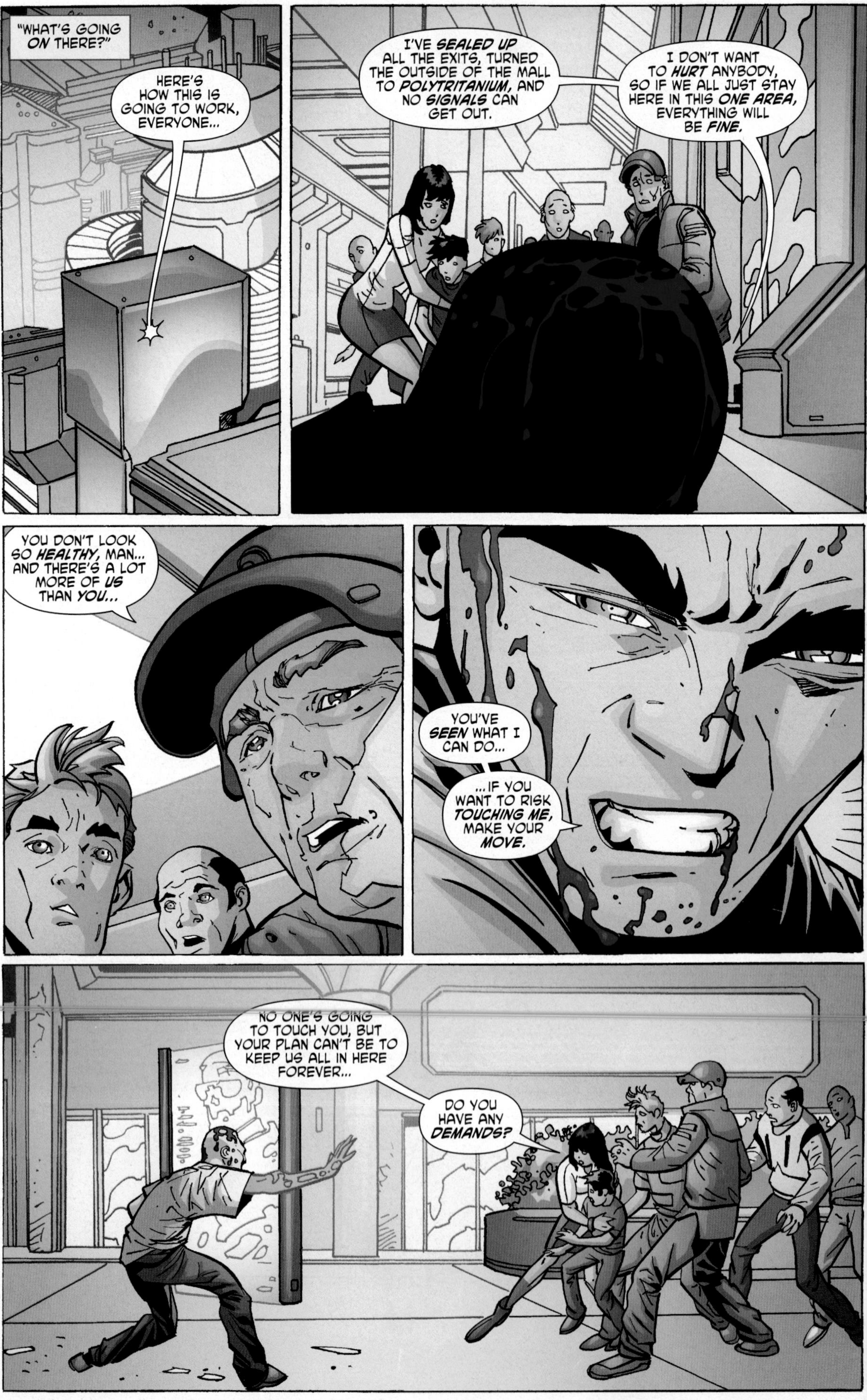
"WHAT'S GOING ON THERE?"
HERE'S HOW THIS IS GOING TO WORK, EVERYONE...
I'VE SEALED UP ALL THE EXITS, TURNED THE OUTSIDE OF THE MALL TO POLYTRITANIUM, AND NO SIGNALS CAN GET OUT.
I DON'T WANT TO HURT ANYBODY, SO IF WE ALL JUST STAY HERE IN THIS ONE AREA, EVERYTHING WILL BE FINE.
YOU DON'T LOOK SO HEALTHY, MAN... AND THERE'S A LOT MORE OF US THAN YOU...
YOU'VE SEEN WHAT I CAN DO...
...IF YOU WANT TO RISK TOUCHING ME, MAKE YOUR MOVE.
NO ONE'S GOING TO TOUCH YOU, BUT YOUR PLAN CAN'T BE TO KEEP US ALL IN HERE FOREVER...
DO YOU HAVE ANY DEMANDS?

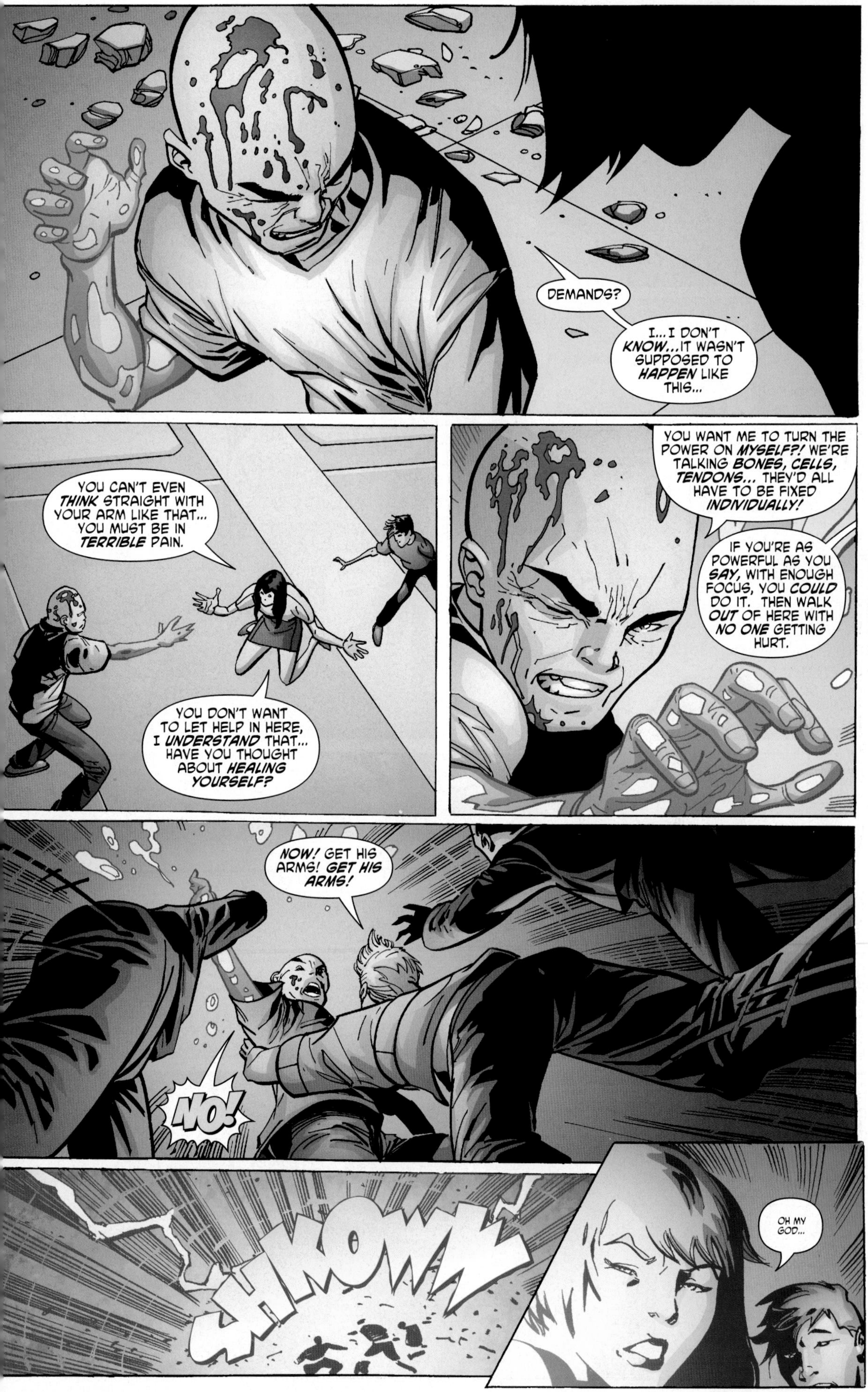
DEMANDS?
I...I DON'T KNOW...IT WASN'T SUPPOSED TO HAPPEN LIKE THIS...
YOU CAN'T EVEN THINK STRAIGHT WITH YOUR ARM LIKE THAT... YOU MUST BE IN TERRIBLE PAIN.
YOU DON'T WANT TO LET HELP IN HERE, I UNDERSTAND THAT... HAVE YOU THOUGHT ABOUT HEALING YOURSELF?
YOU WANT ME TO TURN THE POWER ON MYSELF?! WE'RE TALKING BONES, CELLS, TENDONS... THEY'D ALL HAVE TO BE FIXED INDIVIDUALLY!
IF YOU'RE AS POWERFUL AS YOU SAY, WITH ENOUGH FOCUS, YOU COULD DO IT. THEN WALK OUT OF HERE WITH NO ONE GETTING HURT.
NOW! GET HIS ARMS! GET HIS ARMS!
NO!
WHOOM
OH MY GOD...

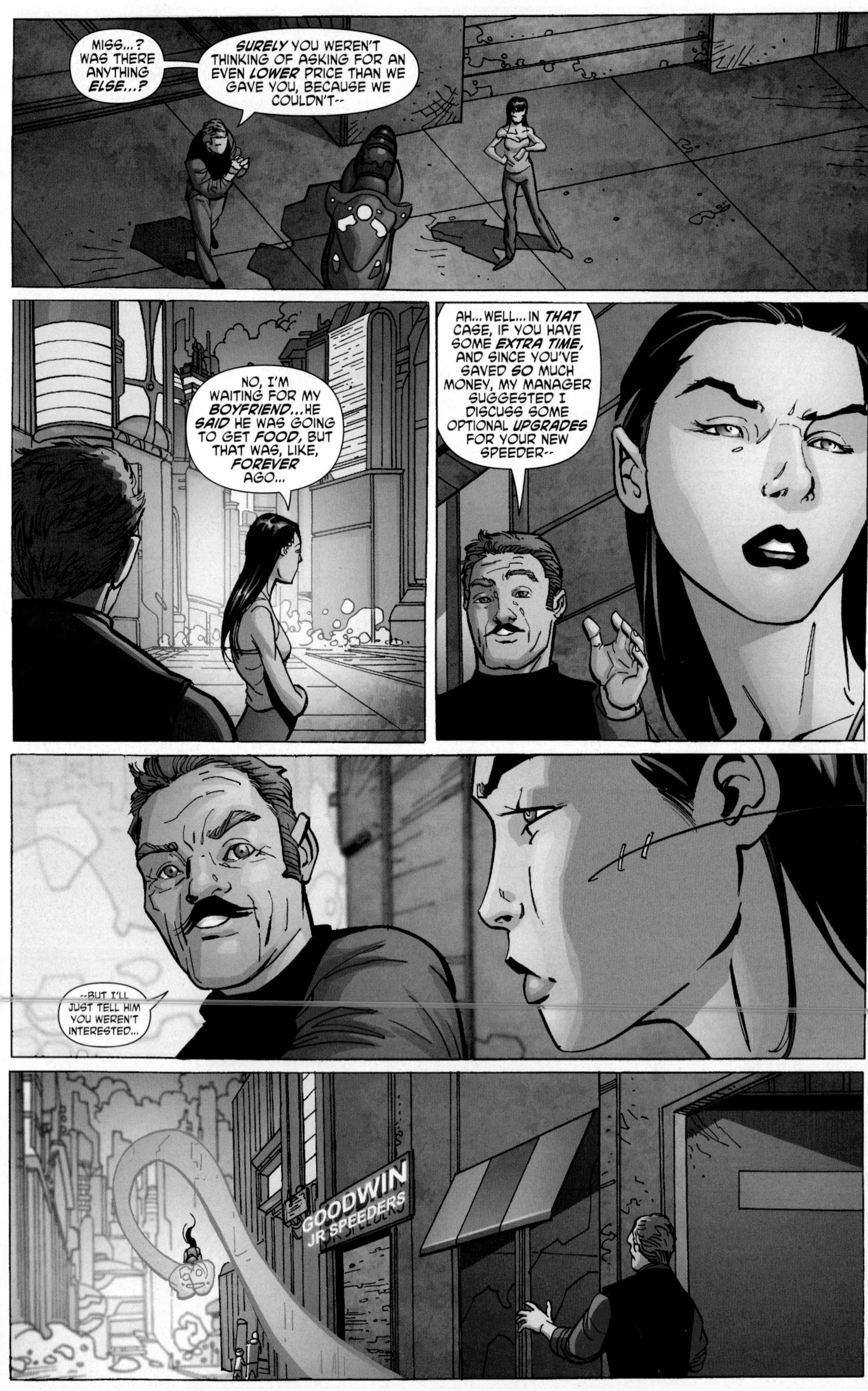
MISS...? WAS THERE ANYTHING ELSE...?
SURELY YOU WEREN'T THINKING OF ASKING FOR AN EVEN LOWER PRICE THAN WE GAVE YOU, BECAUSE WE COULDN'T--
NO, I'M WAITING FOR MY BOYFRIEND... HE SAID HE WAS GOING TO GET FOOD, BUT THAT WAS, LIKE, FOREVER AGO...
AH... WELL... IN THAT CASE, IF YOU HAVE SOME EXTRA TIME, AND SINCE YOU'VE SAVED SO MUCH MONEY, MY MANAGER SUGGESTED I DISCUSS SOME OPTIONAL UPGRADES FOR YOUR NEW SPEEDER--
--BUT I'LL JUST TELL HIM YOU WEREN'T INTERESTED...
GOODWIN
JR SPEEDERS

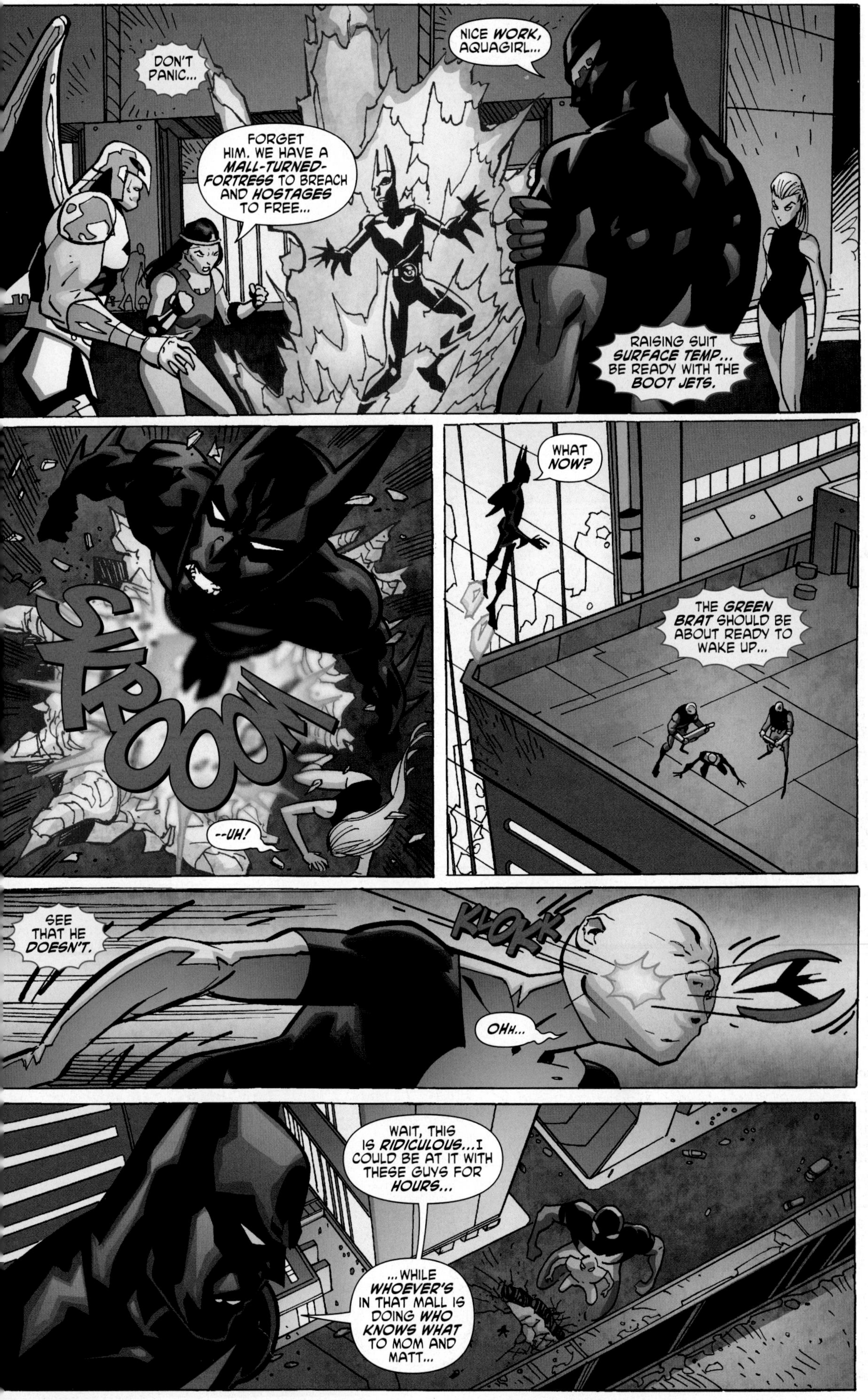
DON'T PANIC...
NICE WORK, AQUAGIRL...
FORGET HIM. WE HAVE A MALL-TURNED-FORTRESS TO BREACH AND HOSTAGES TO FREE...
RAISING SUIT SURFACE TEMP... BE READY WITH THE BOOT JETS.
SKROOOM
--UH!
WHAT NOW?
THE GREEN BRAT SHOULD BE ABOUT READY TO WAKE UP...
SEE THAT HE DOESN'T.
KLOKK
OHH...
WAIT, THIS IS RIDICULOUS...I COULD BE AT IT WITH THESE GUYS FOR HOURS...
...WHILE WHOEVER'S IN THAT MALL IS DOING WHO KNOWS WHAT TO MOM AND MATT...

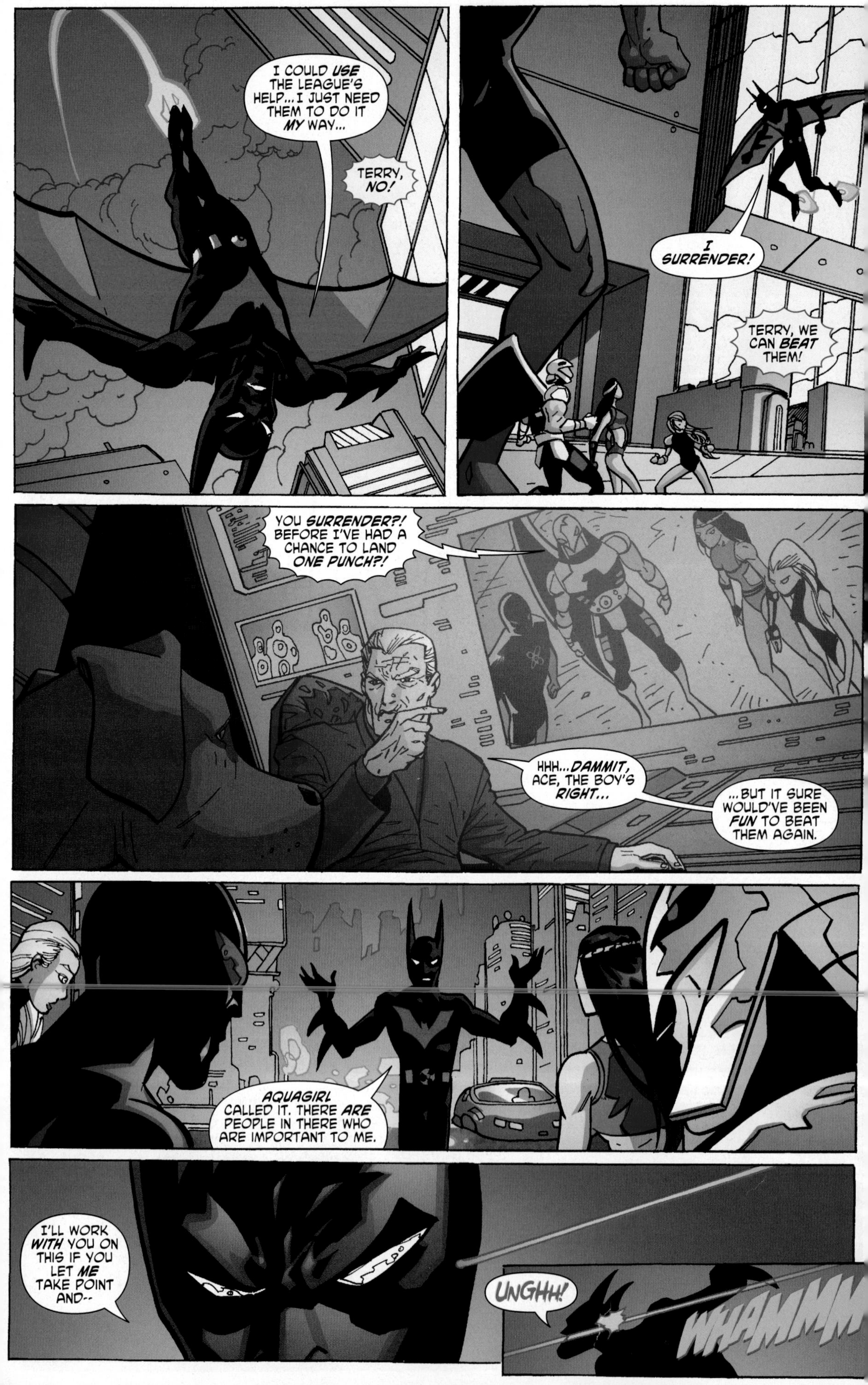

I COULD USE THE LEAGUE'S HELP... I JUST NEED THEM TO DO IT MY WAY...
TERRY, NO!
I SURRENDER!
TERRY, WE CAN BEAT THEM!
YOU SURRENDER?! BEFORE I'VE HAD A CHANCE TO LAND ONE PUNCH?!
HHH...DAMMIT, ACE, THE BOY'S RIGHT...
...BUT IT SURE WOULD'VE BEEN FUN TO BEAT THEM AGAIN.
AQUAGIRL CALLED IT. THERE ARE PEOPLE IN THERE WHO ARE IMPORTANT TO ME.
I'LL WORK WITH YOU ON THIS IF YOU LET ME TAKE POINT AND--
UNGHH!
WHAMMM

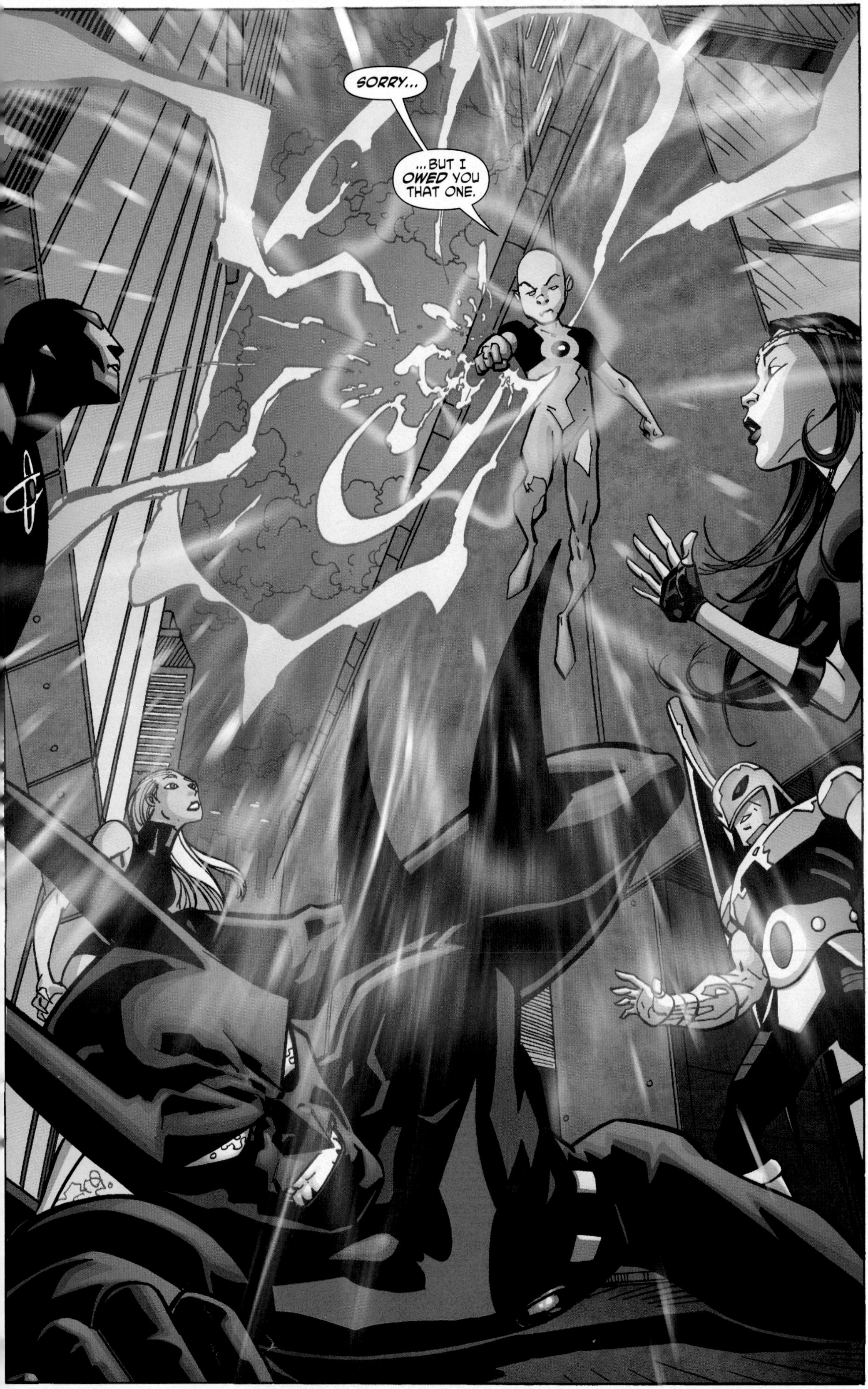
SORRY...
...BUT I OWED YOU THAT ONE.

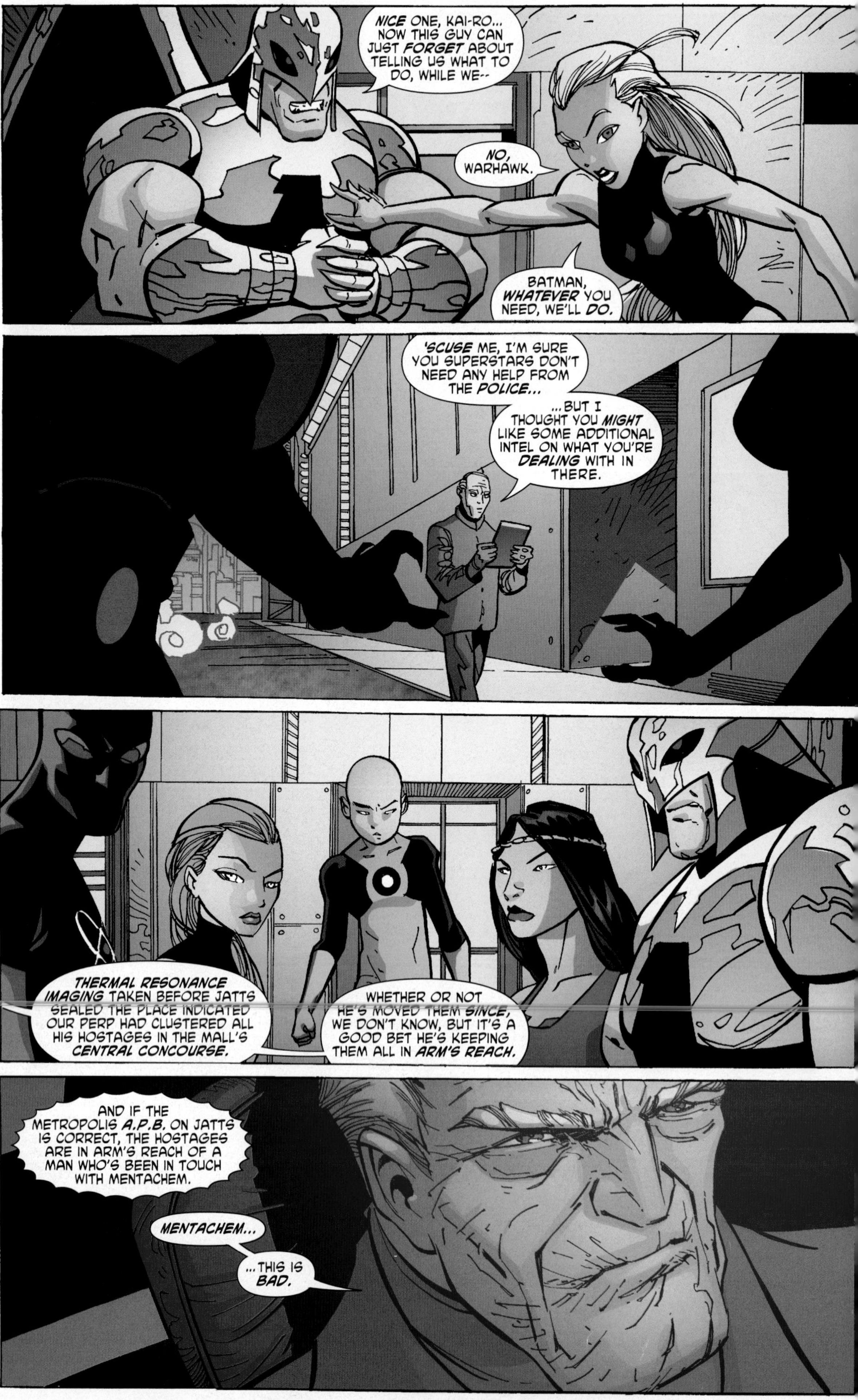
NICE ONE, KAI-RO... NOW THIS GUY CAN JUST FORGET ABOUT TELLING US WHAT TO DO, WHILE WE--
NO, WARHAWK.
BATMAN, WHATEVER YOU NEED, WE'LL DO.
'SCUSE ME, I'M SURE YOU SUPERSTARS DON'T NEED ANY HELP FROM THE POLICE...
...BUT I THOUGHT YOU MIGHT LIKE SOME ADDITIONAL INTEL ON WHAT YOU'RE DEALING WITH IN THERE.
THERMAL RESONANCE IMAGING TAKEN BEFORE JATTS SEALED THE PLACE INDICATED OUR PERP HAD CLUSTERED ALL HIS HOSTAGES IN THE MALL'S CENTRAL CONCOURSE.
WHETHER OR NOT HE'S MOVED THEM SINCE, WE DON'T KNOW, BUT IT'S A GOOD BET HE'S KEEPING THEM ALL IN ARM'S REACH.
AND IF THE METROPOLIS A.P.B. ON JATTS IS CORRECT, THE HOSTAGES ARE IN ARM'S REACH OF A MAN WHO'S BEEN IN TOUCH WITH MENTACHEM.
MENTACHEM...
...THIS IS BAD.

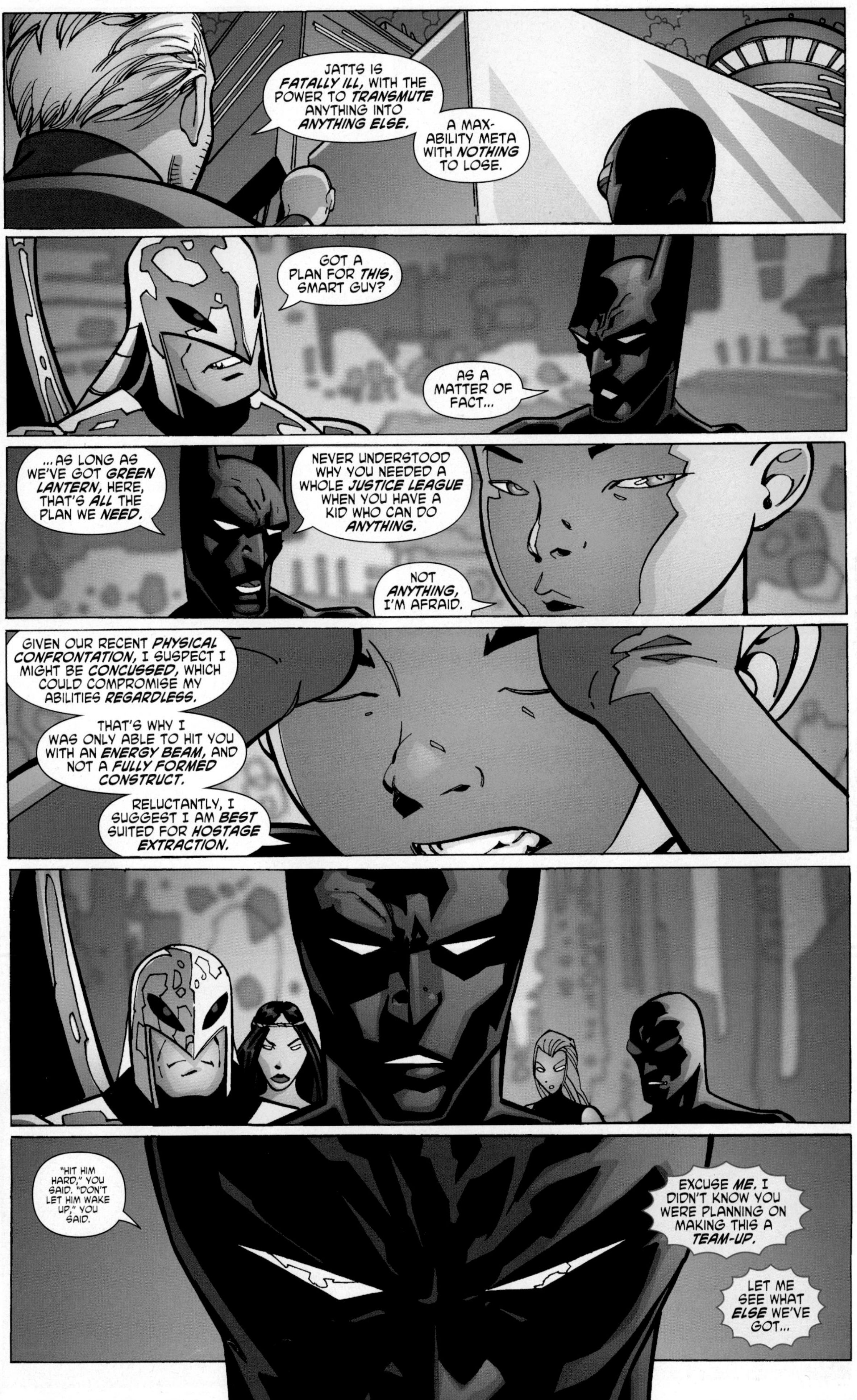
JATTS IS FATALLY ILL, WITH THE POWER TO TRANSMUTE ANYTHING INTO ANYTHING ELSE.
A MAX-ABILITY META WITH NOTHING TO LOSE.
GOT A PLAN FOR THIS, SMART GUY?
AS A MATTER OF FACT...
...AS LONG AS WE'VE GOT GREEN LANTERN, HERE, THAT'S ALL THE PLAN WE NEED.
NEVER UNDERSTOOD WHY YOU NEEDED A WHOLE JUSTICE LEAGUE WHEN YOU HAVE A KID WHO CAN DO ANYTHING.
NOT ANYTHING, I'M AFRAID.
GIVEN OUR RECENT PHYSICAL CONFRONTATION, I SUSPECT I MIGHT BE CONCUSSED, WHICH COULD COMPROMISE MY ABILITIES REGARDLESS.
THAT'S WHY I WAS ONLY ABLE TO HIT YOU WITH AN ENERGY BEAM, AND NOT A FULLY FORMED CONSTRUCT.
RELUCTANTLY, I SUGGEST I AM BEST SUITED FOR HOSTAGE EXTRACTION.
"HIT HIM HARD," YOU SAID. "DON'T LET HIM WAKE UP," YOU SAID.
EXCUSE ME. I DIDN'T KNOW YOU WERE PLANNING ON MAKING THIS A TEAM-UP.
LET ME SEE WHAT ELSE WE'VE GOT...

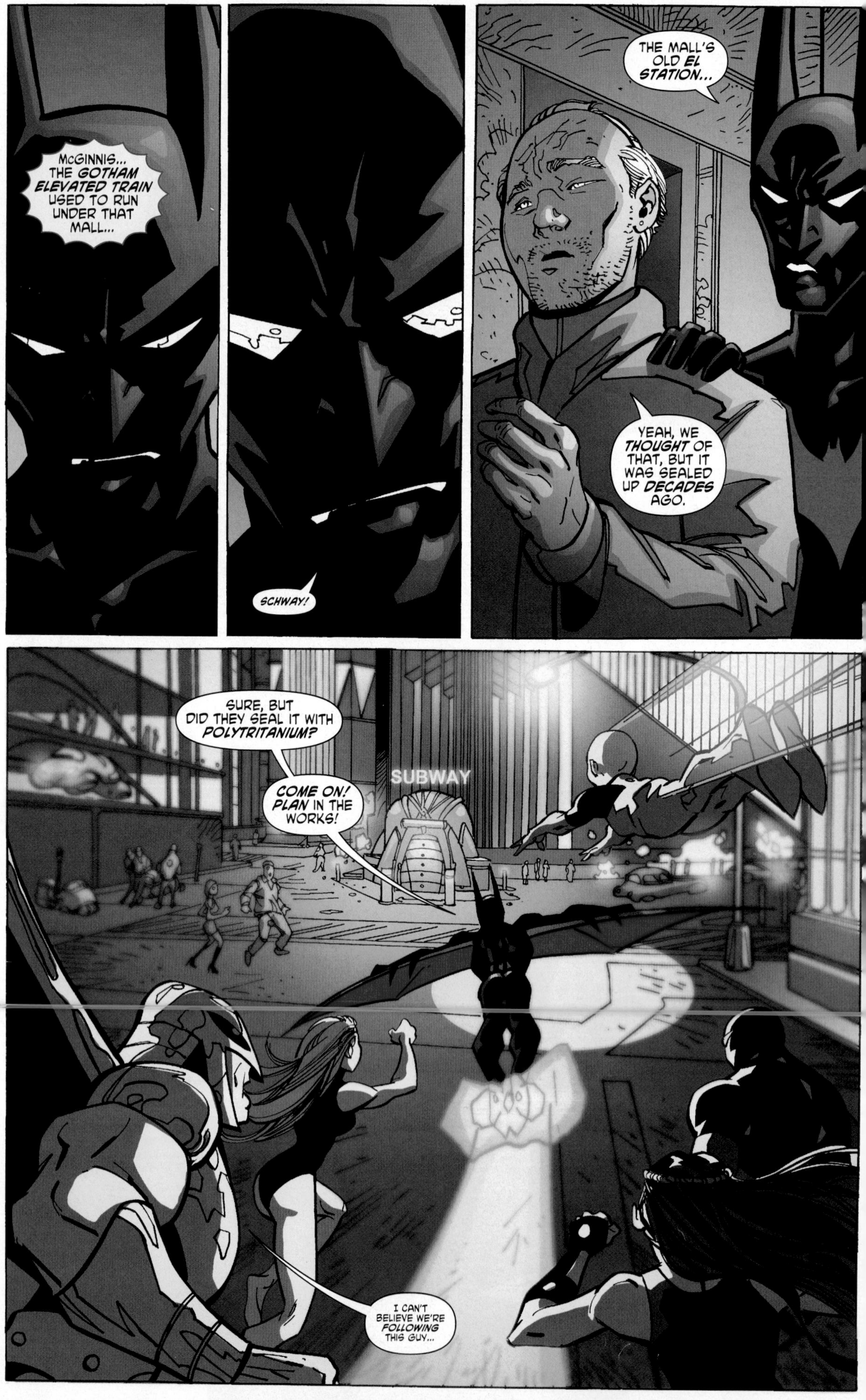
McGINNIS... THE GOTHAM ELEVATED TRAIN USED TO RUN UNDER THAT MALL...
SCHWAY!
THE MALL'S OLD EL STATION...
YEAH, WE THOUGHT OF THAT, BUT IT WAS SEALED UP DECADES AGO.
SURE, BUT DID THEY SEAL IT WITH POLYTRITANIUM?
COME ON! PLAN IN THE WORKS!
SUBWAY
I CAN'T BELIEVE WE'RE FOLLOWING THIS GUY...

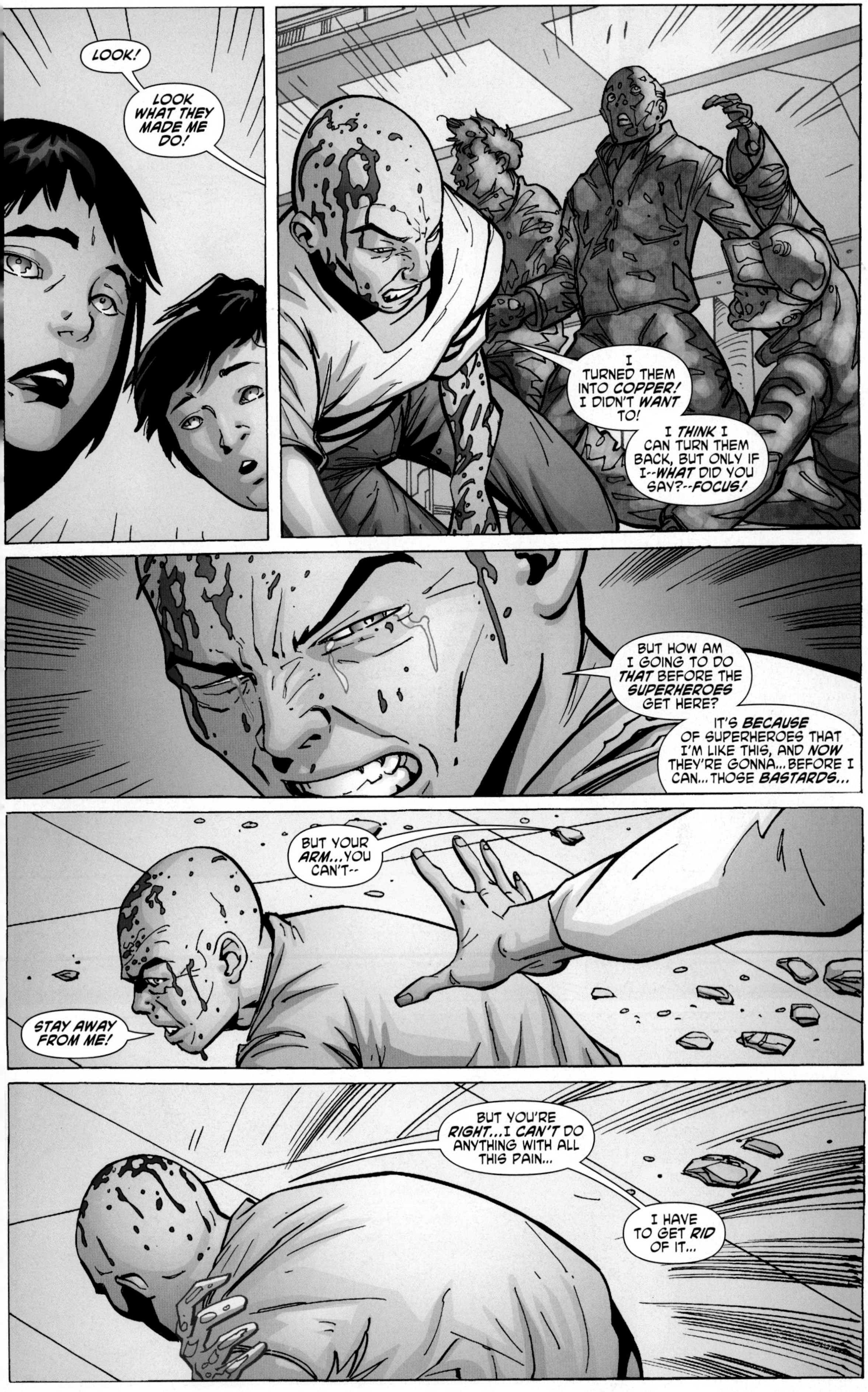
LOOK!
LOOK WHAT THEY MADE ME DO!
I TURNED THEM INTO COPPER! I DIDN'T WANT TO!
I THINK I CAN TURN THEM BACK, BUT ONLY IF I--WHAT DID YOU SAY?--FOCUS!
BUT HOW AM I GOING TO DO THAT BEFORE THE SUPERHEROES GET HERE?
IT'S BECAUSE OF SUPERHEROES THAT I'M LIKE THIS, AND NOW THEY'RE GONNA... BEFORE I CAN... THOSE BASTARDS...
BUT YOUR ARM...YOU CAN'T--
STAY AWAY FROM ME!
BUT YOU'RE RIGHT...I CAN'T DO ANYTHING WITH ALL THIS PAIN...
I HAVE TO GET RID OF IT...

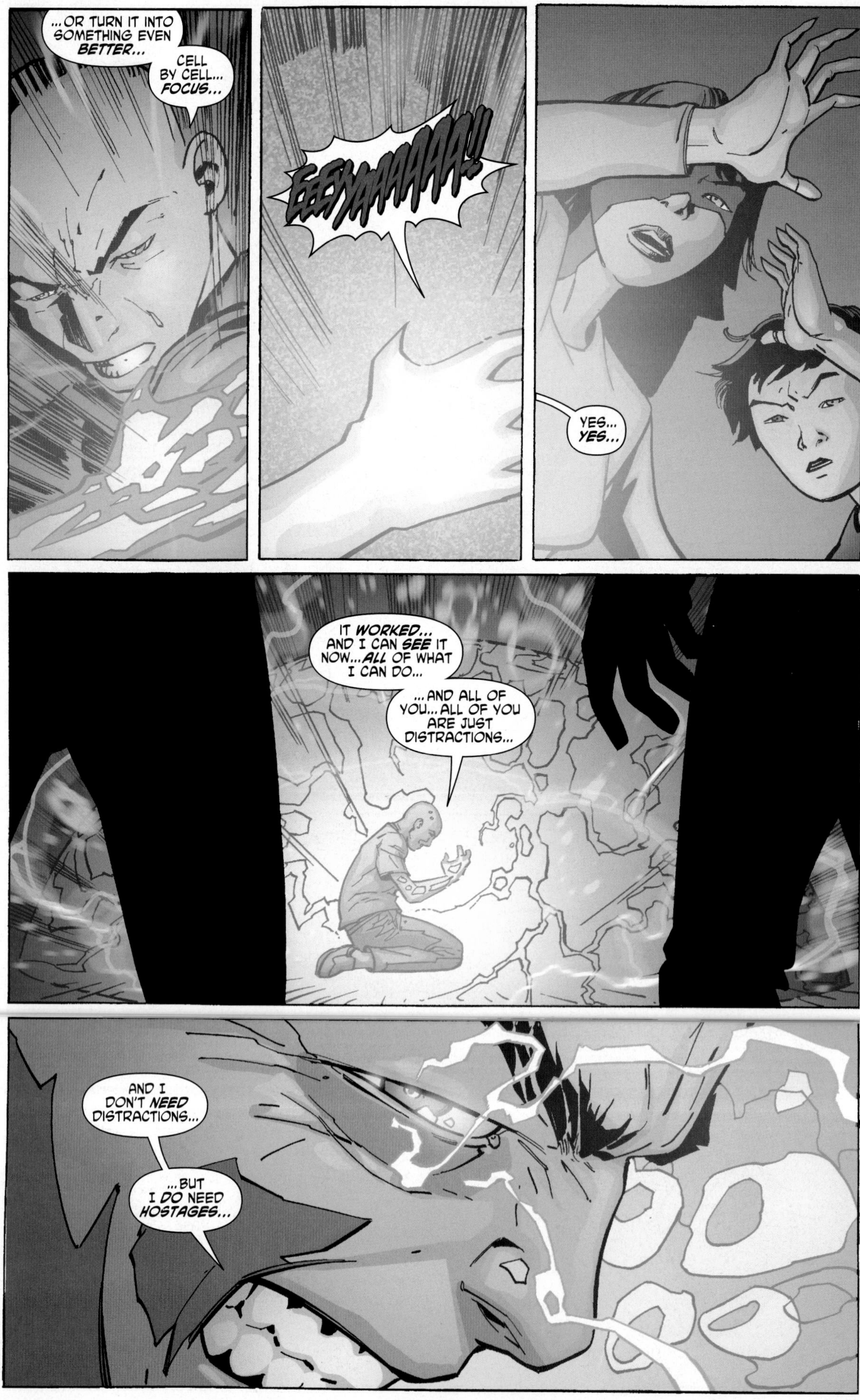
...OR TURN IT INTO SOMETHING EVEN BETTER...
CELL BY CELL... FOCUS...
EEEYYAAAAAA!!
YES... YES...
IT WORKED... AND I CAN SEE IT NOW...ALL OF WHAT I CAN DO...
...AND ALL OF YOU...ALL OF YOU ARE JUST DISTRACTIONS...
AND I DON'T NEED DISTRACTIONS...
...BUT I DO NEED HOSTAGES...

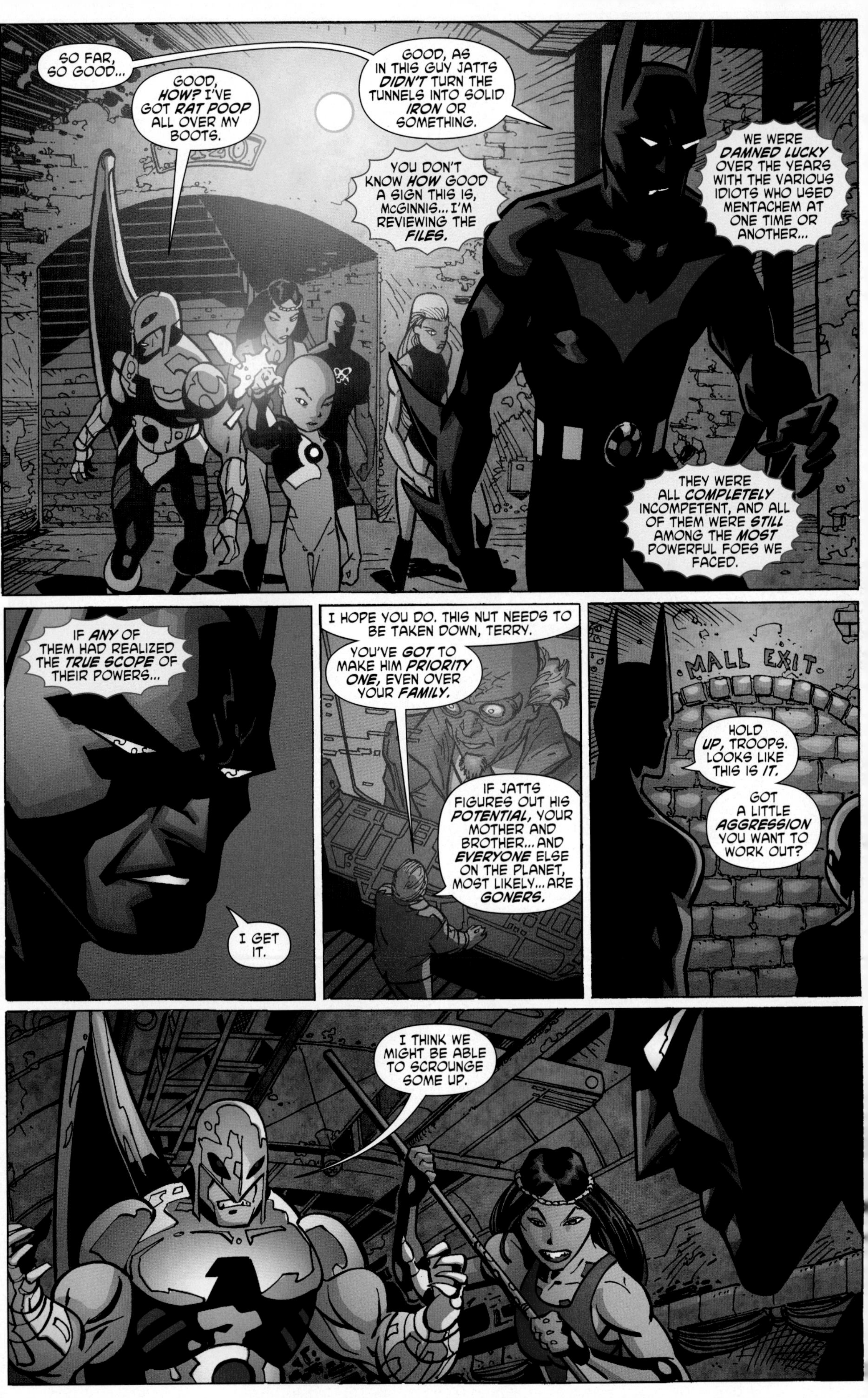
SO FAR, SO GOOD...
GOOD, *HOW?* I'VE GOT *RAT POOP* ALL OVER MY BOOTS.
GOOD, AS IN THIS GUY JATTS *DIDN'T* TURN THE TUNNELS INTO SOLID *IRON* OR SOMETHING.
YOU DON'T KNOW *HOW* GOOD A SIGN THIS IS, McGINNIS... I'M REVIEWING THE *FILES.*
WE WERE *DAMNED LUCKY* OVER THE YEARS WITH THE VARIOUS IDIOTS WHO USED MENTACHEM AT ONE TIME OR ANOTHER...
THEY WERE ALL *COMPLETELY* INCOMPETENT, AND ALL OF THEM WERE *STILL* AMONG THE *MOST* POWERFUL FOES WE FACED.
IF *ANY* OF THEM HAD REALIZED THE *TRUE SCOPE* OF THEIR POWERS...
I GET IT.
I HOPE YOU DO. THIS NUT NEEDS TO BE TAKEN DOWN, TERRY.
YOU'VE *GOT* TO MAKE HIM *PRIORITY ONE,* EVEN OVER YOUR *FAMILY.*
IF JATTS FIGURES OUT HIS *POTENTIAL,* YOUR MOTHER AND BROTHER... AND *EVERYONE* ELSE ON THE PLANET, MOST LIKELY... ARE *GONERS.*
MALL EXIT
HOLD *UP,* TROOPS. LOOKS LIKE THIS IS *IT.*
GOT A LITTLE *AGGRESSION* YOU WANT TO WORK OUT?
I THINK WE MIGHT BE ABLE TO SCROUNGE SOME UP.

KKRAKK ZZAMMM

THANKS FOR-- WHOA-- GETTING THEM TO LISTEN TO ME, BACK THERE.

OF COURSE. I JUST WISH YOU HAD TOLD US YOU NEEDED HELP *SOONER*, SO THE FIGHTING COULD HAVE BEEN *AVOIDED*.

YEAH... I DON'T *TRUST* TOO MANY PEOPLE, I GUESS...

WELL, IF YOU *NEED* A PERSON YOU CAN TRUST...

... I HOPE YOU WILL CONSIDER *ME*.

WE'RE THROUGH!

LOOKS LIKE IT GOES ALL THE WAY UP...

EXCELLENT. LET *ME* GO FIRST...

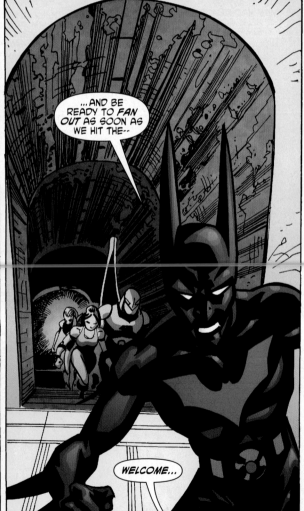

... AND BE READY TO *FAN OUT* AS SOON AS WE HIT THE--

WELCOME...

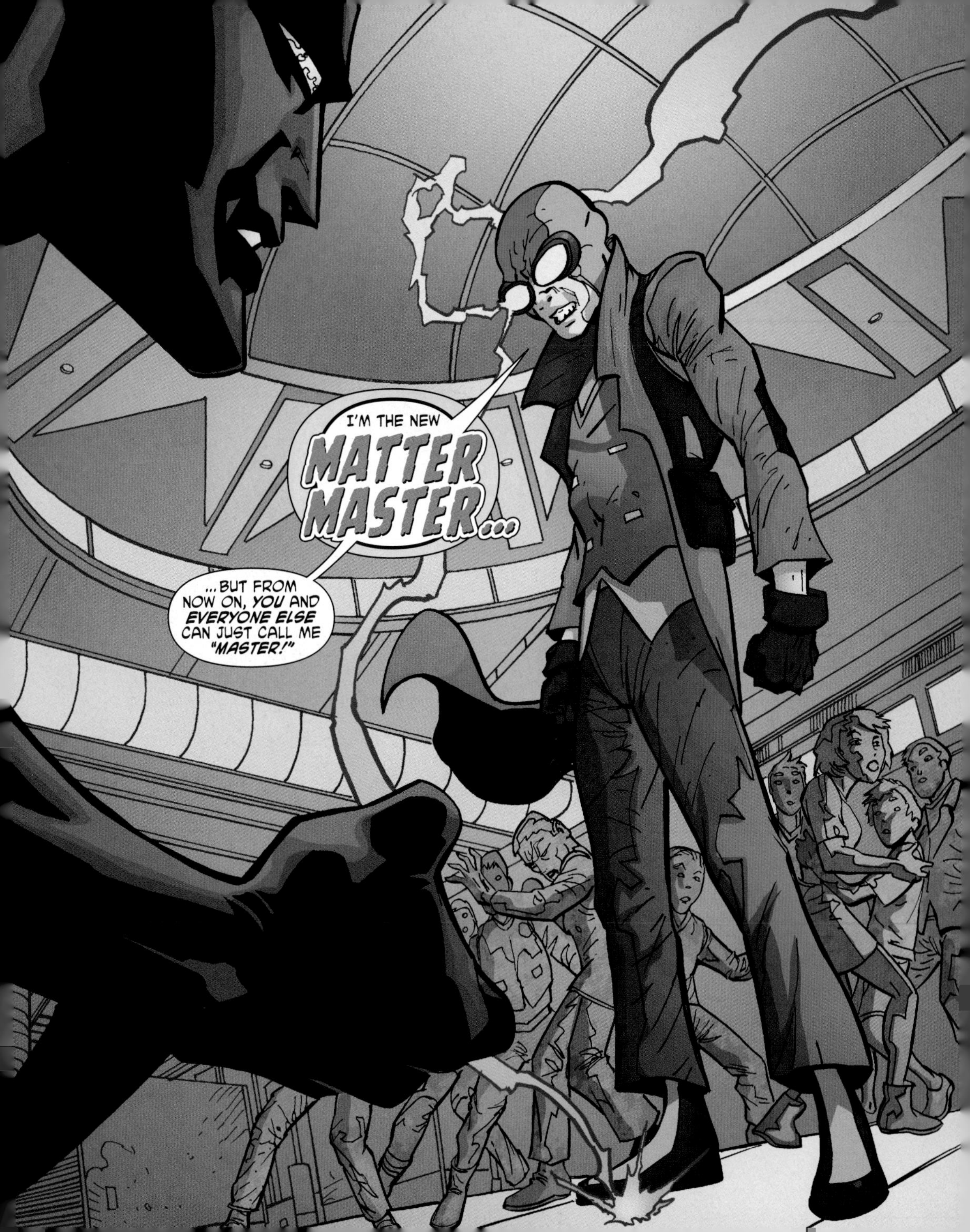
I'M THE NEW MATTER MASTER...
...BUT FROM NOW ON, YOU AND EVERYONE ELSE CAN JUST CALL ME "MASTER!"

THE HEART OF THE MATTER PART 3: COLLATERAL DAMAGE

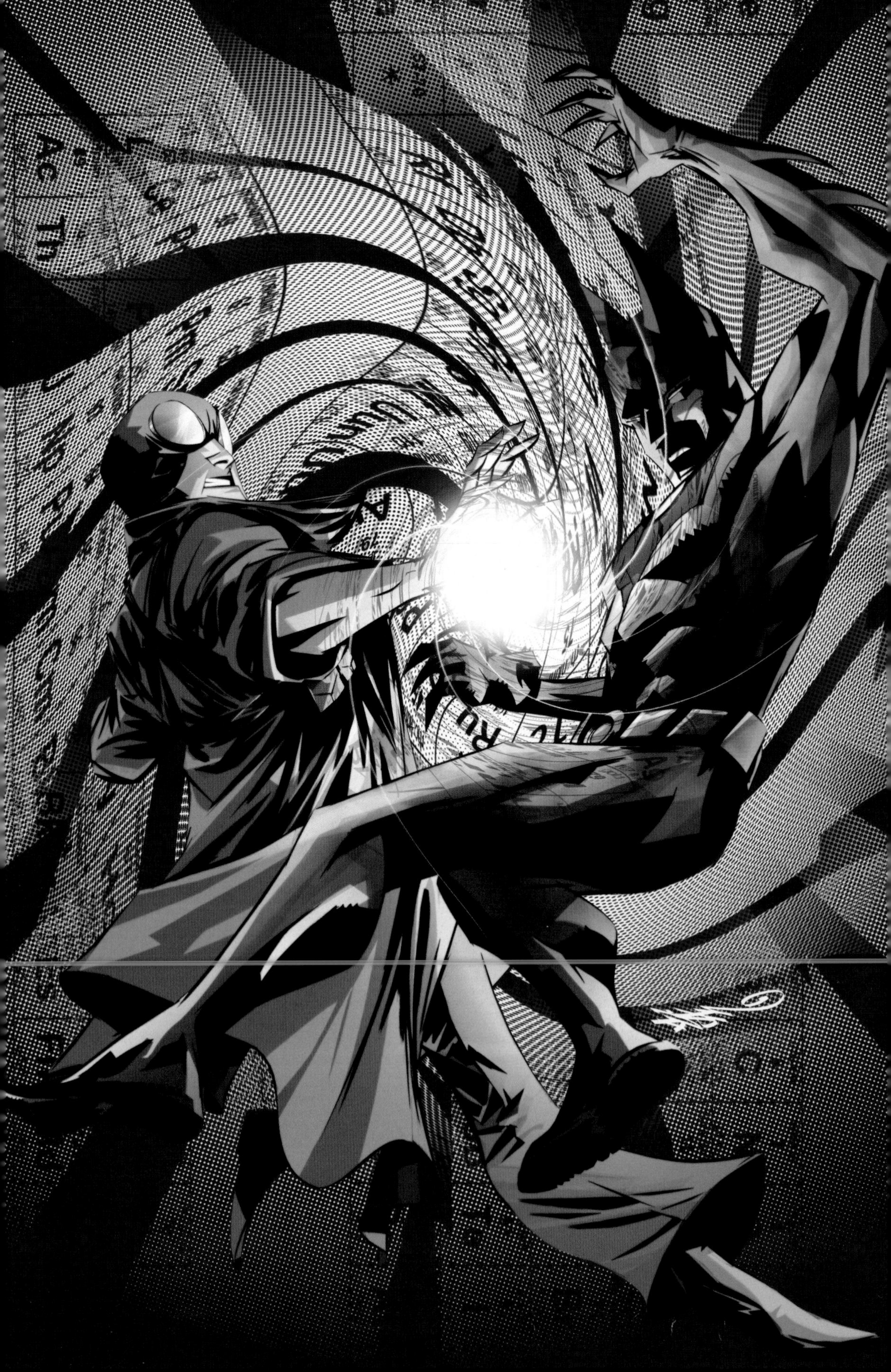

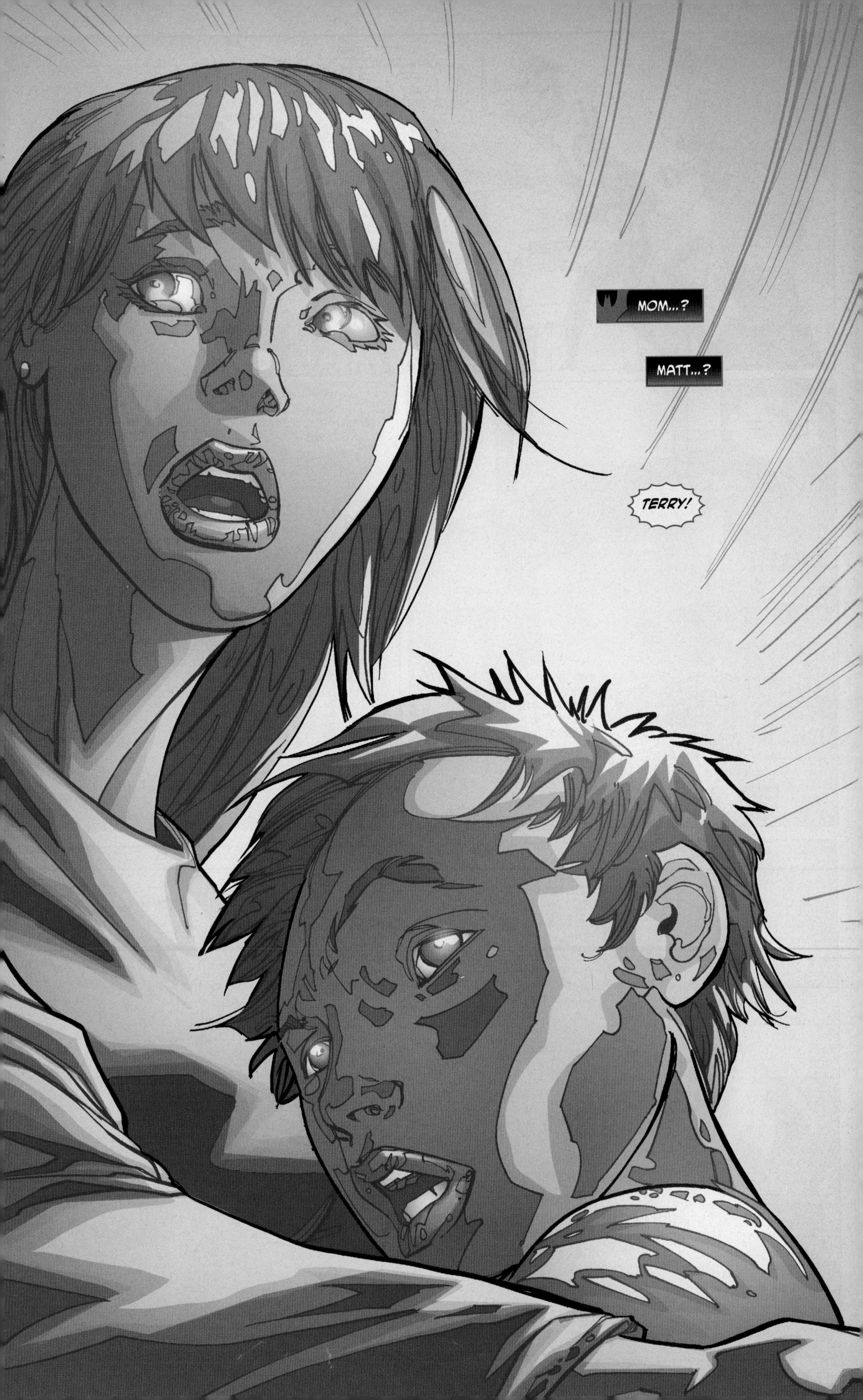
MOM...?
MATT...?
TERRY!

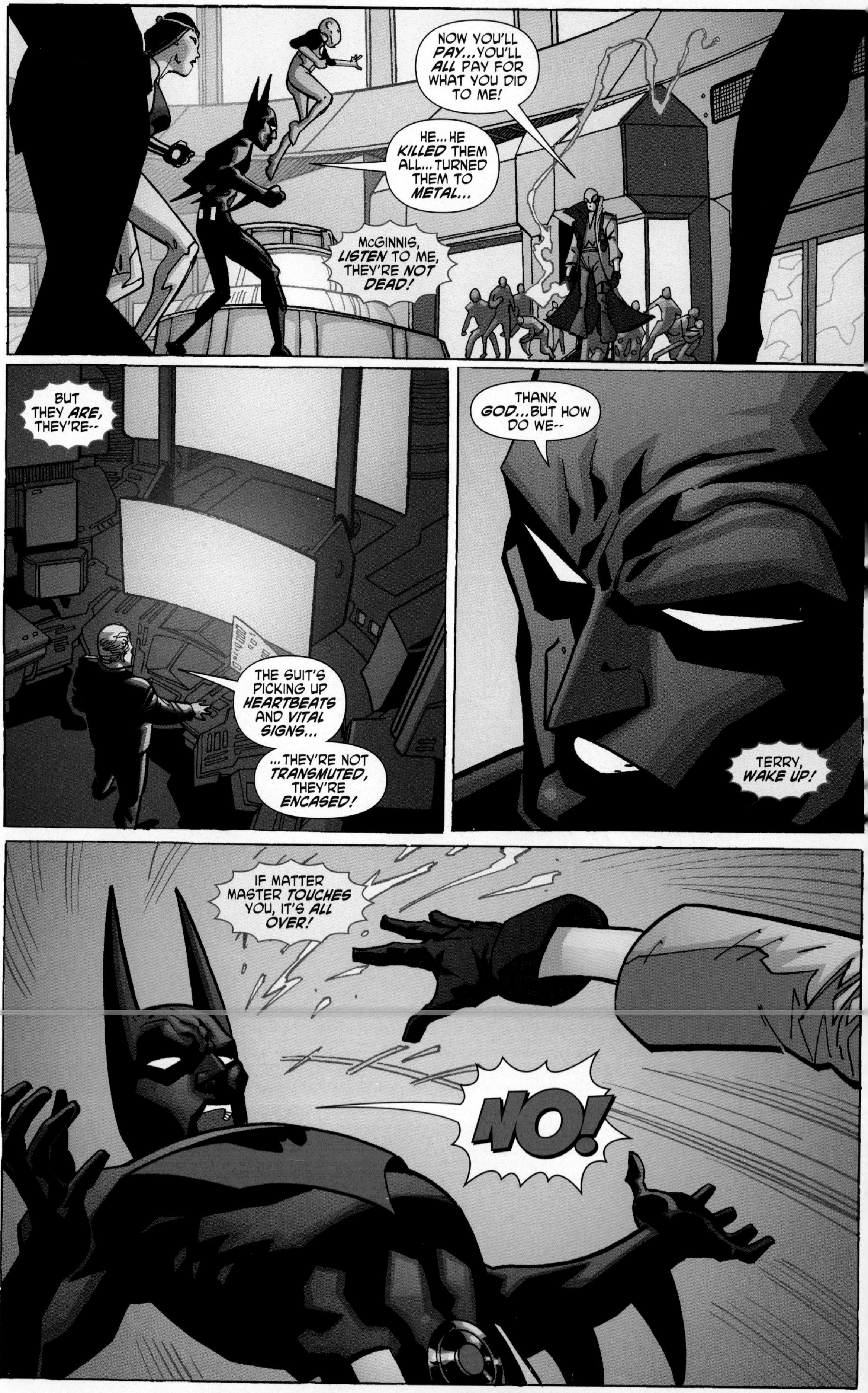
NOW YOU'LL PAY...YOU'LL ALL PAY FOR WHAT YOU DID TO ME!
HE...HE KILLED THEM ALL...TURNED THEM TO METAL...
McGINNIS, LISTEN TO ME, THEY'RE NOT DEAD!
BUT THEY ARE, THEY'RE--
THE SUIT'S PICKING UP HEARTBEATS AND VITAL SIGNS...
...THEY'RE NOT TRANSMUTED, THEY'RE ENCASED!
THANK GOD...BUT HOW DO WE--
TERRY, WAKE UP!
IF MATTER MASTER TOUCHES YOU, IT'S ALL OVER!
NO!

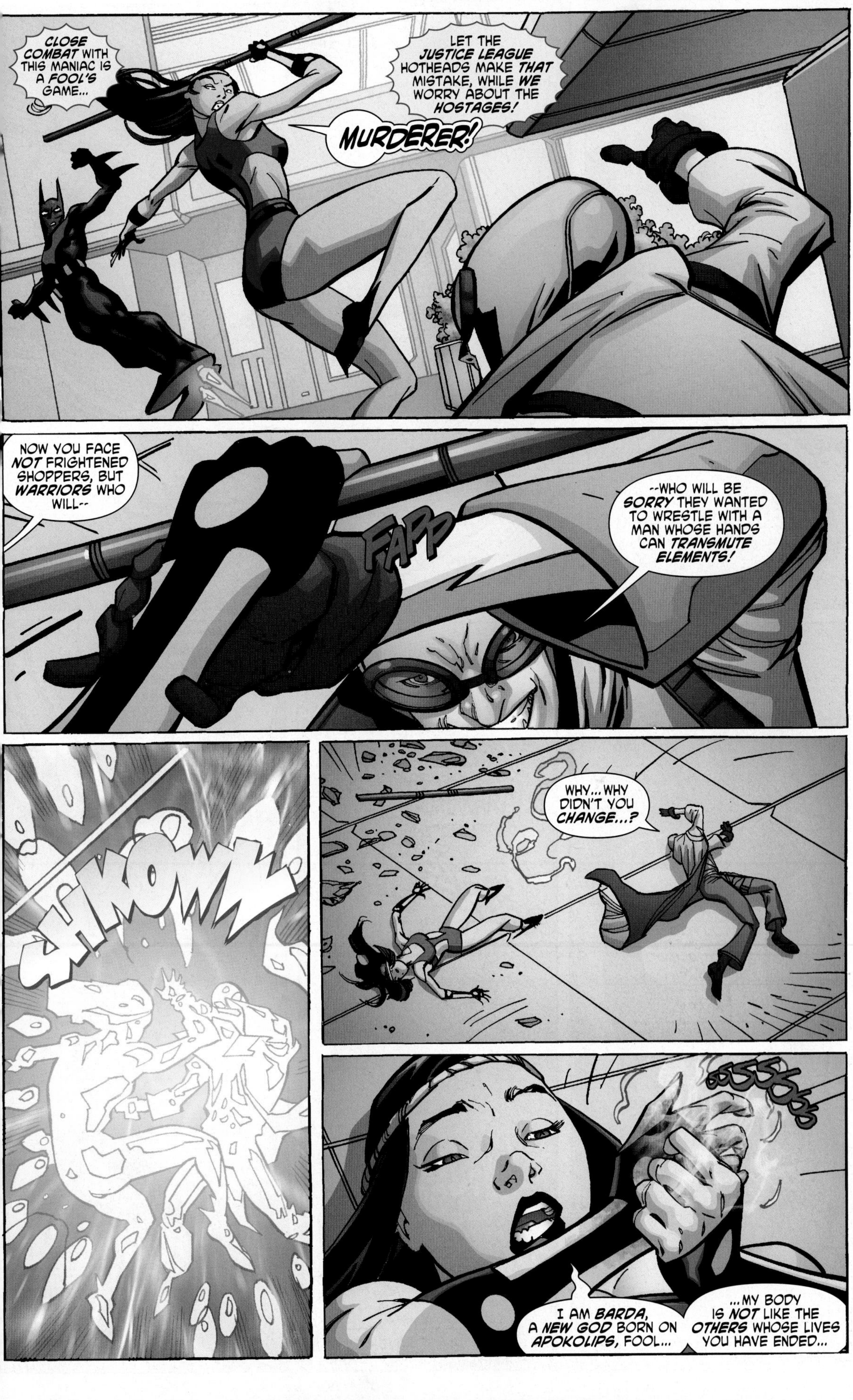

CLOSE COMBAT WITH THIS MANIAC IS A FOOL'S GAME...
LET THE JUSTICE LEAGUE HOTHEADS MAKE THAT MISTAKE, WHILE WE WORRY ABOUT THE HOSTAGES!
MURDERER!
NOW YOU FACE NOT FRIGHTENED SHOPPERS, BUT WARRIORS WHO WILL--
FAPP
--WHO WILL BE SORRY THEY WANTED TO WRESTLE WITH A MAN WHOSE HANDS CAN TRANSMUTE ELEMENTS!
WHY... WHY DIDN'T YOU CHANGE...?
I AM BARDA, A NEW GOD BORN ON APOKOLIPS, FOOL...
...MY BODY IS NOT LIKE THE OTHERS WHOSE LIVES YOU HAVE ENDED...

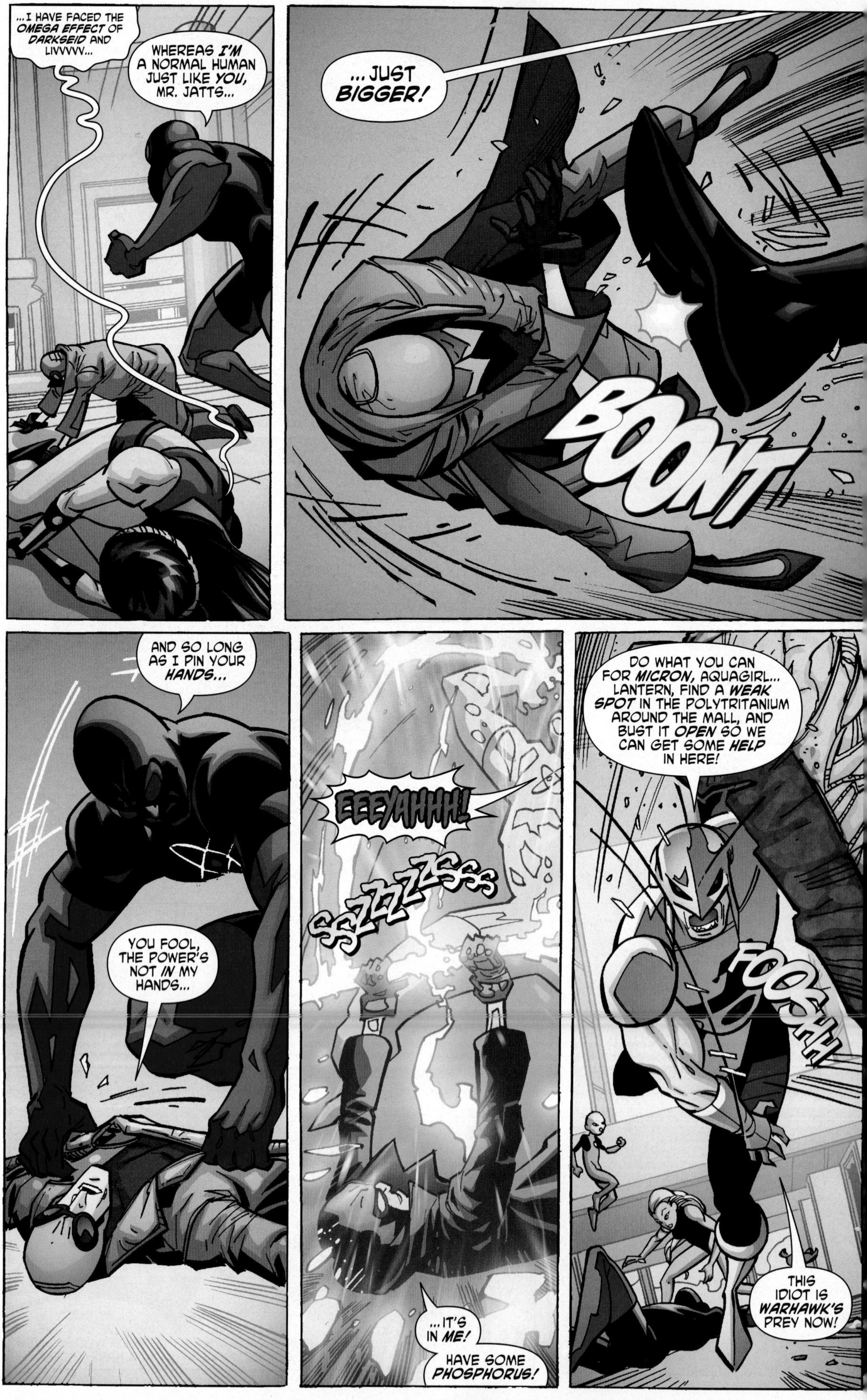
...I HAVE FACED THE OMEGA EFFECT OF DARKSEID AND LIVVVVV...
WHEREAS I'M A NORMAL HUMAN JUST LIKE YOU, MR. JATTS...
...JUST BIGGER!
BOONT
AND SO LONG AS I PIN YOUR HANDS...
YOU FOOL, THE POWER'S NOT IN MY HANDS...
EEEYAHHH!
SSZZZZZSSSS
...IT'S IN ME!
HAVE SOME PHOSPHORUS!
DO WHAT YOU CAN FOR MICRON, AQUAGIRL... LANTERN, FIND A WEAK SPOT IN THE POLYTRITANIUM AROUND THE MALL, AND BUST IT OPEN SO WE CAN GET SOME HELP IN HERE!
FOOSH
THIS IDIOT IS WARHAWK'S PREY NOW!

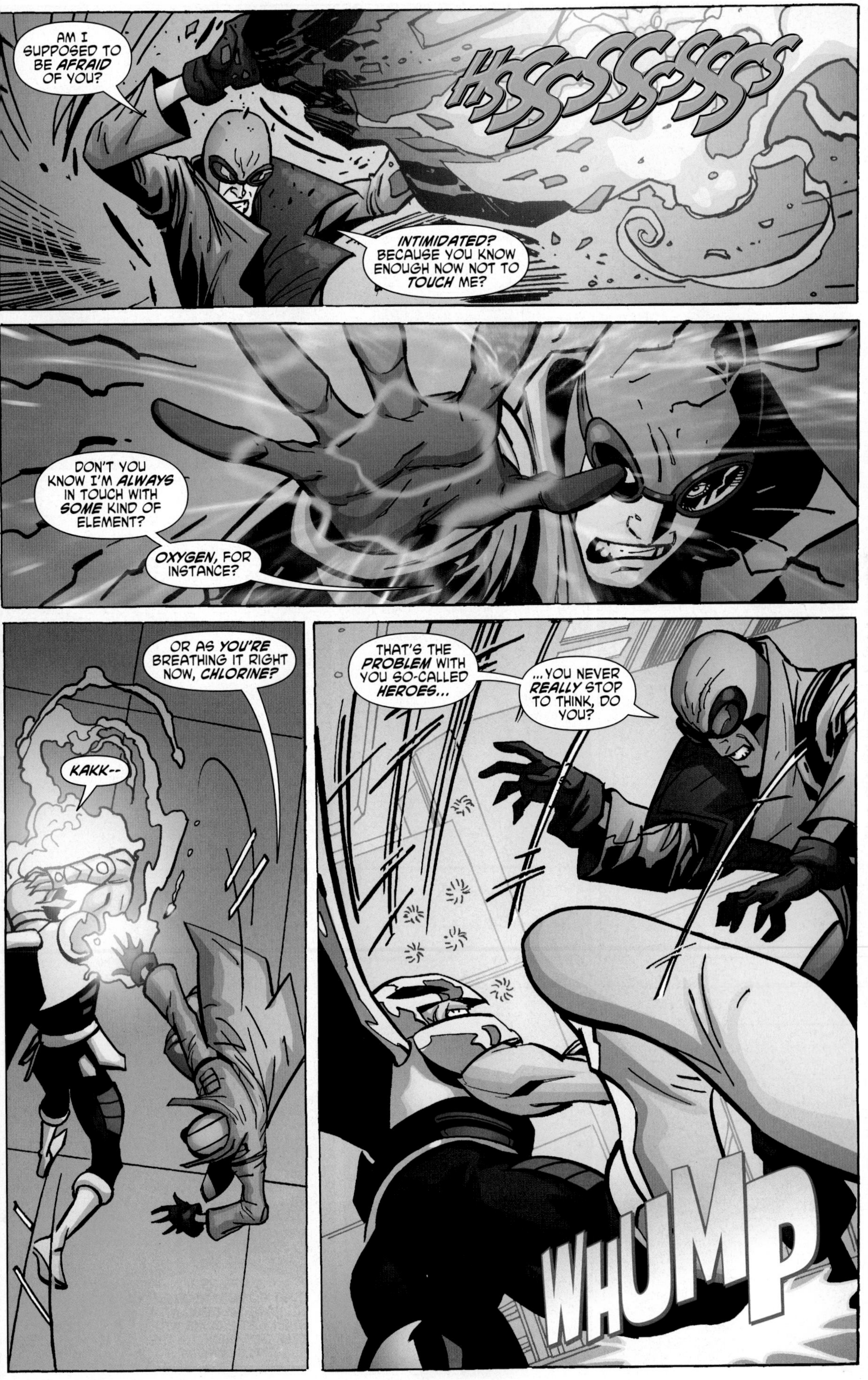

AM I SUPPOSED TO BE AFRAID OF YOU?
HSSSSSSSSS
INTIMIDATED? BECAUSE YOU KNOW ENOUGH NOW NOT TO TOUCH ME?
DON'T YOU KNOW I'M ALWAYS IN TOUCH WITH SOME KIND OF ELEMENT?
OXYGEN, FOR INSTANCE?
OR AS YOU'RE BREATHING IT RIGHT NOW, CHLORINE?
KAKK--
THAT'S THE PROBLEM WITH YOU SO-CALLED HEROES...
...YOU NEVER REALLY STOP TO THINK, DO YOU?
WHUMP

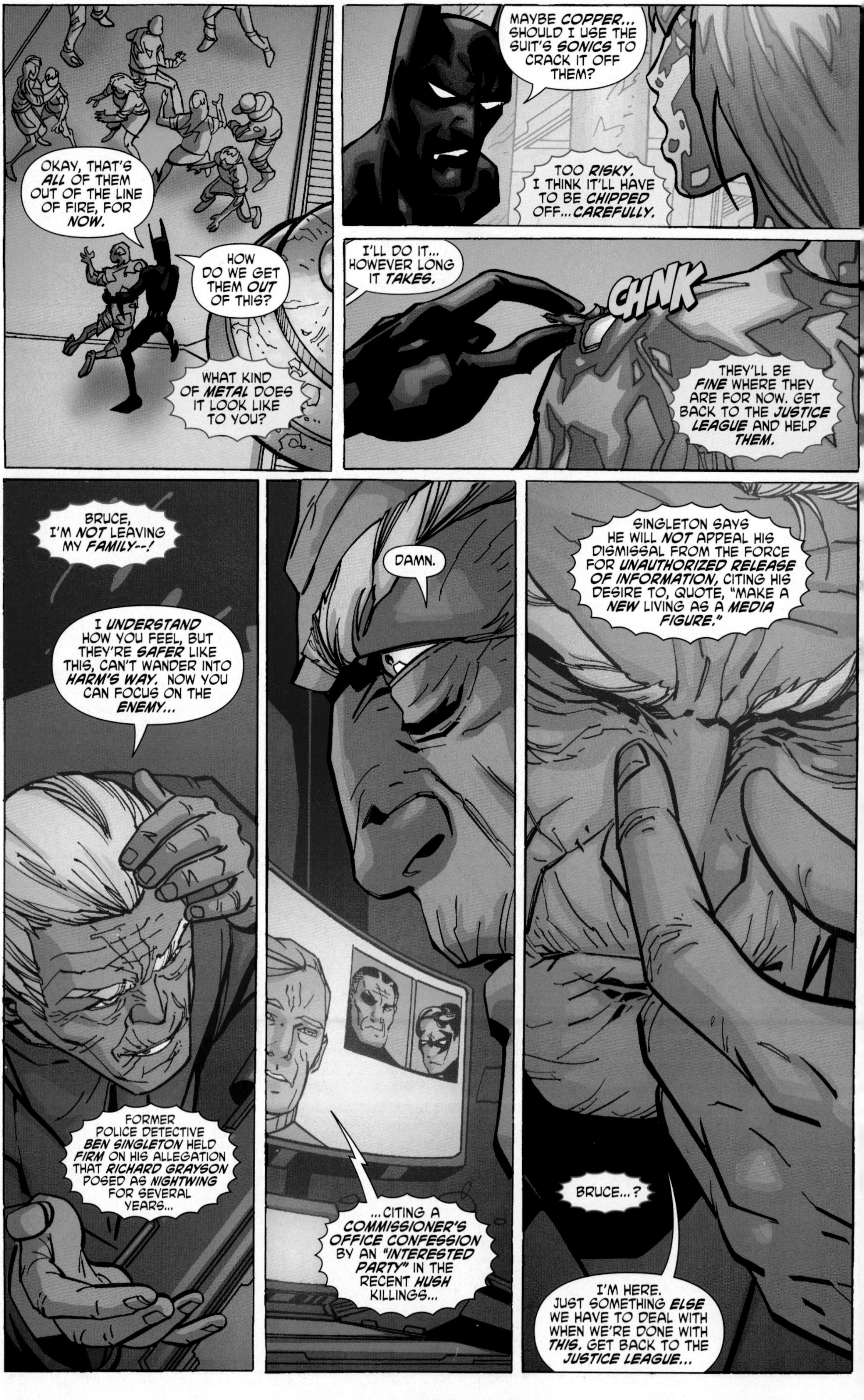
OKAY, THAT'S ALL OF THEM OUT OF THE LINE OF FIRE, FOR NOW.
HOW DO WE GET THEM OUT OF THIS?
WHAT KIND OF METAL DOES IT LOOK LIKE TO YOU?
MAYBE COPPER... SHOULD I USE THE SUIT'S SONICS TO CRACK IT OFF THEM?
TOO RISKY. I THINK IT'LL HAVE TO BE CHIPPED OFF...CAREFULLY.
I'LL DO IT... HOWEVER LONG IT TAKES.
CHNK
THEY'LL BE FINE WHERE THEY ARE FOR NOW. GET BACK TO THE JUSTICE LEAGUE AND HELP THEM.
BRUCE, I'M NOT LEAVING MY FAMILY--!
I UNDERSTAND HOW YOU FEEL, BUT THEY'RE SAFER LIKE THIS, CAN'T WANDER INTO HARM'S WAY. NOW YOU CAN FOCUS ON THE ENEMY...
FORMER POLICE DETECTIVE BEN SINGLETON HELD FIRM ON HIS ALLEGATION THAT RICHARD GRAYSON POSED AS NIGHTWING FOR SEVERAL YEARS...
DAMN.
...CITING A COMMISSIONER'S OFFICE CONFESSION BY AN "INTERESTED PARTY" IN THE RECENT HUSH KILLINGS...
SINGLETON SAYS HE WILL NOT APPEAL HIS DISMISSAL FROM THE FORCE FOR UNAUTHORIZED RELEASE OF INFORMATION, CITING HIS DESIRE TO, QUOTE, "MAKE A NEW LIVING AS A MEDIA FIGURE."
BRUCE...?
I'M HERE. JUST SOMETHING ELSE WE HAVE TO DEAL WITH WHEN WE'RE DONE WITH THIS. GET BACK TO THE JUSTICE LEAGUE...

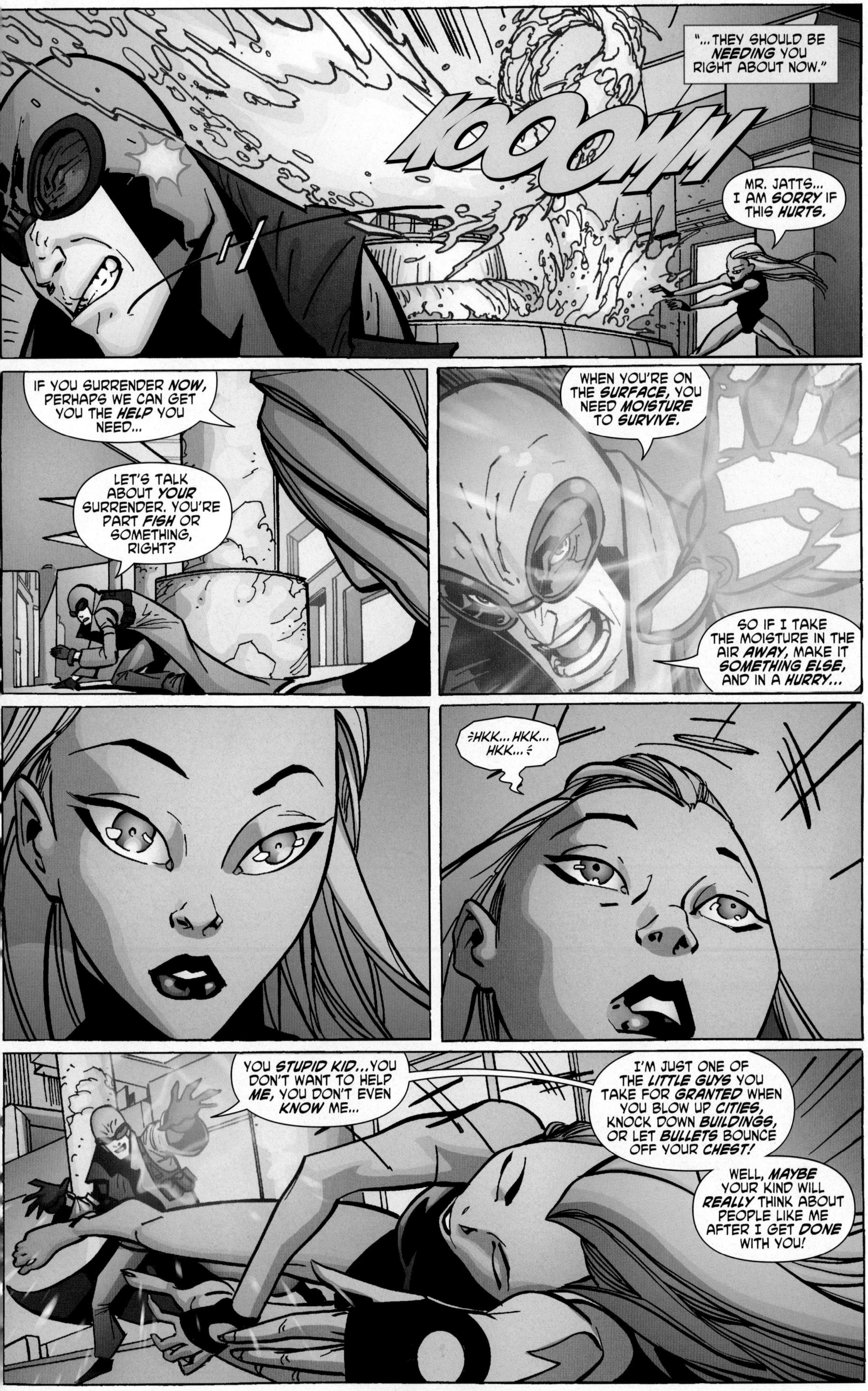
"...THEY SHOULD BE NEEDING YOU RIGHT ABOUT NOW."
KOOOOMM
MR. JATTS... I AM SORRY IF THIS HURTS.
IF YOU SURRENDER NOW, PERHAPS WE CAN GET YOU THE HELP YOU NEED...
LET'S TALK ABOUT YOUR SURRENDER. YOU'RE PART FISH OR SOMETHING, RIGHT?
WHEN YOU'RE ON THE SURFACE, YOU NEED MOISTURE TO SURVIVE.
SO IF I TAKE THE MOISTURE IN THE AIR AWAY, MAKE IT SOMETHING ELSE, AND IN A HURRY...
HKK... HKK... HKK...
YOU STUPID KID...YOU DON'T WANT TO HELP ME, YOU DON'T EVEN KNOW ME...
I'M JUST ONE OF THE LITTLE GUYS YOU TAKE FOR GRANTED WHEN YOU BLOW UP CITIES, KNOCK DOWN BUILDINGS, OR LET BULLETS BOUNCE OFF YOUR CHEST!
WELL, MAYBE YOUR KIND WILL REALLY THINK ABOUT PEOPLE LIKE ME AFTER I GET DONE WITH YOU!

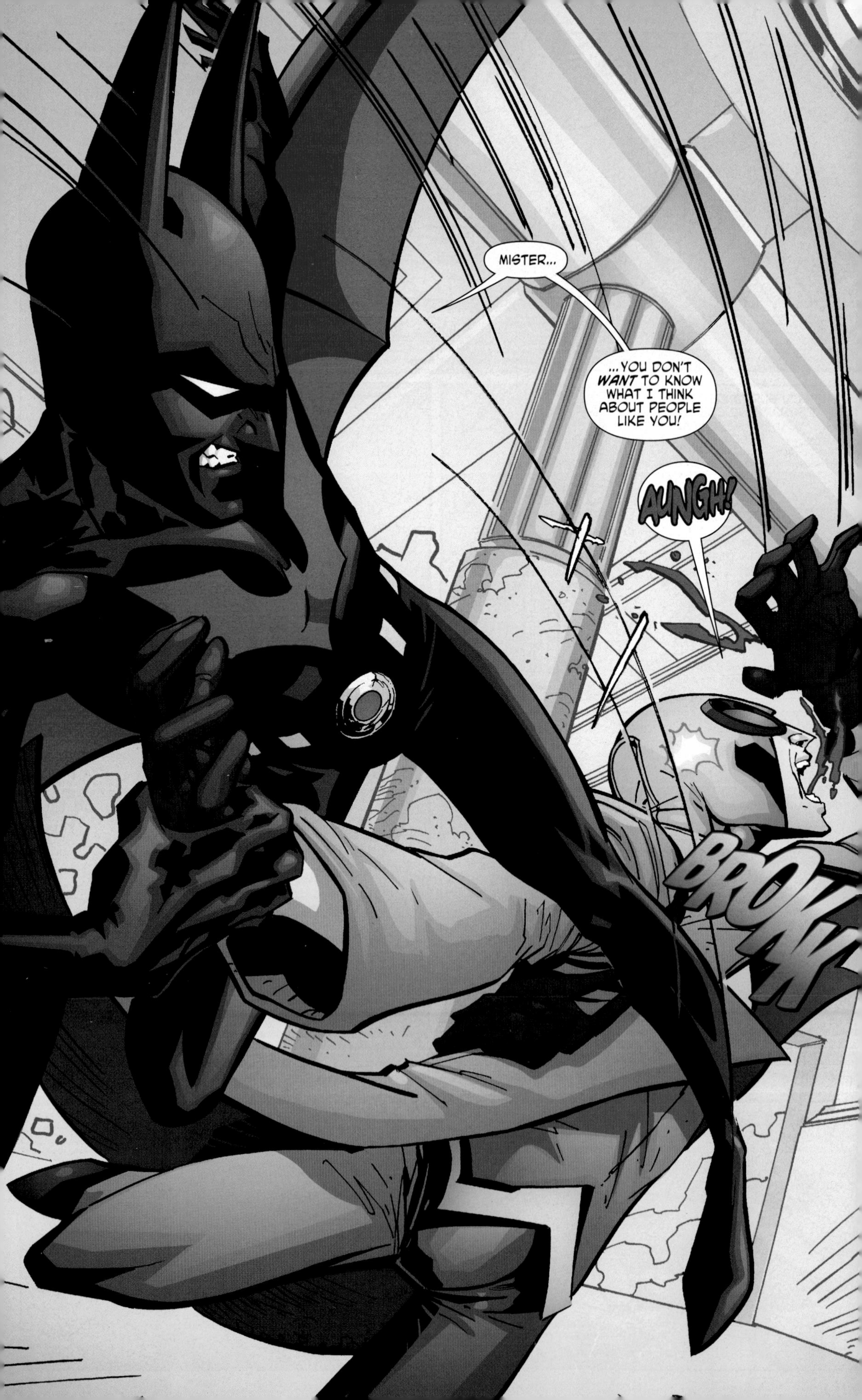
MISTER...
...YOU DON'T WANT TO KNOW WHAT I THINK ABOUT PEOPLE LIKE YOU!
AUNGH!
BRONK

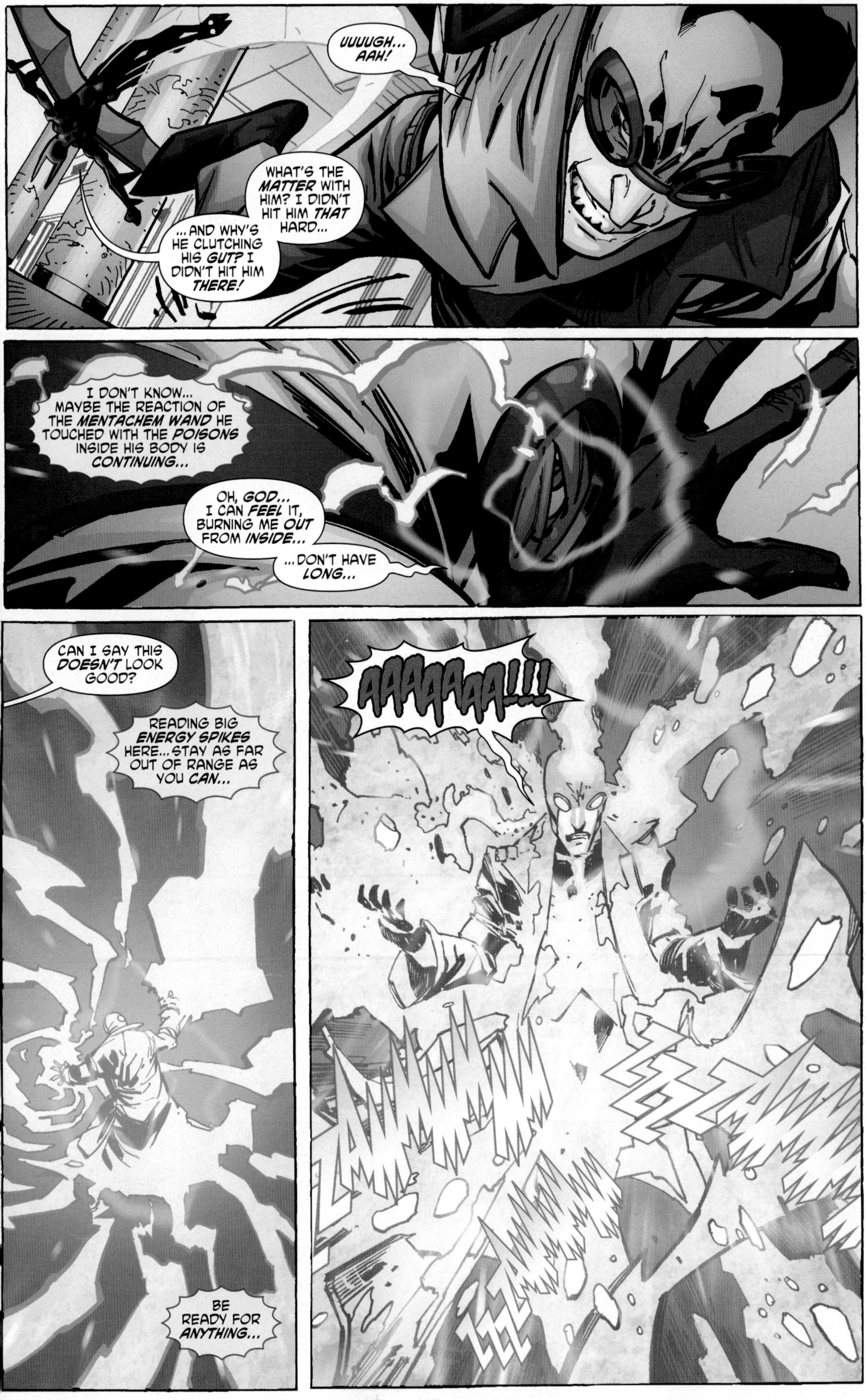
UUUUGH... AAH!
WHAT'S THE MATTER WITH HIM? I DIDN'T HIT HIM THAT HARD...
...AND WHY'S HE CLUTCHING HIS GUT? I DIDN'T HIT HIM THERE!
I DON'T KNOW... MAYBE THE REACTION OF THE MENTACHEM WAND HE TOUCHED WITH THE POISONS INSIDE HIS BODY IS CONTINUING...
OH, GOD... I CAN FEEL IT, BURNING ME OUT FROM INSIDE...
...DON'T HAVE LONG...
CAN I SAY THIS DOESN'T LOOK GOOD?
READING BIG ENERGY SPIKES HERE...STAY AS FAR OUT OF RANGE AS YOU CAN...
BE READY FOR ANYTHING...
AAAAAAA!!!

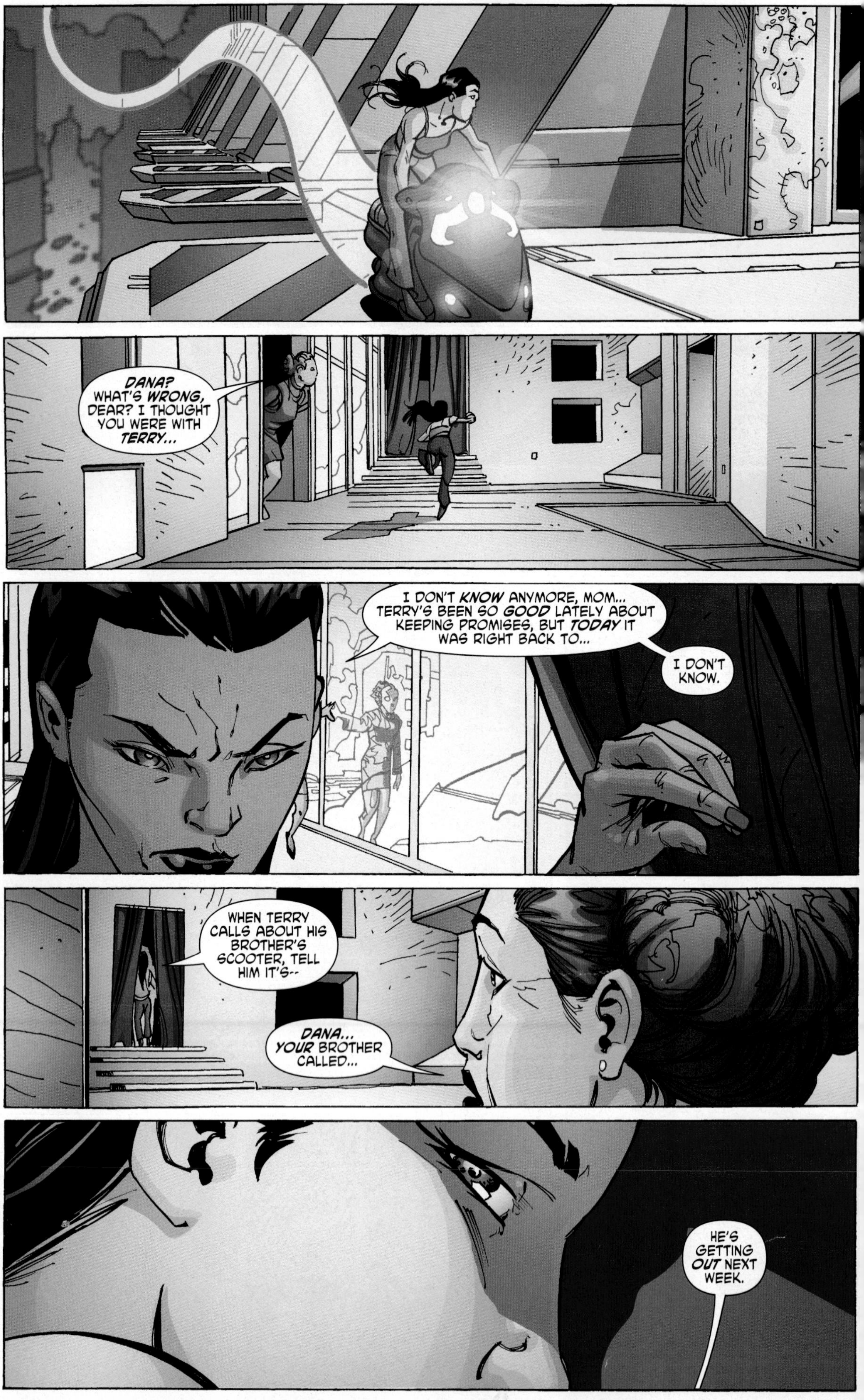
DANA? WHAT'S WRONG, DEAR? I THOUGHT YOU WERE WITH TERRY...
I DON'T KNOW ANYMORE, MOM... TERRY'S BEEN SO GOOD LATELY ABOUT KEEPING PROMISES, BUT TODAY IT WAS RIGHT BACK TO...
I DON'T KNOW.
WHEN TERRY CALLS ABOUT HIS BROTHER'S SCOOTER, TELL HIM IT'S--
DANA... YOUR BROTHER CALLED...
HE'S GETTING OUT NEXT WEEK.

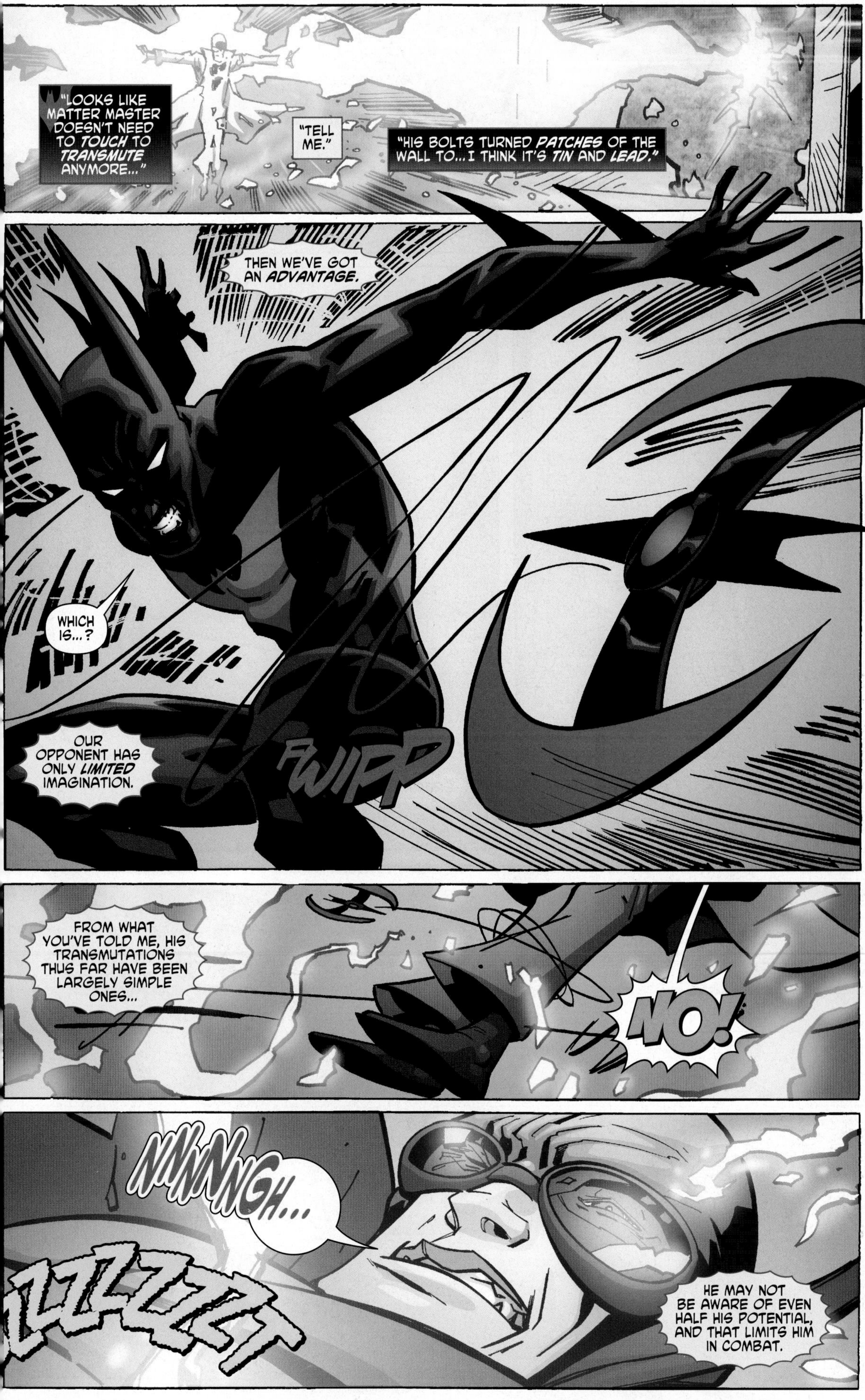
"LOOKS LIKE MATTER MASTER DOESN'T NEED TO TOUCH TO TRANSMUTE ANYMORE..."
"TELL ME."
"HIS BOLTS TURNED PATCHES OF THE WALL TO...I THINK IT'S TIN AND LEAD."
THEN WE'VE GOT AN ADVANTAGE.
WHICH IS...?
OUR OPPONENT HAS ONLY LIMITED IMAGINATION.
FWIPP
FROM WHAT YOU'VE TOLD ME, HIS TRANSMUTATIONS THUS FAR HAVE BEEN LARGELY SIMPLE ONES...
NO!
NNNNNGH...
ZZZZZZT
HE MAY NOT BE AWARE OF EVEN HALF HIS POTENTIAL, AND THAT LIMITS HIM IN COMBAT.

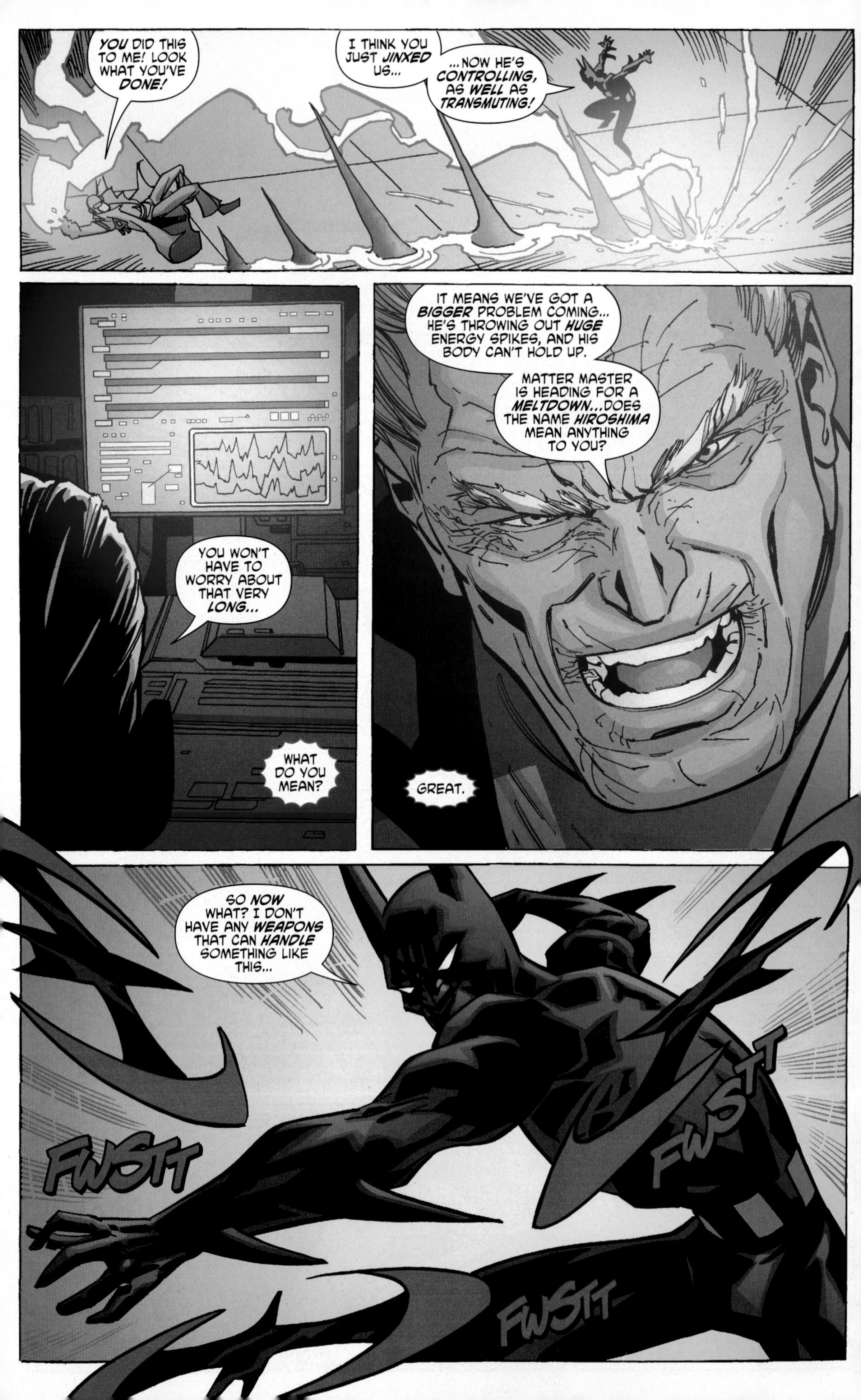
YOU DID THIS TO ME! LOOK WHAT YOU'VE DONE!
I THINK YOU JUST JINXED US...
...NOW HE'S CONTROLLING, AS WELL AS TRANSMUTING!
IT MEANS WE'VE GOT A BIGGER PROBLEM COMING... HE'S THROWING OUT HUGE ENERGY SPIKES, AND HIS BODY CAN'T HOLD UP.
MATTER MASTER IS HEADING FOR A MELTDOWN...DOES THE NAME HIROSHIMA MEAN ANYTHING TO YOU?
YOU WON'T HAVE TO WORRY ABOUT THAT VERY LONG...
WHAT DO YOU MEAN?
GREAT.
SO NOW WHAT? I DON'T HAVE ANY WEAPONS THAT CAN HANDLE SOMETHING LIKE THIS...
FWSTT
FWSTT
FWSTT

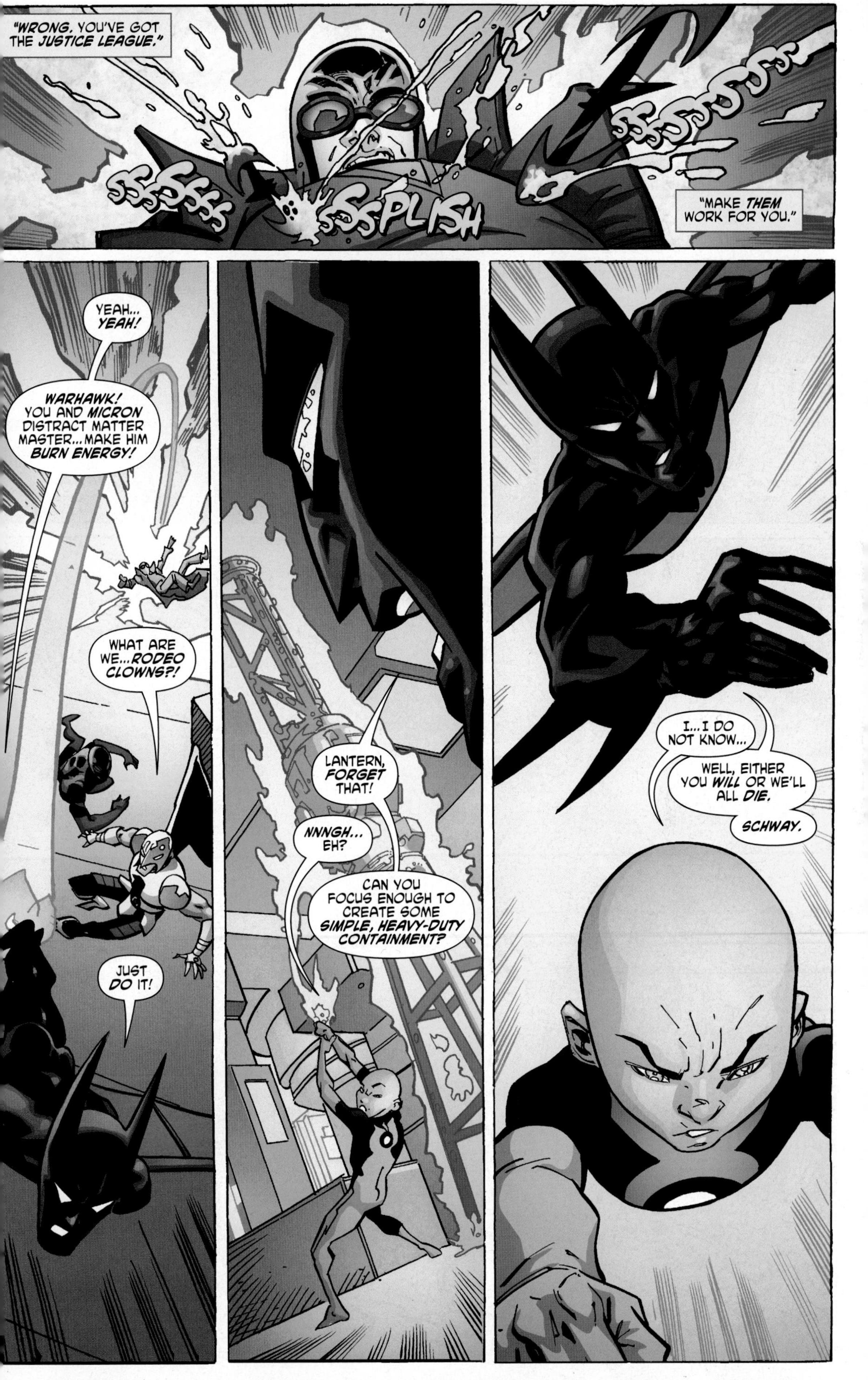

"WRONG. YOU'VE GOT THE JUSTICE LEAGUE."
SSSSSSS
SSSPLISH
SSSSSSS
"MAKE THEM WORK FOR YOU."
YEAH... YEAH!
WARHAWK! YOU AND MICRON DISTRACT MATTER MASTER...MAKE HIM BURN ENERGY!
WHAT ARE WE...RODEO CLOWNS?!
JUST DO IT!
LANTERN, FORGET THAT!
NNNGH... EH?
CAN YOU FOCUS ENOUGH TO CREATE SOME SIMPLE, HEAVY-DUTY CONTAINMENT?
I...I DO NOT KNOW...
WELL, EITHER YOU WILL OR WE'LL ALL DIE.
SCHWAY.

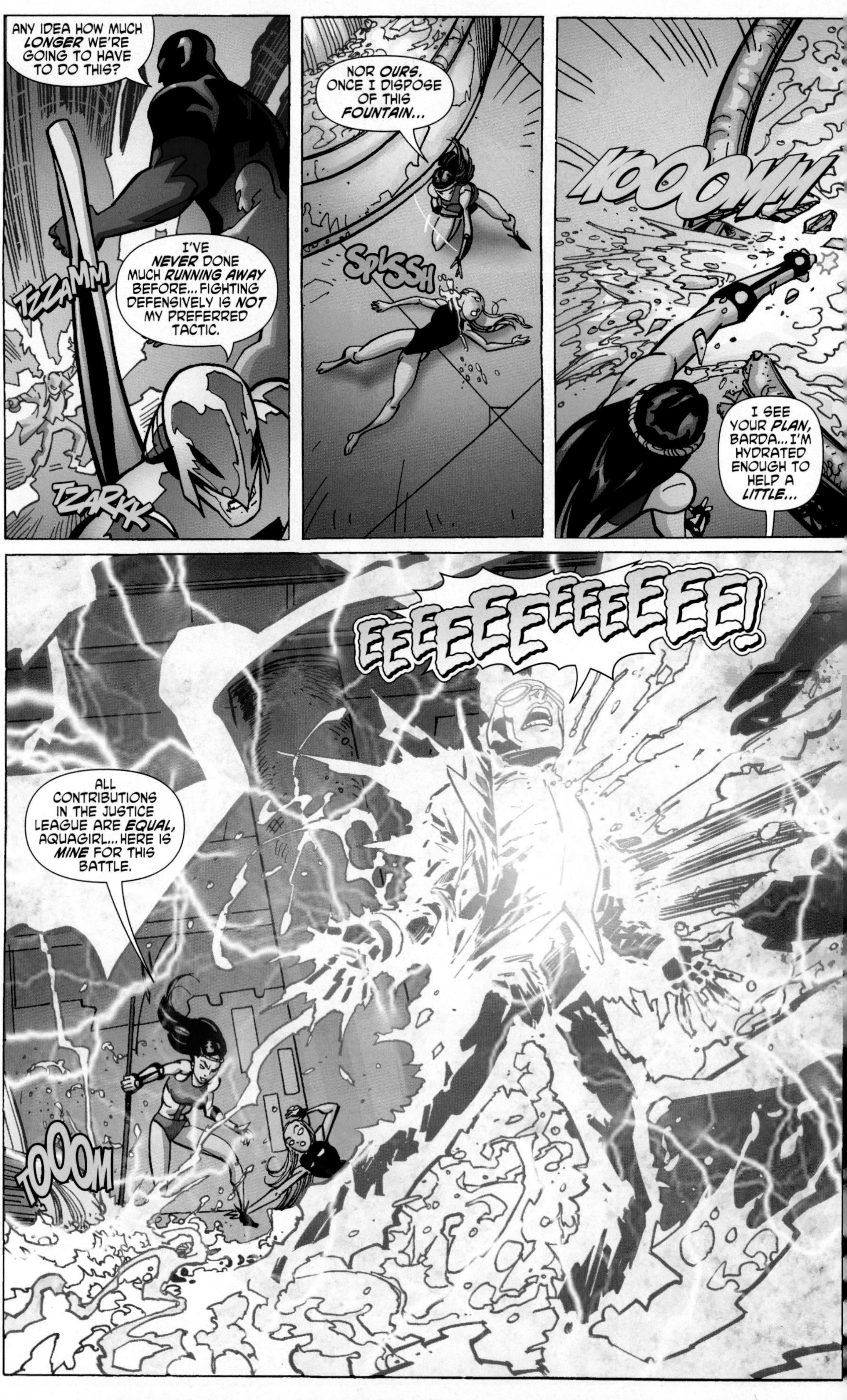
ANY IDEA HOW MUCH LONGER WE'RE GOING TO HAVE TO DO THIS?
TZZAMM
I'VE NEVER DONE MUCH RUNNING AWAY BEFORE...FIGHTING DEFENSIVELY IS NOT MY PREFERRED TACTIC.
TZARKK
NOR OURS. ONCE I DISPOSE OF THIS FOUNTAIN...
SPLSSH
KOOOOMM
I SEE YOUR PLAN, BARDA...I'M HYDRATED ENOUGH TO HELP A LITTLE...
EEEEEEEEEEEEE!
ALL CONTRIBUTIONS IN THE JUSTICE LEAGUE ARE EQUAL, AQUAGIRL...HERE IS MINE FOR THIS BATTLE.
TOOOM

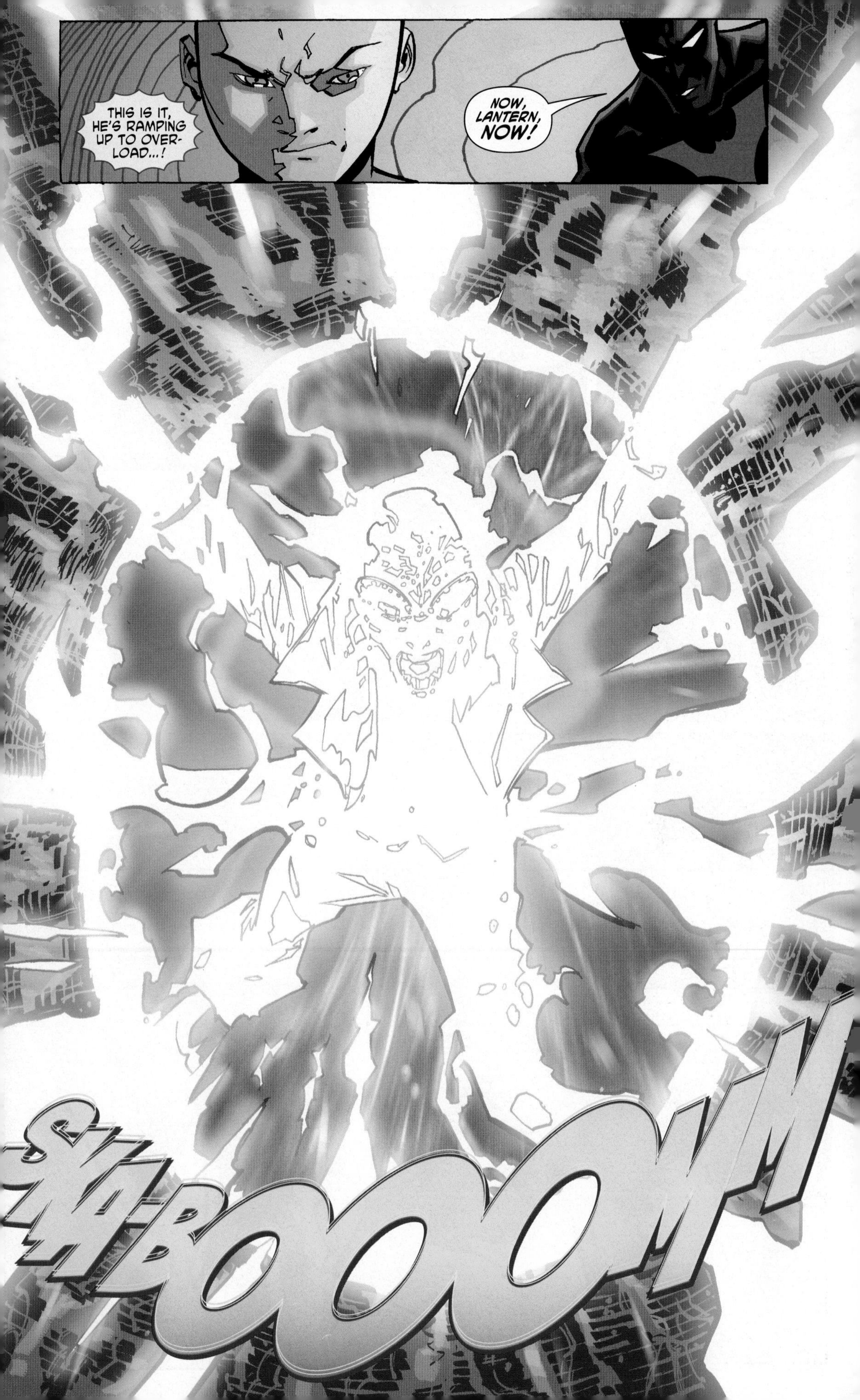
THIS IS IT, HE'S RAMPING UP TO OVER-LOAD...!
NOW, LANTERN, NOW!
SHABOOOOM

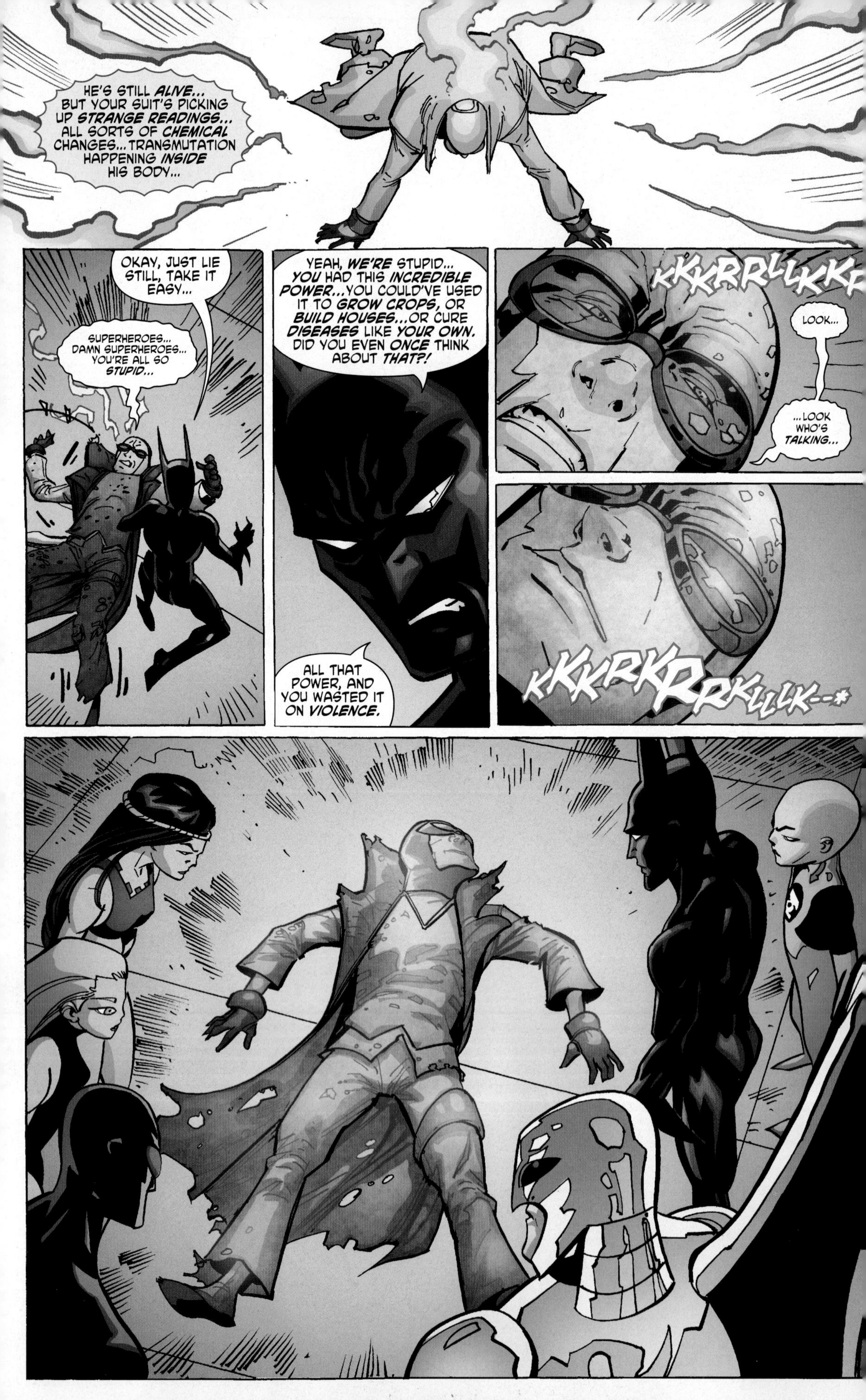
HE'S STILL *ALIVE*... BUT YOUR SUIT'S PICKING UP *STRANGE READINGS*... ALL SORTS OF *CHEMICAL* CHANGES...TRANSMUTATION HAPPENING *INSIDE* HIS BODY...
OKAY, JUST LIE STILL, TAKE IT EASY...
SUPERHEROES... DAMN SUPERHEROES... YOU'RE ALL SO *STUPID*...
YEAH, *WE'RE* STUPID... *YOU* HAD THIS *INCREDIBLE POWER*...YOU COULD'VE USED IT TO *GROW CROPS*, OR *BUILD HOUSES*...OR CURE *DISEASES* LIKE *YOUR OWN*. DID YOU EVEN *ONCE* THINK ABOUT *THAT*?!
ALL THAT POWER, AND YOU WASTED IT ON *VIOLENCE*.
KKKRRRLLKKR
LOOK...
...LOOK WHO'S *TALKING*...
KKKRKRRKLLLK--*

EVERYONE'S OKAY? *REALLY* OKAY?

LOOKS LIKE.

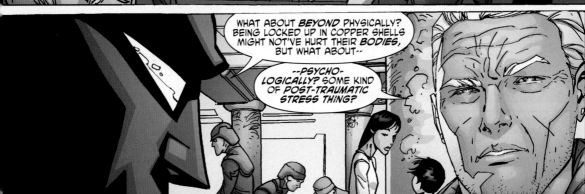

WHAT ABOUT *BEYOND* PHYSICALLY? BEING LOCKED UP IN COPPER SHELLS MIGHT NOT'VE HURT THEIR *BODIES*, BUT WHAT ABOUT--

--PSYCHO-LOGICALLY? SOME KIND OF *POST-TRAUMATIC STRESS* THING?

I'M NOT A *DOCTOR*, BUT EVERYTHING THE E.M.T.s ARE TELLING ME SAYS THE HOSTAGES ARE JUST *SHAKEN UP*.

GOOD... THAT'S GOOD...

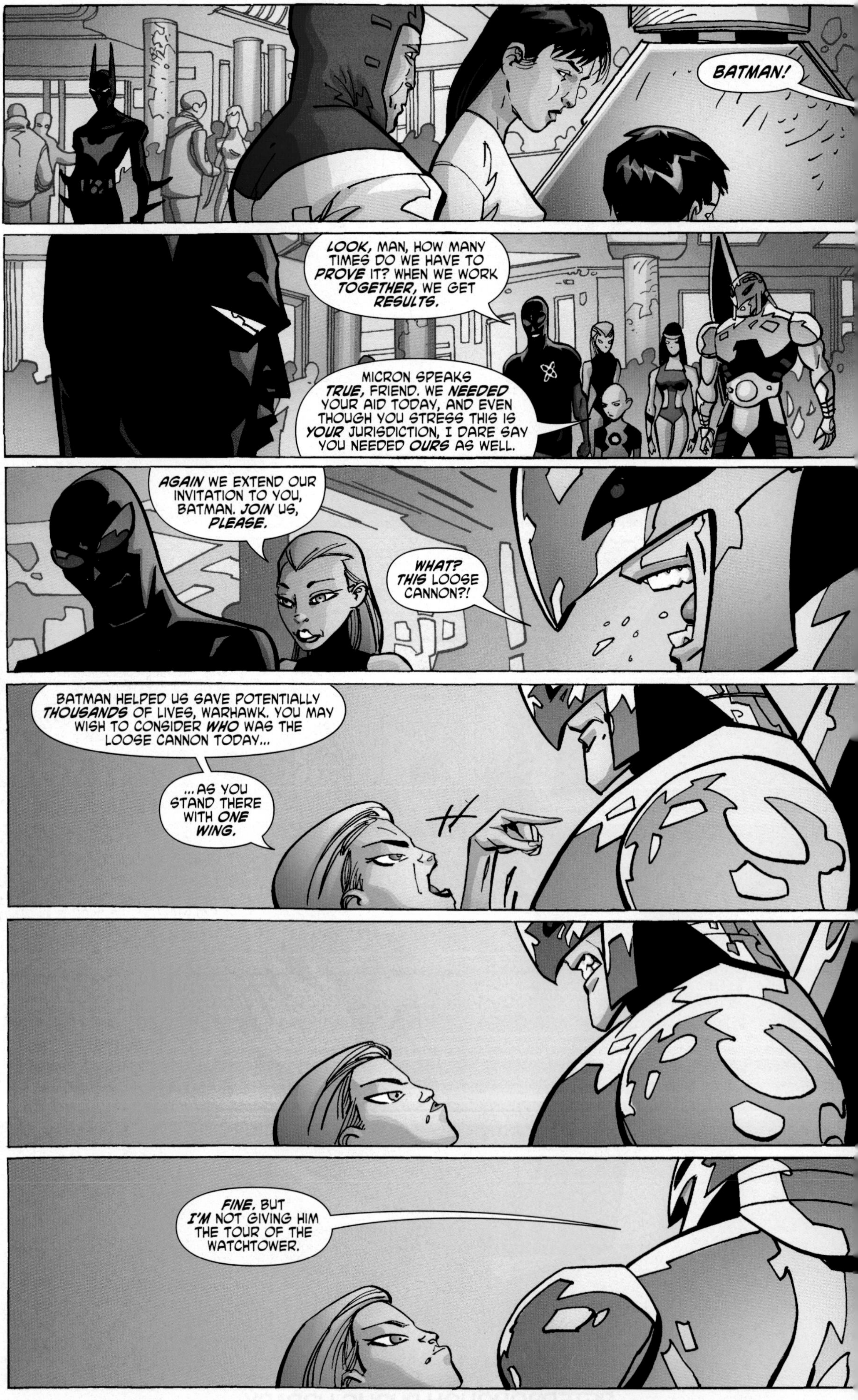
BATMAN!
LOOK, MAN, HOW MANY TIMES DO WE HAVE TO PROVE IT? WHEN WE WORK TOGETHER, WE GET RESULTS.
MICRON SPEAKS TRUE, FRIEND. WE NEEDED YOUR AID TODAY, AND EVEN THOUGH YOU STRESS THIS IS YOUR JURISDICTION, I DARE SAY YOU NEEDED OURS AS WELL.
AGAIN WE EXTEND OUR INVITATION TO YOU, BATMAN. JOIN US, PLEASE.
WHAT? THIS LOOSE CANNON?!
BATMAN HELPED US SAVE POTENTIALLY THOUSANDS OF LIVES, WARHAWK. YOU MAY WISH TO CONSIDER WHO WAS THE LOOSE CANNON TODAY...
...AS YOU STAND THERE WITH ONE WING.
FINE. BUT I'M NOT GIVING HIM THE TOUR OF THE WATCHTOWER.

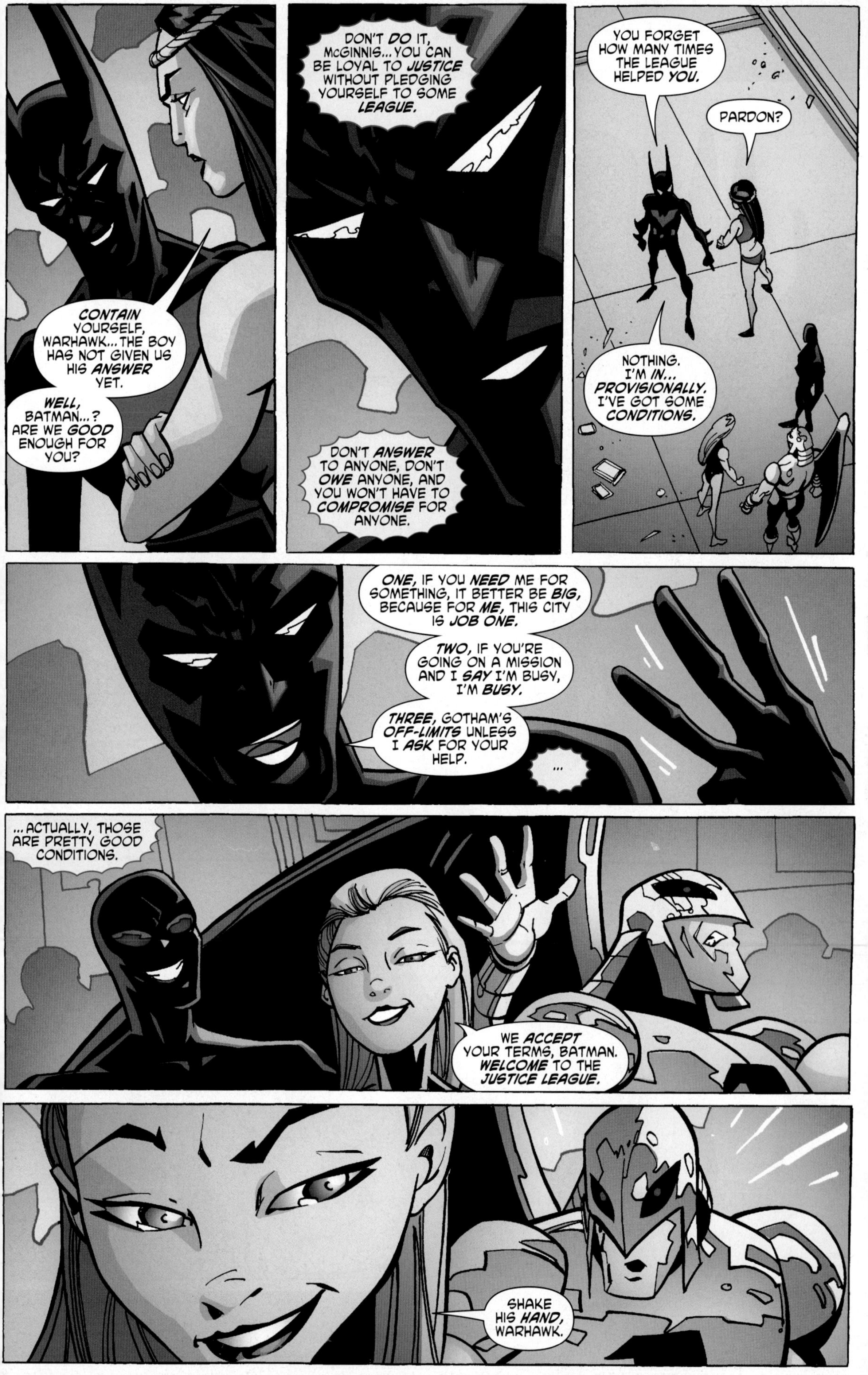
CONTAIN YOURSELF, WARHAWK... THE BOY HAS NOT GIVEN US HIS ANSWER YET.
WELL, BATMAN...? ARE WE GOOD ENOUGH FOR YOU?
DON'T DO IT, McGINNIS... YOU CAN BE LOYAL TO JUSTICE WITHOUT PLEDGING YOURSELF TO SOME LEAGUE.
DON'T ANSWER TO ANYONE, DON'T OWE ANYONE, AND YOU WON'T HAVE TO COMPROMISE FOR ANYONE.
YOU FORGET HOW MANY TIMES THE LEAGUE HELPED YOU.
PARDON?
NOTHING. I'M IN... PROVISIONALLY. I'VE GOT SOME CONDITIONS.
ONE, IF YOU NEED ME FOR SOMETHING, IT BETTER BE BIG, BECAUSE FOR ME, THIS CITY IS JOB ONE.
TWO, IF YOU'RE GOING ON A MISSION AND I SAY I'M BUSY, I'M BUSY.
THREE, GOTHAM'S OFF-LIMITS UNLESS I ASK FOR YOUR HELP.
...
...ACTUALLY, THOSE ARE PRETTY GOOD CONDITIONS.
WE ACCEPT YOUR TERMS, BATMAN. WELCOME TO THE JUSTICE LEAGUE.
SHAKE HIS HAND, WARHAWK.

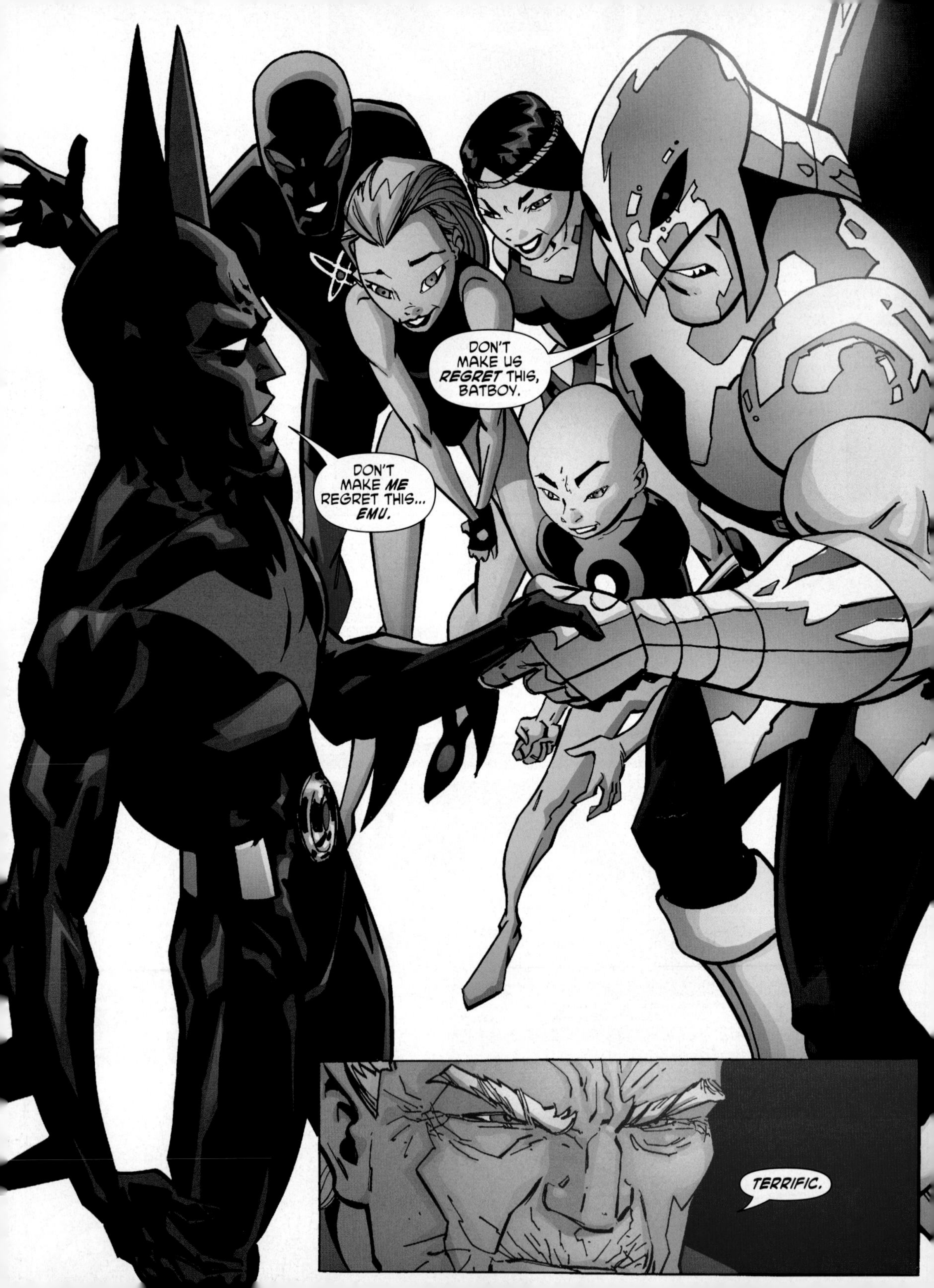
DON'T MAKE US REGRET THIS, BATBOY.
DON'T MAKE ME REGRET THIS... EMU.
TERRIFIC.

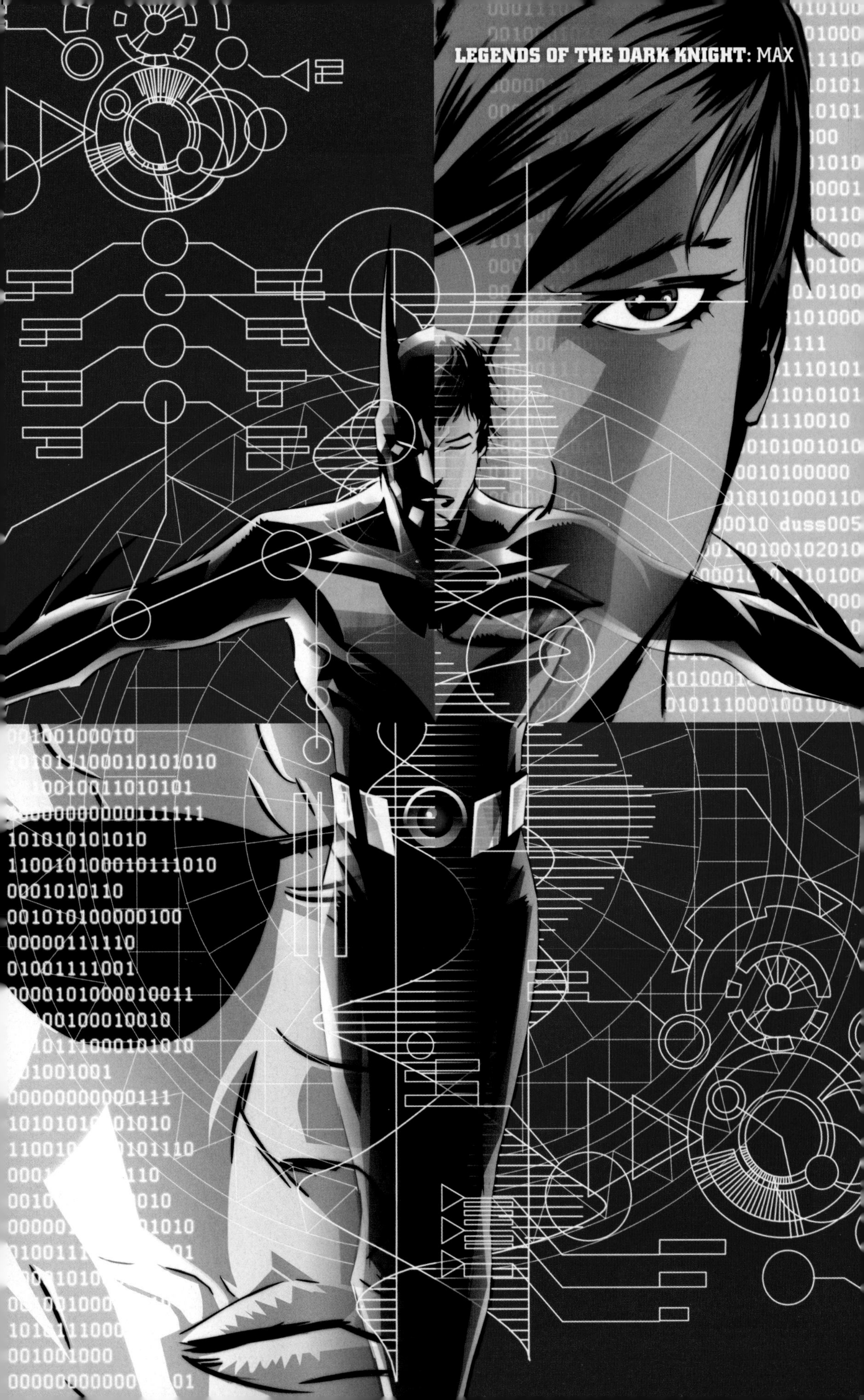
LEGENDS OF THE DARK KNIGHT: MAX

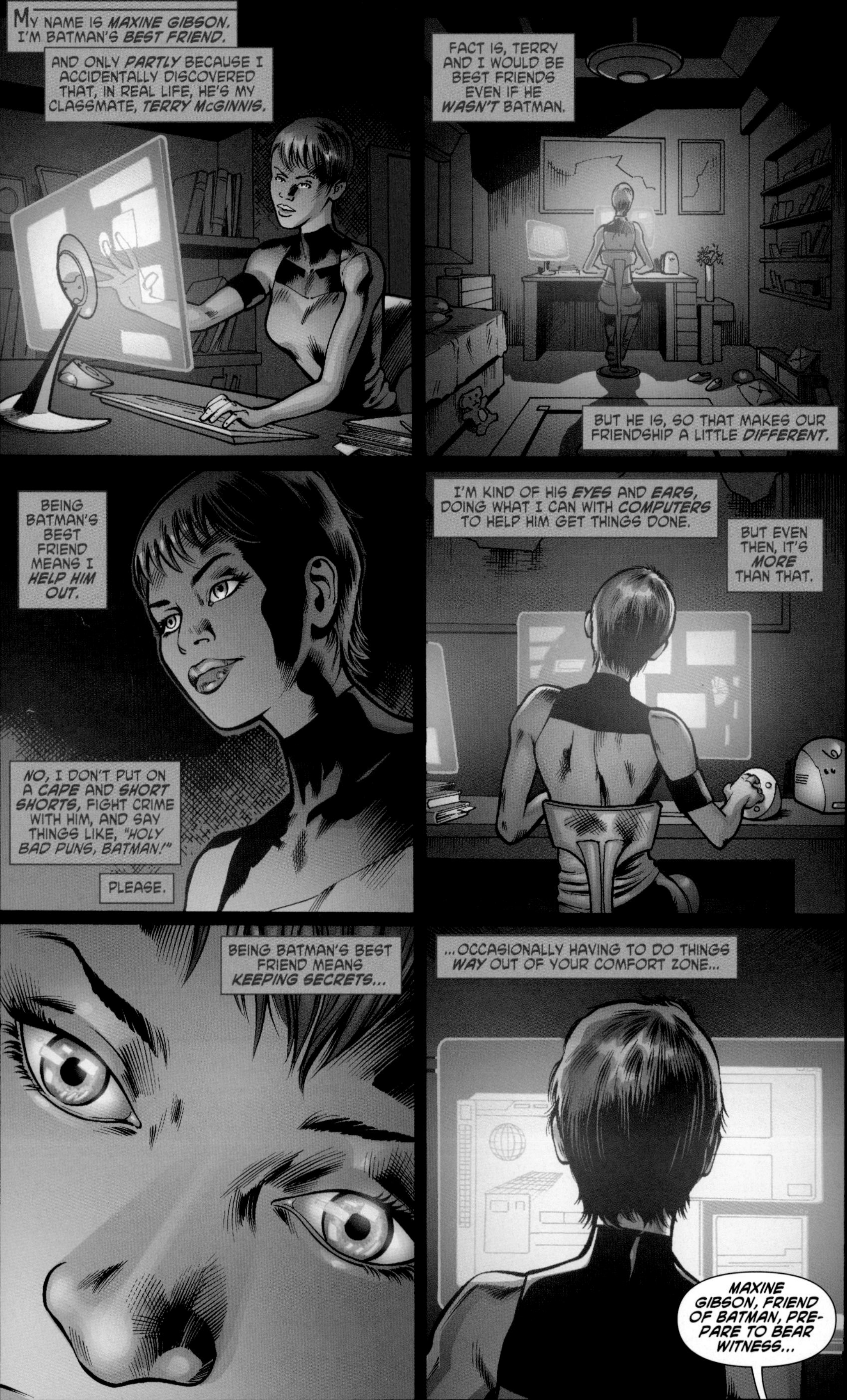

MY NAME IS MAXINE GIBSON. I'M BATMAN'S BEST FRIEND.
AND ONLY PARTLY BECAUSE I ACCIDENTALLY DISCOVERED THAT, IN REAL LIFE, HE'S MY CLASSMATE, TERRY McGINNIS.
FACT IS, TERRY AND I WOULD BE BEST FRIENDS EVEN IF HE WASN'T BATMAN.
BUT HE IS, SO THAT MAKES OUR FRIENDSHIP A LITTLE DIFFERENT.
BEING BATMAN'S BEST FRIEND MEANS I HELP HIM OUT.
NO, I DON'T PUT ON A CAPE AND SHORT SHORTS, FIGHT CRIME WITH HIM, AND SAY THINGS LIKE, "HOLY BAD PUNS, BATMAN!"
PLEASE.
I'M KIND OF HIS EYES AND EARS, DOING WHAT I CAN WITH COMPUTERS TO HELP HIM GET THINGS DONE.
BUT EVEN THEN, IT'S MORE THAN THAT.
BEING BATMAN'S BEST FRIEND MEANS KEEPING SECRETS...
...OCCASIONALLY HAVING TO DO THINGS WAY OUT OF YOUR COMFORT ZONE...
MAXINE GIBSON, FRIEND OF BATMAN, PREPARE TO BEAR WITNESS...

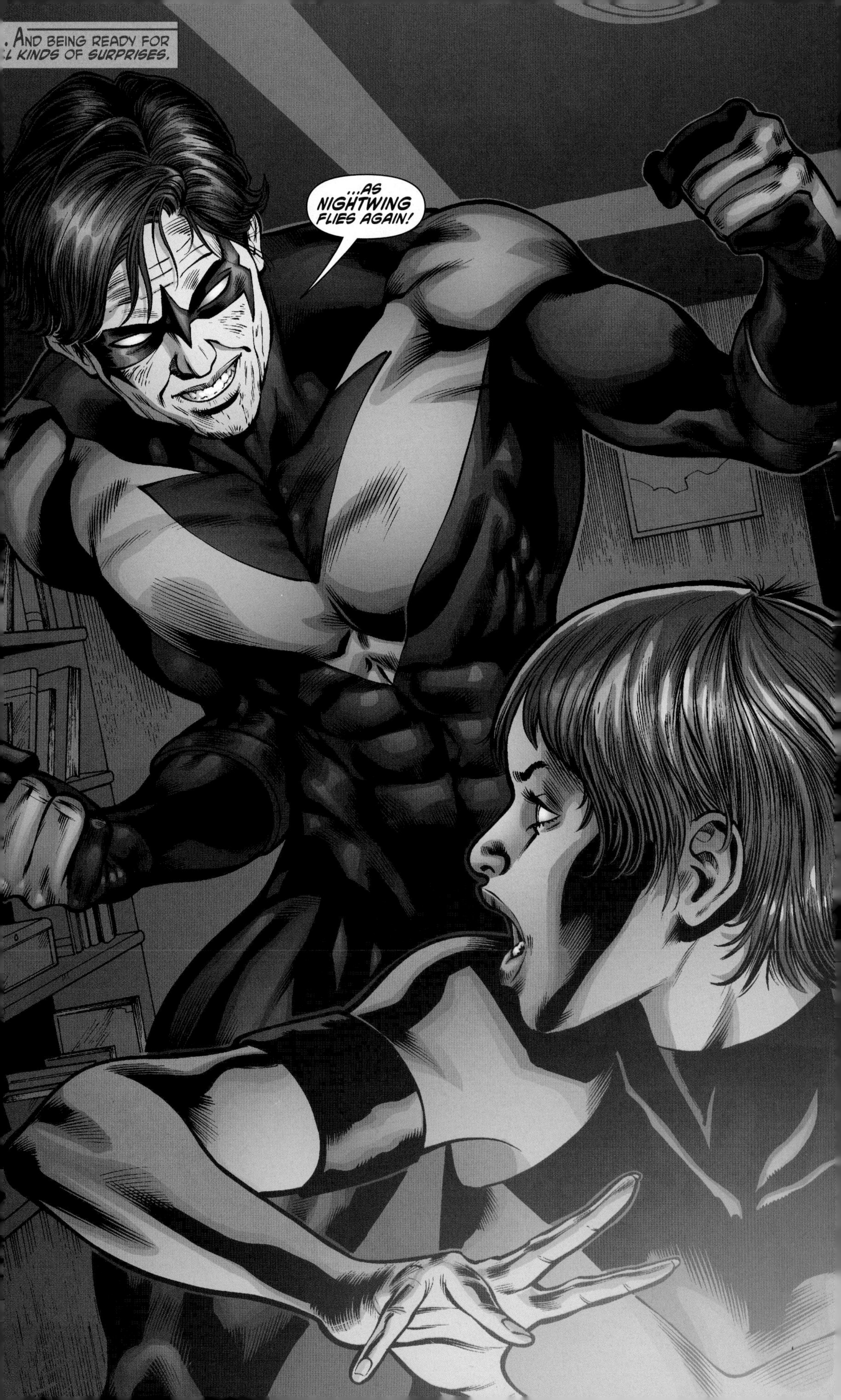
...AND BEING READY FOR
ALL KINDS OF SURPRISES.
...AS NIGHTWING FLIES AGAIN!

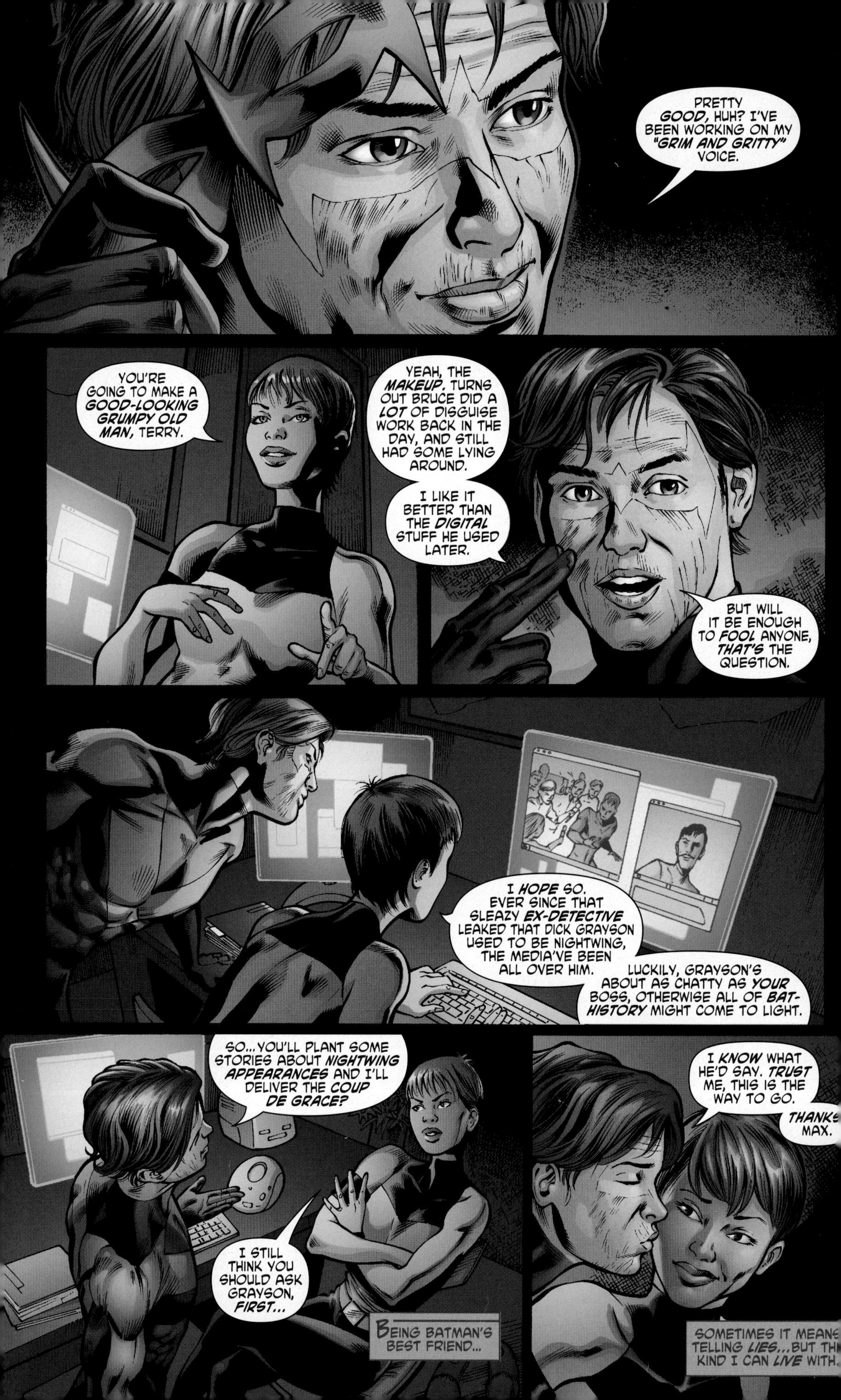

PRETTY GOOD, HUH? I'VE BEEN WORKING ON MY "GRIM AND GRITTY" VOICE.
YOU'RE GOING TO MAKE A GOOD-LOOKING GRUMPY OLD MAN, TERRY.
YEAH, THE MAKEUP. TURNS OUT BRUCE DID A LOT OF DISGUISE WORK BACK IN THE DAY, AND STILL HAD SOME LYING AROUND.
I LIKE IT BETTER THAN THE DIGITAL STUFF HE USED LATER.
BUT WILL IT BE ENOUGH TO FOOL ANYONE, THAT'S THE QUESTION.
I HOPE SO. EVER SINCE THAT SLEAZY EX-DETECTIVE LEAKED THAT DICK GRAYSON USED TO BE NIGHTWING, THE MEDIA'VE BEEN ALL OVER HIM.
LUCKILY, GRAYSON'S ABOUT AS CHATTY AS YOUR BOSS, OTHERWISE ALL OF BAT-HISTORY MIGHT COME TO LIGHT.
SO...YOU'LL PLANT SOME STORIES ABOUT NIGHTWING APPEARANCES AND I'LL DELIVER THE COUP DE GRACE?
I STILL THINK YOU SHOULD ASK GRAYSON, FIRST...
BEING BATMAN'S BEST FRIEND...
I KNOW WHAT HE'D SAY. TRUST ME, THIS IS THE WAY TO GO.
THANKS MAX.
SOMETIMES IT MEANS TELLING LIES...BUT THE KIND I CAN LIVE WITH.

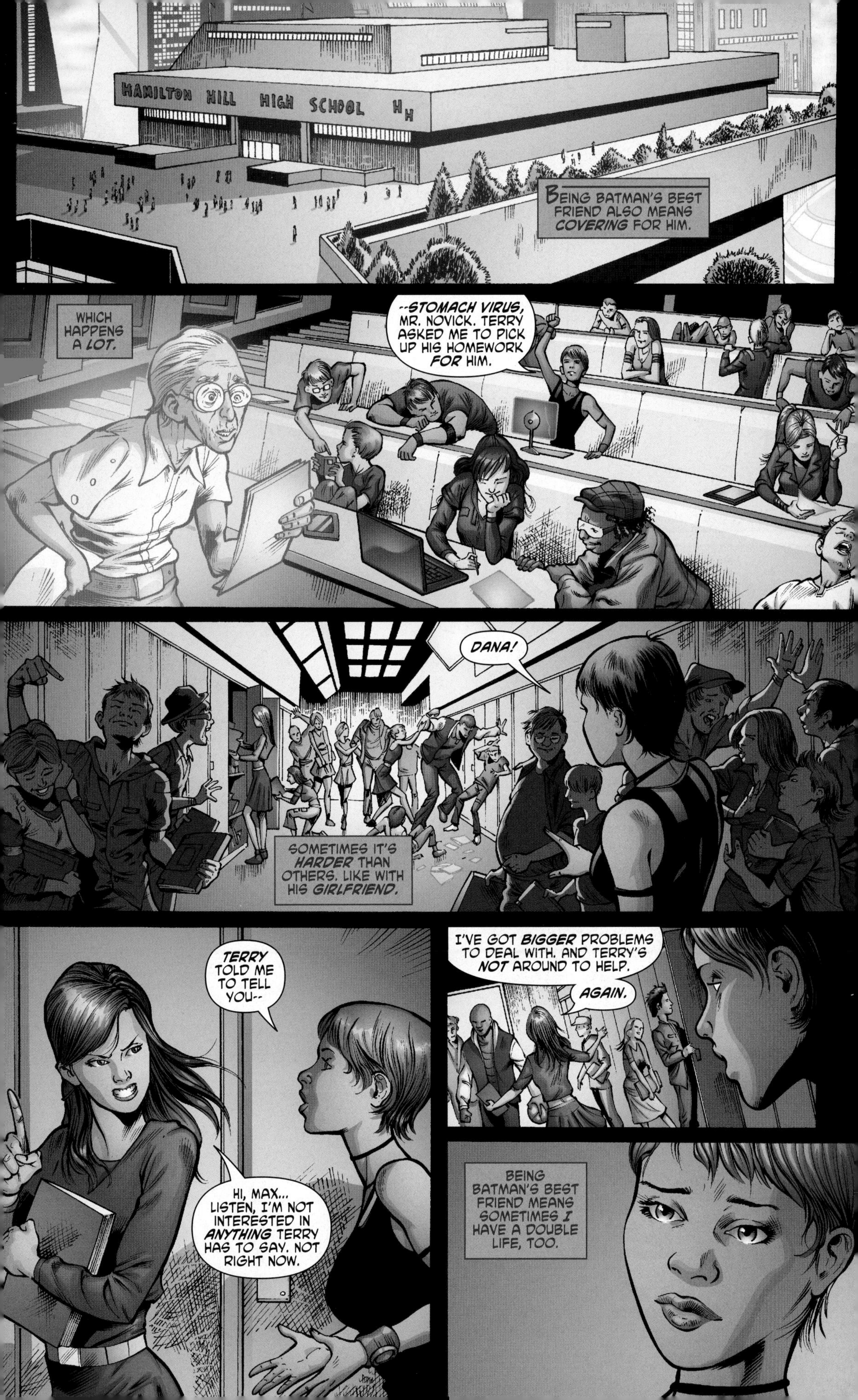

HAMILTON HILL HIGH SCHOOL HH
BEING BATMAN'S BEST FRIEND ALSO MEANS COVERING FOR HIM.
WHICH HAPPENS A LOT.
--STOMACH VIRUS, MR. NOVICK. TERRY ASKED ME TO PICK UP HIS HOMEWORK FOR HIM.
DANA!
SOMETIMES IT'S HARDER THAN OTHERS. LIKE WITH HIS GIRLFRIEND.
TERRY TOLD ME TO TELL YOU--
HI, MAX... LISTEN, I'M NOT INTERESTED IN ANYTHING TERRY HAS TO SAY. NOT RIGHT NOW.
I'VE GOT BIGGER PROBLEMS TO DEAL WITH. AND TERRY'S NOT AROUND TO HELP.
AGAIN.
BEING BATMAN'S BEST FRIEND MEANS SOMETIMES I HAVE A DOUBLE LIFE, TOO.

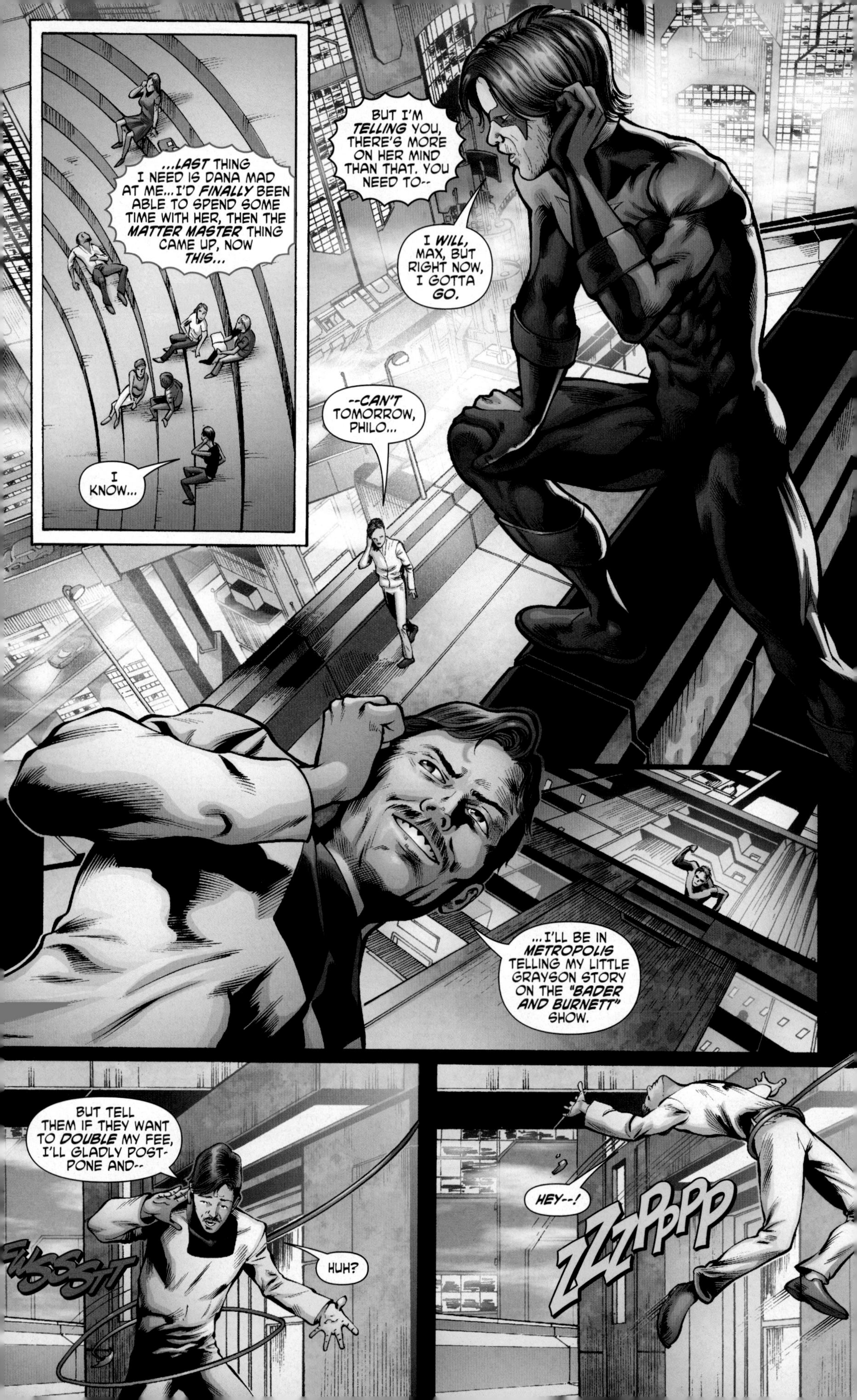
...LAST THING I NEED IS DANA MAD AT ME...I'D FINALLY BEEN ABLE TO SPEND SOME TIME WITH HER, THEN THE MATTER MASTER THING CAME UP, NOW THIS...
I KNOW...
BUT I'M TELLING YOU, THERE'S MORE ON HER MIND THAN THAT. YOU NEED TO--
I WILL, MAX, BUT RIGHT NOW, I GOTTA GO.
--CAN'T TOMORROW, PHILO...
...I'LL BE IN METROPOLIS TELLING MY LITTLE GRAYSON STORY ON THE "BADER AND BURNETT" SHOW.
BUT TELL THEM IF THEY WANT TO DOUBLE MY FEE, I'LL GLADLY POST-PONE AND--
FWSSSTT
HUH?
HEY--!
ZZZPPPP

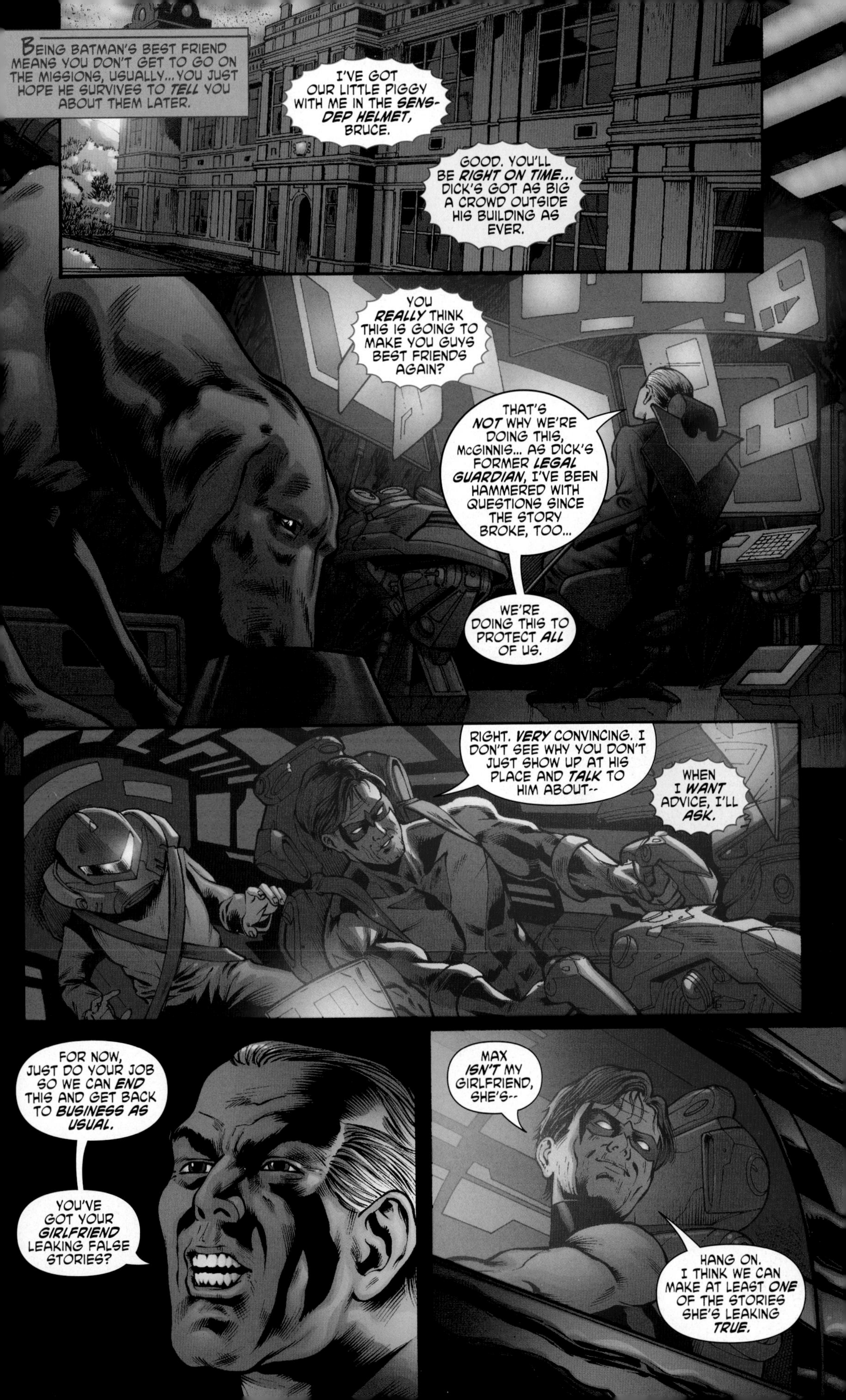
BEING BATMAN'S BEST FRIEND MEANS YOU DON'T GET TO GO ON THE MISSIONS, USUALLY... YOU JUST HOPE HE SURVIVES TO TELL YOU ABOUT THEM LATER.
I'VE GOT OUR LITTLE PIGGY WITH ME IN THE SENS-DEP HELMET, BRUCE.
GOOD. YOU'LL BE RIGHT ON TIME... DICK'S GOT AS BIG A CROWD OUTSIDE HIS BUILDING AS EVER.
YOU REALLY THINK THIS IS GOING TO MAKE YOU GUYS BEST FRIENDS AGAIN?
THAT'S NOT WHY WE'RE DOING THIS, McGINNIS... AS DICK'S FORMER LEGAL GUARDIAN, I'VE BEEN HAMMERED WITH QUESTIONS SINCE THE STORY BROKE, TOO...
WE'RE DOING THIS TO PROTECT ALL OF US.
RIGHT. VERY CONVINCING. I DON'T SEE WHY YOU DON'T JUST SHOW UP AT HIS PLACE AND TALK TO HIM ABOUT--
WHEN I WANT ADVICE, I'LL ASK.
FOR NOW, JUST DO YOUR JOB SO WE CAN END THIS AND GET BACK TO BUSINESS AS USUAL.
YOU'VE GOT YOUR GIRLFRIEND LEAKING FALSE STORIES?
MAX ISN'T MY GIRLFRIEND, SHE'S--
HANG ON. I THINK WE CAN MAKE AT LEAST ONE OF THE STORIES SHE'S LEAKING TRUE.

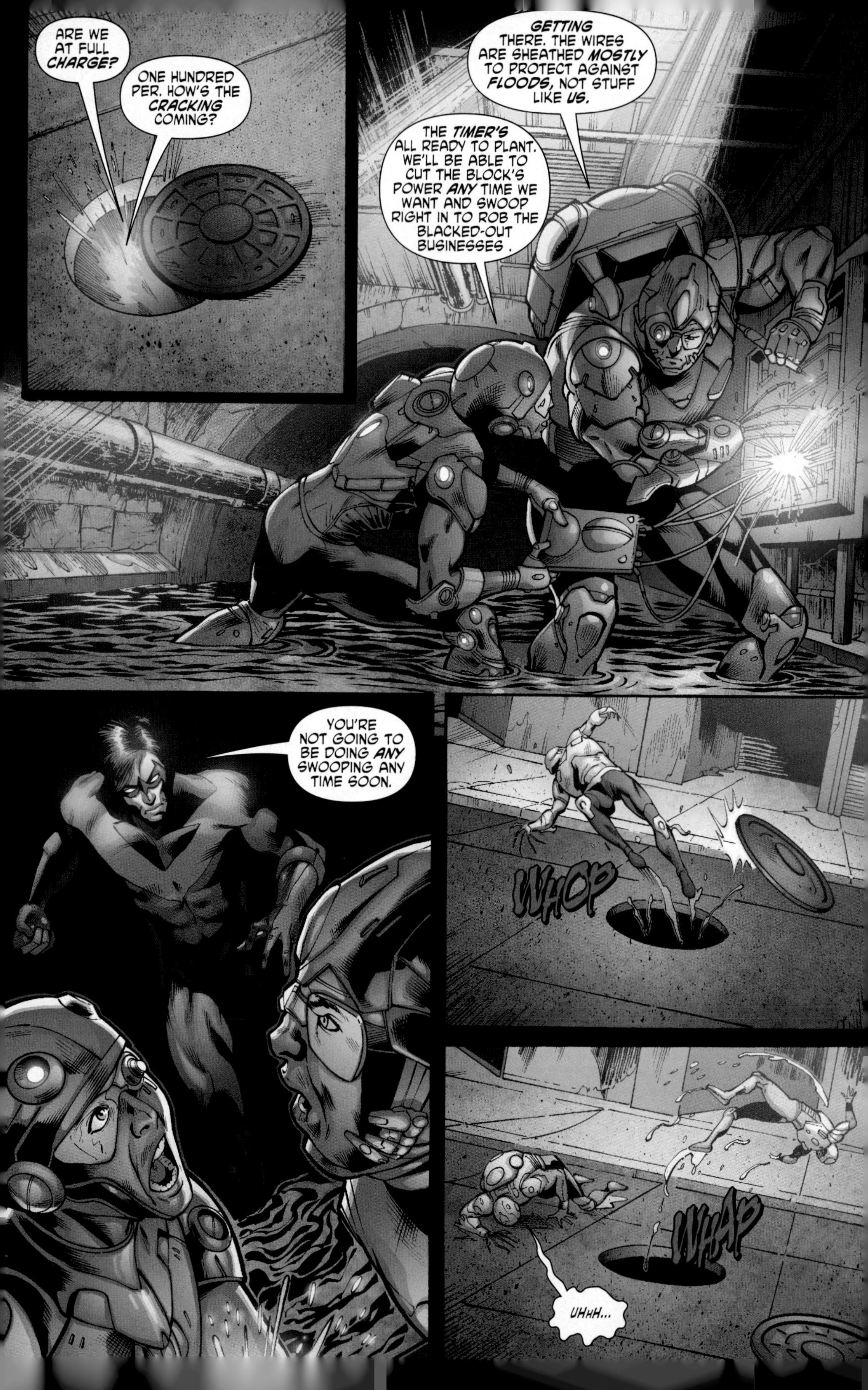
ARE WE AT FULL CHARGE?
ONE HUNDRED PER. HOW'S THE CRACKING COMING?
GETTING THERE. THE WIRES ARE SHEATHED MOSTLY TO PROTECT AGAINST FLOODS, NOT STUFF LIKE US.
THE TIMER'S ALL READY TO PLANT. WE'LL BE ABLE TO CUT THE BLOCK'S POWER ANY TIME WE WANT AND SWOOP RIGHT IN TO ROB THE BLACKED-OUT BUSINESSES .
YOU'RE NOT GOING TO BE DOING ANY SWOOPING ANY TIME SOON.
WHOP
WHAP
UHHH...

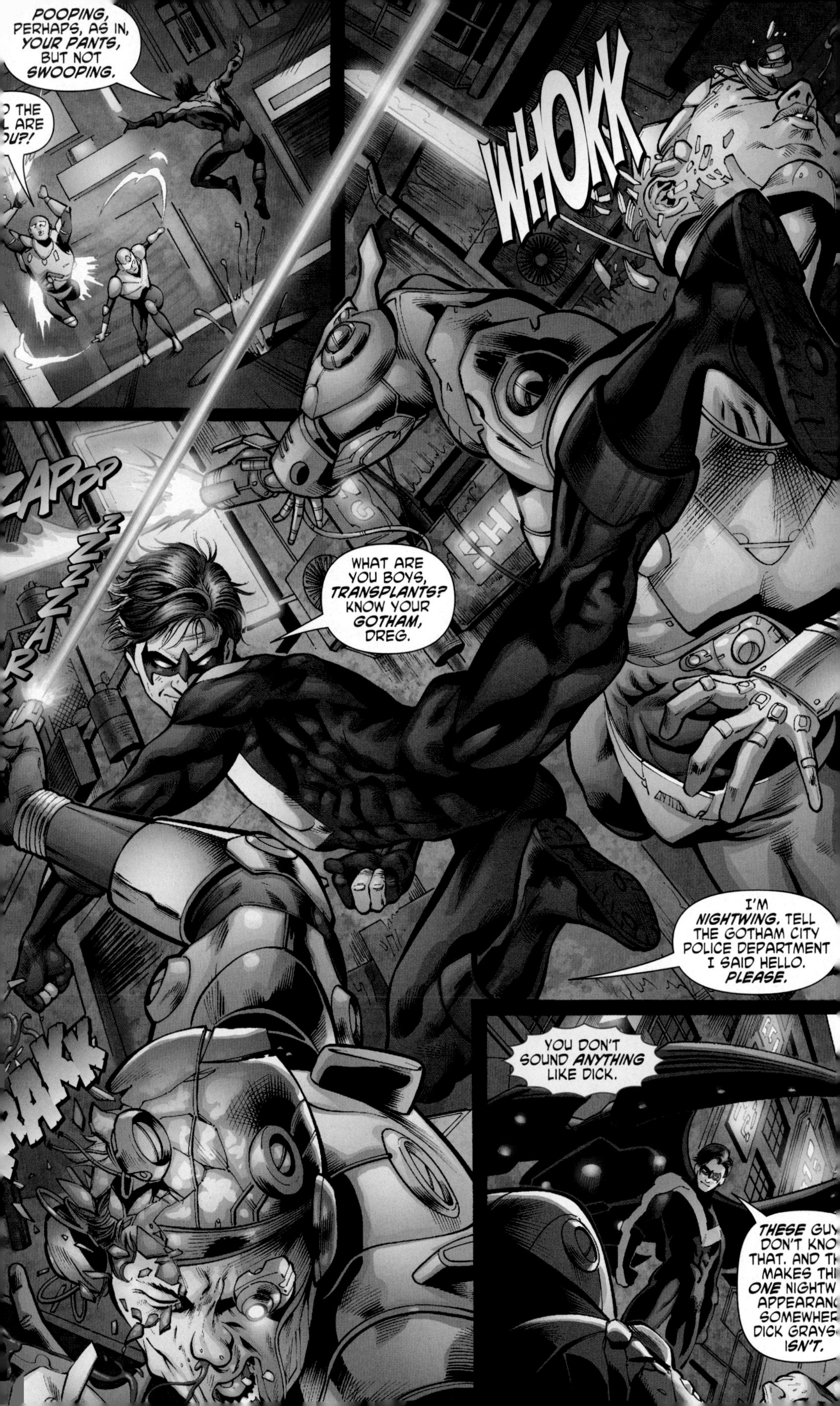

POOPING, PERHAPS, AS IN, YOUR PANTS, BUT NOT SWOOPING.
WHOKK
ZAPPP
ZZZZAR
WHAT ARE YOU BOYS, TRANSPLANTS? KNOW YOUR GOTHAM, DREG.
I'M NIGHTWING. TELL THE GOTHAM CITY POLICE DEPARTMENT I SAID HELLO. PLEASE.
YOU DON'T SOUND ANYTHING LIKE DICK.

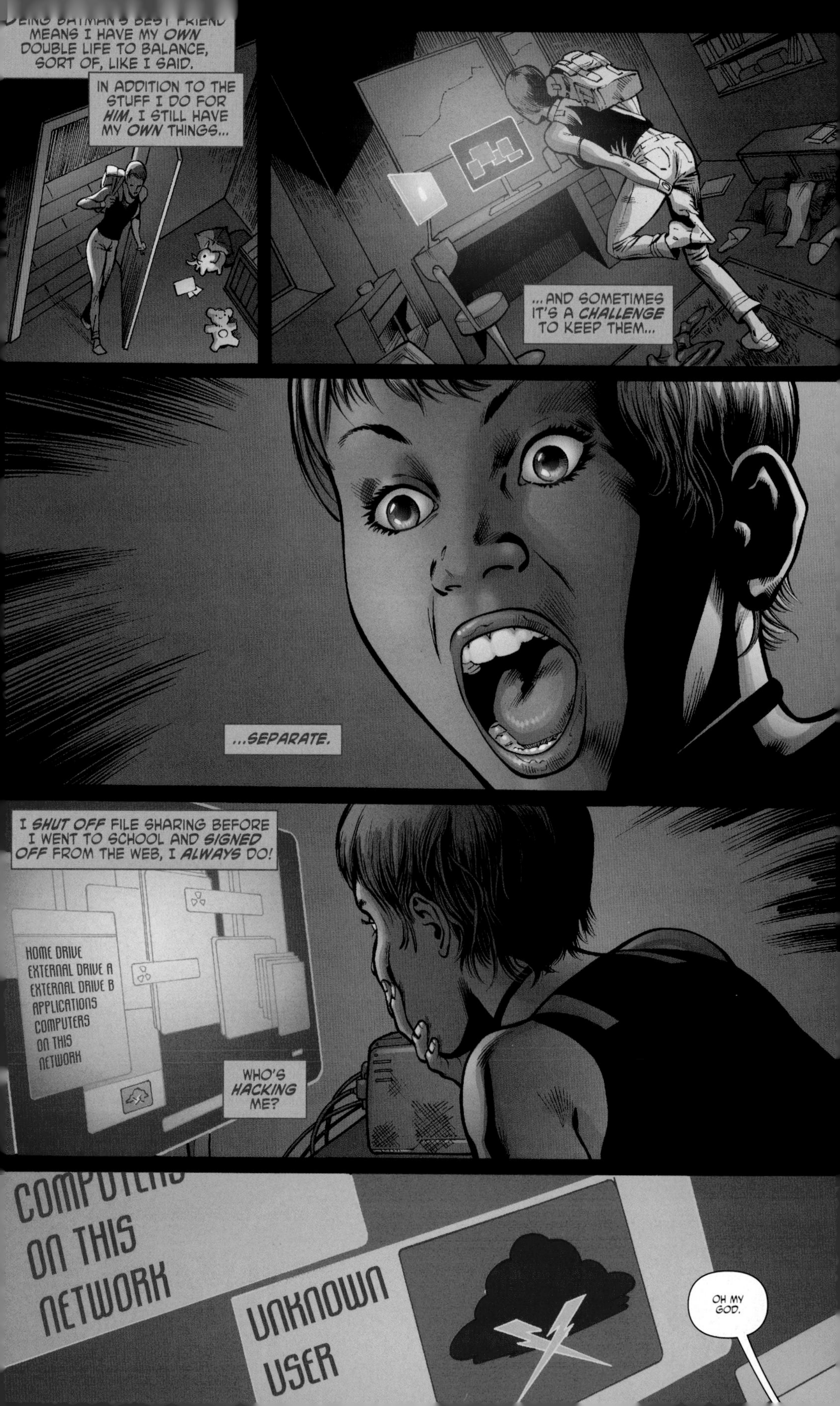

BEING BATMAN'S BEST FRIEND MEANS I HAVE MY OWN DOUBLE LIFE TO BALANCE, SORT OF, LIKE I SAID.
IN ADDITION TO THE STUFF I DO FOR HIM, I STILL HAVE MY OWN THINGS...
...AND SOMETIMES IT'S A CHALLENGE TO KEEP THEM...
...SEPARATE.
I SHUT OFF FILE SHARING BEFORE I WENT TO SCHOOL AND SIGNED OFF FROM THE WEB, I ALWAYS DO!
HOME DRIVE
EXTERNAL DRIVE A
EXTERNAL DRIVE B
APPLICATIONS
COMPUTERS ON THIS NETWORK
WHO'S HACKING ME?
COMPUTERS ON THIS NETWORK
UNKNOWN USER
OH MY GOD.

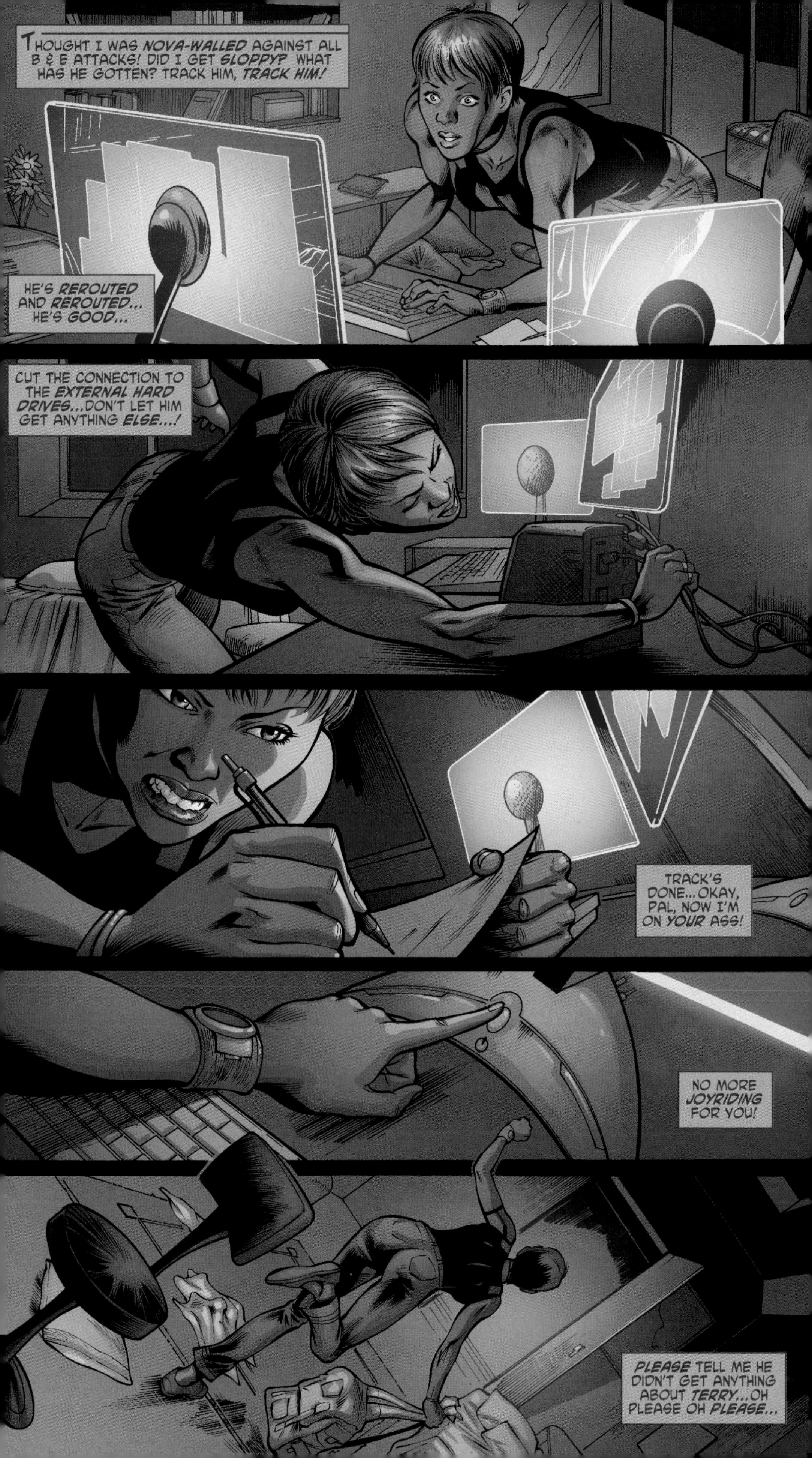
THOUGHT I WAS NOVA-WALLED AGAINST ALL B & E ATTACKS! DID I GET SLOPPY? WHAT HAS HE GOTTEN? TRACK HIM, TRACK HIM!
HE'S REROUTED AND REROUTED... HE'S GOOD...
CUT THE CONNECTION TO THE EXTERNAL HARD DRIVES...DON'T LET HIM GET ANYTHING ELSE...!
TRACK'S DONE...OKAY, PAL, NOW I'M ON YOUR ASS!
NO MORE JOYRIDING FOR YOU!
PLEASE TELL ME HE DIDN'T GET ANYTHING ABOUT TERRY...OH PLEASE OH PLEASE...

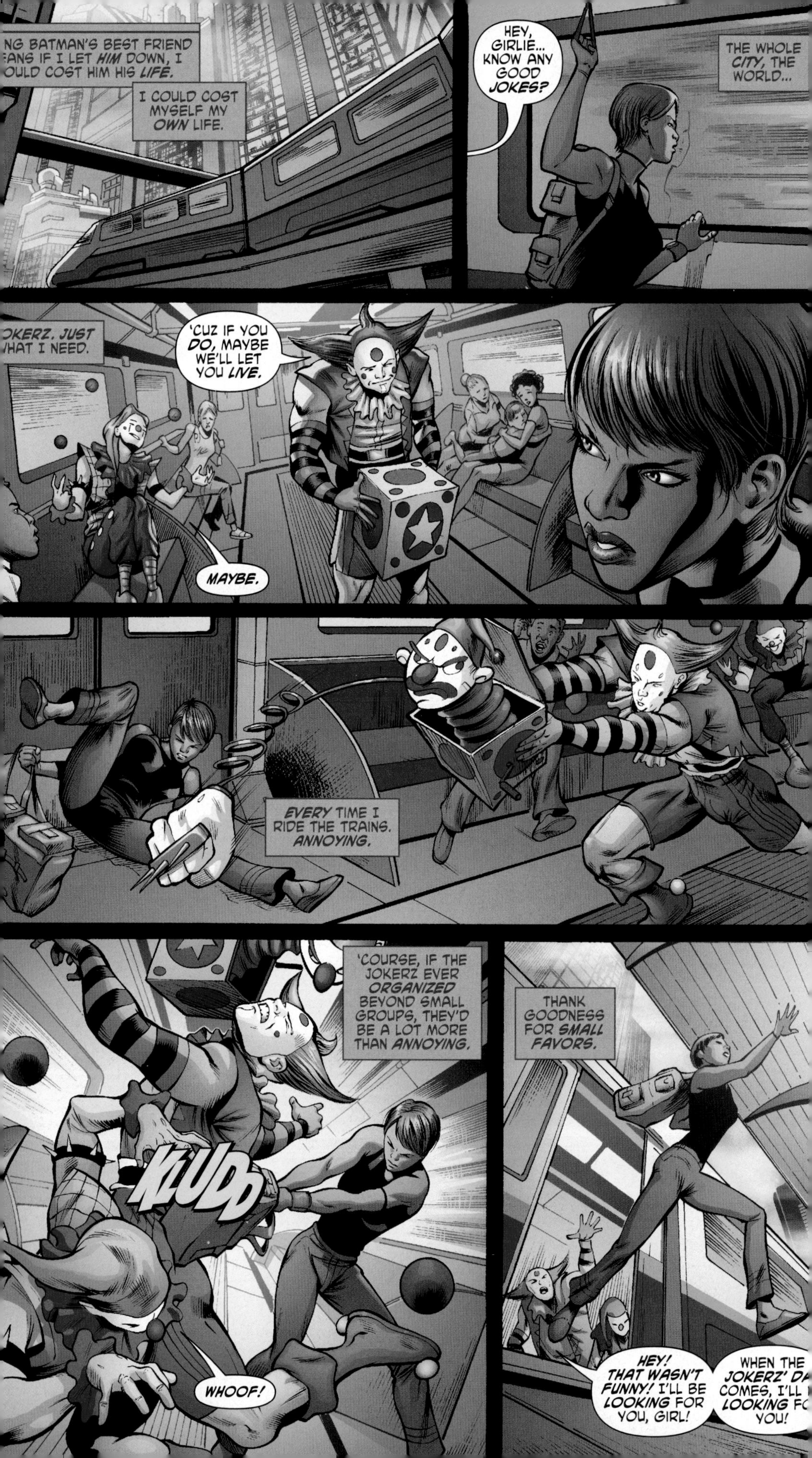

NG BATMAN'S BEST FRIEND
FANS IF I LET HIM DOWN, I
OULD COST HIM HIS LIFE.
I COULD COST MYSELF MY OWN LIFE.
HEY, GIRLIE... KNOW ANY GOOD JOKES?
THE WHOLE CITY, THE WORLD...
OKERZ. JUST WHAT I NEED.
'CUZ IF YOU DO, MAYBE WE'LL LET YOU LIVE.
MAYBE.
EVERY TIME I RIDE THE TRAINS. ANNOYING.
'COURSE, IF THE JOKERZ EVER ORGANIZED BEYOND SMALL GROUPS, THEY'D BE A LOT MORE THAN ANNOYING.
KLUDD
WHOOF!
THANK GOODNESS FOR SMALL FAVORS.
HEY! THAT WASN'T FUNNY! I'LL BE LOOKING FOR YOU, GIRL!
WHEN THE JOKERZ' DA
COMES, I'LL
LOOKING FO
YOU!

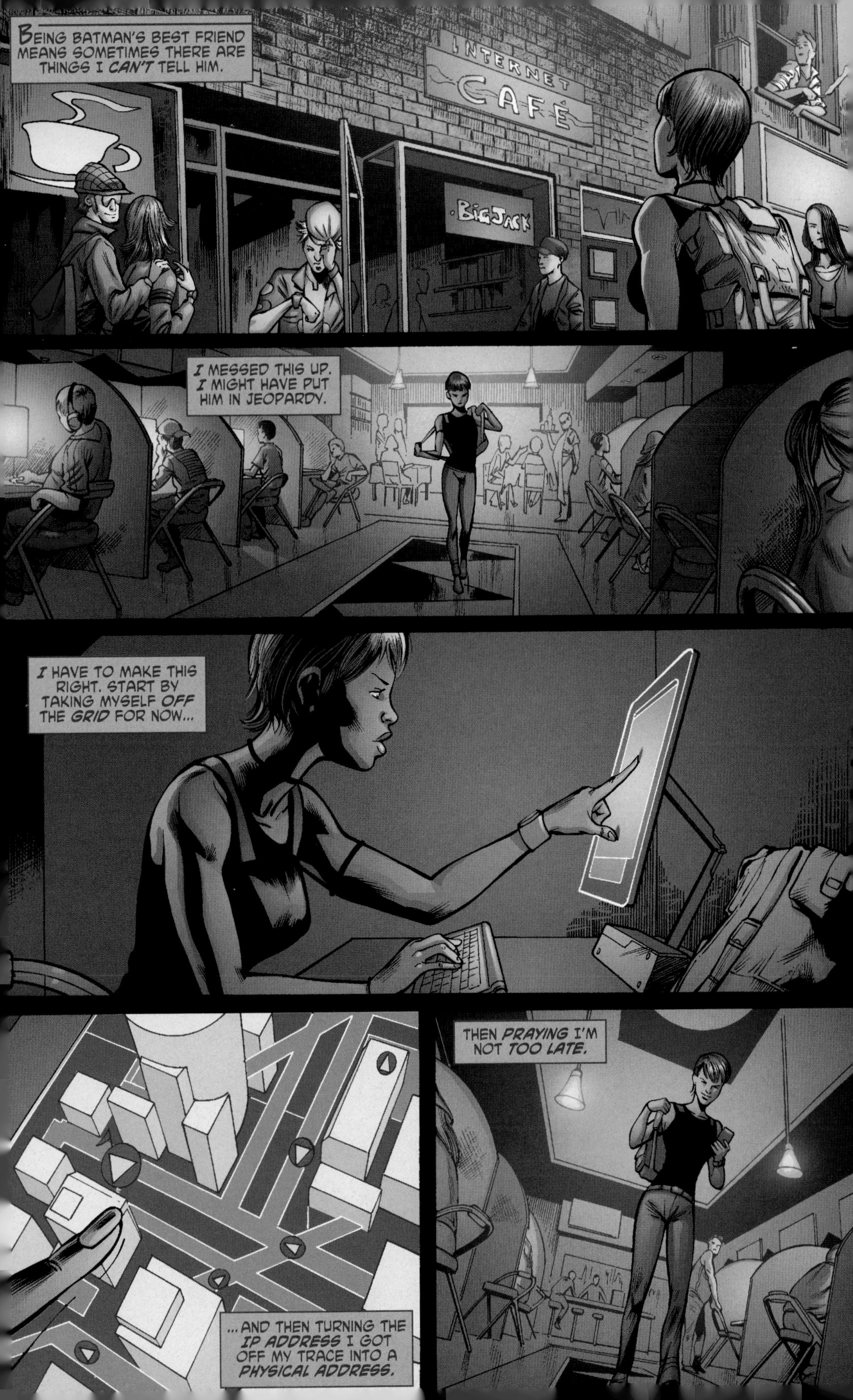
BEING BATMAN'S BEST FRIEND MEANS SOMETIMES THERE ARE THINGS I *CAN'T* TELL HIM.
INTERNET CAFÉ
BIG JACK
I MESSED THIS UP. *I* MIGHT HAVE PUT HIM IN JEOPARDY.
I HAVE TO MAKE THIS RIGHT. START BY TAKING MYSELF *OFF* THE *GRID* FOR NOW...
...AND THEN TURNING THE *IP ADDRESS* I GOT OFF MY TRACE INTO A *PHYSICAL ADDRESS.*
THEN *PRAYING* I'M NOT *TOO LATE.*

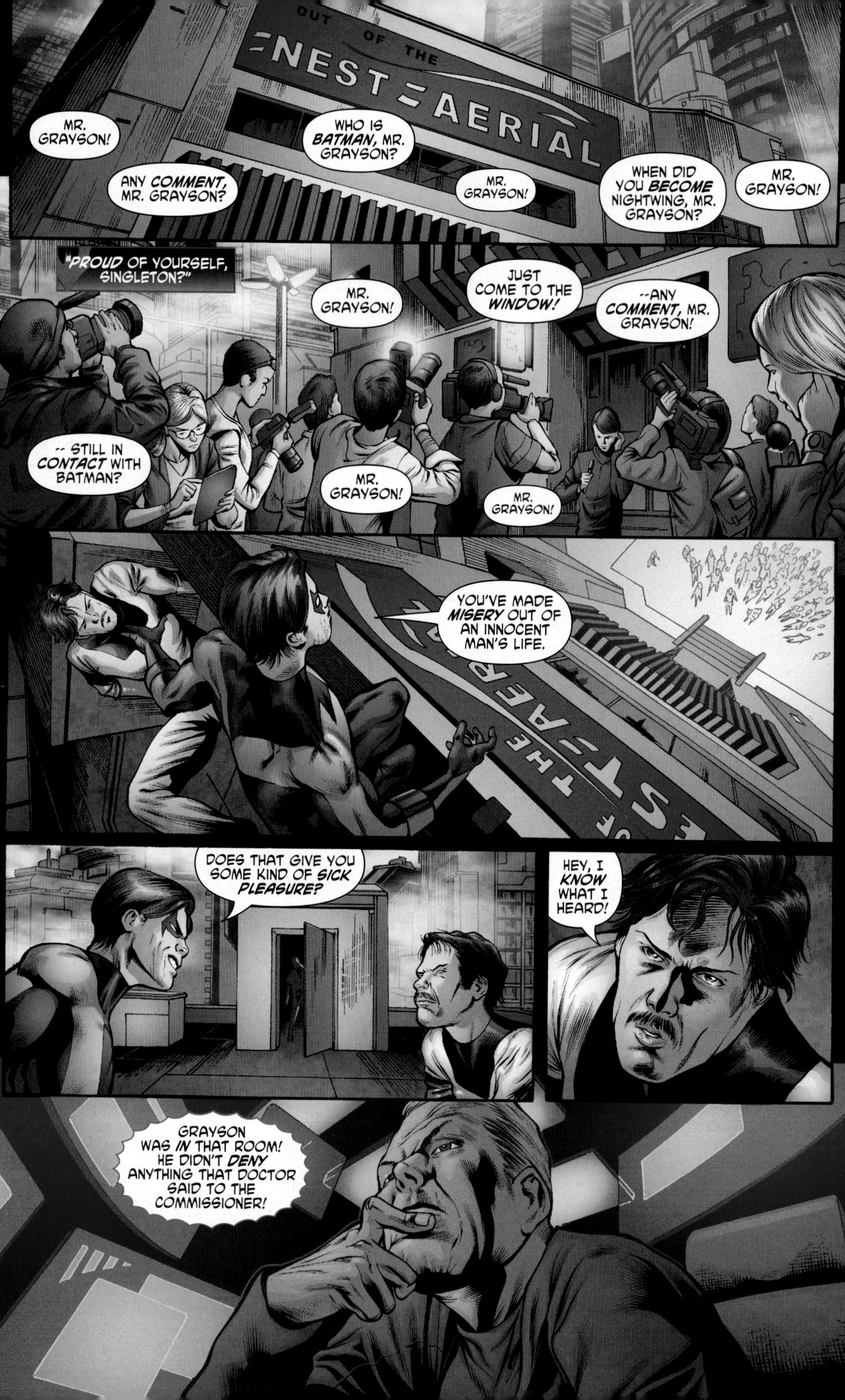
OUT OF THE NEST AERIAL
MR. GRAYSON!
WHO IS BATMAN, MR. GRAYSON?
ANY COMMENT, MR. GRAYSON?
MR. GRAYSON!
WHEN DID YOU BECOME NIGHTWING, MR. GRAYSON?
MR. GRAYSON!
"PROUD OF YOURSELF, SINGLETON?"
MR. GRAYSON!
JUST COME TO THE WINDOW!
--ANY COMMENT, MR. GRAYSON!
-- STILL IN CONTACT WITH BATMAN?
MR. GRAYSON!
MR. GRAYSON!
YOU'VE MADE MISERY OUT OF AN INNOCENT MAN'S LIFE.
DOES THAT GIVE YOU SOME KIND OF SICK PLEASURE?
HEY, I KNOW WHAT I HEARD!
GRAYSON WAS IN THAT ROOM! HE DIDN'T DENY ANYTHING THAT DOCTOR SAID TO THE COMMISSIONER!

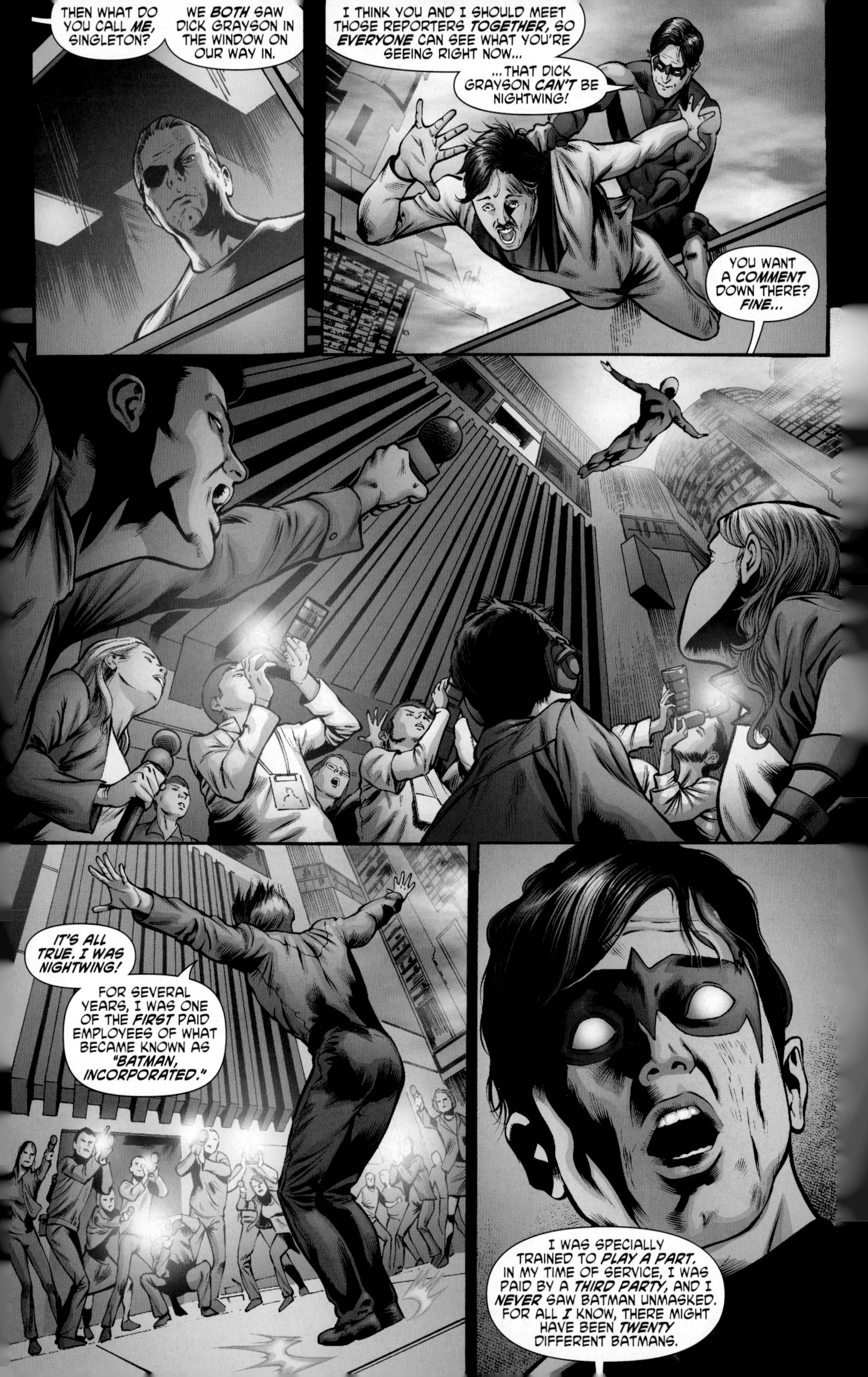
THEN WHAT DO YOU CALL *ME*, SINGLETON?
WE *BOTH* SAW DICK GRAYSON IN THE WINDOW ON OUR WAY IN.
I THINK YOU AND I SHOULD MEET THOSE REPORTERS *TOGETHER*, SO *EVERYONE* CAN SEE WHAT YOU'RE SEEING RIGHT NOW...
...THAT DICK GRAYSON *CAN'T* BE NIGHTWING!
YOU WANT A *COMMENT* DOWN THERE? *FINE*...
IT'S ALL TRUE. I WAS NIGHTWING!
FOR SEVERAL YEARS, I WAS ONE OF THE *FIRST* PAID EMPLOYEES OF WHAT BECAME KNOWN AS *"BATMAN, INCORPORATED."*
I WAS SPECIALLY TRAINED TO *PLAY A PART*. IN MY TIME OF SERVICE, I WAS PAID BY A *THIRD PARTY*, AND I *NEVER* SAW BATMAN UNMASKED. FOR ALL *I* KNOW, THERE MIGHT HAVE BEEN *TWENTY* DIFFERENT BATMANS.

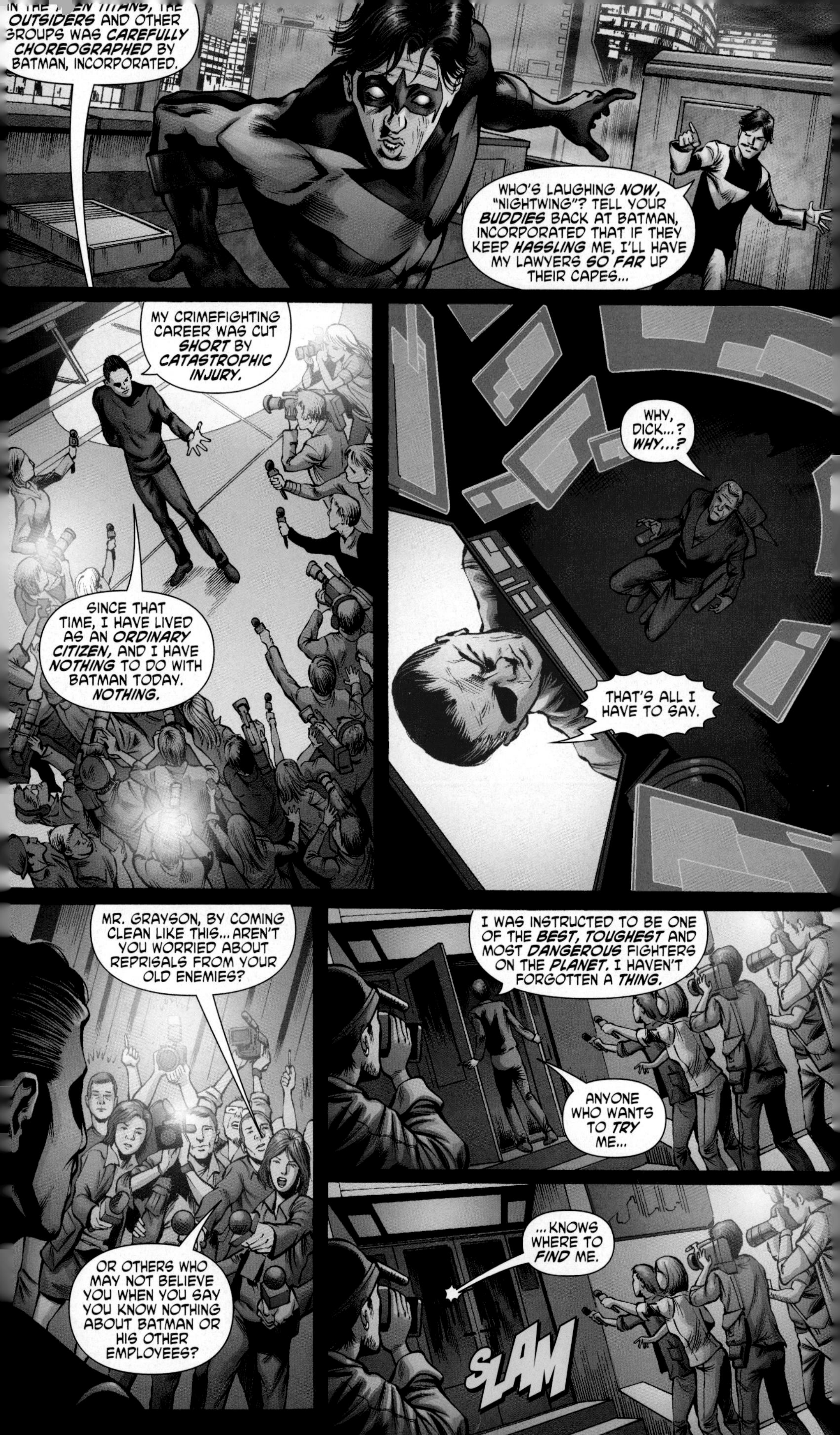
IN THE ...EN TITANS, THE OUTSIDERS AND OTHER GROUPS WAS CAREFULLY CHOREOGRAPHED BY BATMAN, INCORPORATED.
WHO'S LAUGHING NOW, "NIGHTWING"? TELL YOUR BUDDIES BACK AT BATMAN, INCORPORATED THAT IF THEY KEEP HASSLING ME, I'LL HAVE MY LAWYERS SO FAR UP THEIR CAPES...
MY CRIMEFIGHTING CAREER WAS CUT SHORT BY CATASTROPHIC INJURY.
SINCE THAT TIME, I HAVE LIVED AS AN ORDINARY CITIZEN, AND I HAVE NOTHING TO DO WITH BATMAN TODAY. NOTHING.
WHY, DICK...? WHY...?
THAT'S ALL I HAVE TO SAY.
MR. GRAYSON, BY COMING CLEAN LIKE THIS... AREN'T YOU WORRIED ABOUT REPRISALS FROM YOUR OLD ENEMIES?
OR OTHERS WHO MAY NOT BELIEVE YOU WHEN YOU SAY YOU KNOW NOTHING ABOUT BATMAN OR HIS OTHER EMPLOYEES?
I WAS INSTRUCTED TO BE ONE OF THE BEST, TOUGHEST AND MOST DANGEROUS FIGHTERS ON THE PLANET. I HAVEN'T FORGOTTEN A THING.
ANYONE WHO WANTS TO TRY ME...
...KNOWS WHERE TO FIND ME.
SLAM

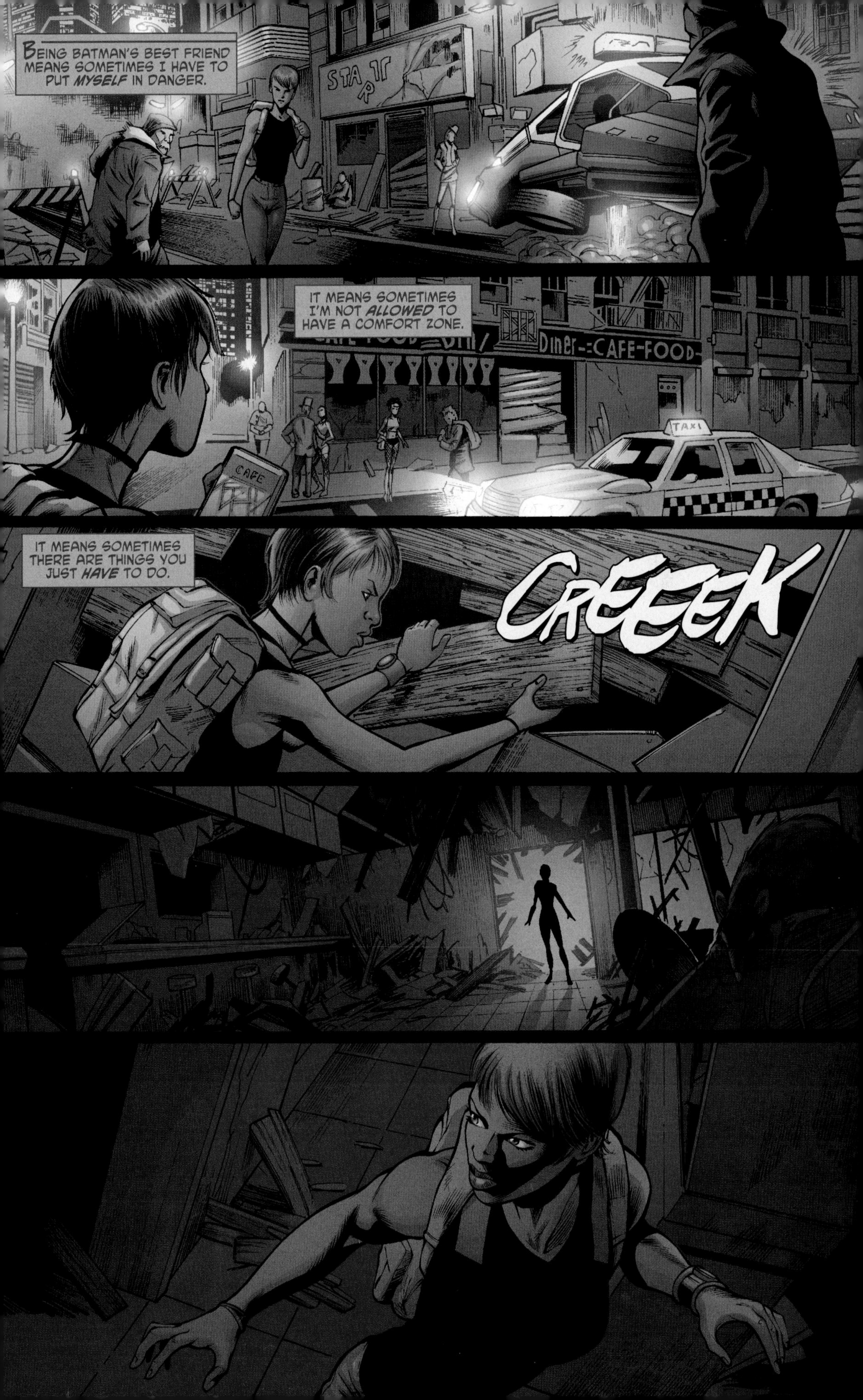

BEING BATMAN'S BEST FRIEND MEANS SOMETIMES I HAVE TO PUT *MYSELF* IN DANGER.
IT MEANS SOMETIMES I'M NOT *ALLOWED* TO HAVE A COMFORT ZONE.
Diner-CAFE-FOOD
TAXI
CAFE
IT MEANS SOMETIMES THERE ARE THINGS YOU JUST *HAVE* TO DO.
CREEEK

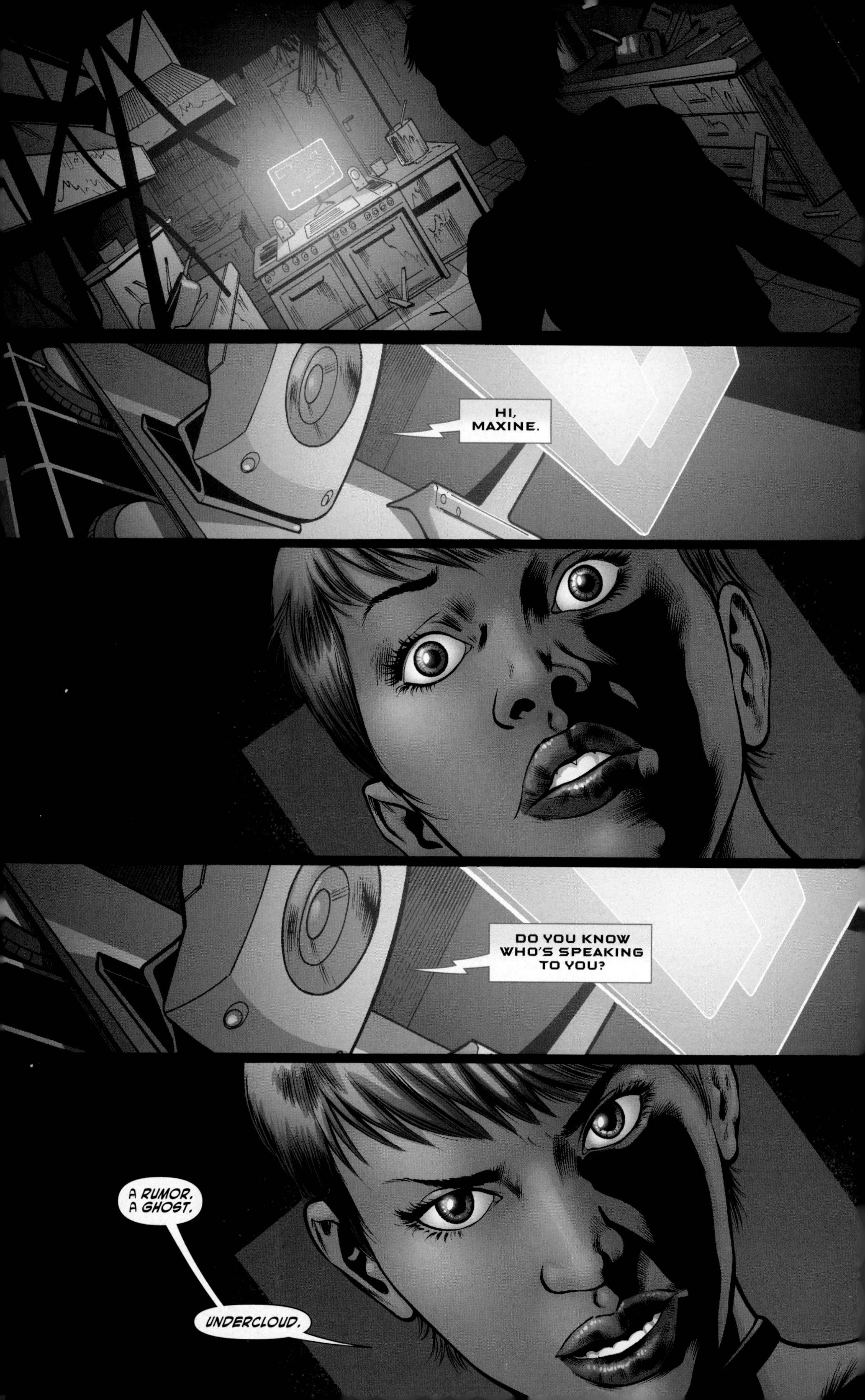
HI, MAXINE.
DO YOU KNOW WHO'S SPEAKING TO YOU?
A RUMOR. A GHOST.
UNDERCLOUD.

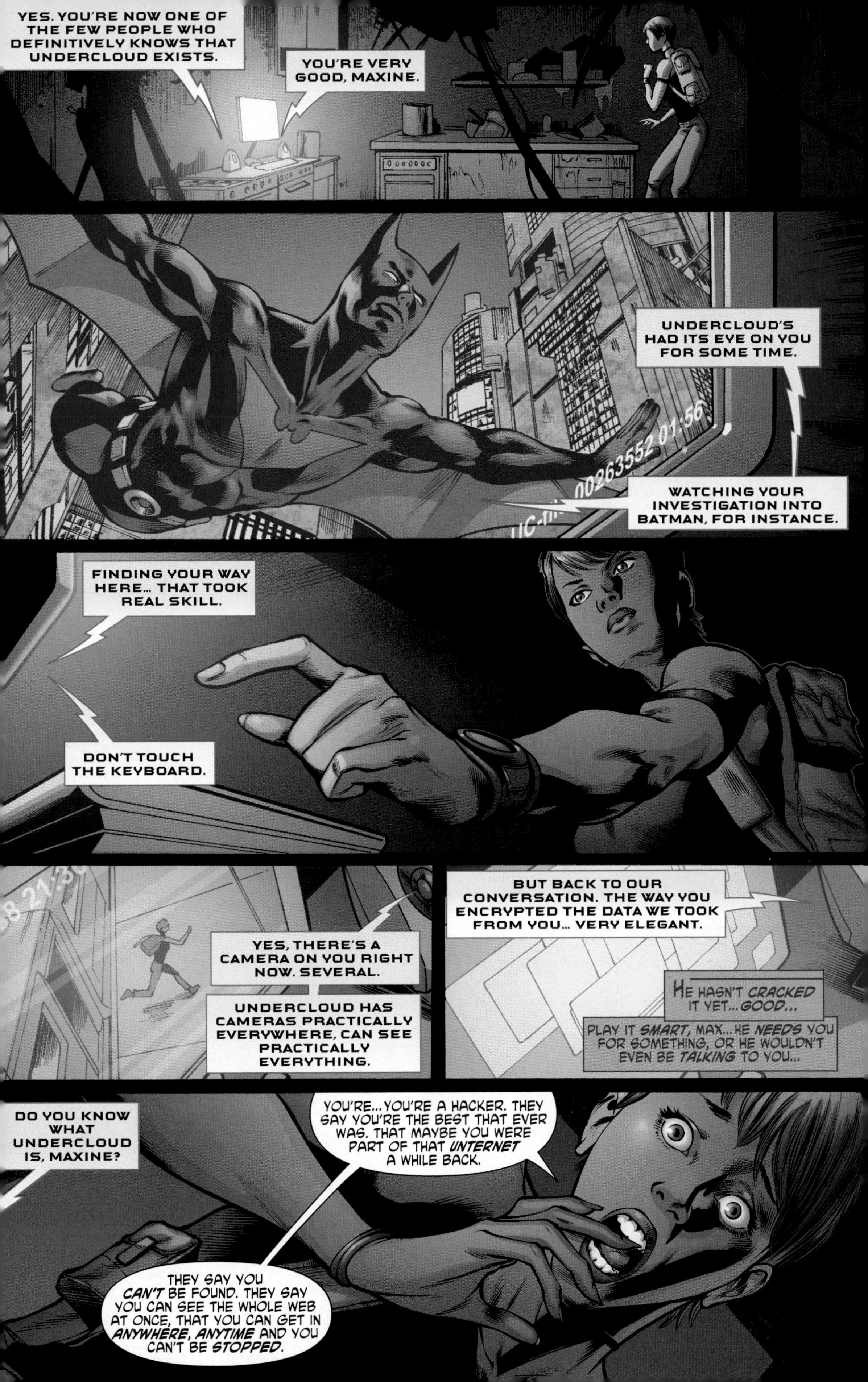
YES. YOU'RE NOW ONE OF THE FEW PEOPLE WHO DEFINITIVELY KNOWS THAT UNDERCLOUD EXISTS.
YOU'RE VERY GOOD, MAXINE.
UNDERCLOUD'S HAD ITS EYE ON YOU FOR SOME TIME.
WATCHING YOUR INVESTIGATION INTO BATMAN, FOR INSTANCE.
FINDING YOUR WAY HERE... THAT TOOK REAL SKILL.
DON'T TOUCH THE KEYBOARD.
YES, THERE'S A CAMERA ON YOU RIGHT NOW. SEVERAL.
UNDERCLOUD HAS CAMERAS PRACTICALLY EVERYWHERE, CAN SEE PRACTICALLY EVERYTHING.
BUT BACK TO OUR CONVERSATION. THE WAY YOU ENCRYPTED THE DATA WE TOOK FROM YOU... VERY ELEGANT.
HE HASN'T CRACKED IT YET... GOOD...
PLAY IT SMART, MAX... HE NEEDS YOU FOR SOMETHING, OR HE WOULDN'T EVEN BE TALKING TO YOU...
DO YOU KNOW WHAT UNDERCLOUD IS, MAXINE?
YOU'RE... YOU'RE A HACKER. THEY SAY YOU'RE THE BEST THAT EVER WAS. THAT MAYBE YOU WERE PART OF THAT UNTERNET A WHILE BACK.
THEY SAY YOU CAN'T BE FOUND. THEY SAY YOU CAN SEE THE WHOLE WEB AT ONCE, THAT YOU CAN GET IN ANYWHERE, ANYTIME AND YOU CAN'T BE STOPPED.

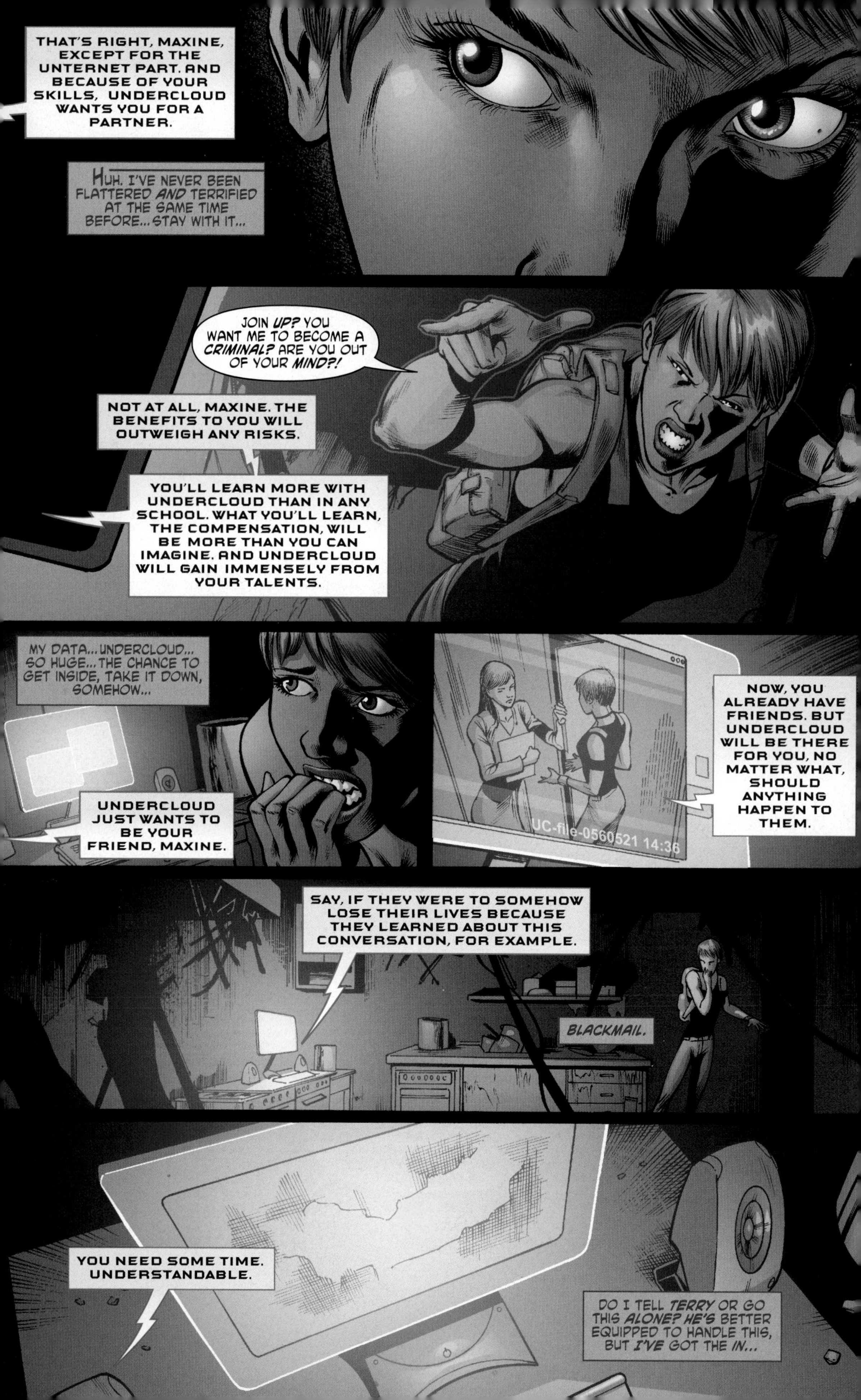

THAT'S RIGHT, MAXINE, EXCEPT FOR THE UNTERNET PART. AND BECAUSE OF YOUR SKILLS, UNDERCLOUD WANTS YOU FOR A PARTNER.
HUH. I'VE NEVER BEEN FLATTERED AND TERRIFIED AT THE SAME TIME BEFORE... STAY WITH IT...
JOIN UP? YOU WANT ME TO BECOME A CRIMINAL? ARE YOU OUT OF YOUR MIND?!
NOT AT ALL, MAXINE. THE BENEFITS TO YOU WILL OUTWEIGH ANY RISKS.
YOU'LL LEARN MORE WITH UNDERCLOUD THAN IN ANY SCHOOL. WHAT YOU'LL LEARN, THE COMPENSATION, WILL BE MORE THAN YOU CAN IMAGINE. AND UNDERCLOUD WILL GAIN IMMENSELY FROM YOUR TALENTS.
MY DATA... UNDERCLOUD... SO HUGE... THE CHANCE TO GET INSIDE, TAKE IT DOWN, SOMEHOW...
UNDERCLOUD JUST WANTS TO BE YOUR FRIEND, MAXINE.
UC-file-0560521 14:36
NOW, YOU ALREADY HAVE FRIENDS. BUT UNDERCLOUD WILL BE THERE FOR YOU, NO MATTER WHAT, SHOULD ANYTHING HAPPEN TO THEM.
SAY, IF THEY WERE TO SOMEHOW LOSE THEIR LIVES BECAUSE THEY LEARNED ABOUT THIS CONVERSATION, FOR EXAMPLE.
BLACKMAIL.
YOU NEED SOME TIME. UNDERSTANDABLE.
DO I TELL TERRY OR GO THIS ALONE? HE'S BETTER EQUIPPED TO HANDLE THIS, BUT I'VE GOT THE IN...

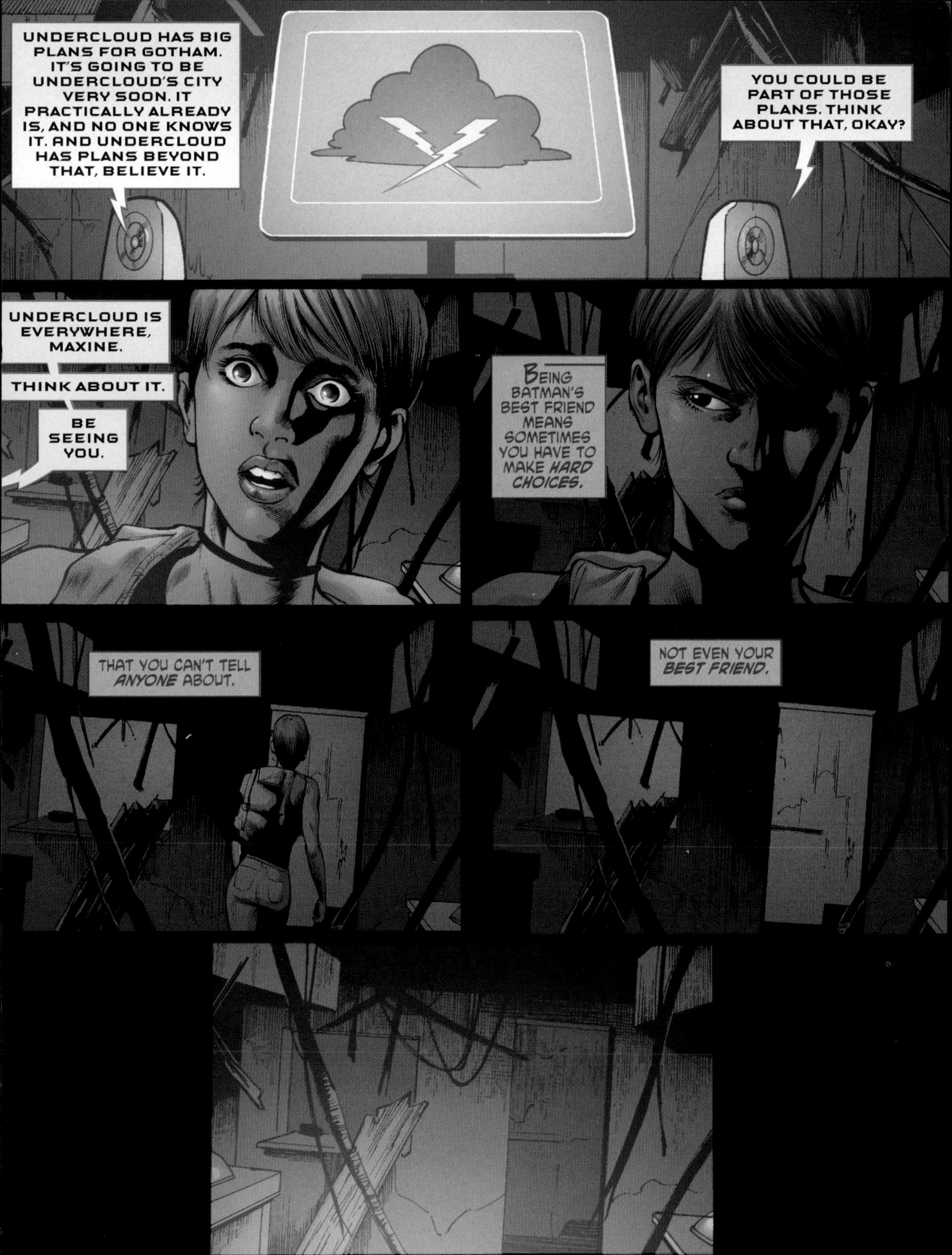
UNDERCLOUD HAS BIG PLANS FOR GOTHAM. IT'S GOING TO BE UNDERCLOUD'S CITY VERY SOON. IT PRACTICALLY ALREADY IS, AND NO ONE KNOWS IT. AND UNDERCLOUD HAS PLANS BEYOND THAT, BELIEVE IT.
YOU COULD BE PART OF THOSE PLANS. THINK ABOUT THAT, OKAY?
UNDERCLOUD IS EVERYWHERE, MAXINE.
THINK ABOUT IT.
BE SEEING YOU.
BEING BATMAN'S BEST FRIEND MEANS SOMETIMES YOU HAVE TO MAKE HARD CHOICES.
THAT YOU CAN'T TELL ANYONE ABOUT.
NOT EVEN YOUR BEST FRIEND.

INDUSTRIAL REVOLUTION PART 1: A RIOT GOING ON

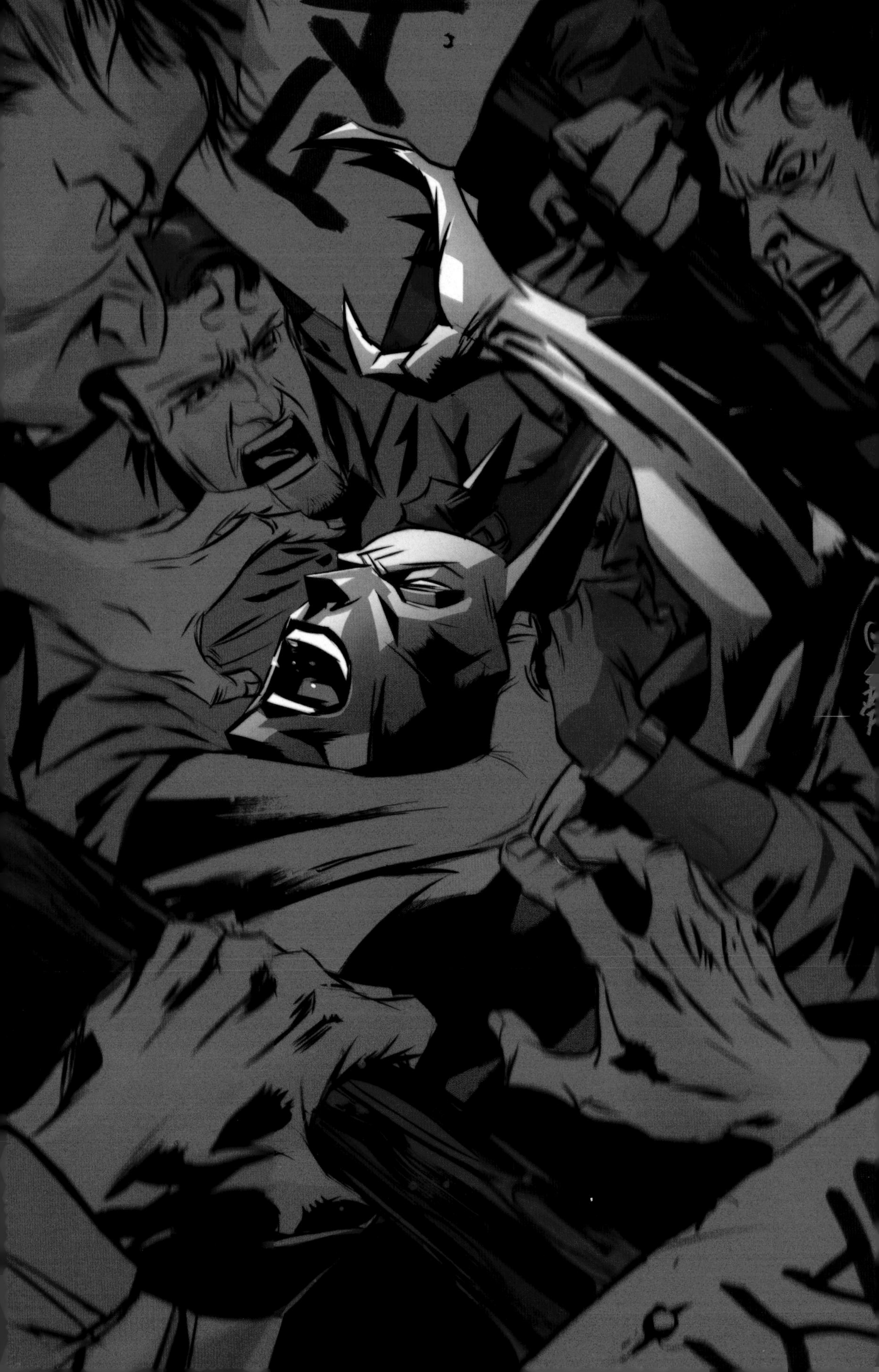

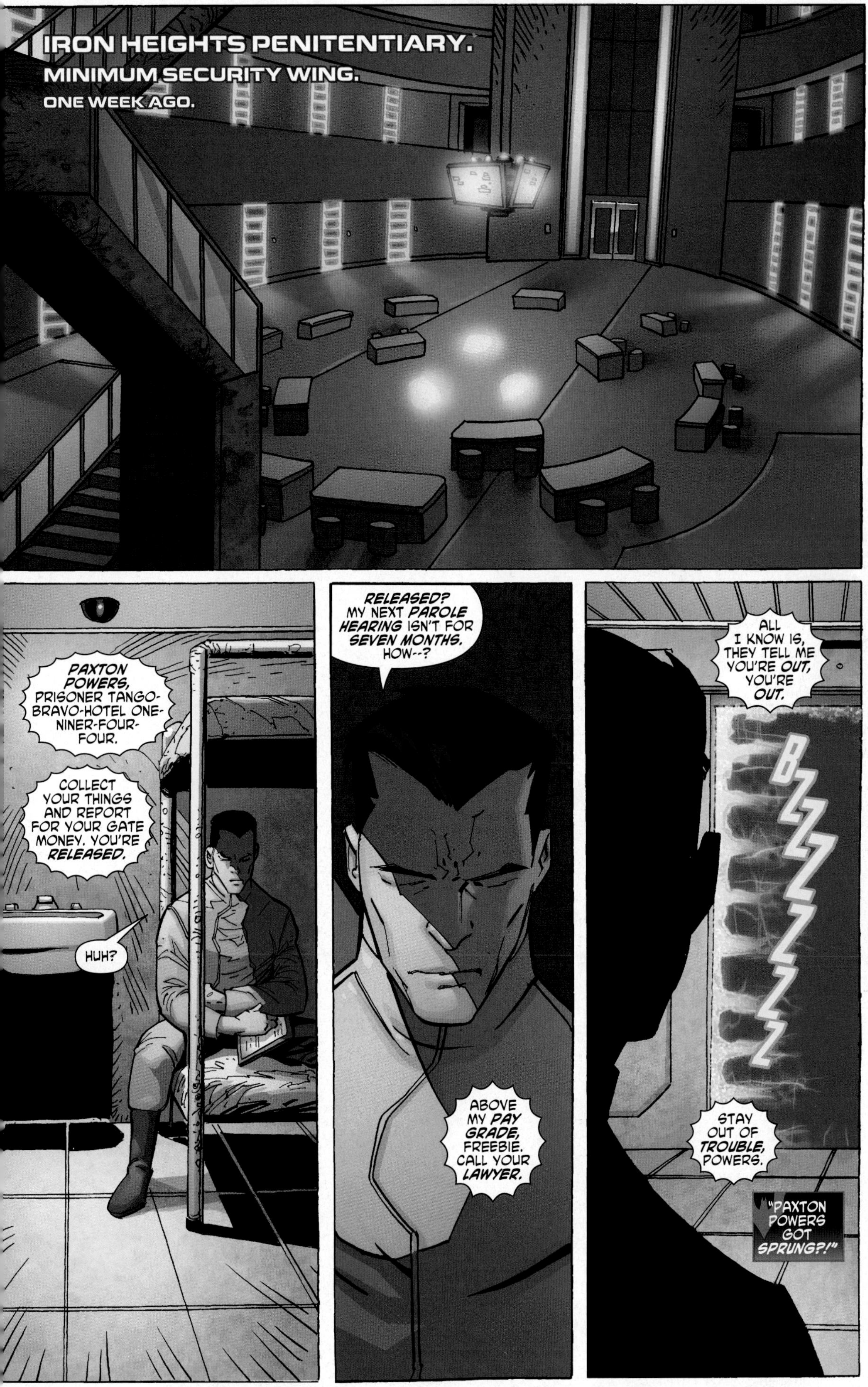
IRON HEIGHTS PENITENTIARY.
MINIMUM SECURITY WING.
ONE WEEK AGO.
PAXTON POWERS, PRISONER TANGO-BRAVO-HOTEL ONE-NINER-FOUR-FOUR.
COLLECT YOUR THINGS AND REPORT FOR YOUR GATE MONEY. YOU'RE RELEASED.
HUH?
RELEASED? MY NEXT PAROLE HEARING ISN'T FOR SEVEN MONTHS. HOW--?
ABOVE MY PAY GRADE, FREEBIE. CALL YOUR LAWYER.
ALL I KNOW IS, THEY TELL ME YOU'RE OUT, YOU'RE OUT.
BZZZZZZ
STAY OUT OF TROUBLE, POWERS.
"PAXTON POWERS GOT SPRUNG?!"

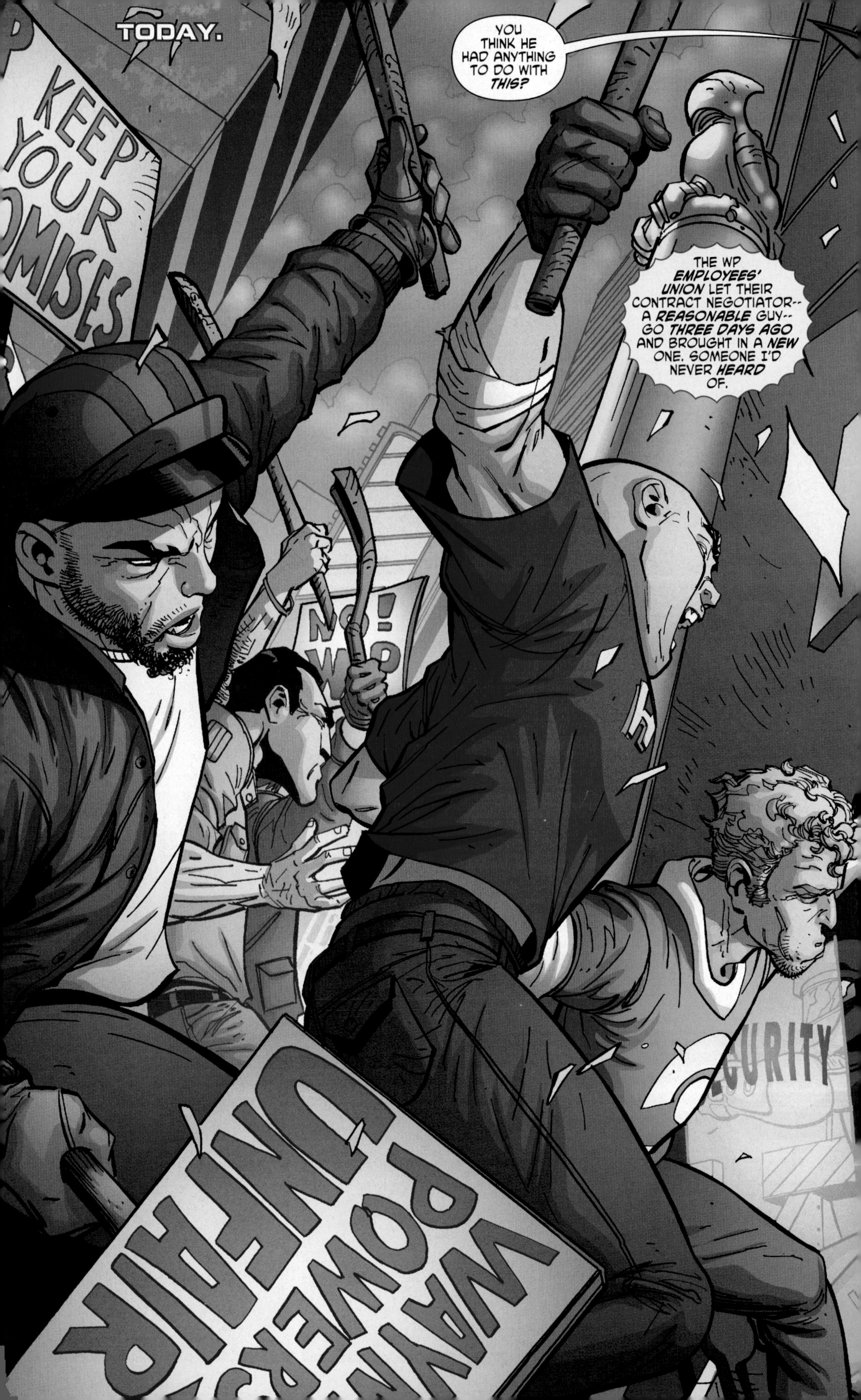
TODAY.
YOU THINK HE HAD ANYTHING TO DO WITH *THIS?*
THE WP *EMPLOYEES' UNION* LET THEIR CONTRACT NEGOTIATOR-- A *REASONABLE* GUY-- GO *THREE DAYS AGO* AND BROUGHT IN A *NEW* ONE. SOMEONE I'D NEVER *HEARD* OF.
KEEP YOUR

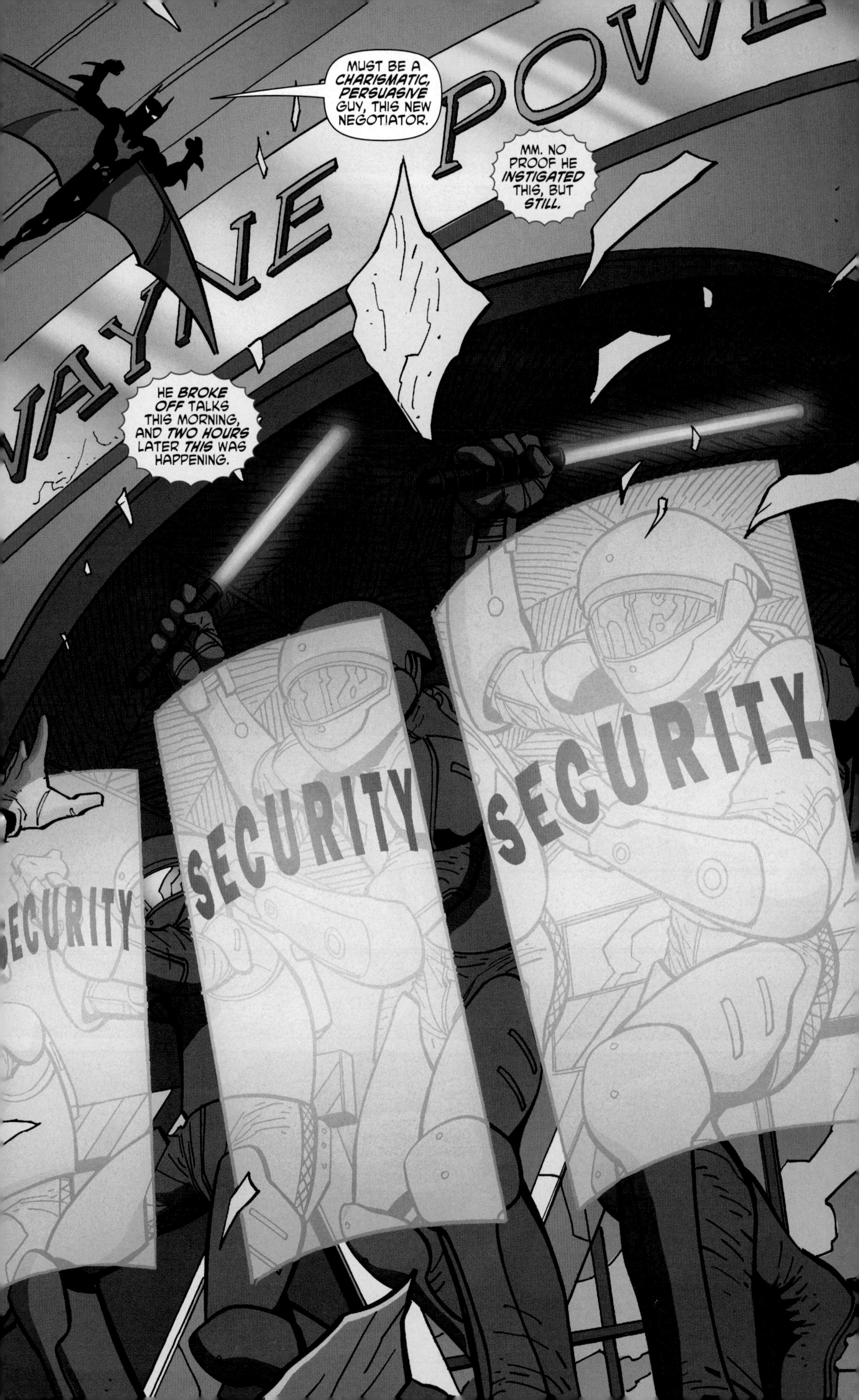

MUST BE A CHARISMATIC, PERSUASIVE GUY, THIS NEW NEGOTIATOR.
MM. NO PROOF HE INSTIGATED THIS, BUT STILL.
HE BROKE OFF TALKS THIS MORNING, AND TWO HOURS LATER THIS WAS HAPPENING.
SECURITY
SECURITY
ECURITY

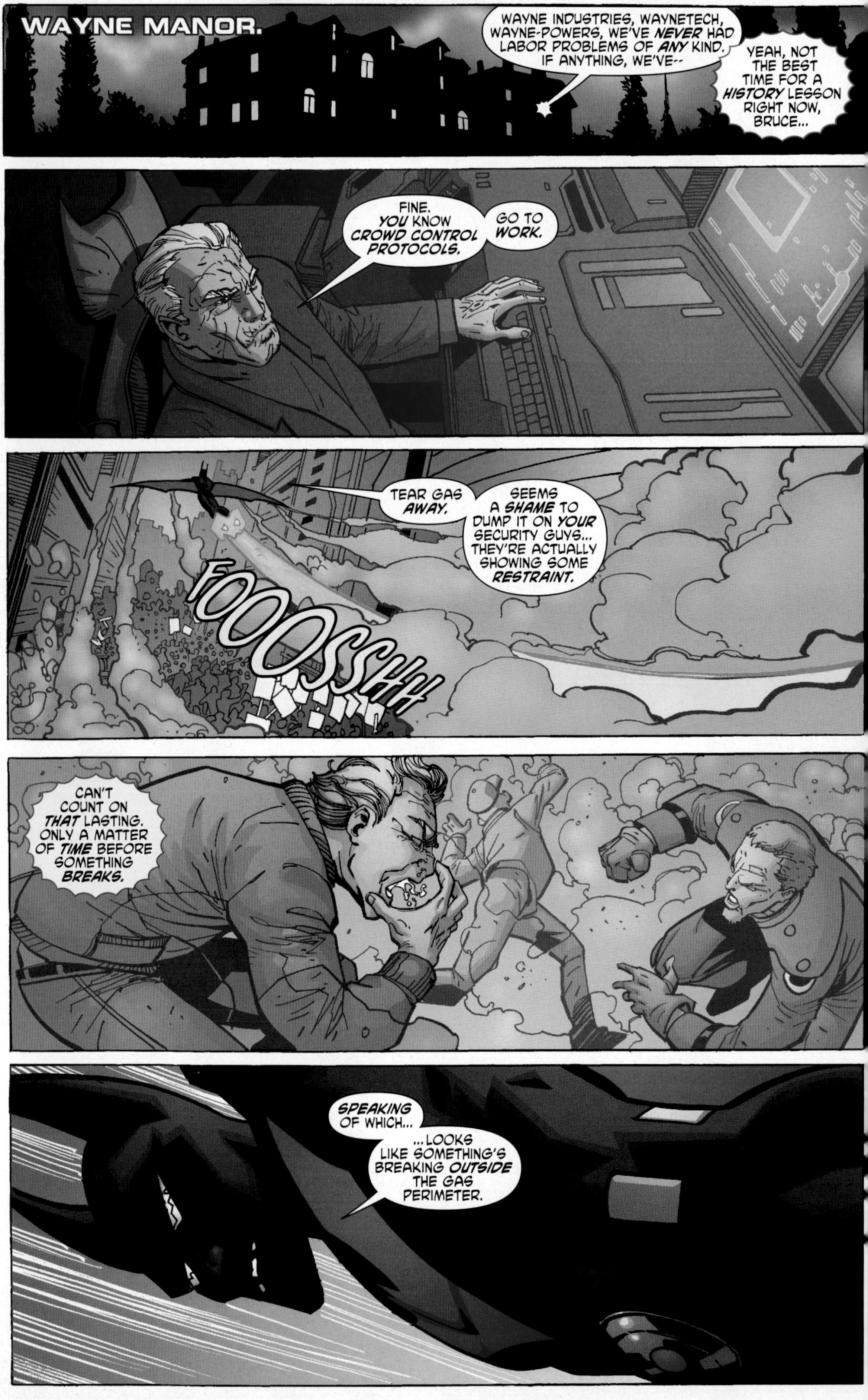
WAYNE MANOR.
WAYNE INDUSTRIES, WAYNETECH, WAYNE-POWERS, WE'VE NEVER HAD LABOR PROBLEMS OF ANY KIND. IF ANYTHING, WE'VE--
YEAH, NOT THE BEST TIME FOR A HISTORY LESSON RIGHT NOW, BRUCE...
FINE. YOU KNOW CROWD CONTROL PROTOCOLS.
GO TO WORK.
TEAR GAS AWAY.
SEEMS A SHAME TO DUMP IT ON YOUR SECURITY GUYS... THEY'RE ACTUALLY SHOWING SOME RESTRAINT.
FOOOSSHH
CAN'T COUNT ON THAT LASTING. ONLY A MATTER OF TIME BEFORE SOMETHING BREAKS.
SPEAKING OF WHICH...
...LOOKS LIKE SOMETHING'S BREAKING OUTSIDE THE GAS PERIMETER.

HEY! EVERYONE SLOW-PULSE IT!

BATMAAAAN!

CAREFUL...

REMEMBER, THESE AREN'T META-CRIMINALS, THEY'RE NORMAL PEOPLE. YOU'RE THEIR PROTECTOR.

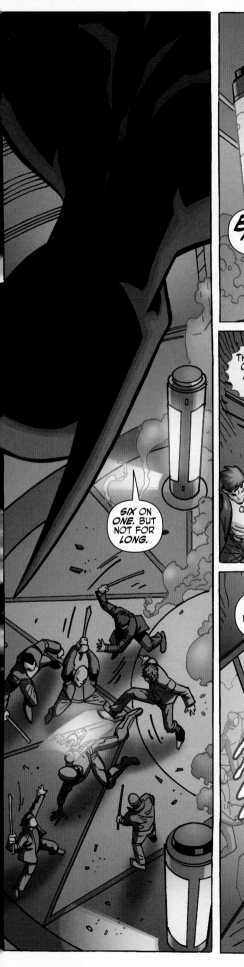

SIX ON ONE, BUT NOT FOR LONG.

HE'S JUST A STOOGE FOR WAYNE! GET HIM!

KREESHH

THEN I GUESS THIS IS WHAT YOU MIGHT CALL IRONIC.

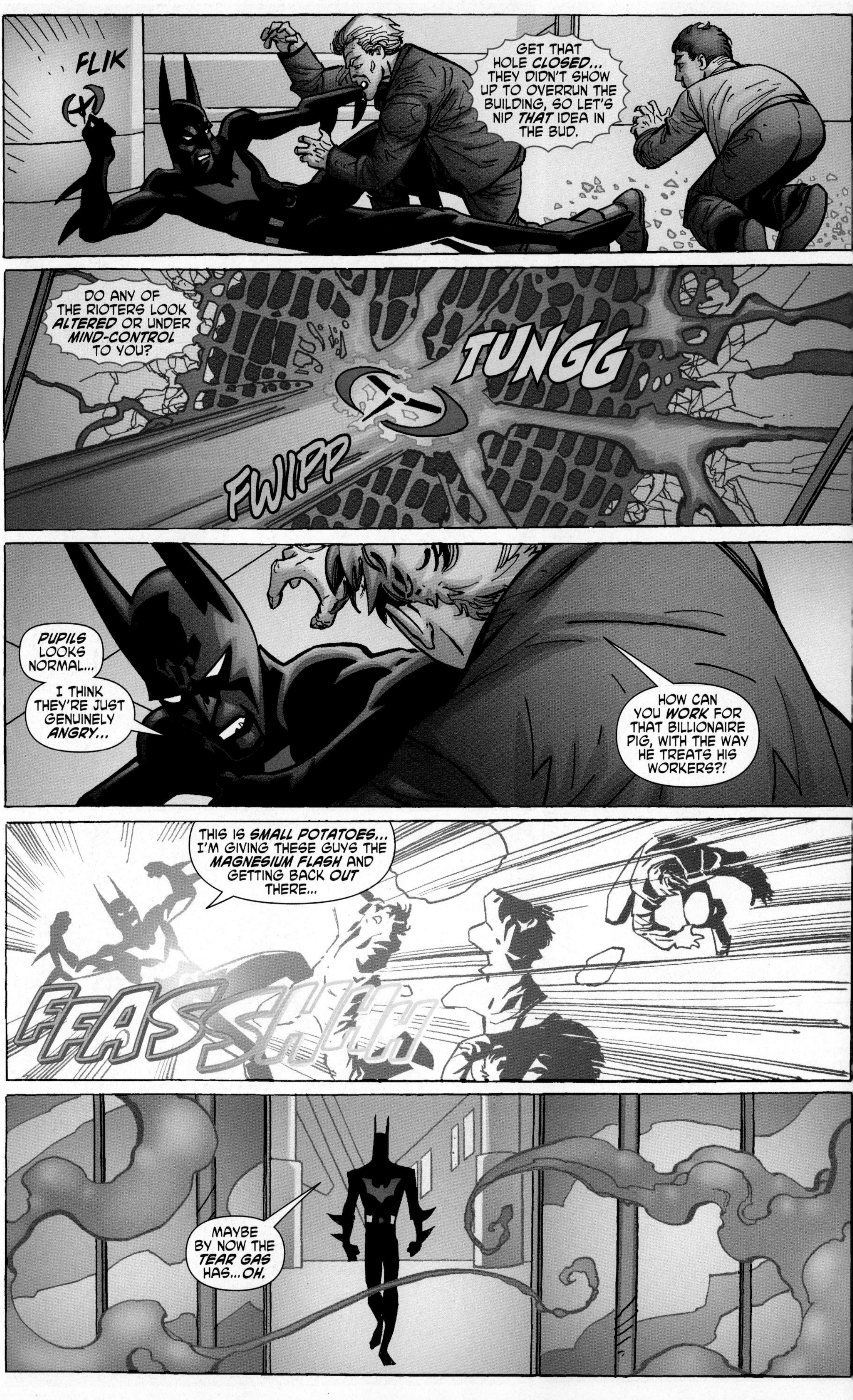
FLIK
GET THAT HOLE CLOSED... THEY DIDN'T SHOW UP TO OVERRUN THE BUILDING, SO LET'S NIP THAT IDEA IN THE BUD.
DO ANY OF THE RIOTERS LOOK ALTERED OR UNDER MIND-CONTROL TO YOU?
TUNGG
FWIPP
PUPILS LOOKS NORMAL...
I THINK THEY'RE JUST GENUINELY ANGRY...
HOW CAN YOU WORK FOR THAT BILLIONAIRE PIG, WITH THE WAY HE TREATS HIS WORKERS?!
THIS IS SMALL POTATOES... I'M GIVING THESE GUYS THE MAGNESIUM FLASH AND GETTING BACK OUT THERE...
FFASSHHH
MAYBE BY NOW THE TEAR GAS HAS...OH.

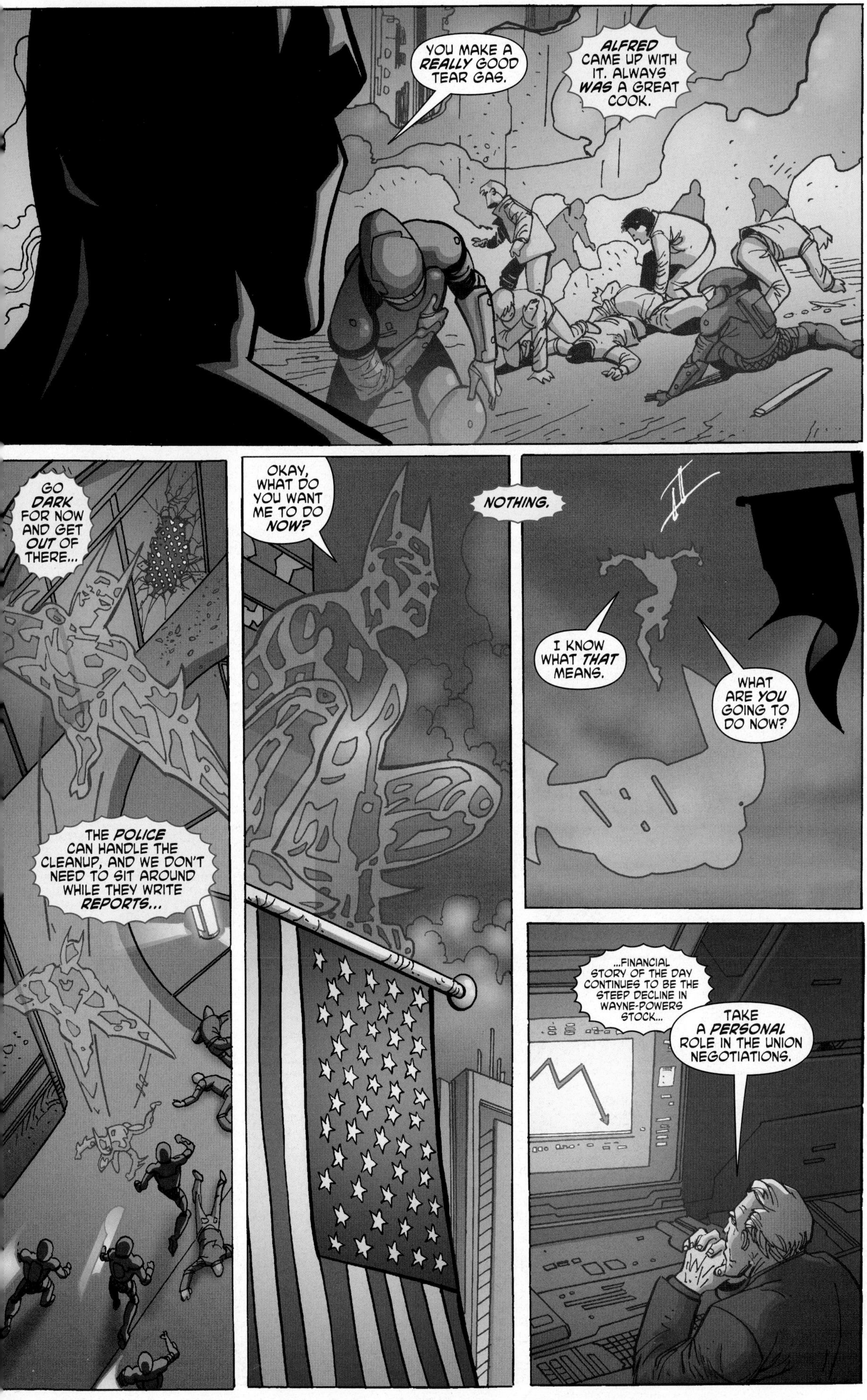
YOU MAKE A REALLY GOOD TEAR GAS.
ALFRED CAME UP WITH IT. ALWAYS WAS A GREAT COOK.
GO DARK FOR NOW AND GET OUT OF THERE...
THE POLICE CAN HANDLE THE CLEANUP, AND WE DON'T NEED TO SIT AROUND WHILE THEY WRITE REPORTS...
OKAY, WHAT DO YOU WANT ME TO DO NOW?
NOTHING.
I KNOW WHAT THAT MEANS.
WHAT ARE YOU GOING TO DO NOW?
...FINANCIAL STORY OF THE DAY CONTINUES TO BE THE STEEP DECLINE IN WAYNE-POWERS STOCK...
TAKE A PERSONAL ROLE IN THE UNION NEGOTIATIONS.

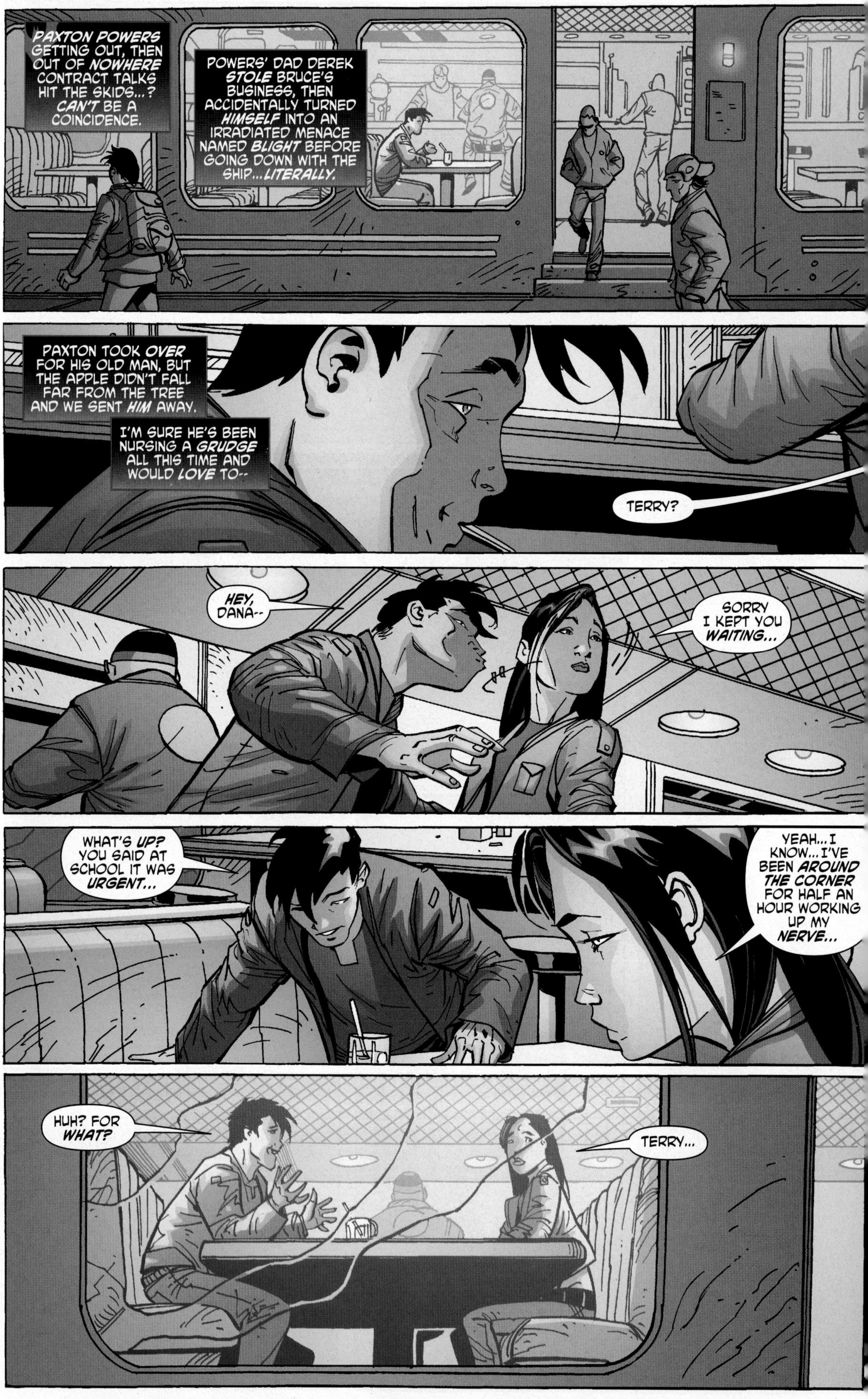
PAXTON POWERS GETTING OUT, THEN OUT OF NOWHERE CONTRACT TALKS HIT THE SKIDS...? CAN'T BE A COINCIDENCE.
POWERS' DAD DEREK STOLE BRUCE'S BUSINESS, THEN ACCIDENTALLY TURNED HIMSELF INTO AN IRRADIATED MENACE NAMED BLIGHT BEFORE GOING DOWN WITH THE SHIP...LITERALLY.
PAXTON TOOK OVER FOR HIS OLD MAN, BUT THE APPLE DIDN'T FALL FAR FROM THE TREE AND WE SENT HIM AWAY.
I'M SURE HE'S BEEN NURSING A GRUDGE ALL THIS TIME AND WOULD LOVE TO--
TERRY?
HEY, DANA--
SORRY I KEPT YOU WAITING...
WHAT'S UP? YOU SAID AT SCHOOL IT WAS URGENT...
YEAH...I KNOW...I'VE BEEN AROUND THE CORNER FOR HALF AN HOUR WORKING UP MY NERVE...
TERRY...
HUH? FOR WHAT?

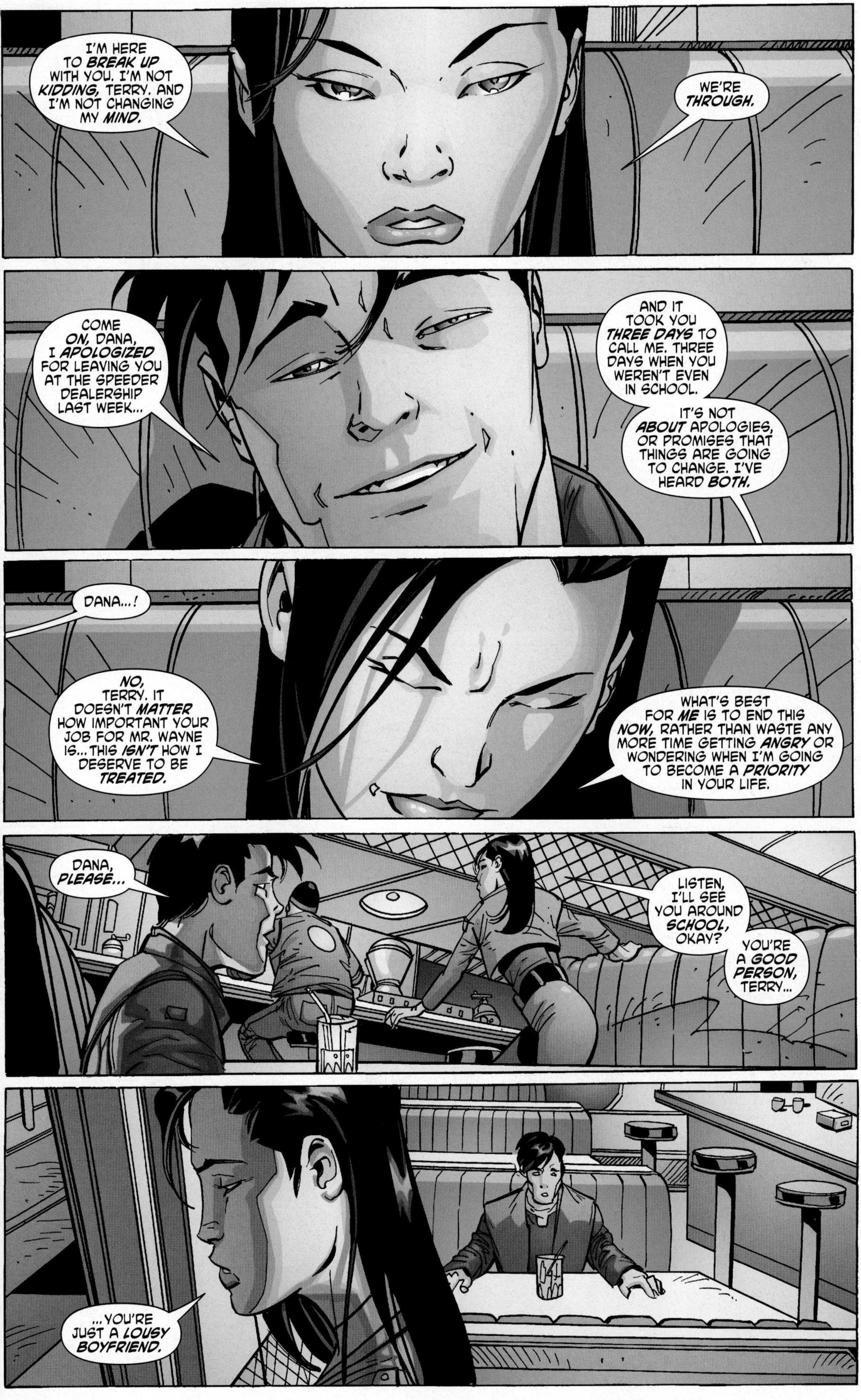
I'M HERE TO BREAK UP WITH YOU. I'M NOT KIDDING, TERRY. AND I'M NOT CHANGING MY MIND.
WE'RE THROUGH.
COME ON, DANA, I APOLOGIZED FOR LEAVING YOU AT THE SPEEDER DEALERSHIP LAST WEEK...
AND IT TOOK YOU THREE DAYS TO CALL ME. THREE DAYS WHEN YOU WEREN'T EVEN IN SCHOOL.
IT'S NOT ABOUT APOLOGIES, OR PROMISES THAT THINGS ARE GOING TO CHANGE. I'VE HEARD BOTH.
DANA...!
NO, TERRY. IT DOESN'T MATTER HOW IMPORTANT YOUR JOB FOR MR. WAYNE IS... THIS ISN'T HOW I DESERVE TO BE TREATED.
WHAT'S BEST FOR ME IS TO END THIS NOW, RATHER THAN WASTE ANY MORE TIME GETTING ANGRY OR WONDERING WHEN I'M GOING TO BECOME A PRIORITY IN YOUR LIFE.
DANA, PLEASE...
LISTEN, I'LL SEE YOU AROUND SCHOOL, OKAY?
YOU'RE A GOOD PERSON, TERRY...
...YOU'RE JUST A LOUSY BOYFRIEND.

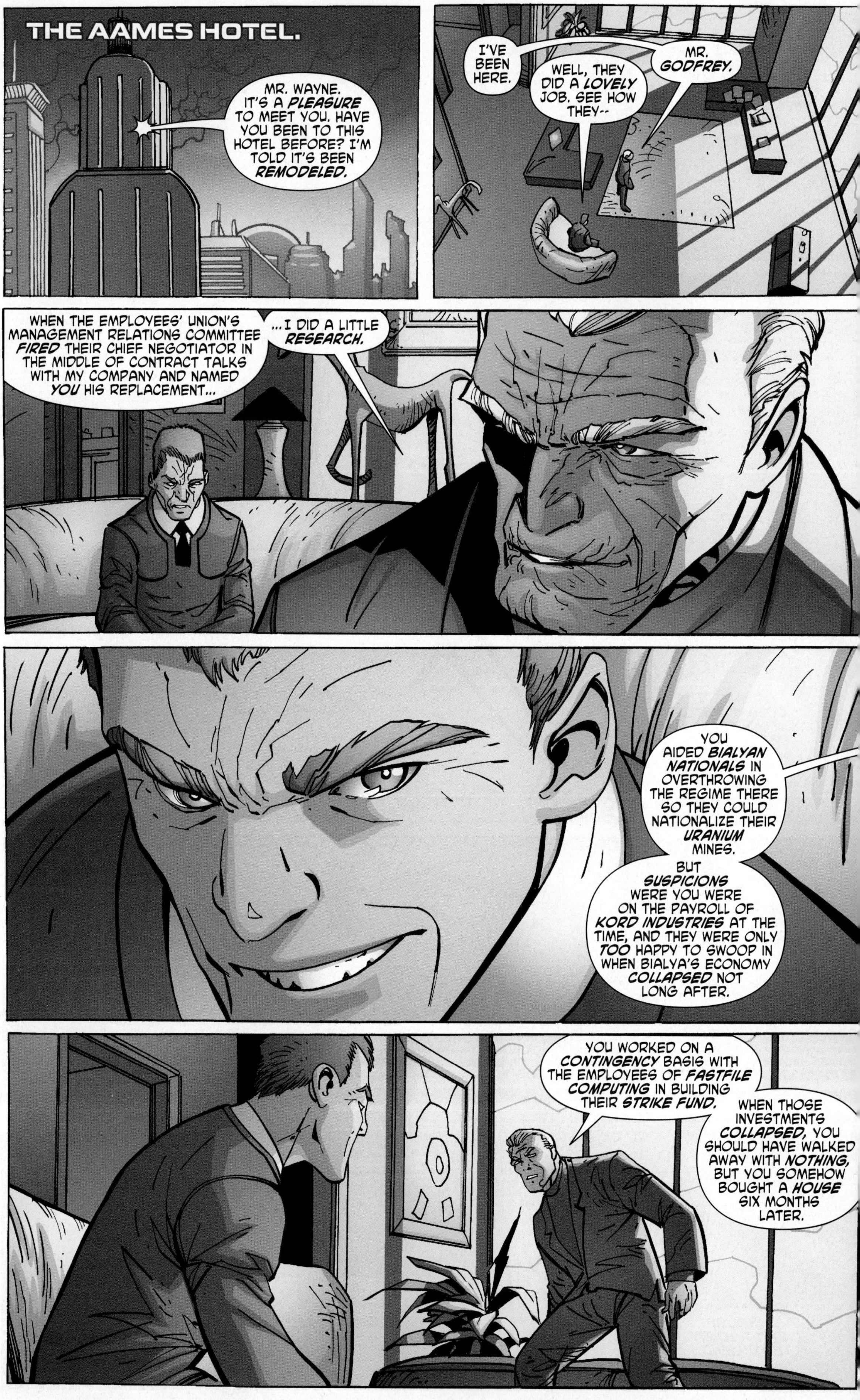
THE AAMES HOTEL.
MR. WAYNE. IT'S A PLEASURE TO MEET YOU. HAVE YOU BEEN TO THIS HOTEL BEFORE? I'M TOLD IT'S BEEN REMODELED.
I'VE BEEN HERE.
WELL, THEY DID A LOVELY JOB. SEE HOW THEY--
MR. GODFREY.
WHEN THE EMPLOYEES' UNION'S MANAGEMENT RELATIONS COMMITTEE FIRED THEIR CHIEF NEGOTIATOR IN THE MIDDLE OF CONTRACT TALKS WITH MY COMPANY AND NAMED YOU HIS REPLACEMENT...
...I DID A LITTLE RESEARCH.
YOU AIDED BIALYAN NATIONALS IN OVERTHROWING THE REGIME THERE SO THEY COULD NATIONALIZE THEIR URANIUM MINES.
BUT SUSPICIONS WERE YOU WERE ON THE PAYROLL OF KORD INDUSTRIES AT THE TIME, AND THEY WERE ONLY TOO HAPPY TO SWOOP IN WHEN BIALYA'S ECONOMY COLLAPSED NOT LONG AFTER.
YOU WORKED ON A CONTINGENCY BASIS WITH THE EMPLOYEES OF FASTFILE COMPUTING IN BUILDING THEIR STRIKE FUND.
WHEN THOSE INVESTMENTS COLLAPSED, YOU SHOULD HAVE WALKED AWAY WITH NOTHING, BUT YOU SOMEHOW BOUGHT A HOUSE SIX MONTHS LATER.

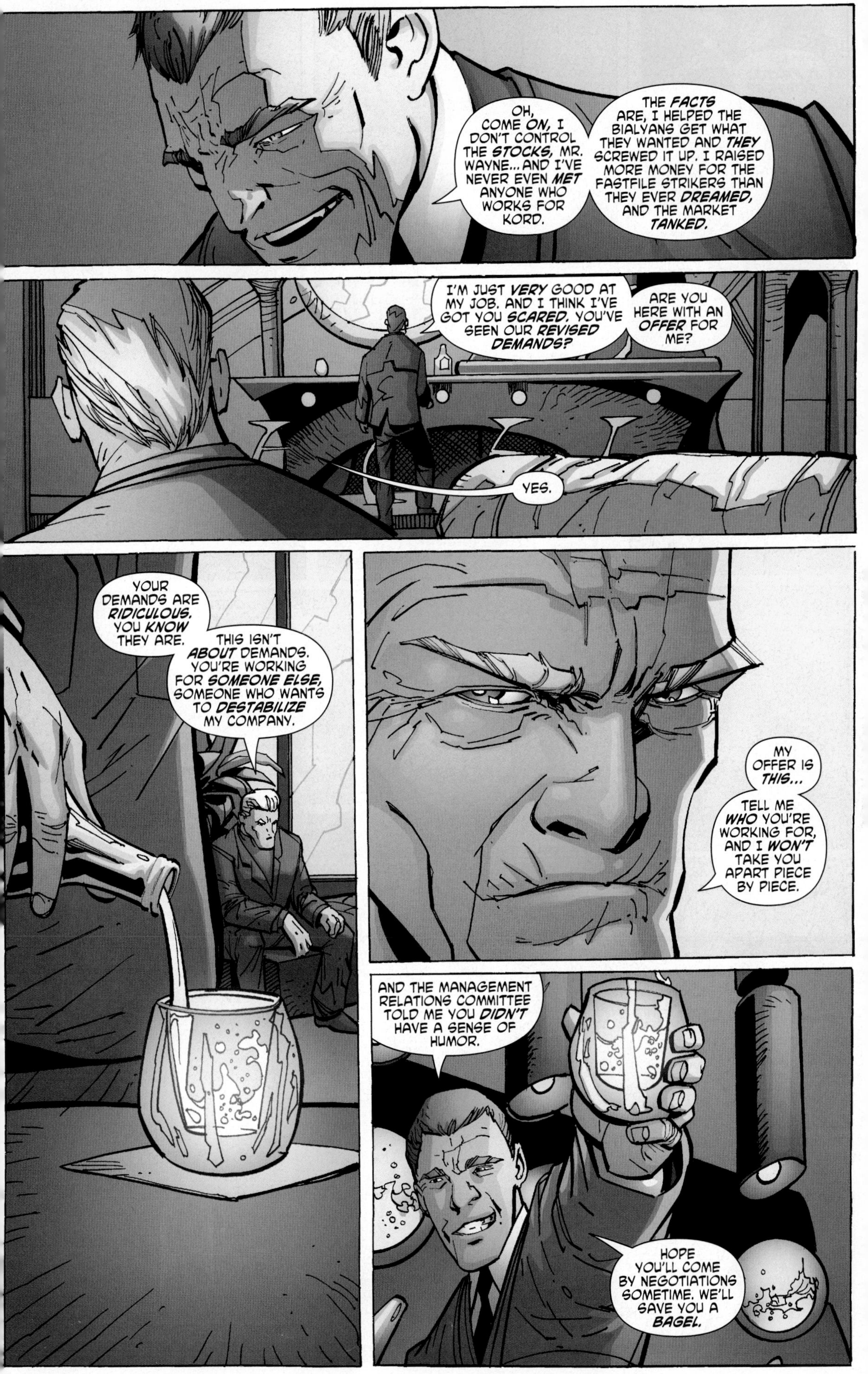

OH, COME ON, I DON'T CONTROL THE STOCKS, MR. WAYNE... AND I'VE NEVER EVEN MET ANYONE WHO WORKS FOR KORD.
THE FACTS ARE, I HELPED THE BIALYANS GET WHAT THEY WANTED AND THEY SCREWED IT UP. I RAISED MORE MONEY FOR THE FASTFILE STRIKERS THAN THEY EVER DREAMED, AND THE MARKET TANKED.
I'M JUST VERY GOOD AT MY JOB. AND I THINK I'VE GOT YOU SCARED. YOU'VE SEEN OUR REVISED DEMANDS?
ARE YOU HERE WITH AN OFFER FOR ME?
YES.
YOUR DEMANDS ARE RIDICULOUS. YOU KNOW THEY ARE.
THIS ISN'T ABOUT DEMANDS. YOU'RE WORKING FOR SOMEONE ELSE, SOMEONE WHO WANTS TO DESTABILIZE MY COMPANY.
MY OFFER IS THIS...
TELL ME WHO YOU'RE WORKING FOR, AND I WON'T TAKE YOU APART PIECE BY PIECE.
AND THE MANAGEMENT RELATIONS COMMITTEE TOLD ME YOU DIDN'T HAVE A SENSE OF HUMOR.
HOPE YOU'LL COME BY NEGOTIATIONS SOMETIME. WE'LL SAVE YOU A BAGEL.

IS IT *PAXTON POWERS?*

... NEVER MET *HIM*, EITHER. ISN'T HE IN *PRISON?*

I'LL SHOW MYSELF OUT.

OH, ONE *MORE* THING. I *KNEW* A MAN NAMED GODFREY ONCE. A G. GORDON GODFREY.

YES, THE MAN WHO TRIED TO TURN THE POPULATION AGAINST METAHUMANS SEVERAL *DECADES* AGO. I GET THAT QUESTION A *LOT.*

NO, *NO* RELATION. BUT I CERTAINLY ADMIRE HIS *SKILL.*

HAVE A GOOD NIGHT, MR. WAYNE.

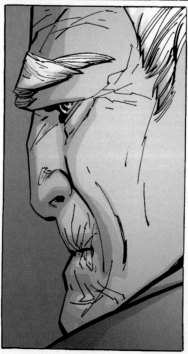

KLAK

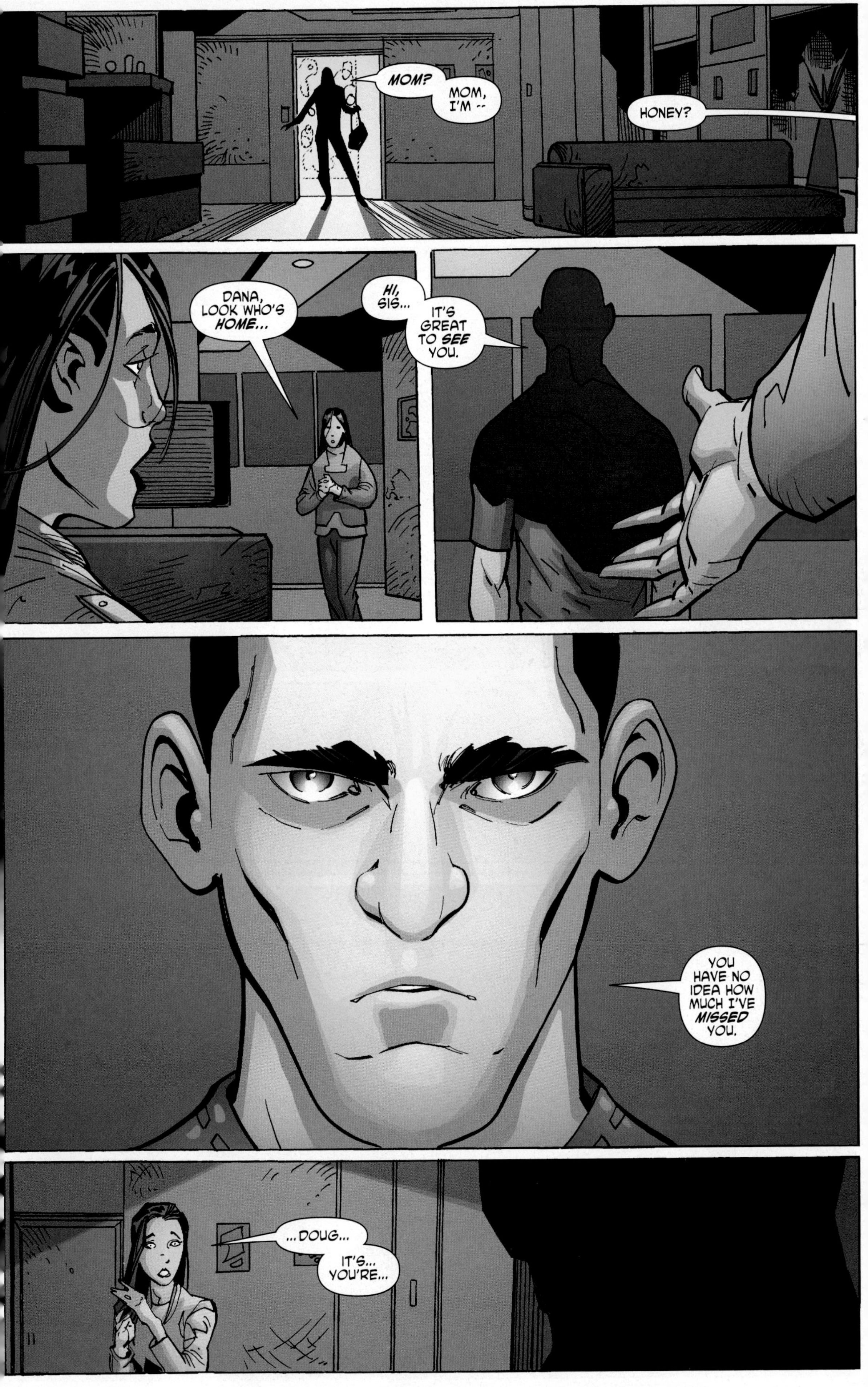
MOM?
MOM, I'M --
HONEY?
DANA, LOOK WHO'S HOME...
HI, SIS...
IT'S GREAT TO SEE YOU.
YOU HAVE NO IDEA HOW MUCH I'VE MISSED YOU.
...DOUG...
IT'S... YOU'RE...

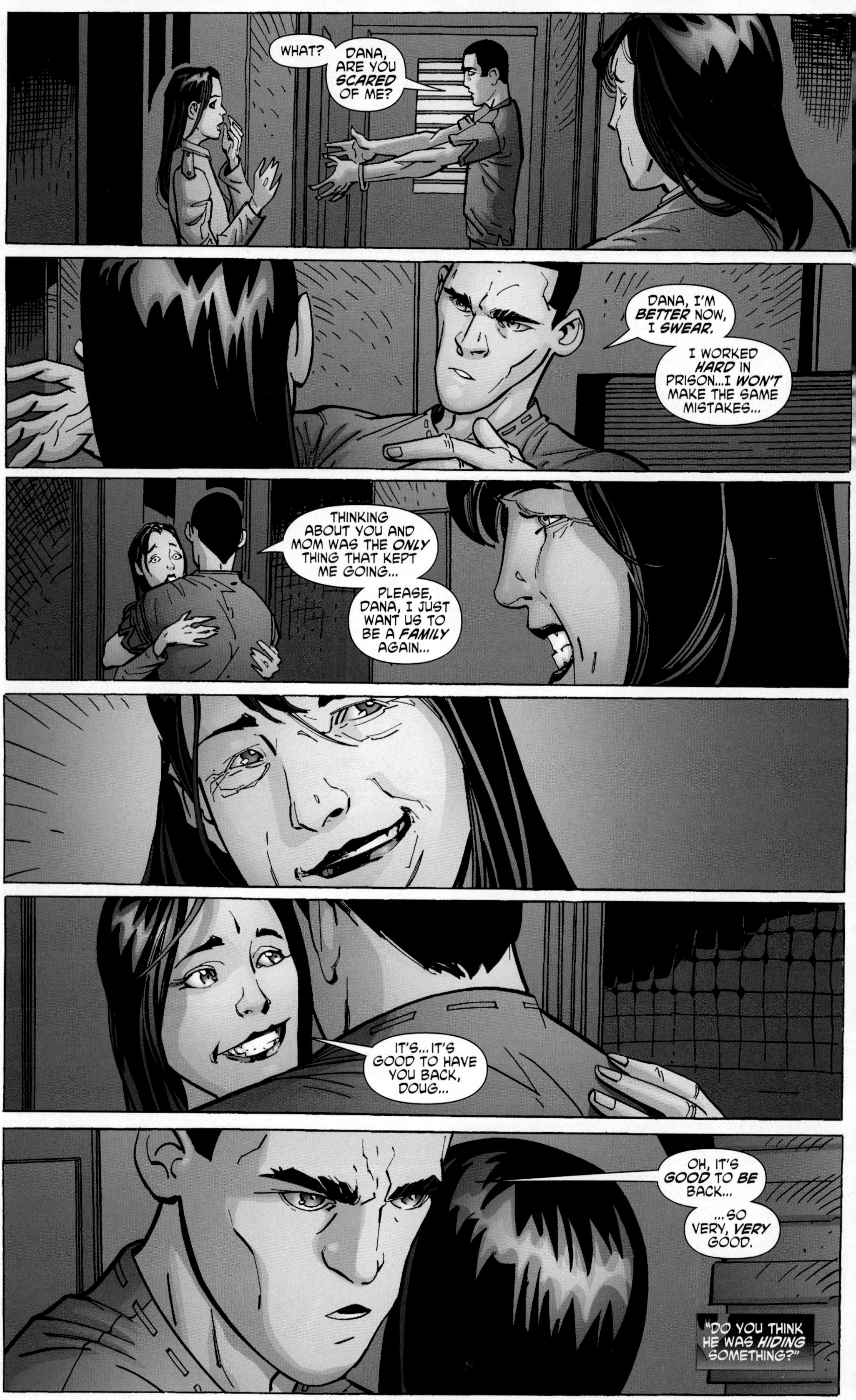

WHAT?
DANA, ARE YOU SCARED OF ME?
DANA, I'M BETTER NOW, I SWEAR.
I WORKED HARD IN PRISON...I WON'T MAKE THE SAME MISTAKES...
THINKING ABOUT YOU AND MOM WAS THE ONLY THING THAT KEPT ME GOING...
PLEASE, DANA, I JUST WANT US TO BE A FAMILY AGAIN...
IT'S...IT'S GOOD TO HAVE YOU BACK, DOUG...
OH, IT'S GOOD TO BE BACK...
...SO VERY, VERY GOOD.
"DO YOU THINK HE WAS HIDING SOMETHING?"

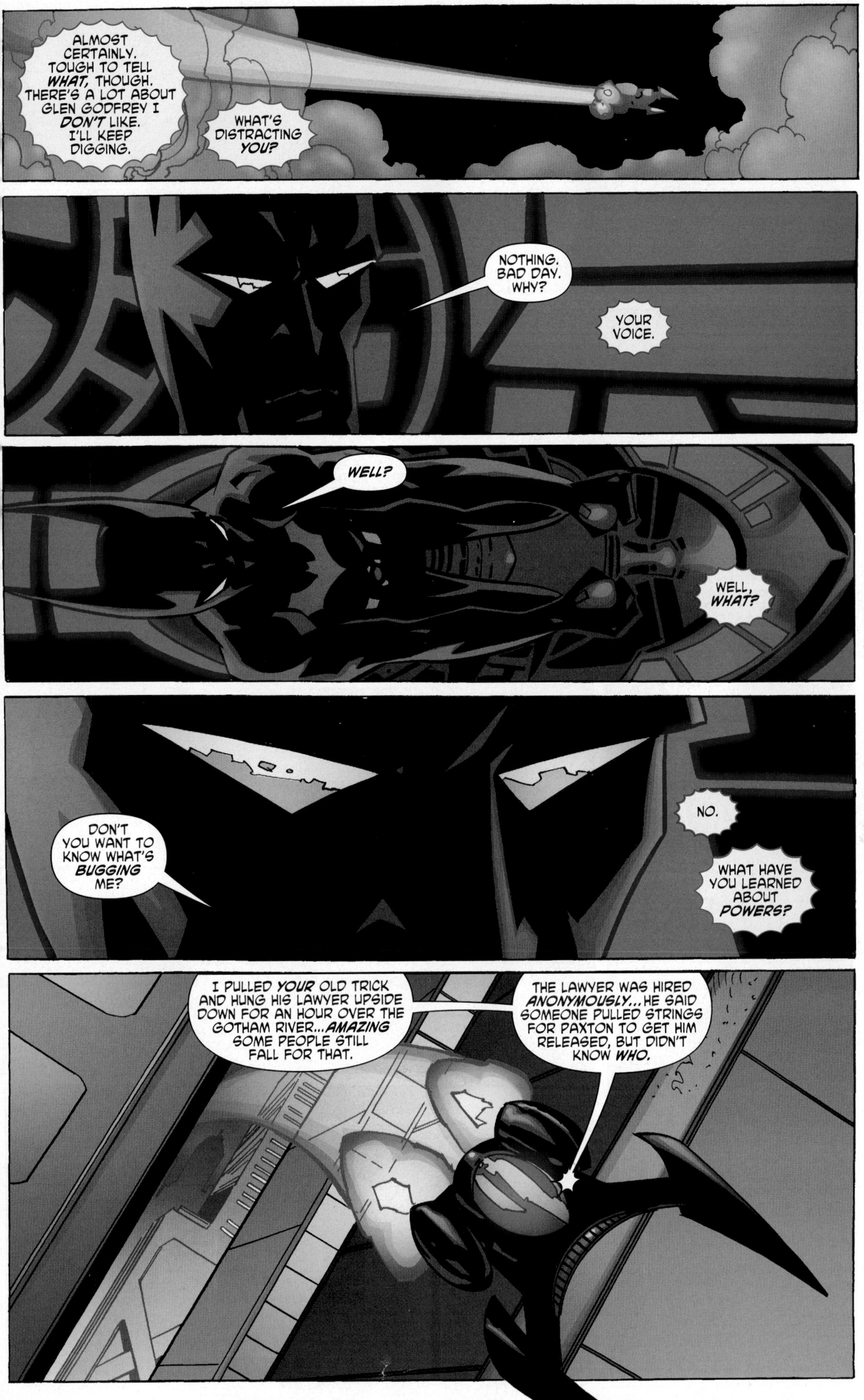
ALMOST CERTAINLY. TOUGH TO TELL WHAT, THOUGH. THERE'S A LOT ABOUT GLEN GODFREY I DON'T LIKE. I'LL KEEP DIGGING.
WHAT'S DISTRACTING YOU?
NOTHING. BAD DAY. WHY?
YOUR VOICE.
WELL?
WELL, WHAT?
DON'T YOU WANT TO KNOW WHAT'S BUGGING ME?
NO.
WHAT HAVE YOU LEARNED ABOUT POWERS?
I PULLED YOUR OLD TRICK AND HUNG HIS LAWYER UPSIDE DOWN FOR AN HOUR OVER THE GOTHAM RIVER... AMAZING SOME PEOPLE STILL FALL FOR THAT.
THE LAWYER WAS HIRED ANONYMOUSLY... HE SAID SOMEONE PULLED STRINGS FOR PAXTON TO GET HIM RELEASED, BUT DIDN'T KNOW WHO.

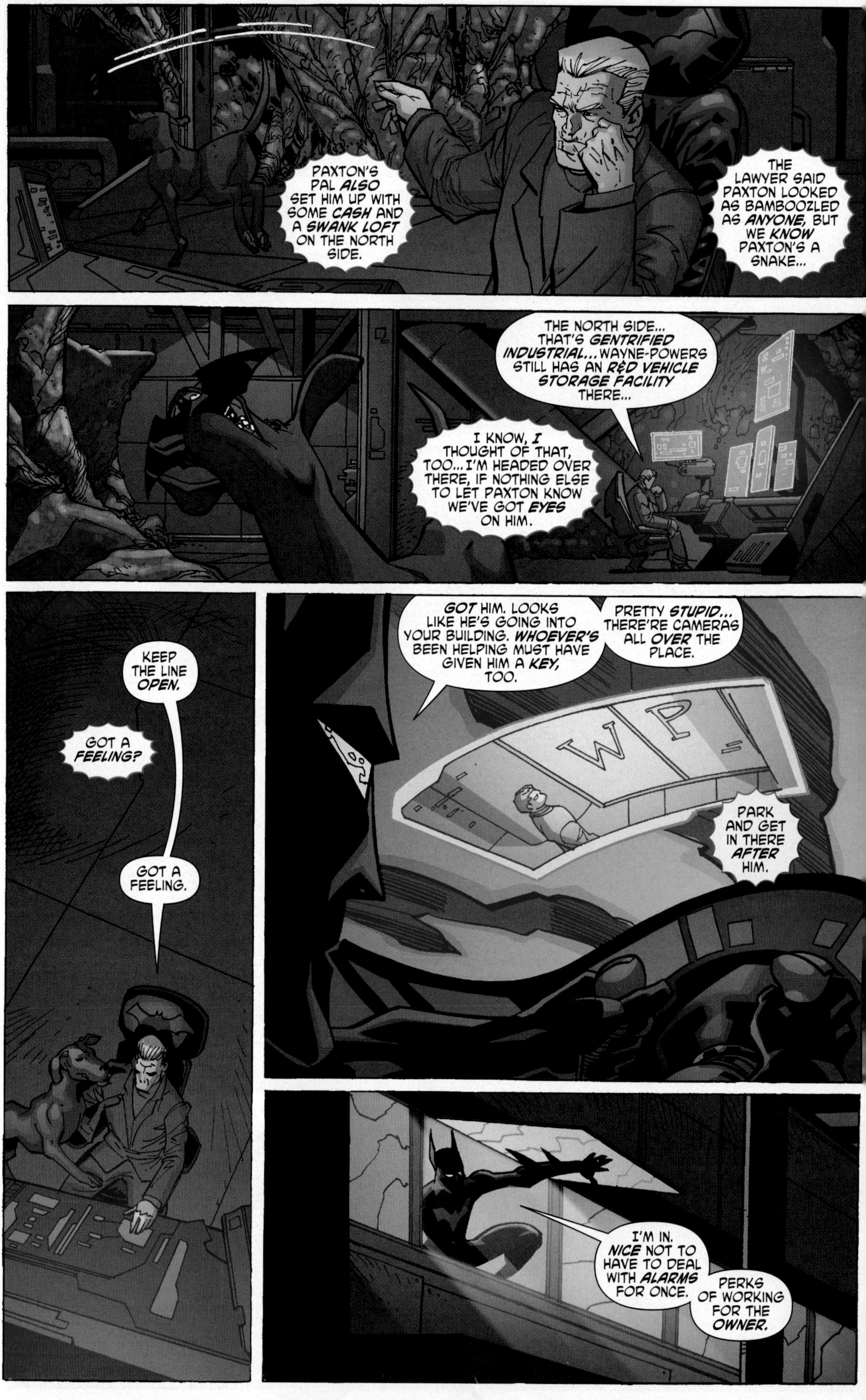
PAXTON'S PAL ALSO SET HIM UP WITH SOME CASH AND A SWANK LOFT ON THE NORTH SIDE.
THE LAWYER SAID PAXTON LOOKED AS BAMBOOZLED AS ANYONE, BUT WE KNOW PAXTON'S A SNAKE...
THE NORTH SIDE... THAT'S GENTRIFIED INDUSTRIAL... WAYNE-POWERS STILL HAS AN R&D VEHICLE STORAGE FACILITY THERE...
I KNOW, I THOUGHT OF THAT, TOO... I'M HEADED OVER THERE, IF NOTHING ELSE TO LET PAXTON KNOW WE'VE GOT EYES ON HIM.
KEEP THE LINE OPEN.
GOT A FEELING?
GOT A FEELING.
GOT HIM. LOOKS LIKE HE'S GOING INTO YOUR BUILDING. WHOEVER'S BEEN HELPING MUST HAVE GIVEN HIM A KEY, TOO.
PRETTY STUPID... THERE'RE CAMERAS ALL OVER THE PLACE.
WP
PARK AND GET IN THERE AFTER HIM.
I'M IN. NICE NOT TO HAVE TO DEAL WITH ALARMS FOR ONCE.
PERKS OF WORKING FOR THE OWNER.

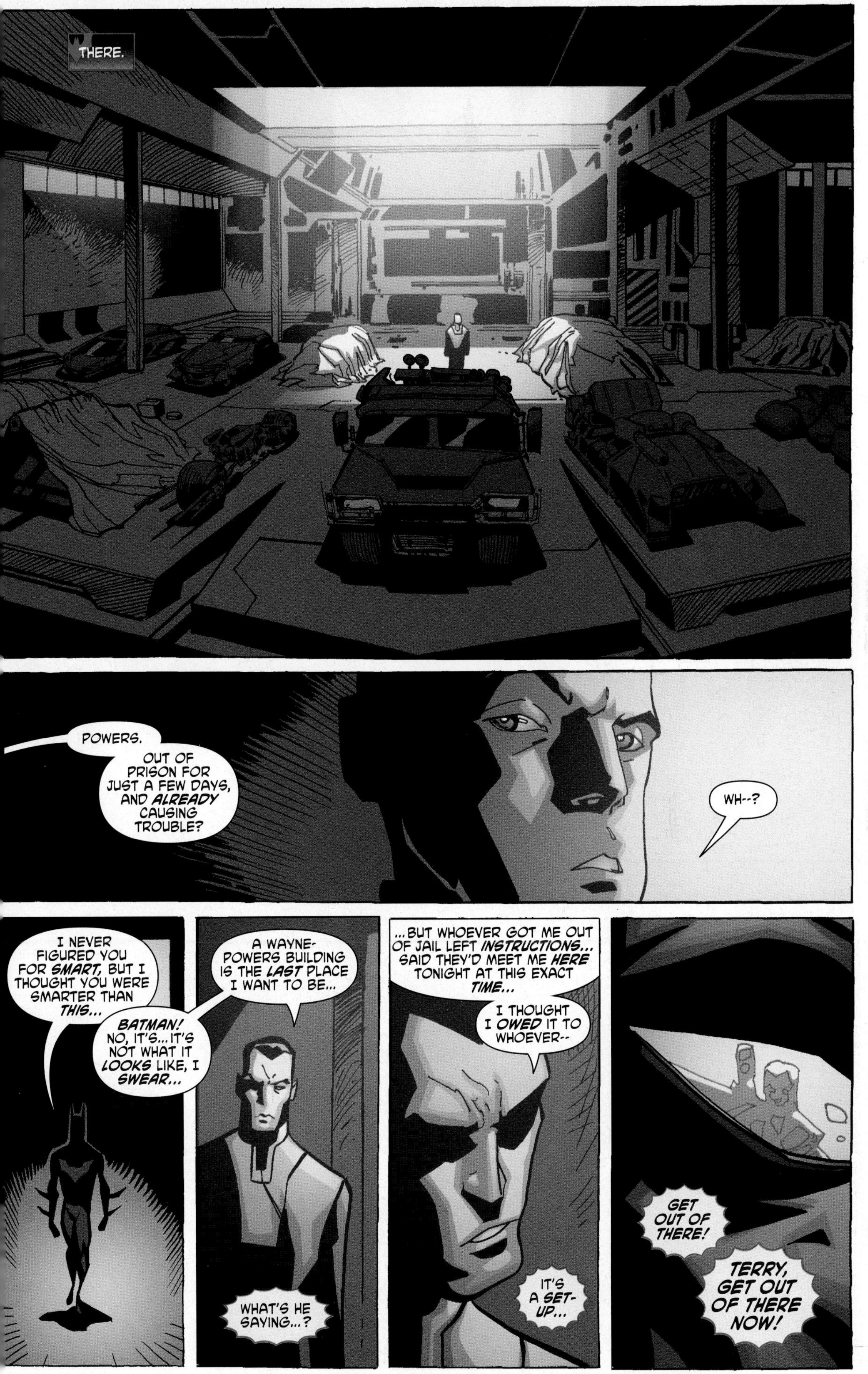
THERE.
POWERS.
OUT OF PRISON FOR JUST A FEW DAYS, AND ALREADY CAUSING TROUBLE?
WH--?
I NEVER FIGURED YOU FOR SMART, BUT I THOUGHT YOU WERE SMARTER THAN THIS...
BATMAN! NO, IT'S... IT'S NOT WHAT IT LOOKS LIKE, I SWEAR...
A WAYNE-POWERS BUILDING IS THE LAST PLACE I WANT TO BE...
WHAT'S HE SAYING...?
...BUT WHOEVER GOT ME OUT OF JAIL LEFT INSTRUCTIONS... SAID THEY'D MEET ME HERE TONIGHT AT THIS EXACT TIME...
I THOUGHT I OWED IT TO WHOEVER--
IT'S A SET-UP...
GET OUT OF THERE!
TERRY, GET OUT OF THERE NOW!

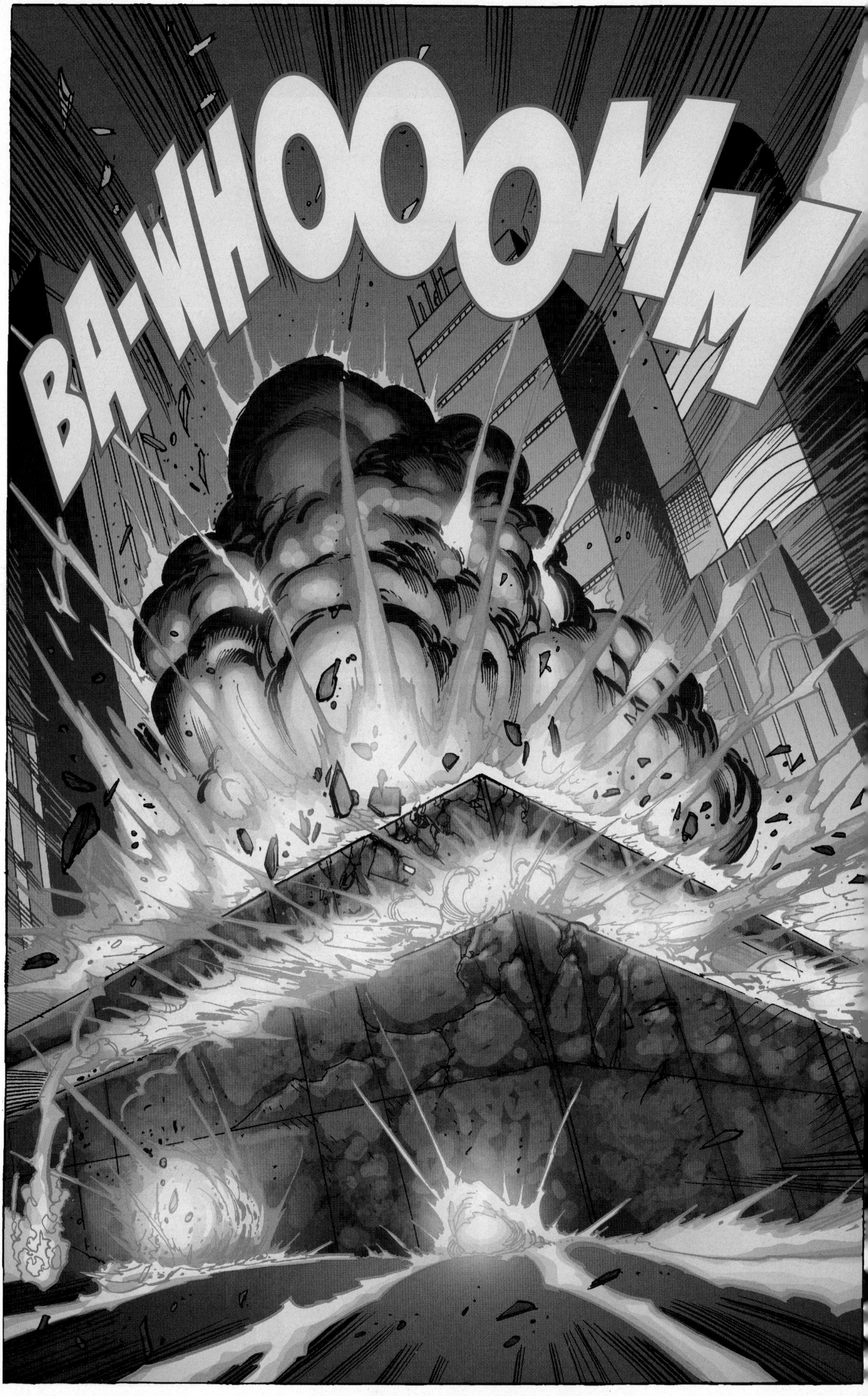
BA-WHOOOMM

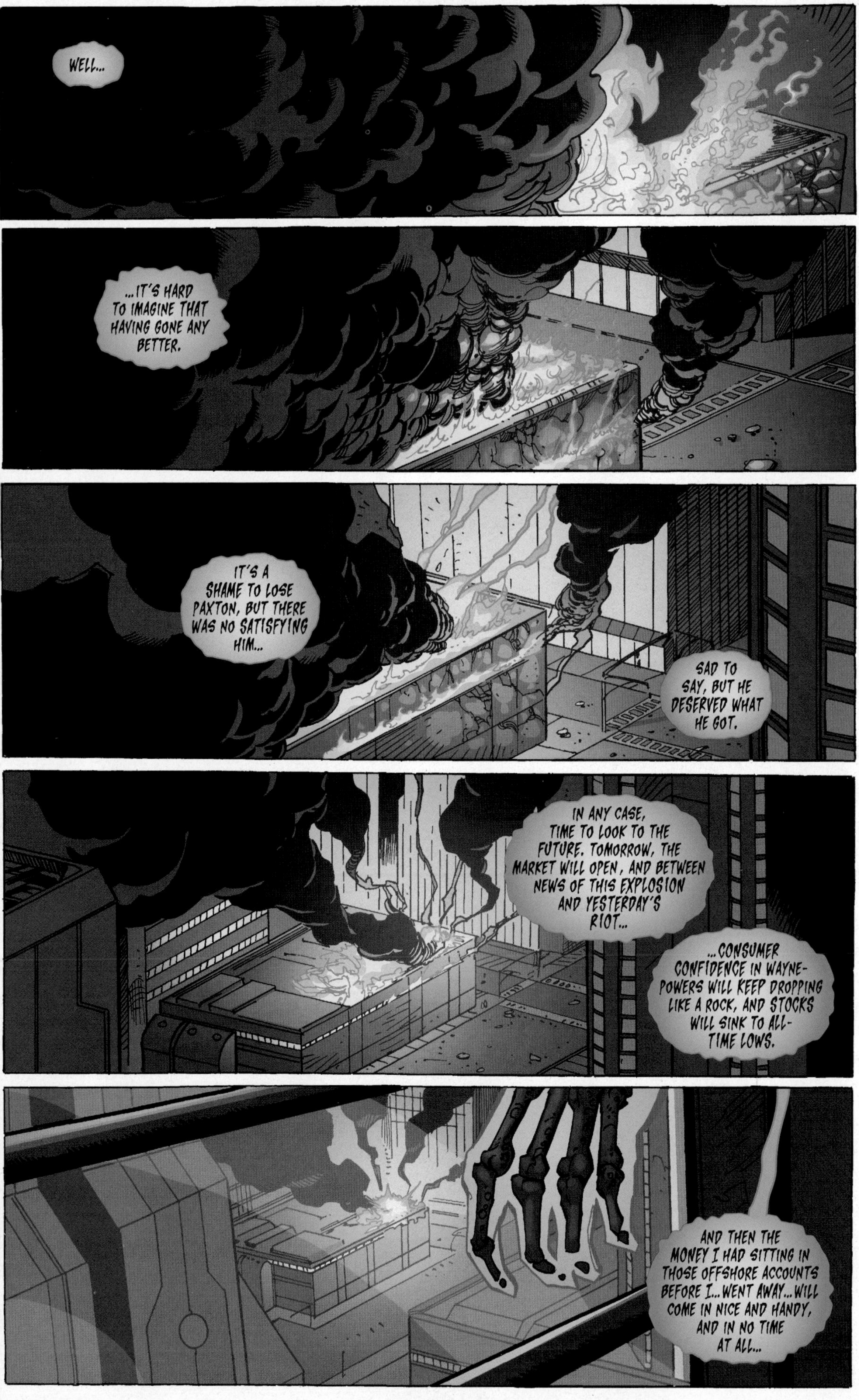
WELL...
...IT'S HARD TO IMAGINE THAT HAVING GONE ANY BETTER.
IT'S A SHAME TO LOSE PAXTON, BUT THERE WAS NO SATISFYING HIM...
SAD TO SAY, BUT HE DESERVED WHAT HE GOT.
IN ANY CASE, TIME TO LOOK TO THE FUTURE. TOMORROW, THE MARKET WILL OPEN, AND BETWEEN NEWS OF THIS EXPLOSION AND YESTERDAY'S RIOT...
...CONSUMER CONFIDENCE IN WAYNE-POWERS WILL KEEP DROPPING LIKE A ROCK, AND STOCKS WILL SINK TO ALL-TIME LOWS.
AND THEN THE MONEY I HAD SITTING IN THOSE OFFSHORE ACCOUNTS BEFORE I...WENT AWAY...WILL COME IN NICE AND HANDY, AND IN NO TIME AT ALL...

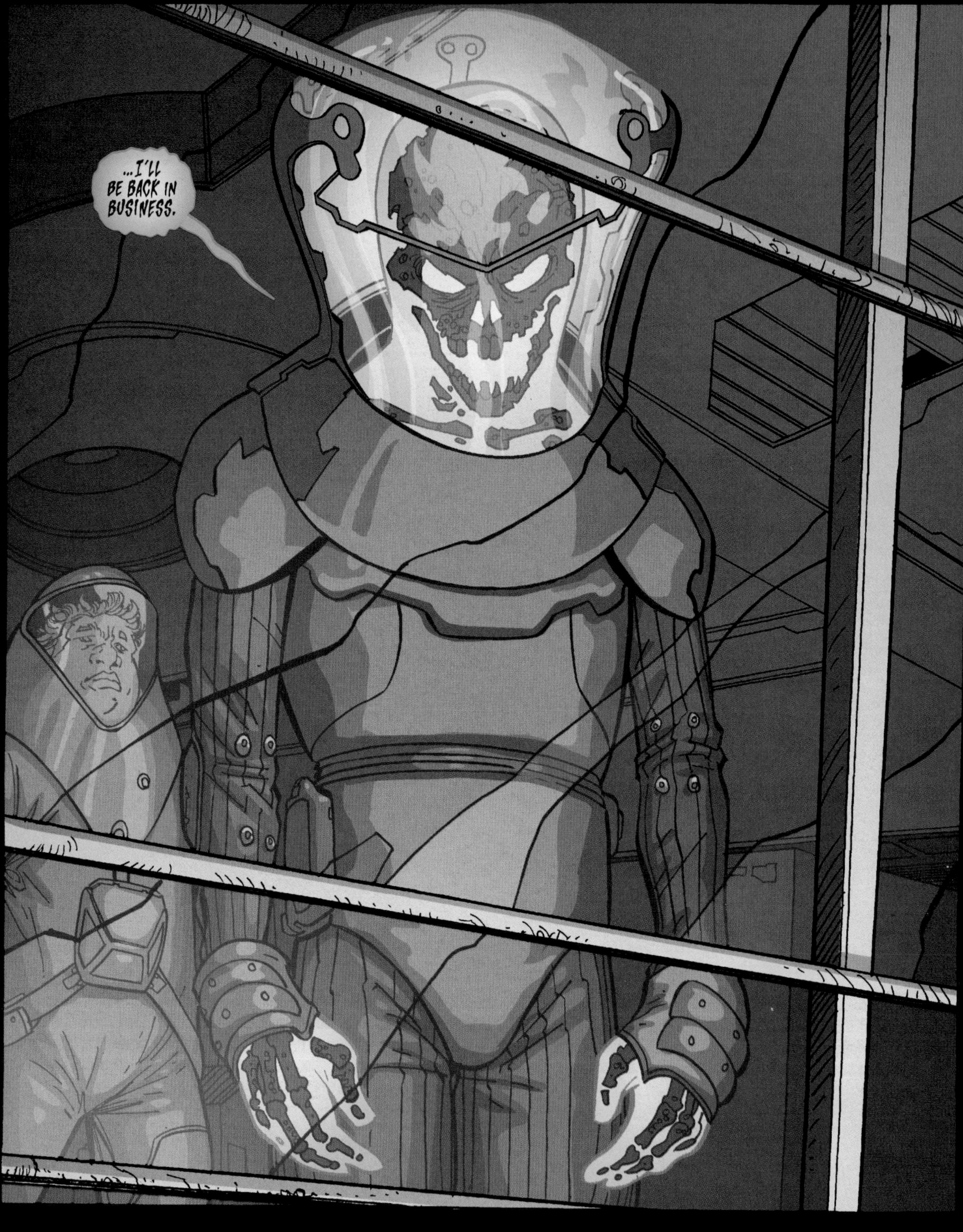
...I'LL BE BACK IN BUSINESS.

INDUSTRIAL REVOLUTION PART 2: INDUSTRIAL DISEASE

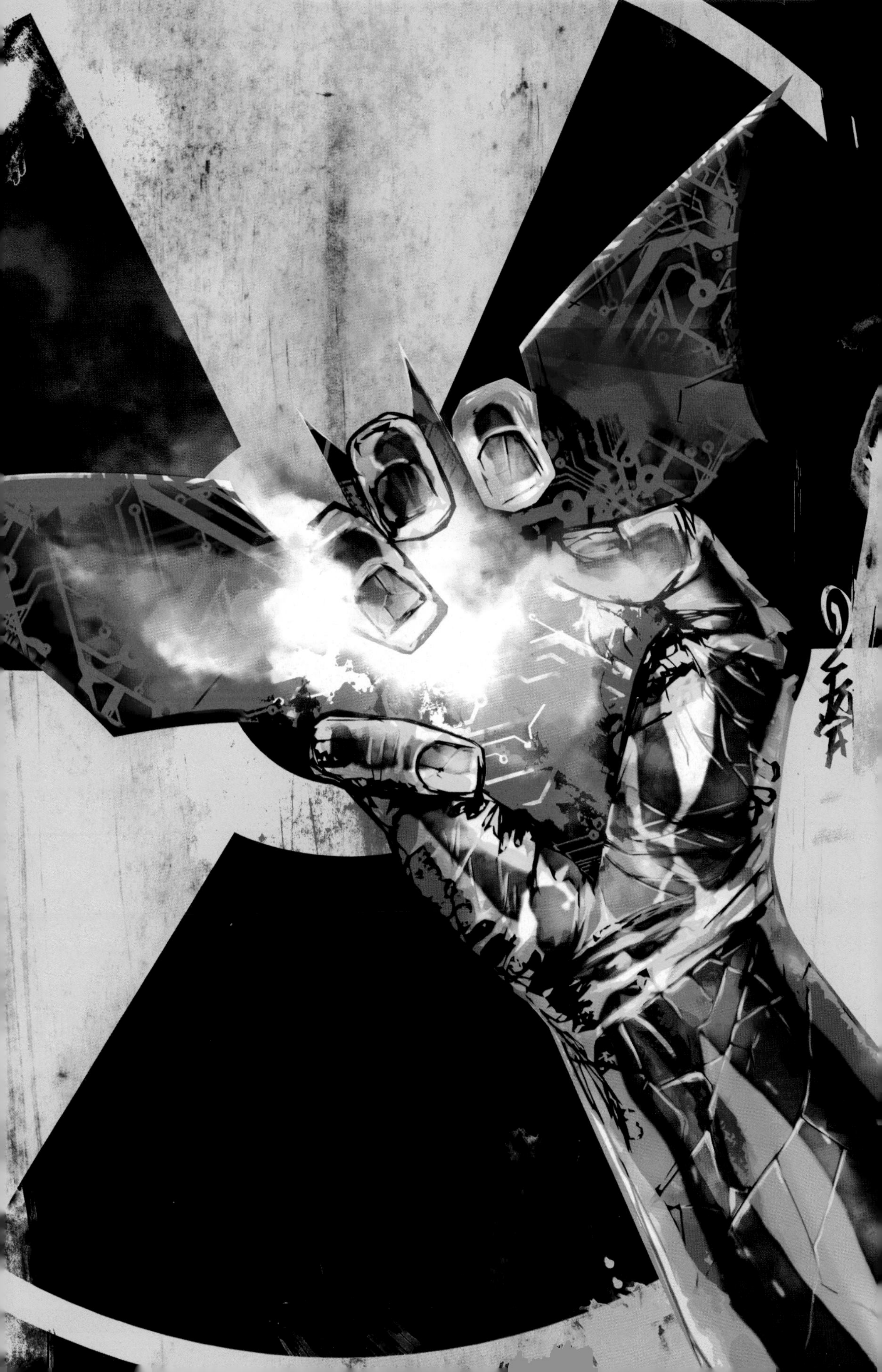

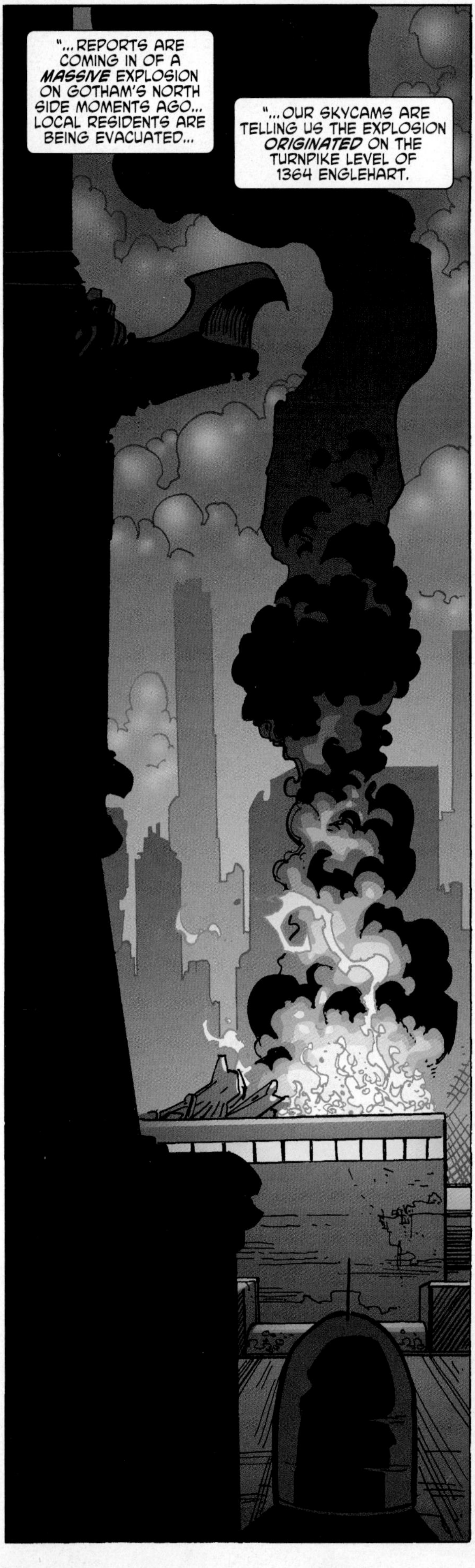
"...REPORTS ARE COMING IN OF A *MASSIVE* EXPLOSION ON GOTHAM'S NORTH SIDE MOMENTS AGO... LOCAL RESIDENTS ARE BEING EVACUATED...
"...OUR SKYCAMS ARE TELLING US THE EXPLOSION *ORIGINATED* ON THE TURNPIKE LEVEL OF 1364 ENGLEHART.

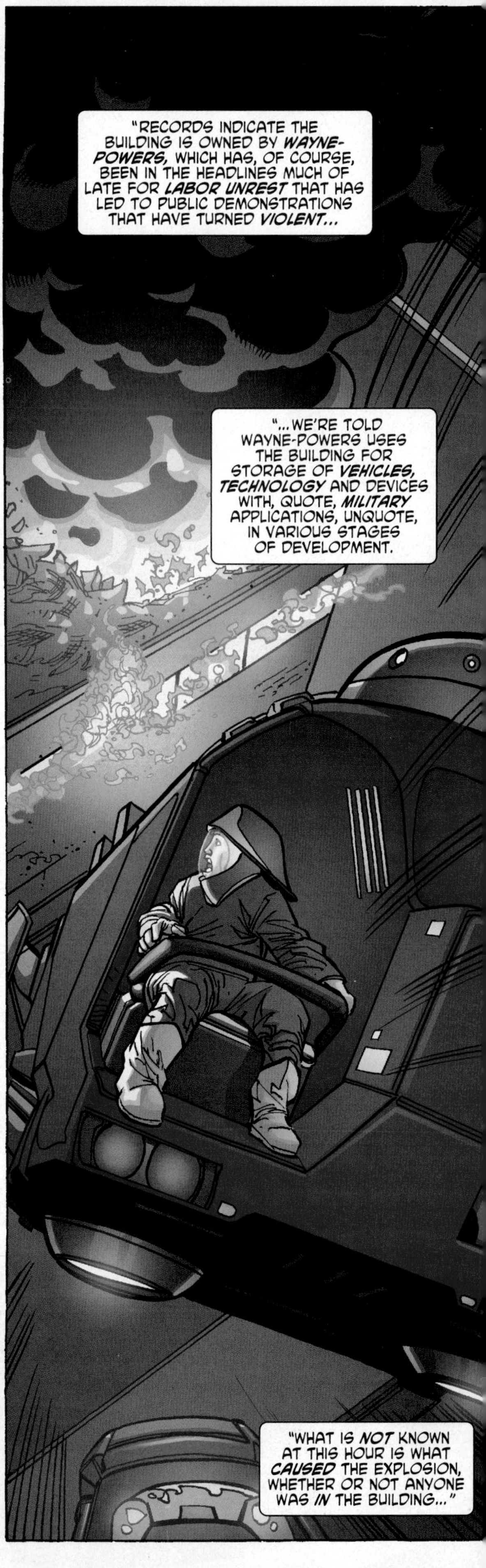
"RECORDS INDICATE THE BUILDING IS OWNED BY *WAYNE-POWERS,* WHICH HAS, OF COURSE, BEEN IN THE HEADLINES MUCH OF LATE FOR *LABOR UNREST* THAT HAS LED TO PUBLIC DEMONSTRATIONS THAT HAVE TURNED *VIOLENT...*
"...WE'RE TOLD WAYNE-POWERS USES THE BUILDING FOR STORAGE OF *VEHICLES, TECHNOLOGY* AND DEVICES WITH, QUOTE, *MILITARY* APPLICATIONS, UNQUOTE, IN VARIOUS STAGES OF DEVELOPMENT.
"WHAT IS *NOT* KNOWN AT THIS HOUR IS WHAT *CAUSED* THE EXPLOSION, WHETHER OR NOT ANYONE WAS *IN* THE BUILDING..."

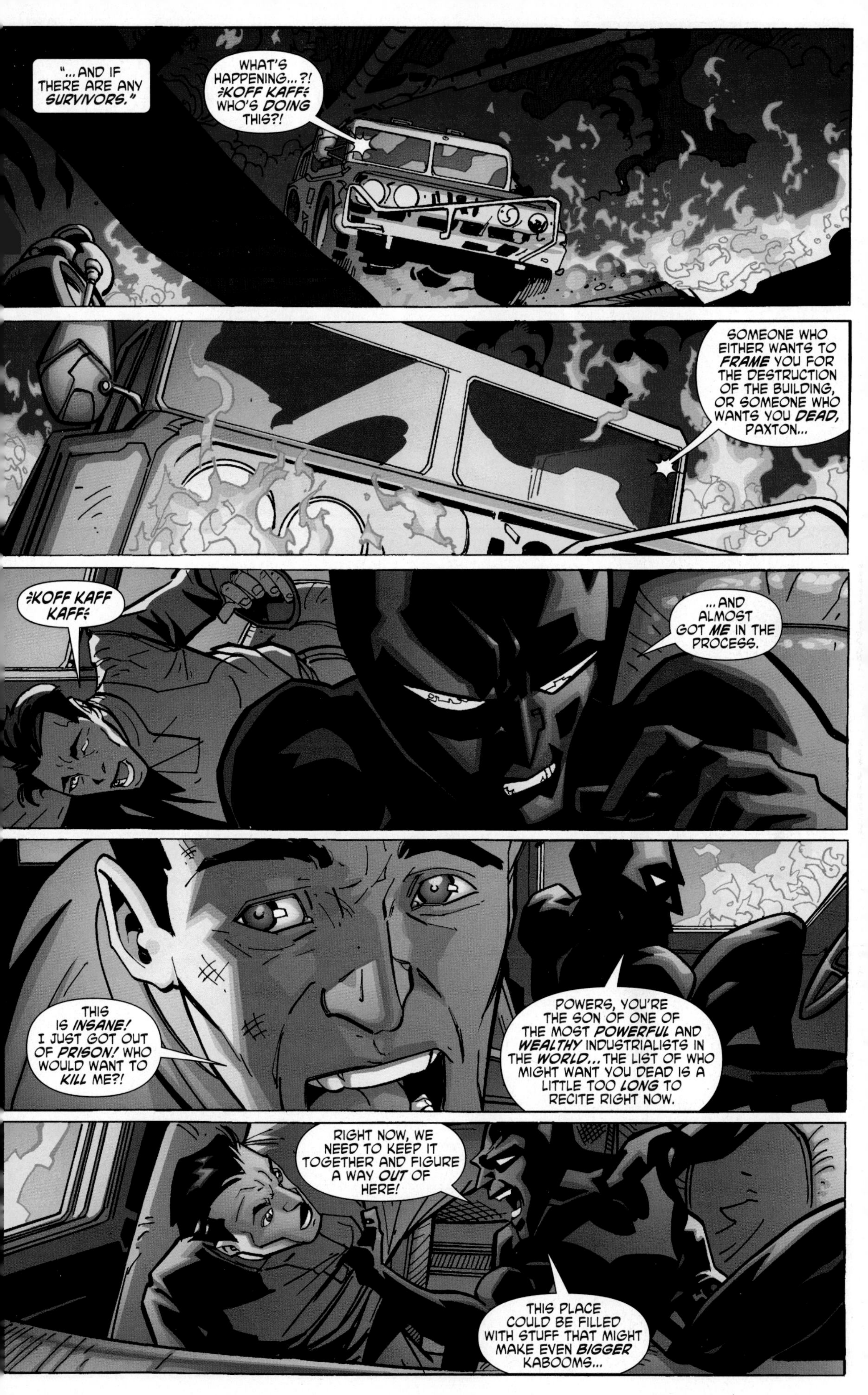
"...AND IF THERE ARE ANY SURVIVORS."
WHAT'S HAPPENING...?! ⸗KOFF KAFF⸗ WHO'S DOING THIS?!
SOMEONE WHO EITHER WANTS TO FRAME YOU FOR THE DESTRUCTION OF THE BUILDING, OR SOMEONE WHO WANTS YOU DEAD, PAXTON...
⸗KOFF KAFF KAFF⸗
...AND ALMOST GOT ME IN THE PROCESS.
THIS IS INSANE! I JUST GOT OUT OF PRISON! WHO WOULD WANT TO KILL ME?!
POWERS, YOU'RE THE SON OF ONE OF THE MOST POWERFUL AND WEALTHY INDUSTRIALISTS IN THE WORLD... THE LIST OF WHO MIGHT WANT YOU DEAD IS A LITTLE TOO LONG TO RECITE RIGHT NOW.
RIGHT NOW, WE NEED TO KEEP IT TOGETHER AND FIGURE A WAY OUT OF HERE!
THIS PLACE COULD BE FILLED WITH STUFF THAT MIGHT MAKE EVEN BIGGER KABOOMS...

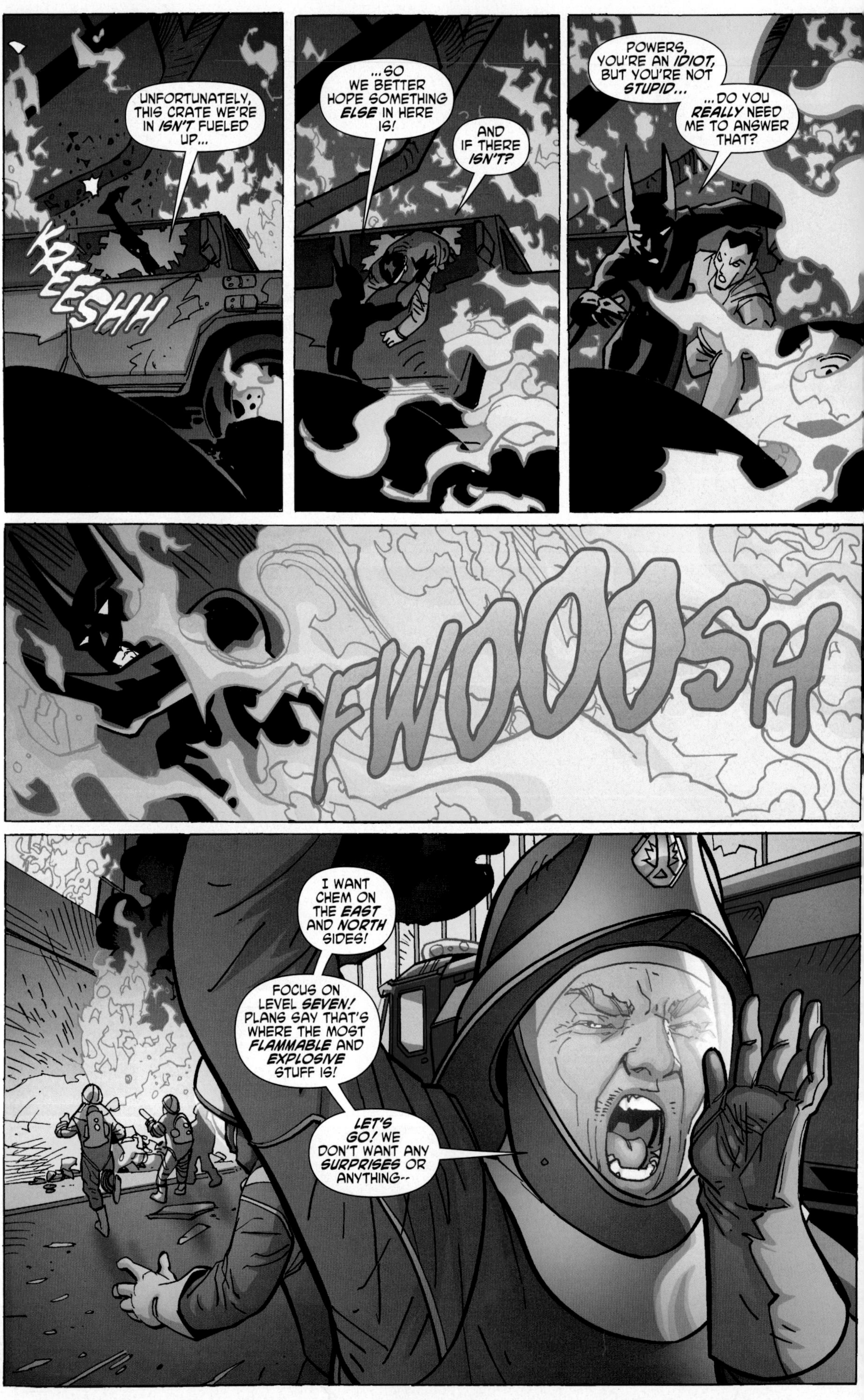
UNFORTUNATELY, THIS CRATE WE'RE IN *ISN'T* FUELED UP...
KREESHH
...SO WE BETTER HOPE SOMETHING *ELSE* IN HERE IS!
AND IF THERE *ISN'T?*
POWERS, YOU'RE AN *IDIOT,* BUT YOU'RE NOT *STUPID...*
...DO YOU *REALLY* NEED ME TO ANSWER THAT?
FWOOOSH
I WANT CHEM ON THE *EAST* AND *NORTH* SIDES!
FOCUS ON LEVEL *SEVEN!* PLANS SAY THAT'S WHERE THE MOST *FLAMMABLE* AND *EXPLOSIVE* STUFF IS!
LET'S GO! WE DON'T WANT ANY *SURPRISES* OR ANYTHING--

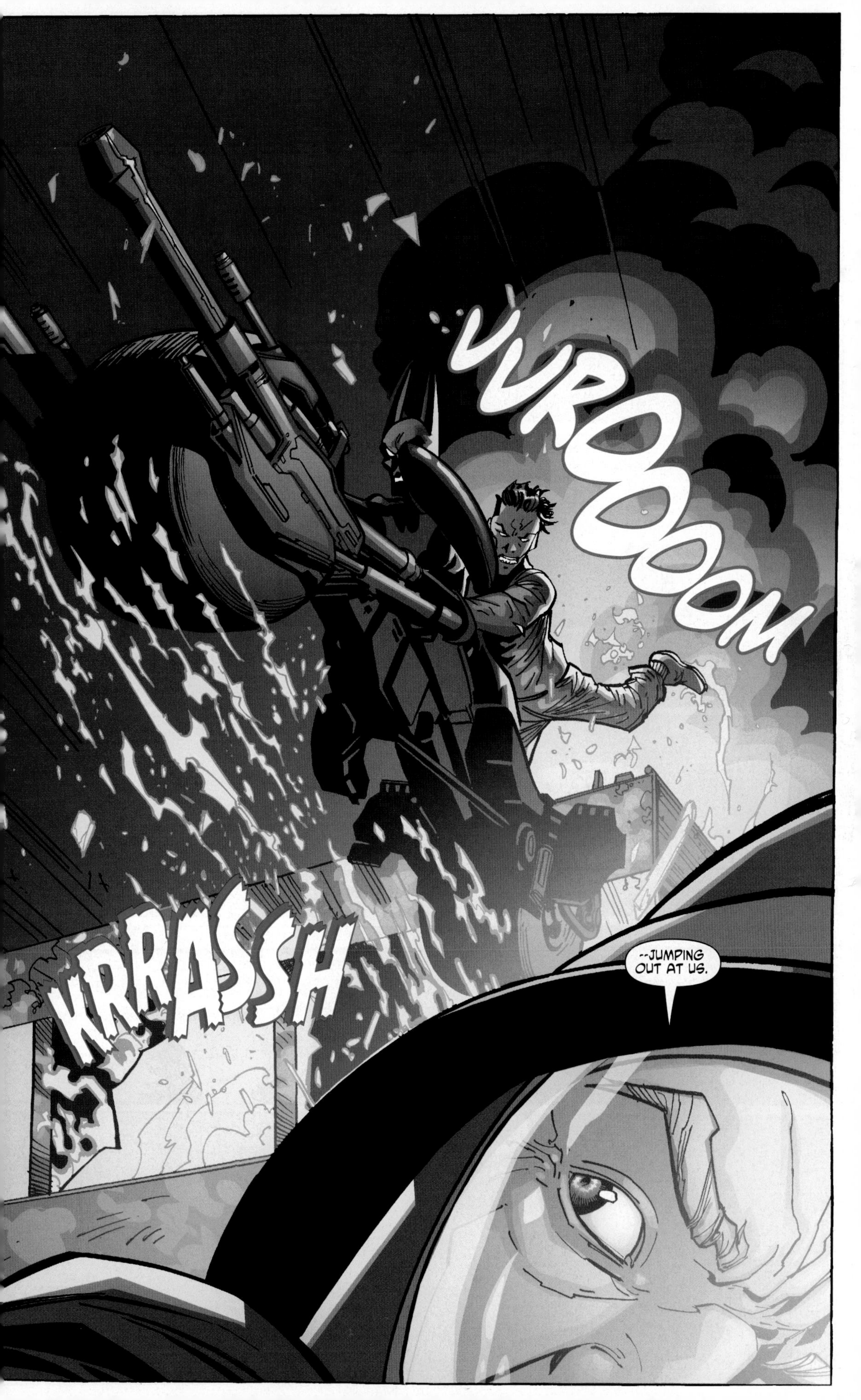
VVROOOOOM
KRRASSH
--JUMPING OUT AT US.

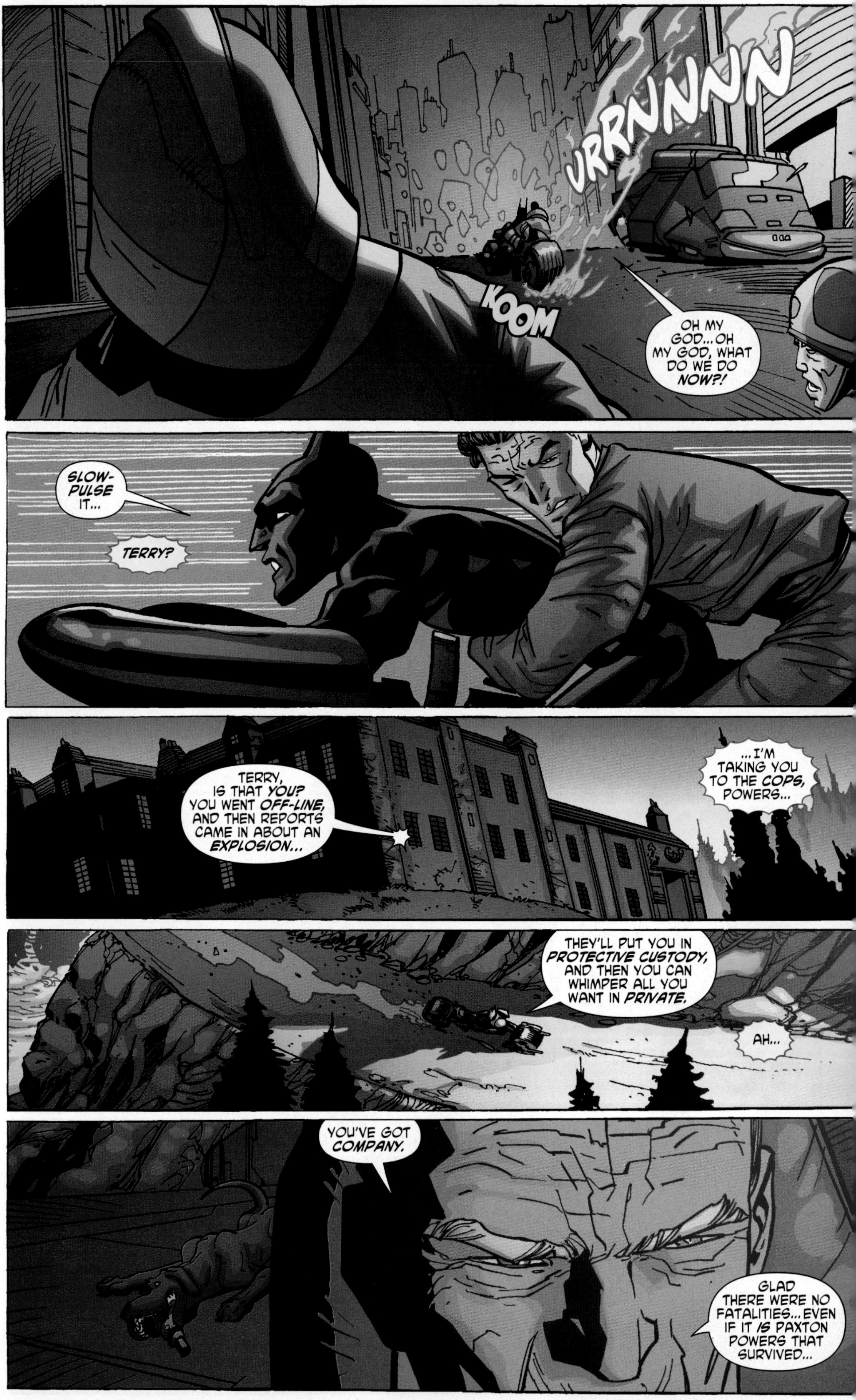
URRNNNN
KOOM
OH MY GOD... OH MY GOD, WHAT DO WE DO NOW?!
SLOW-PULSE IT...
TERRY?
TERRY, IS THAT YOU? YOU WENT OFF-LINE, AND THEN REPORTS CAME IN ABOUT AN EXPLOSION...
...I'M TAKING YOU TO THE COPS, POWERS...
THEY'LL PUT YOU IN PROTECTIVE CUSTODY, AND THEN YOU CAN WHIMPER ALL YOU WANT IN PRIVATE.
AH...
YOU'VE GOT COMPANY.
GLAD THERE WERE NO FATALITIES... EVEN IF IT IS PAXTON POWERS THAT SURVIVED...

"...SOMETIMES, YOU HAVE TO TAKE THE GOOD WITH THE *BAD.*"

BEAUTIFUL, ISN'T IT, DOCTOR FRENCH?

I'M MORE CONCERNED WITH YOUR *CONTAINMENT SUIT.*

IT'S HAVING TROUBLE KEEPING PACE WITH THE *PROGRESSION* OF YOUR ILLNESS.

WE NEED TO MAKE SOME *ADJUSTMENTS.*

DO *WHATEVER* YOU HAVE TO DO TO KEEP ME UP AND *MOVING,* OLD FRIEND.

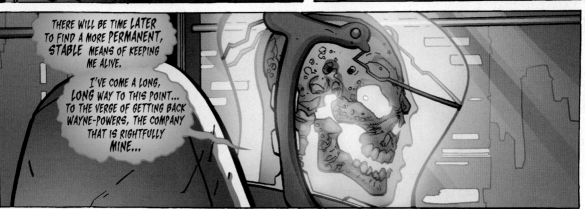

THERE WILL BE TIME *LATER* TO FIND A MORE *PERMANENT, STABLE* MEANS OF KEEPING ME ALIVE.

I'VE COME A LONG, *LONG* WAY TO THIS POINT... TO THE VERGE OF GETTING BACK WAYNE-POWERS, THE COMPANY THAT IS RIGHTFULLY *MINE...*

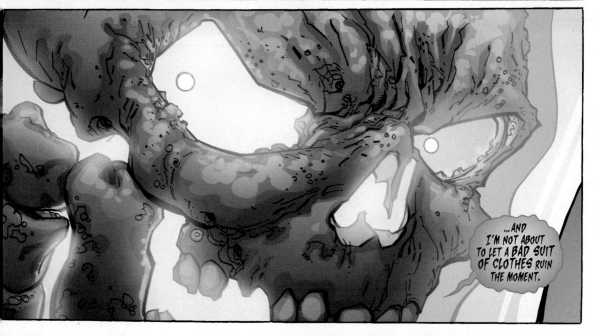

...AND I'M NOT ABOUT TO LET A *BAD SUIT* OF CLOTHES RUIN THE MOMENT.

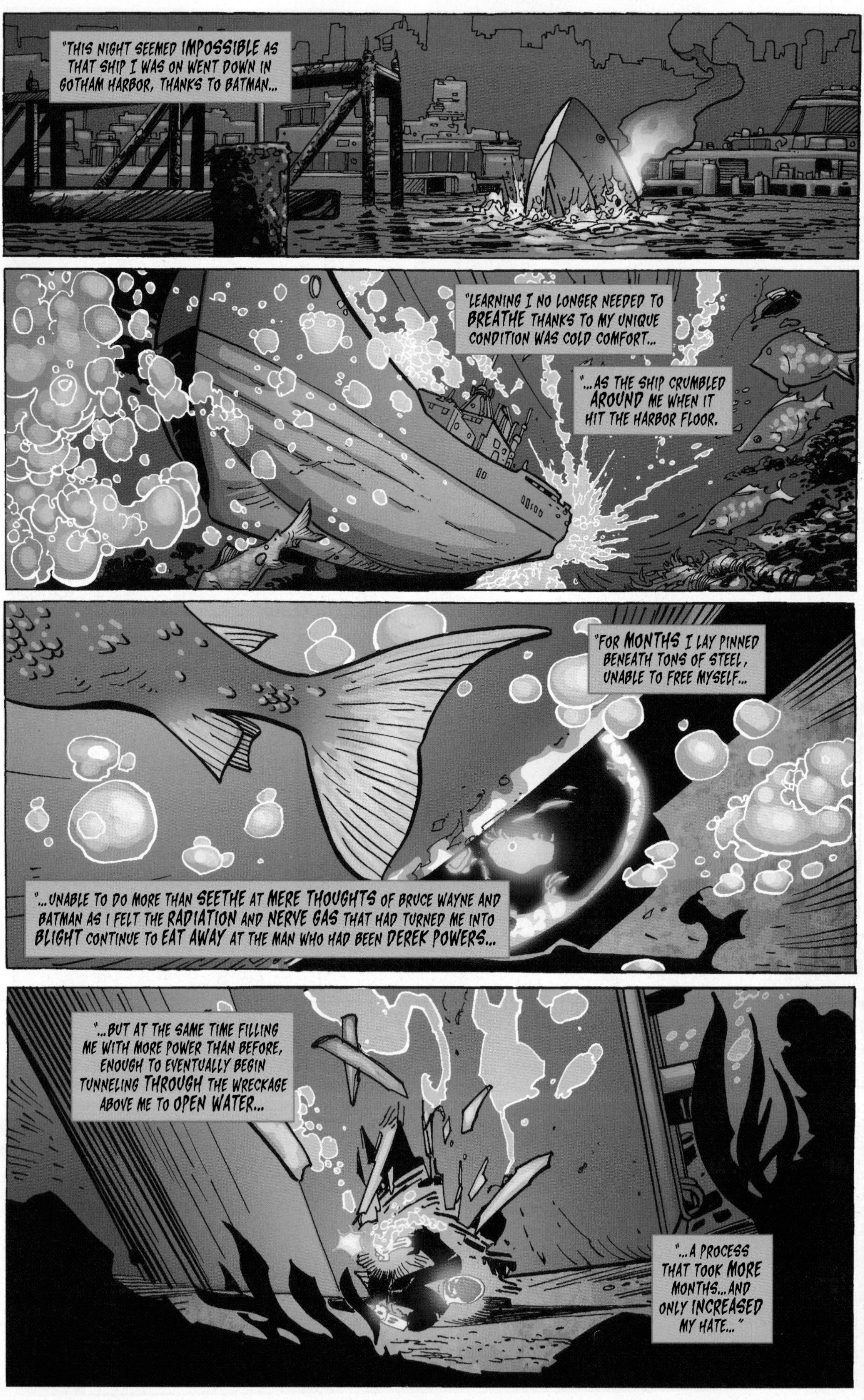
"THIS NIGHT SEEMED IMPOSSIBLE AS THAT SHIP I WAS ON WENT DOWN IN GOTHAM HARBOR, THANKS TO BATMAN...
"LEARNING I NO LONGER NEEDED TO BREATHE THANKS TO MY UNIQUE CONDITION WAS COLD COMFORT...
"...AS THE SHIP CRUMBLED AROUND ME WHEN IT HIT THE HARBOR FLOOR.
"FOR MONTHS I LAY PINNED BENEATH TONS OF STEEL, UNABLE TO FREE MYSELF...
"...UNABLE TO DO MORE THAN SEETHE AT MERE THOUGHTS OF BRUCE WAYNE AND BATMAN AS I FELT THE RADIATION AND NERVE GAS THAT HAD TURNED ME INTO BLIGHT CONTINUE TO EAT AWAY AT THE MAN WHO HAD BEEN DEREK POWERS...
"...BUT AT THE SAME TIME FILLING ME WITH MORE POWER THAN BEFORE, ENOUGH TO EVENTUALLY BEGIN TUNNELING THROUGH THE WRECKAGE ABOVE ME TO OPEN WATER...
"...A PROCESS THAT TOOK MORE MONTHS...AND ONLY INCREASED MY HATE..."

"I EMERGED WITH MY PLANS TO RECLAIM ALL I HAD LOST, BURN BRUCE WAYNE TO THE GROUND, AND SHRED THE BATMAN... AND THE OPPORTUNITY TO MAKE THOSE PLANS REALITY.

"AND SO I CAME TO YOU. YOUR SCIENTIFIC GENIUS AND MY BUSINESS ACUMEN HELPED ME RAISE THE MONEY TO BUY WAYNE-POWERS IN THE FIRST PLACE.

"BUT WITH MY... REMOVAL FROM THE COMPANY, YOU TOO HAD BEEN CAST ASIDE."

BUT YOU HELPED KEEP ME ALIVE BY BUILDING THIS SUIT, HELPED ME CONTROL MY GROWING STRENGTH, WHILE I CAUGHT UP ON ALL I HAD-- AAAARGH!

S-SORRY...

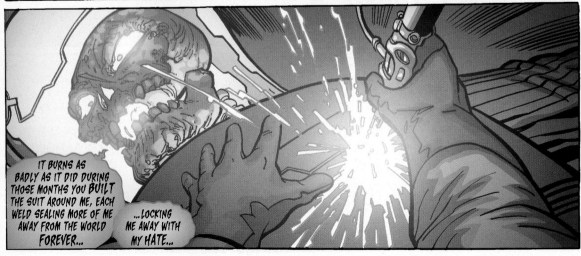

IT BURNS AS BADLY AS IT DID DURING THOSE MONTHS YOU BUILT THE SUIT AROUND ME, EACH WELD SEALING MORE OF ME AWAY FROM THE WORLD FOREVER...

...LOCKING ME AWAY WITH MY HATE...

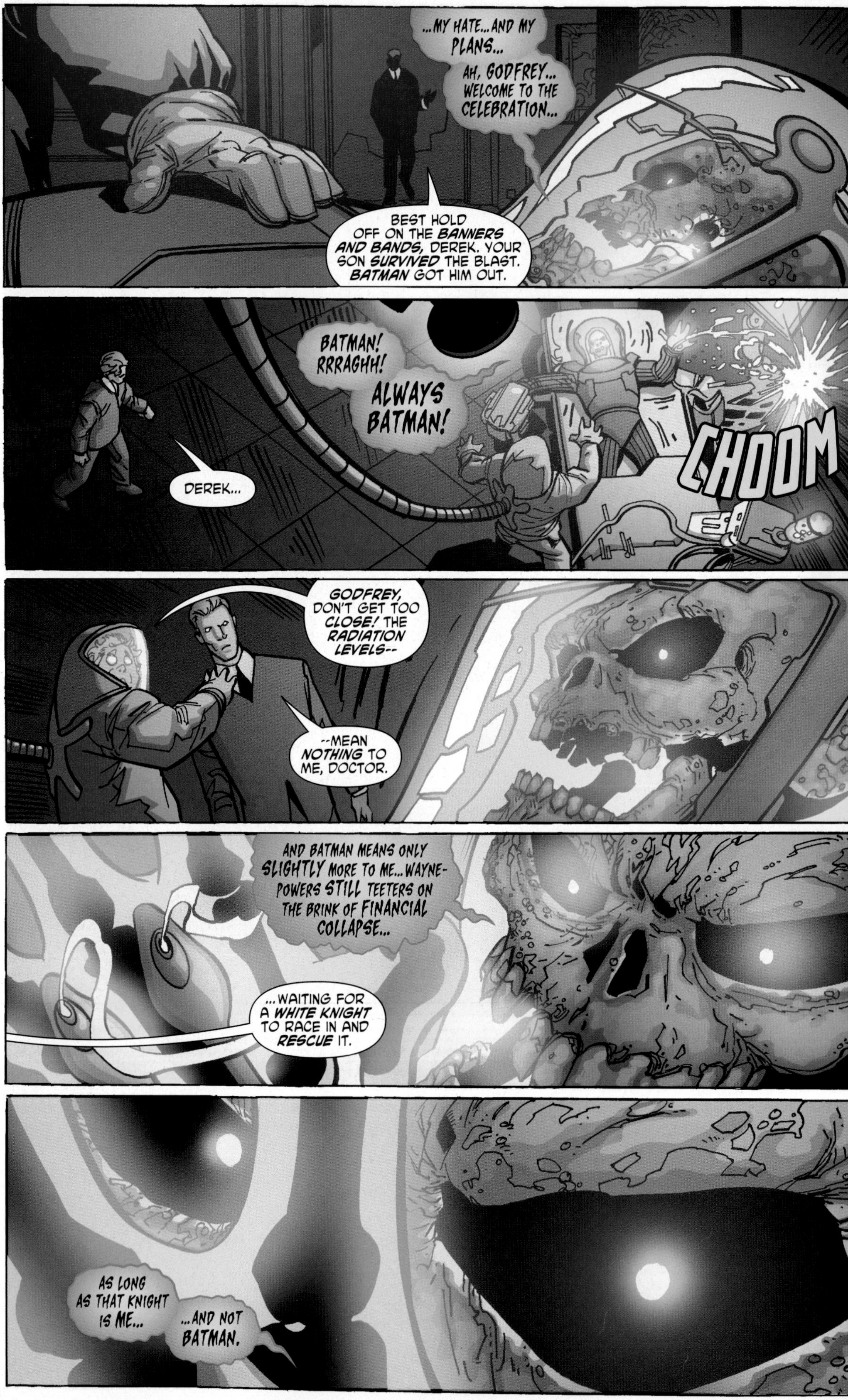
...MY HATE...AND MY PLANS...
AH, GODFREY... WELCOME TO THE CELEBRATION...
BEST HOLD OFF ON THE BANNERS AND BANDS, DEREK. YOUR SON SURVIVED THE BLAST. BATMAN GOT HIM OUT.
BATMAN! RRRAGHH!
ALWAYS BATMAN!
DEREK...
CHOOM
GODFREY, DON'T GET TOO CLOSE! THE RADIATION LEVELS--
--MEAN NOTHING TO ME, DOCTOR.
AND BATMAN MEANS ONLY SLIGHTLY MORE TO ME...WAYNE-POWERS STILL TEETERS ON THE BRINK OF FINANCIAL COLLAPSE...
...WAITING FOR A WHITE KNIGHT TO RACE IN AND RESCUE IT.
AS LONG AS THAT KNIGHT IS ME...
...AND NOT BATMAN.

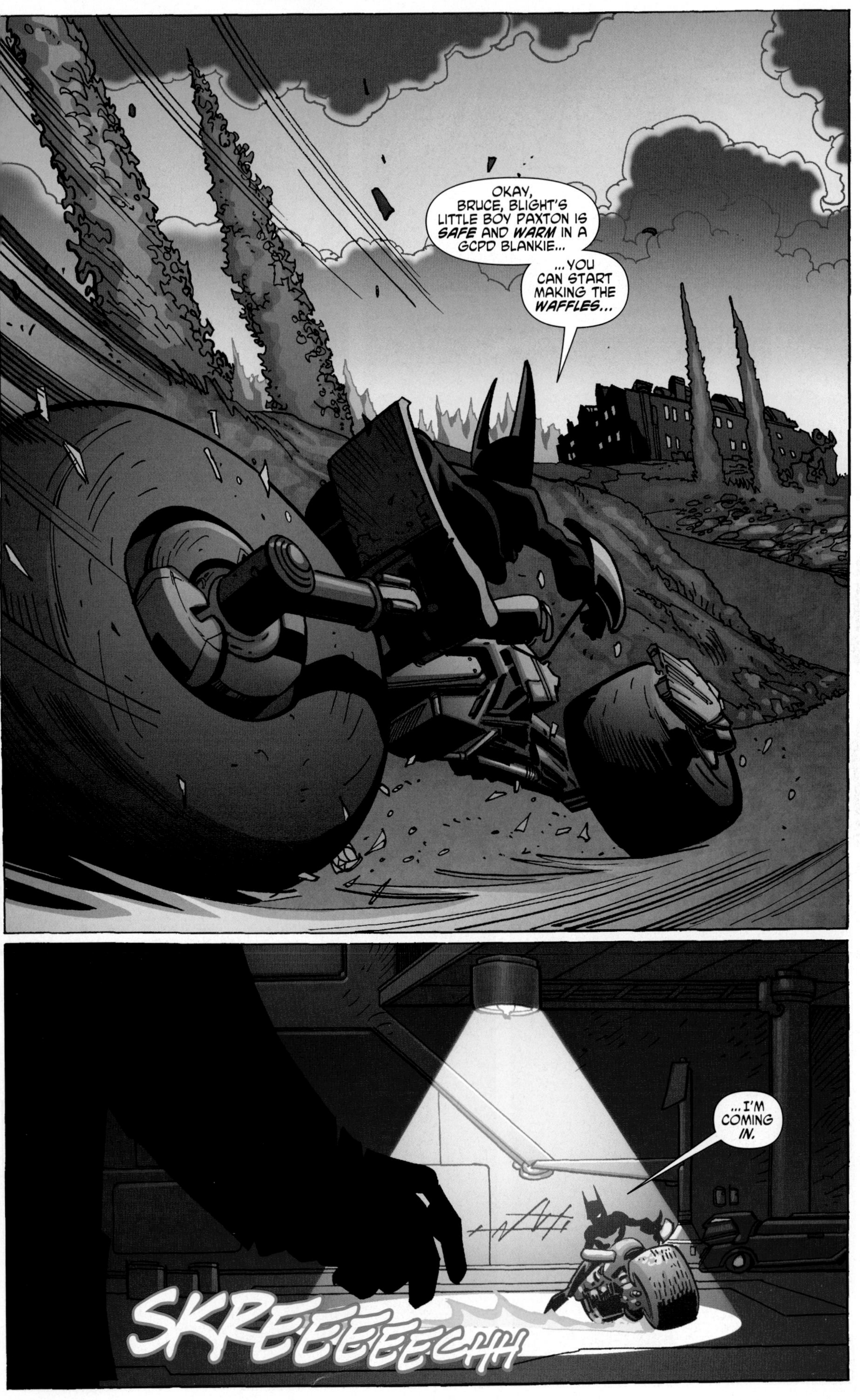
OKAY, BRUCE, BLIGHT'S LITTLE BOY PAXTON IS SAFE AND WARM IN A GCPD BLANKIE...
...YOU CAN START MAKING THE WAFFLES...
...I'M COMING IN.
SKREEEEEECHH

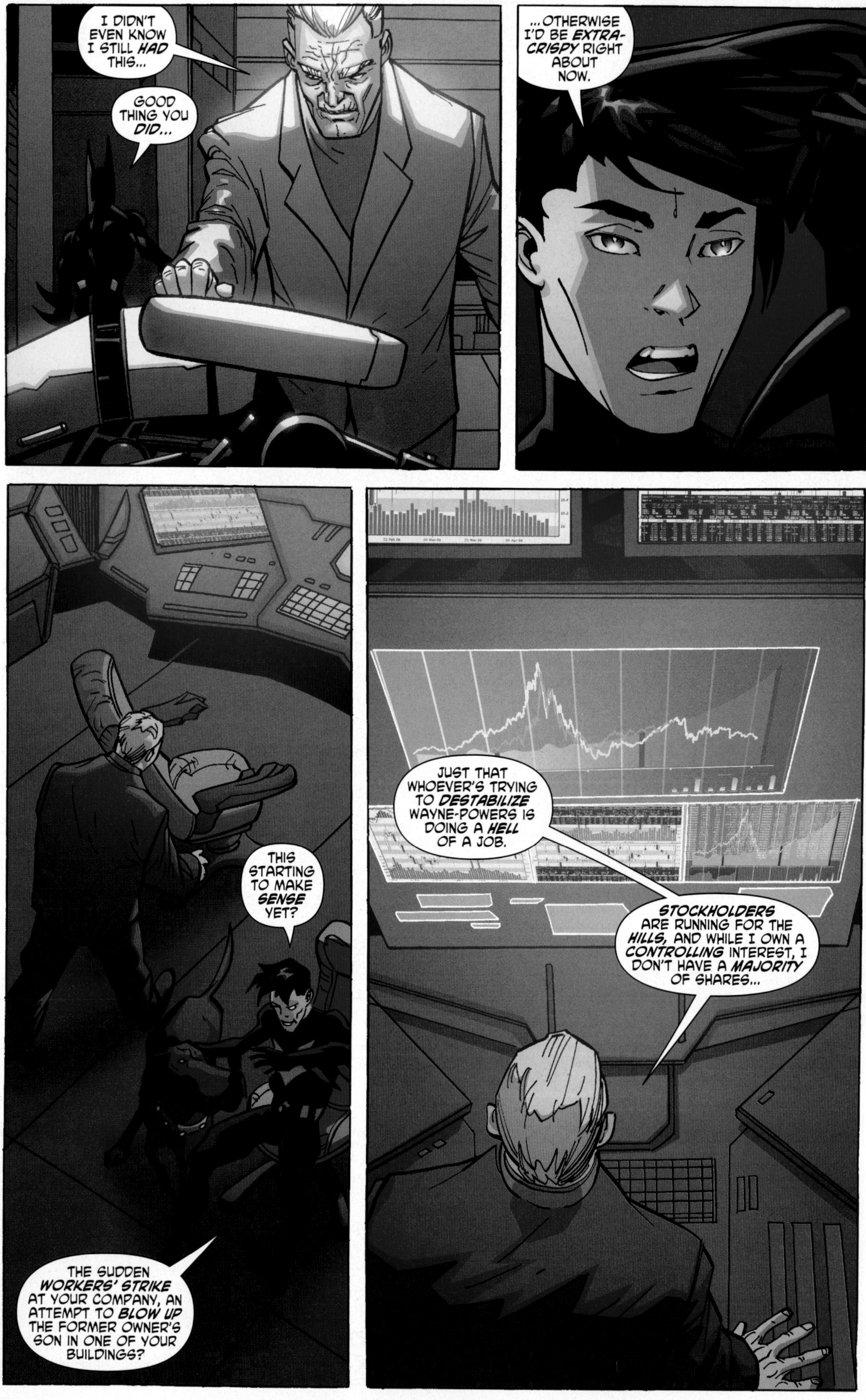
I DIDN'T EVEN KNOW I STILL *HAD* THIS...
GOOD THING YOU *DID*...
...OTHERWISE I'D BE *EXTRA-CRISPY* RIGHT ABOUT NOW.
THIS STARTING TO MAKE *SENSE* YET?
THE SUDDEN *WORKERS' STRIKE* AT YOUR COMPANY, AN ATTEMPT TO *BLOW UP* THE FORMER OWNER'S SON IN ONE OF YOUR BUILDINGS?
JUST THAT WHOEVER'S TRYING TO *DESTABILIZE* WAYNE-POWERS IS DOING A *HELL* OF A JOB.
STOCKHOLDERS ARE RUNNING FOR THE *HILLS,* AND WHILE I OWN A *CONTROLLING* INTEREST, I DON'T HAVE A *MAJORITY* OF SHARES...

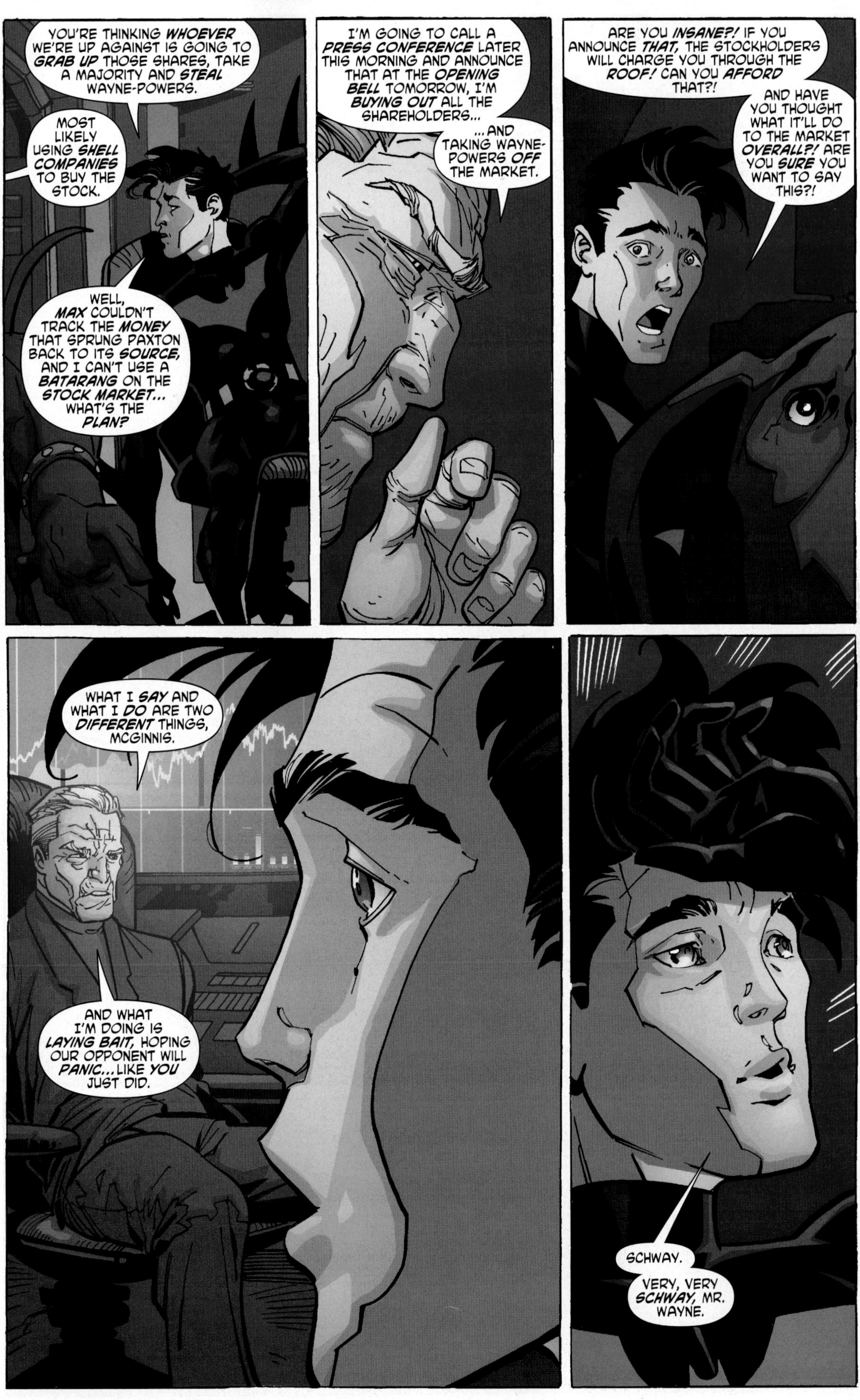
YOU'RE THINKING WHOEVER WE'RE UP AGAINST IS GOING TO GRAB UP THOSE SHARES, TAKE A MAJORITY AND STEAL WAYNE-POWERS.
MOST LIKELY USING SHELL COMPANIES TO BUY THE STOCK.
WELL, MAX COULDN'T TRACK THE MONEY THAT SPRUNG PAXTON BACK TO ITS SOURCE, AND I CAN'T USE A BATARANG ON THE STOCK MARKET... WHAT'S THE PLAN?
I'M GOING TO CALL A PRESS CONFERENCE LATER THIS MORNING AND ANNOUNCE THAT AT THE OPENING BELL TOMORROW, I'M BUYING OUT ALL THE SHAREHOLDERS...
...AND TAKING WAYNE-POWERS OFF THE MARKET.
ARE YOU INSANE?! IF YOU ANNOUNCE THAT, THE STOCKHOLDERS WILL CHARGE YOU THROUGH THE ROOF! CAN YOU AFFORD THAT?!
AND HAVE YOU THOUGHT WHAT IT'LL DO TO THE MARKET OVERALL?! ARE YOU SURE YOU WANT TO SAY THIS?!
WHAT I SAY AND WHAT I DO ARE TWO DIFFERENT THINGS, MCGINNIS.
AND WHAT I'M DOING IS LAYING BAIT, HOPING OUR OPPONENT WILL PANIC... LIKE YOU JUST DID.
SCHWAY.
VERY, VERY SCHWAY, MR. WAYNE.

--DANA AVOIDS ME LIKE THE *PLAGUE* AT SCHOOL, AND SHE WON'T RETURN MY *CALLS*...

IT'S GOING TO TAKE HER SOME *TIME*, TERRY. AND YOUR *BREAKUP* ISN'T THE *ONLY* THING SHE'S DEALING WITH RIGHT NOW.

SHE TOLD ME NOT TO SAY ANYTHING TO ANYONE, *ESPECIALLY* YOU...SHE WANTED TO KEEP THIS *TOTALLY* PRIVATE, BUT...

...SHE TOLD ME HER *BROTHER* IS BACK.

DANA HAS A *BROTHER*?

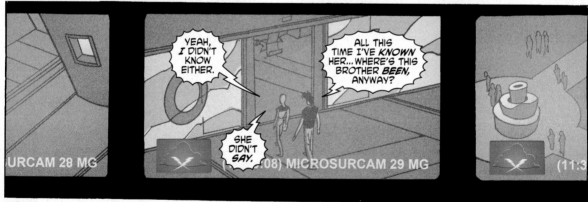

YEAH, *I* DIDN'T KNOW EITHER.

ALL THIS TIME I'VE *KNOWN* HER...WHERE'S THIS BROTHER *BEEN*, ANYWAY?

SHE DIDN'T *SAY*.

SURCAM 28 MG

(...08) MICROSURCAM 29 MG

(11:3

MY *POINT* IS, GIVE HER SOME *ROOM*.

BUT I *MISS* HER, MAX.

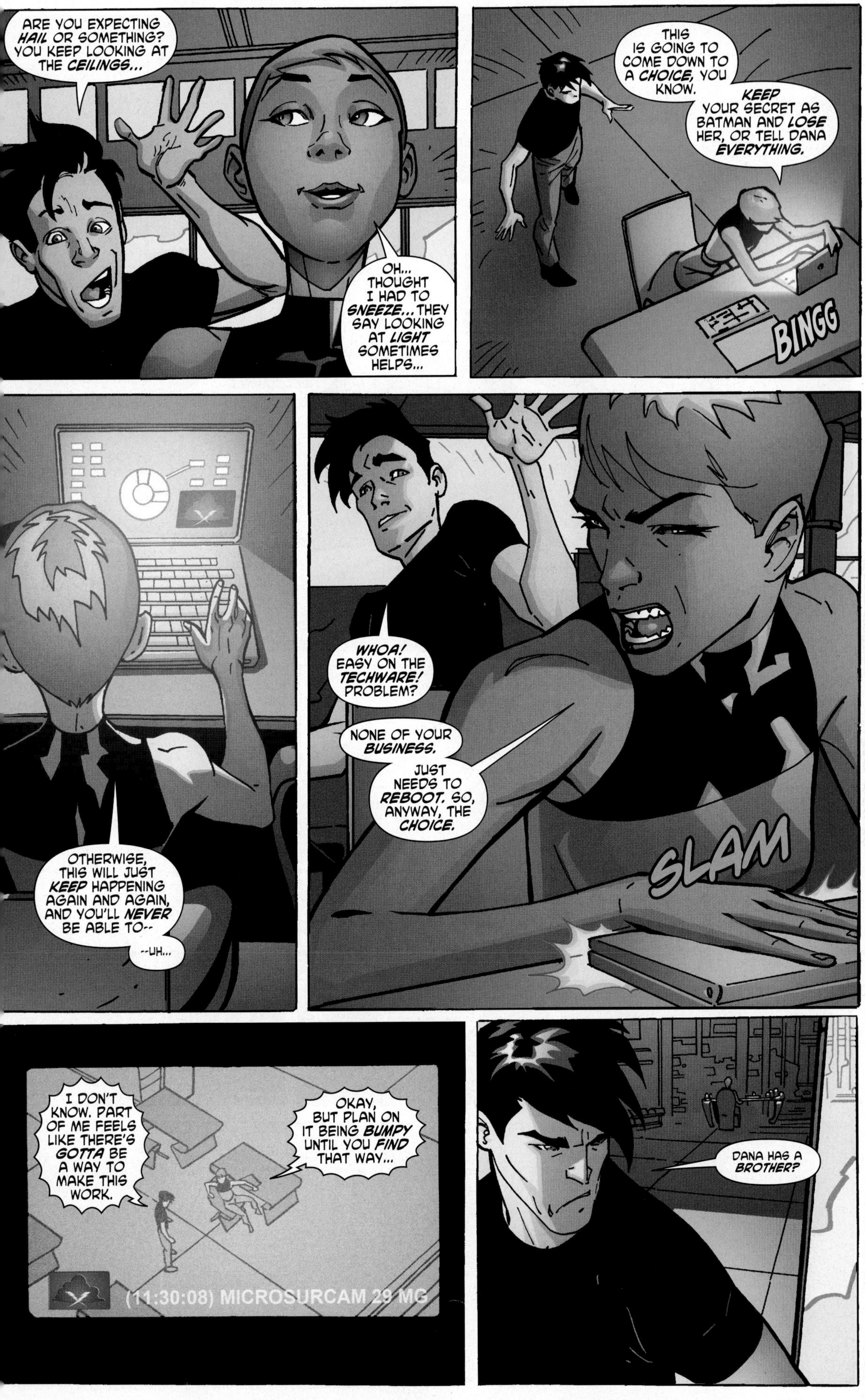
ARE YOU EXPECTING HAIL OR SOMETHING? YOU KEEP LOOKING AT THE CEILINGS...
OH... THOUGHT I HAD TO SNEEZE... THEY SAY LOOKING AT LIGHT SOMETIMES HELPS...
THIS IS GOING TO COME DOWN TO A CHOICE, YOU KNOW.
KEEP YOUR SECRET AS BATMAN AND LOSE HER, OR TELL DANA EVERYTHING.
BINGG
OTHERWISE, THIS WILL JUST KEEP HAPPENING AGAIN AND AGAIN, AND YOU'LL NEVER BE ABLE TO--
--UH...
WHOA! EASY ON THE TECHWARE! PROBLEM?
NONE OF YOUR BUSINESS.
JUST NEEDS TO REBOOT. SO, ANYWAY, THE CHOICE.
SLAM
I DON'T KNOW. PART OF ME FEELS LIKE THERE'S GOTTA BE A WAY TO MAKE THIS WORK.
OKAY, BUT PLAN ON IT BEING BUMPY UNTIL YOU FIND THAT WAY...
(11:30:08) MICROSURCAM 29 MG
DANA HAS A BROTHER?

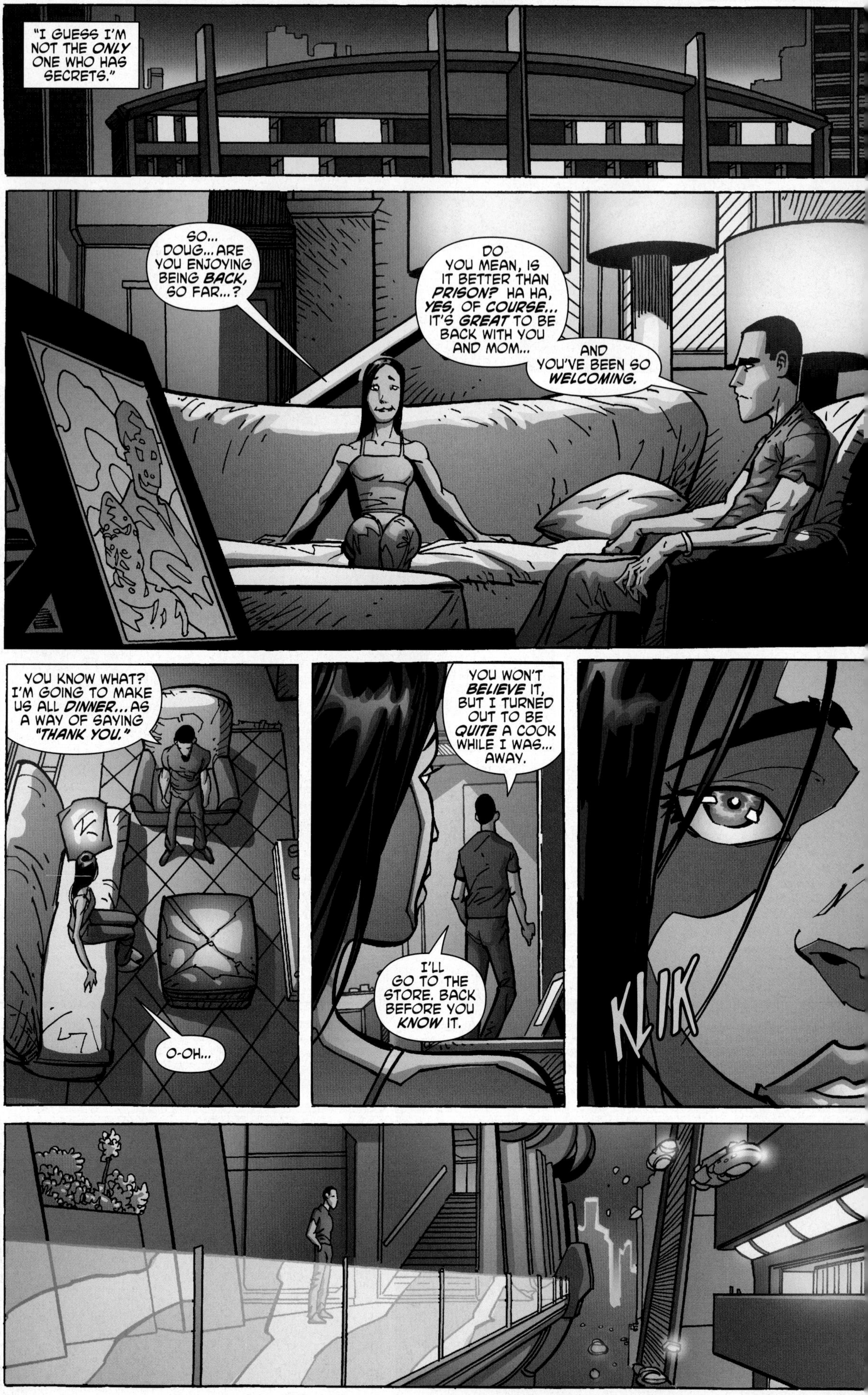
"I GUESS I'M NOT THE ONLY ONE WHO HAS SECRETS."
SO... DOUG...ARE YOU ENJOYING BEING BACK, SO FAR...?
DO YOU MEAN, IS IT BETTER THAN PRISON? HA HA, YES, OF COURSE... IT'S GREAT TO BE BACK WITH YOU AND MOM...
AND YOU'VE BEEN SO WELCOMING.
YOU KNOW WHAT? I'M GOING TO MAKE US ALL DINNER...AS A WAY OF SAYING "THANK YOU."
O-OH...
YOU WON'T BELIEVE IT, BUT I TURNED OUT TO BE QUITE A COOK WHILE I WAS... AWAY.
I'LL GO TO THE STORE. BACK BEFORE YOU KNOW IT.
KLIK

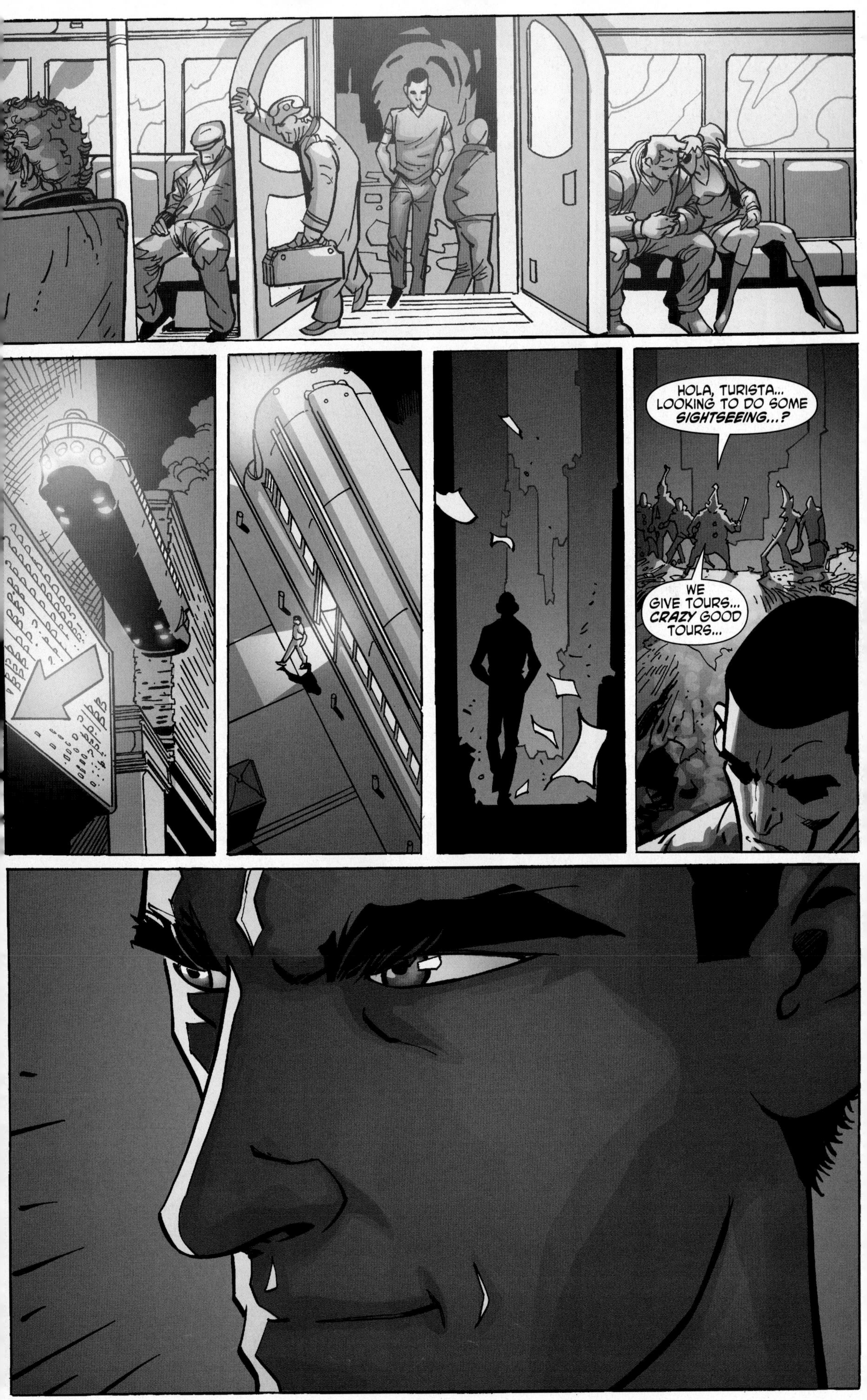
HOLA, TURISTA... LOOKING TO DO SOME *SIGHTSEEING*...?
WE GIVE TOURS... *CRAZY* GOOD TOURS...

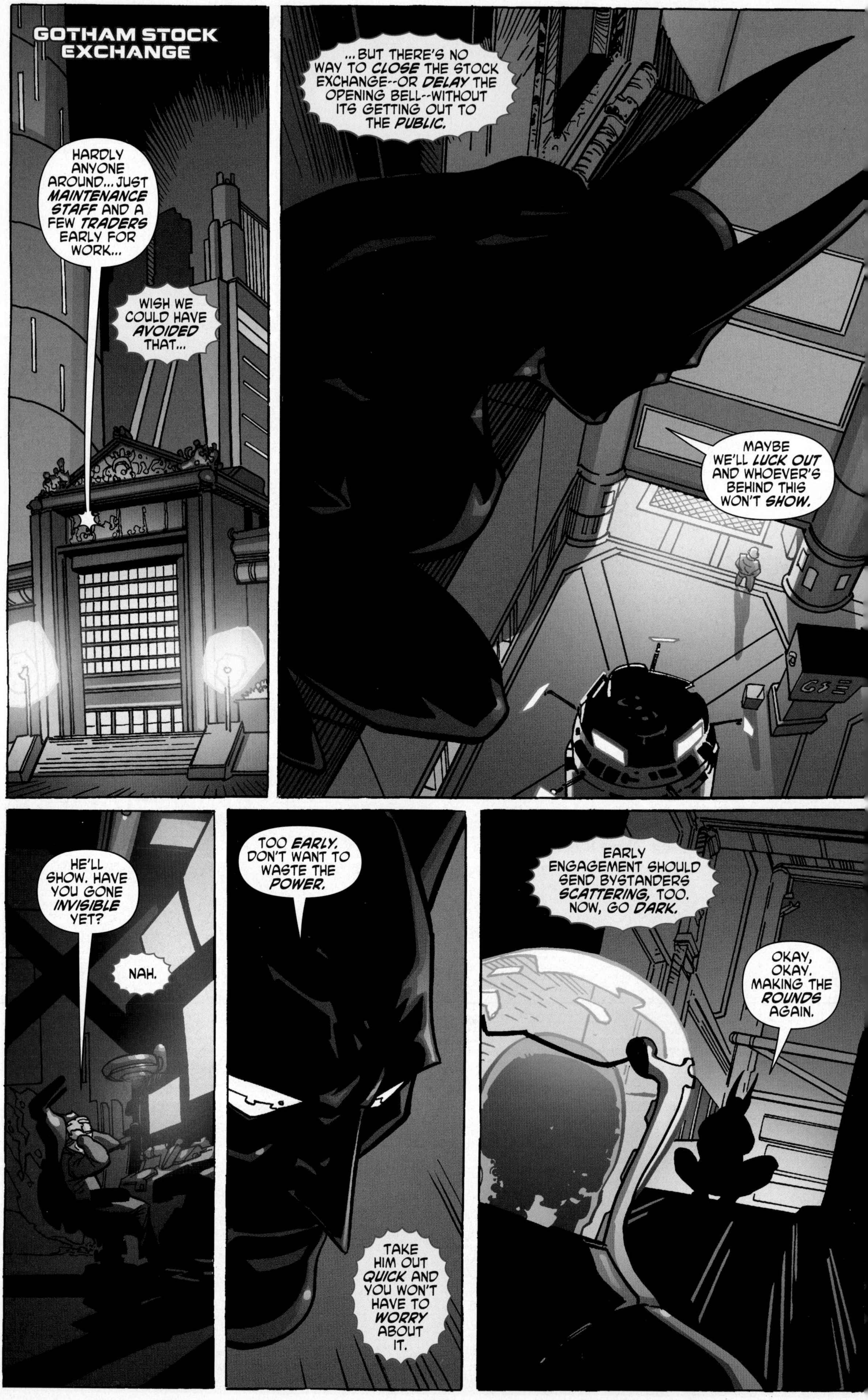
GOTHAM STOCK EXCHANGE
HARDLY ANYONE AROUND... JUST MAINTENANCE STAFF AND A FEW TRADERS EARLY FOR WORK...
WISH WE COULD HAVE AVOIDED THAT...
...BUT THERE'S NO WAY TO CLOSE THE STOCK EXCHANGE--OR DELAY THE OPENING BELL--WITHOUT ITS GETTING OUT TO THE PUBLIC.
MAYBE WE'LL LUCK OUT AND WHOEVER'S BEHIND THIS WON'T SHOW.
HE'LL SHOW. HAVE YOU GONE INVISIBLE YET?
NAH.
TOO EARLY. DON'T WANT TO WASTE THE POWER.
TAKE HIM OUT QUICK AND YOU WON'T HAVE TO WORRY ABOUT IT.
EARLY ENGAGEMENT SHOULD SEND BYSTANDERS SCATTERING, TOO. NOW, GO DARK.
OKAY, OKAY. MAKING THE ROUNDS AGAIN.

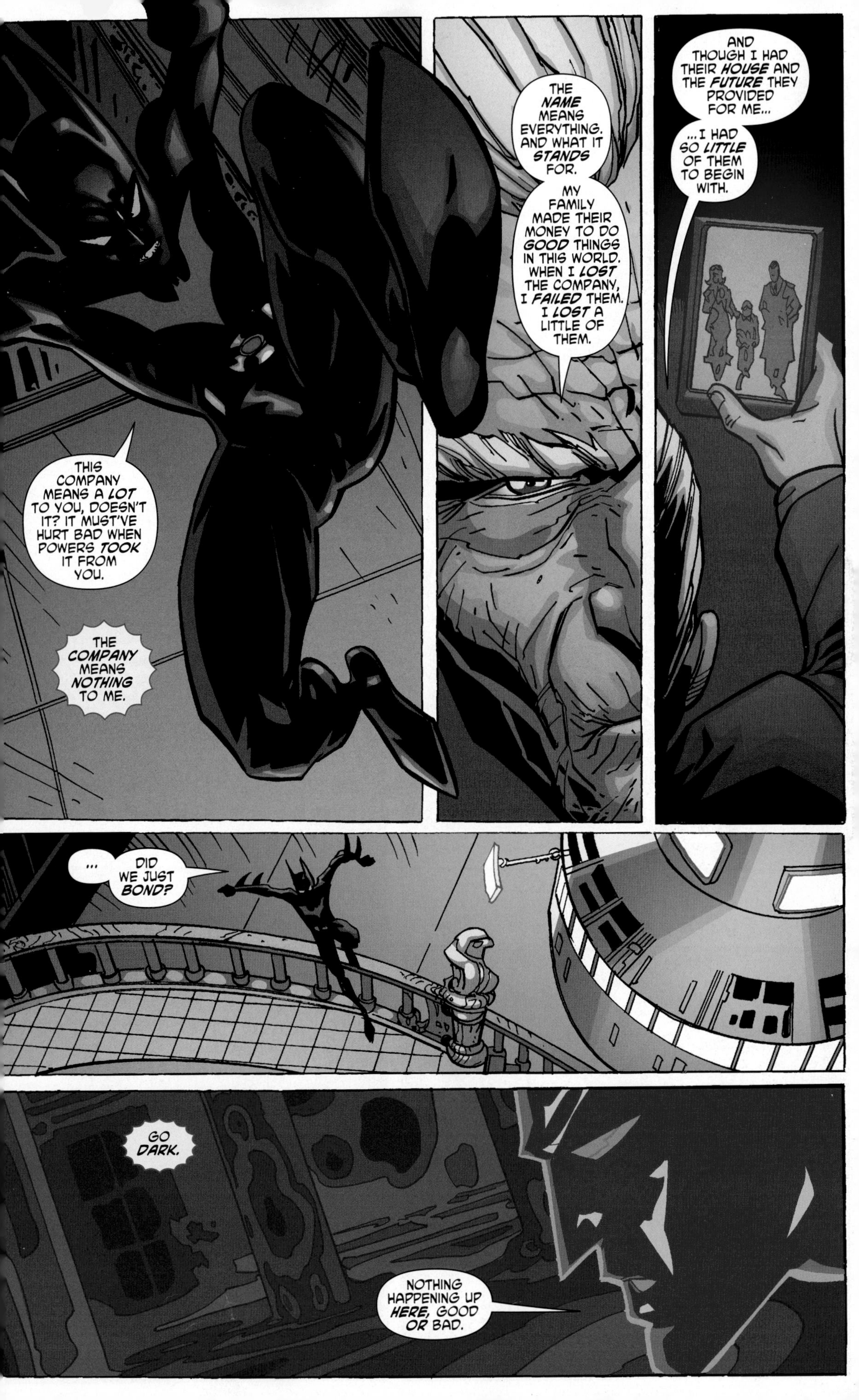
THIS COMPANY MEANS A LOT TO YOU, DOESN'T IT? IT MUST'VE HURT BAD WHEN POWERS TOOK IT FROM YOU.
THE COMPANY MEANS NOTHING TO ME.
THE NAME MEANS EVERYTHING. AND WHAT IT STANDS FOR.
MY FAMILY MADE THEIR MONEY TO DO GOOD THINGS IN THIS WORLD. WHEN I LOST THE COMPANY, I FAILED THEM. I LOST A LITTLE OF THEM.
AND THOUGH I HAD THEIR HOUSE AND THE FUTURE THEY PROVIDED FOR ME...
...I HAD SO LITTLE OF THEM TO BEGIN WITH.
...
DID WE JUST BOND?
GO DARK.
NOTHING HAPPENING UP HERE, GOOD OR BAD.

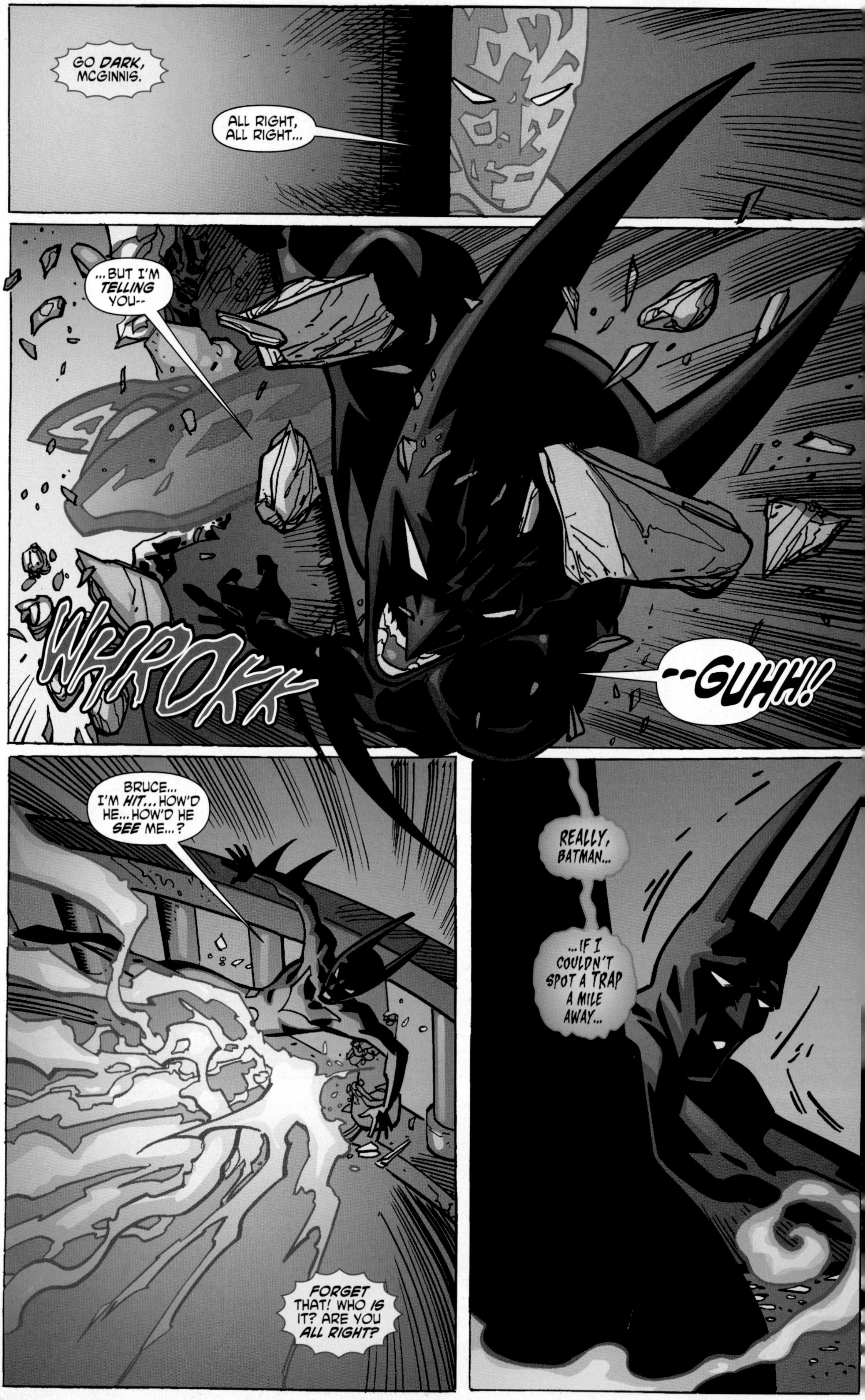
GO DARK, MCGINNIS.
ALL RIGHT, ALL RIGHT...
...BUT I'M TELLING YOU--
WHROKK
--GUHH!
BRUCE... I'M HIT... HOW'D HE... HOW'D HE SEE ME...?
FORGET THAT! WHO IS IT? ARE YOU ALL RIGHT?
REALLY, BATMAN...
...IF I COULDN'T SPOT A TRAP A MILE AWAY...

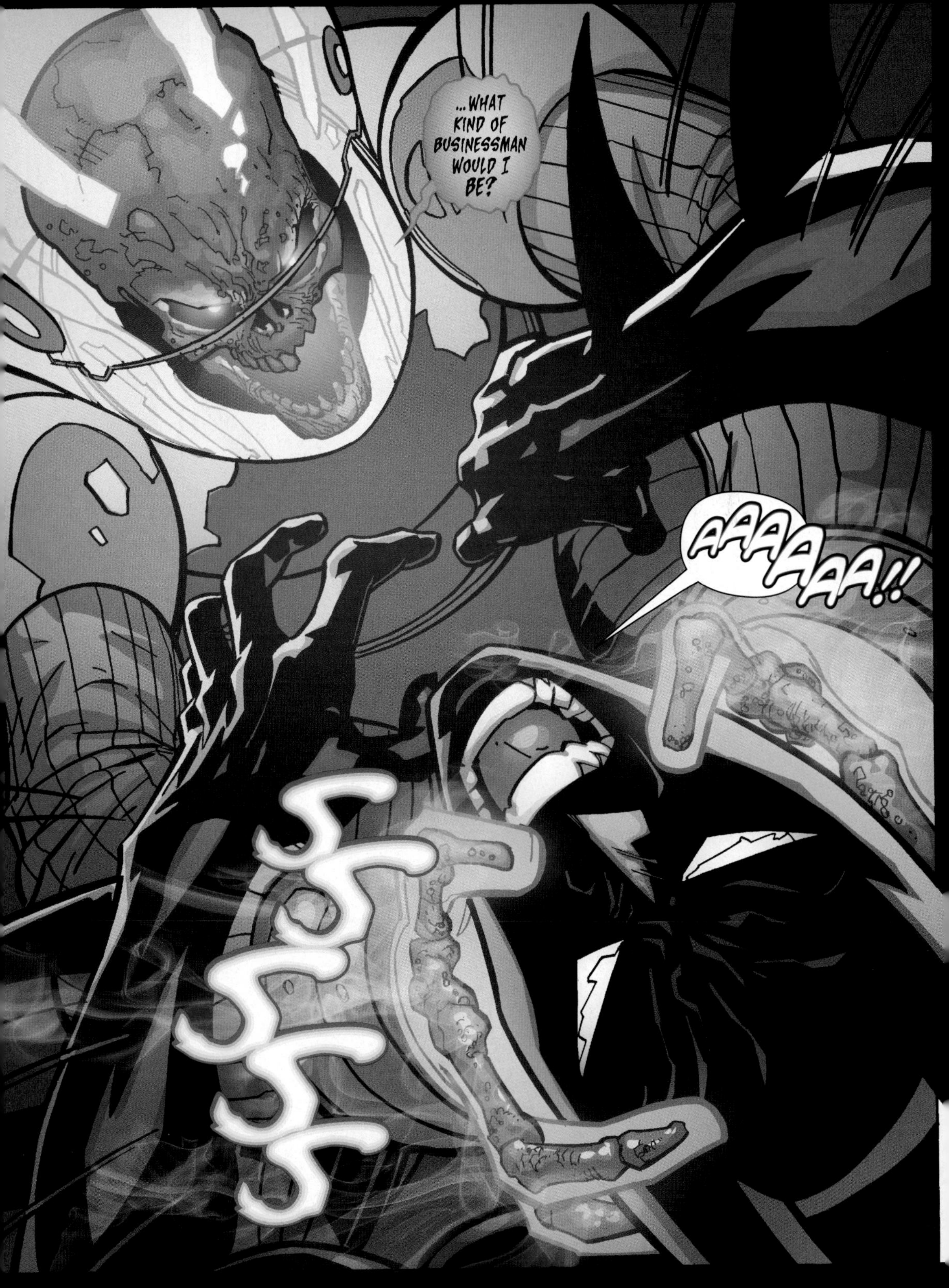
...WHAT KIND OF BUSINESSMAN WOULD I BE?
AAAAAAA!!
SSSSS

INDUSTRIAL REVOLUTION PART 3: BAD FOR BUSINESS

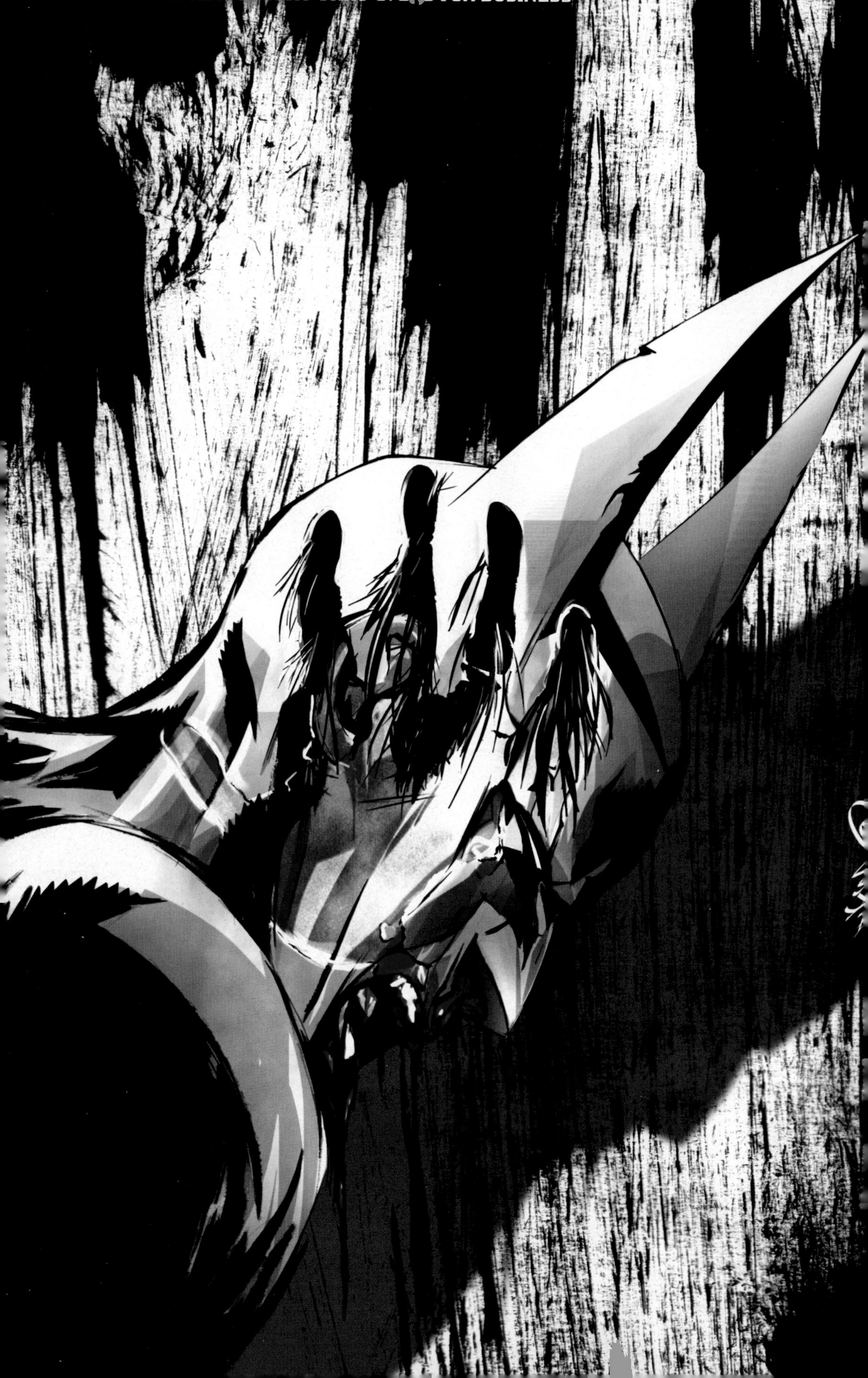

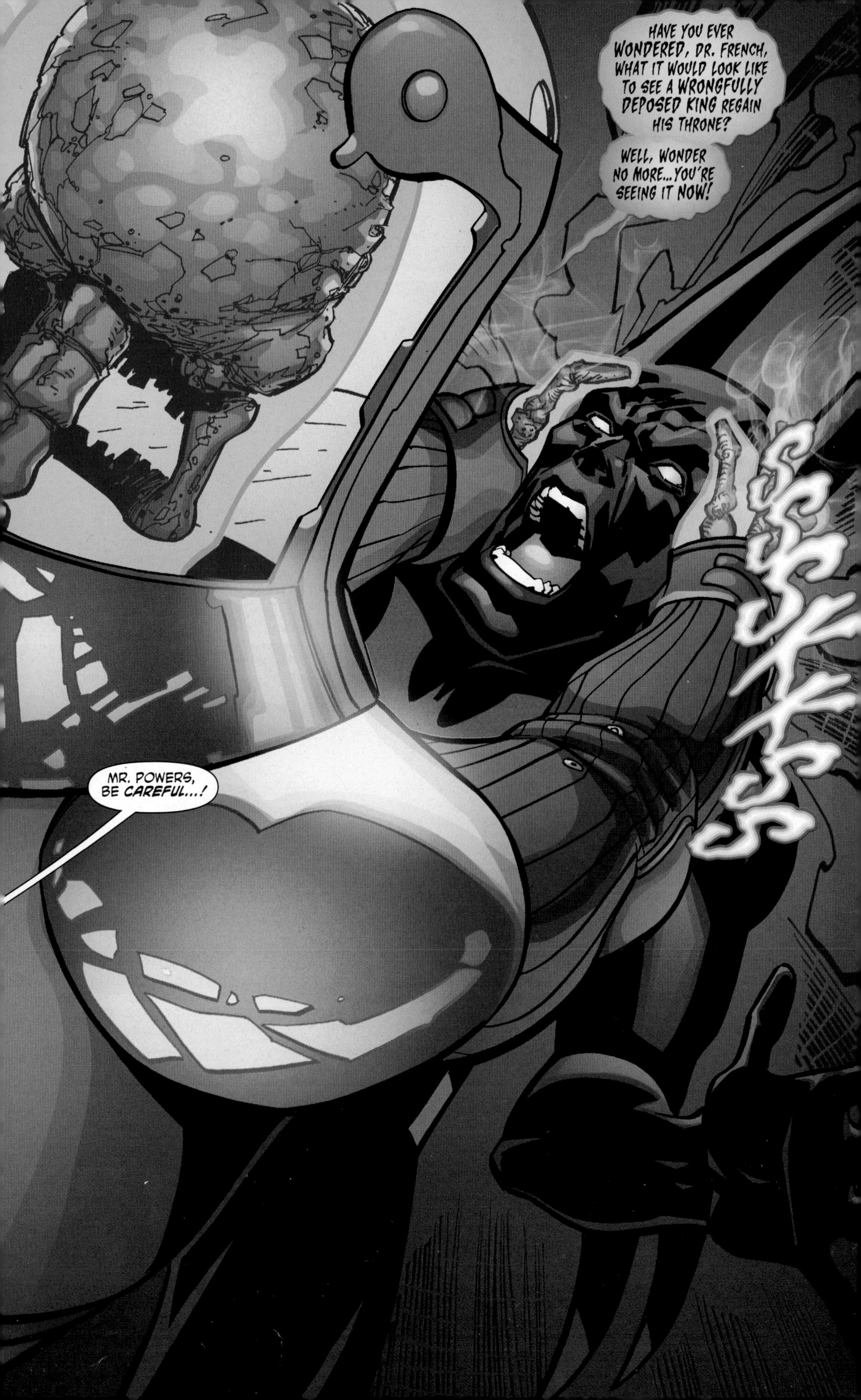
HAVE YOU EVER WONDERED, DR. FRENCH, WHAT IT WOULD LOOK LIKE TO SEE A WRONGFULLY DEPOSED KING REGAIN HIS THRONE?
WELL, WONDER NO MORE...YOU'RE SEEING IT NOW!
SSSKKSSS
MR. POWERS, BE CAREFUL...!

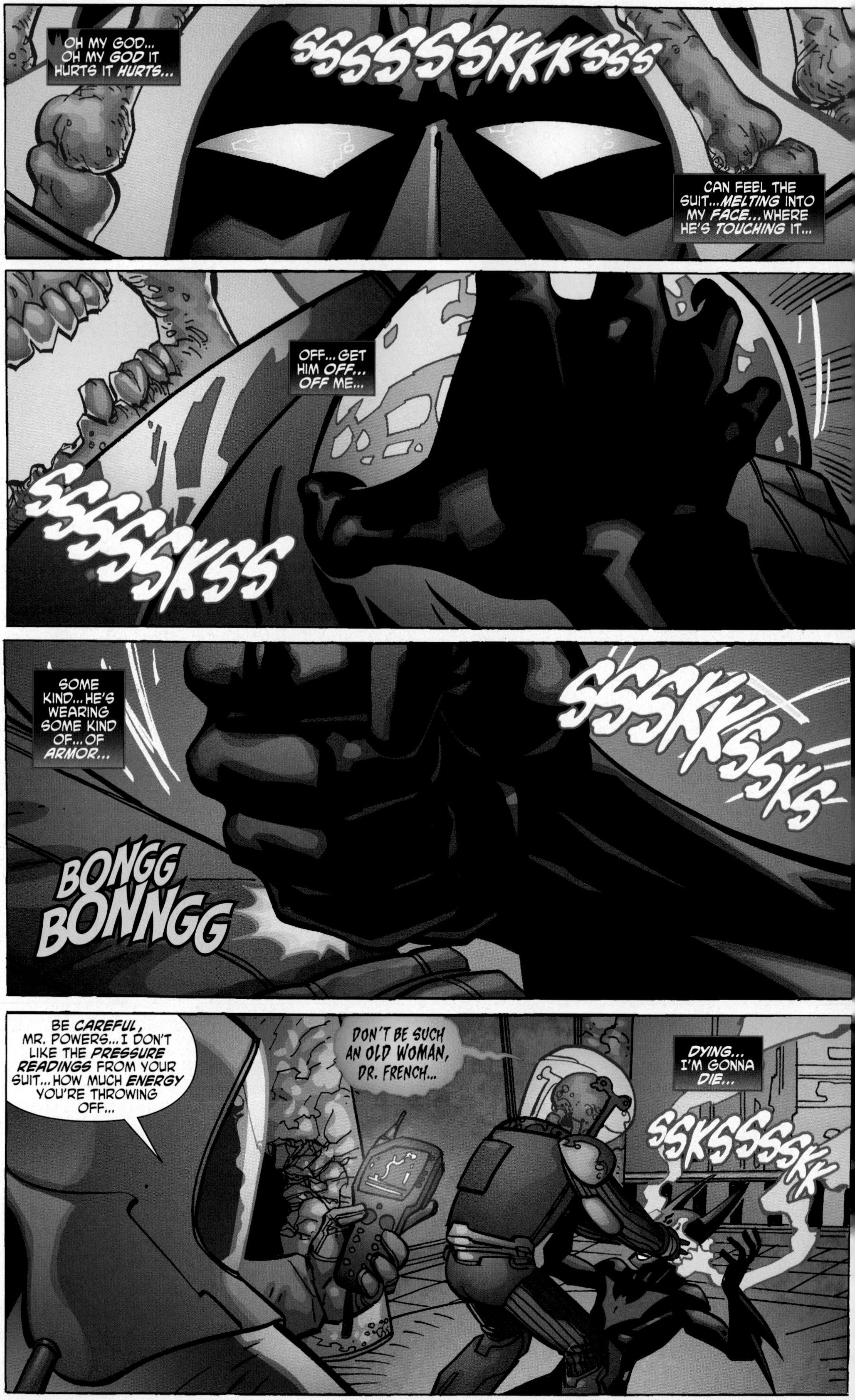
OH MY GOD... OH MY GOD IT HURTS IT HURTS...
SSSSSSKKKSSS
CAN FEEL THE SUIT...MELTING INTO MY FACE...WHERE HE'S TOUCHING IT...
OFF... GET HIM OFF... OFF ME...
SSSSSKSS
SOME KIND... HE'S WEARING SOME KIND OF...OF ARMOR...
SSSKKSSSKS
BONGG BONNGG
BE CAREFUL, MR. POWERS...I DON'T LIKE THE PRESSURE READINGS FROM YOUR SUIT...HOW MUCH ENERGY YOU'RE THROWING OFF...
DON'T BE SUCH AN OLD WOMAN, DR. FRENCH...
DYING... I'M GONNA DIE...
SSKSSSSSKK

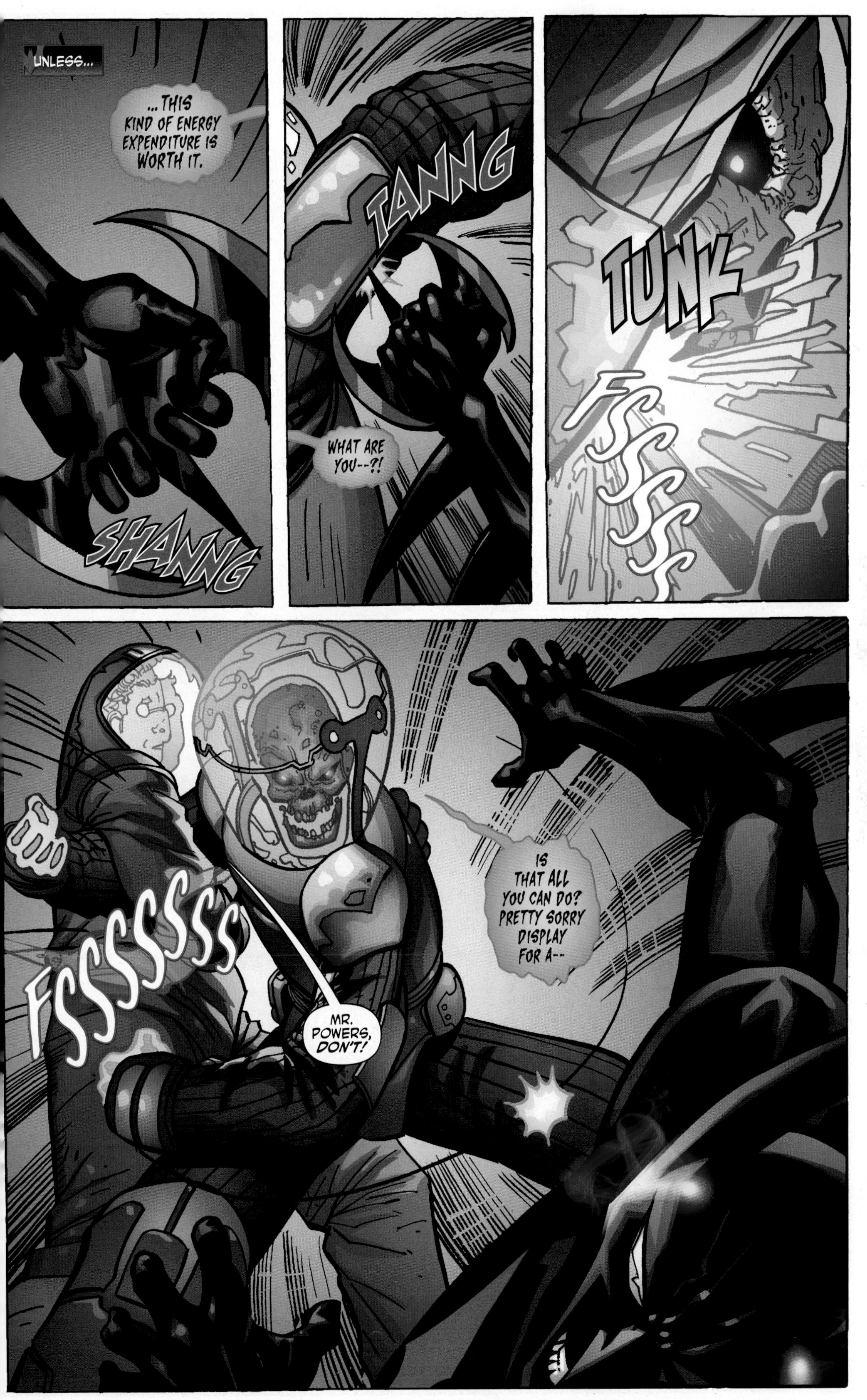
UNLESS...
...THIS KIND OF ENERGY EXPENDITURE IS WORTH IT.
SHANNG
TANNG
WHAT ARE YOU--?!
TUNK
FSSSSS
IS THAT ALL YOU CAN DO? PRETTY SORRY DISPLAY FOR A--
MR. POWERS, DON'T!
FSSSSSSS

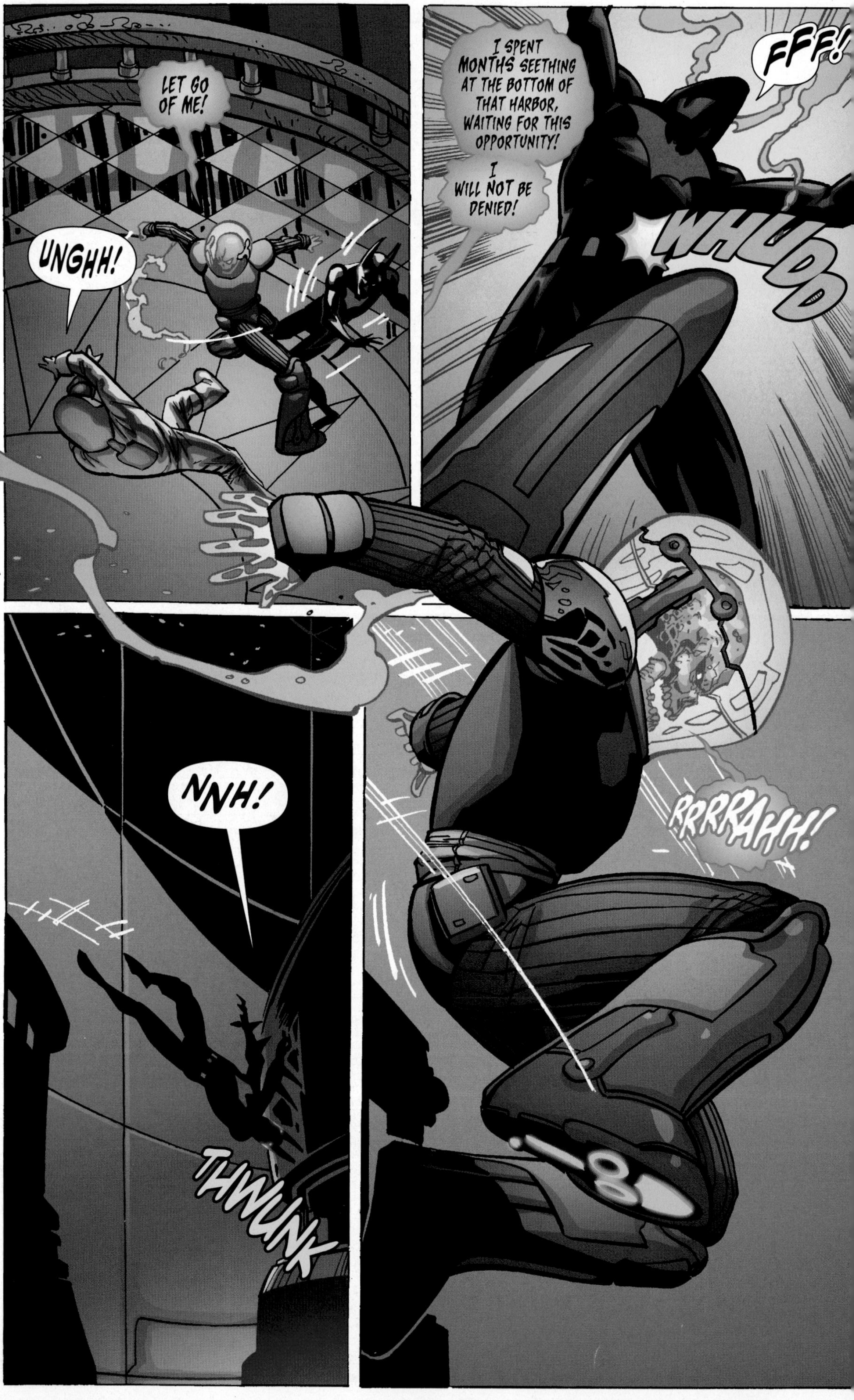
LET GO OF ME!
UNGHH!
I SPENT MONTHS SEETHING AT THE BOTTOM OF THAT HARBOR, WAITING FOR THIS OPPORTUNITY!
I WILL NOT BE DENIED!
FFF!
WHUDD
NNH!
RRRRAHH!
THWUNK

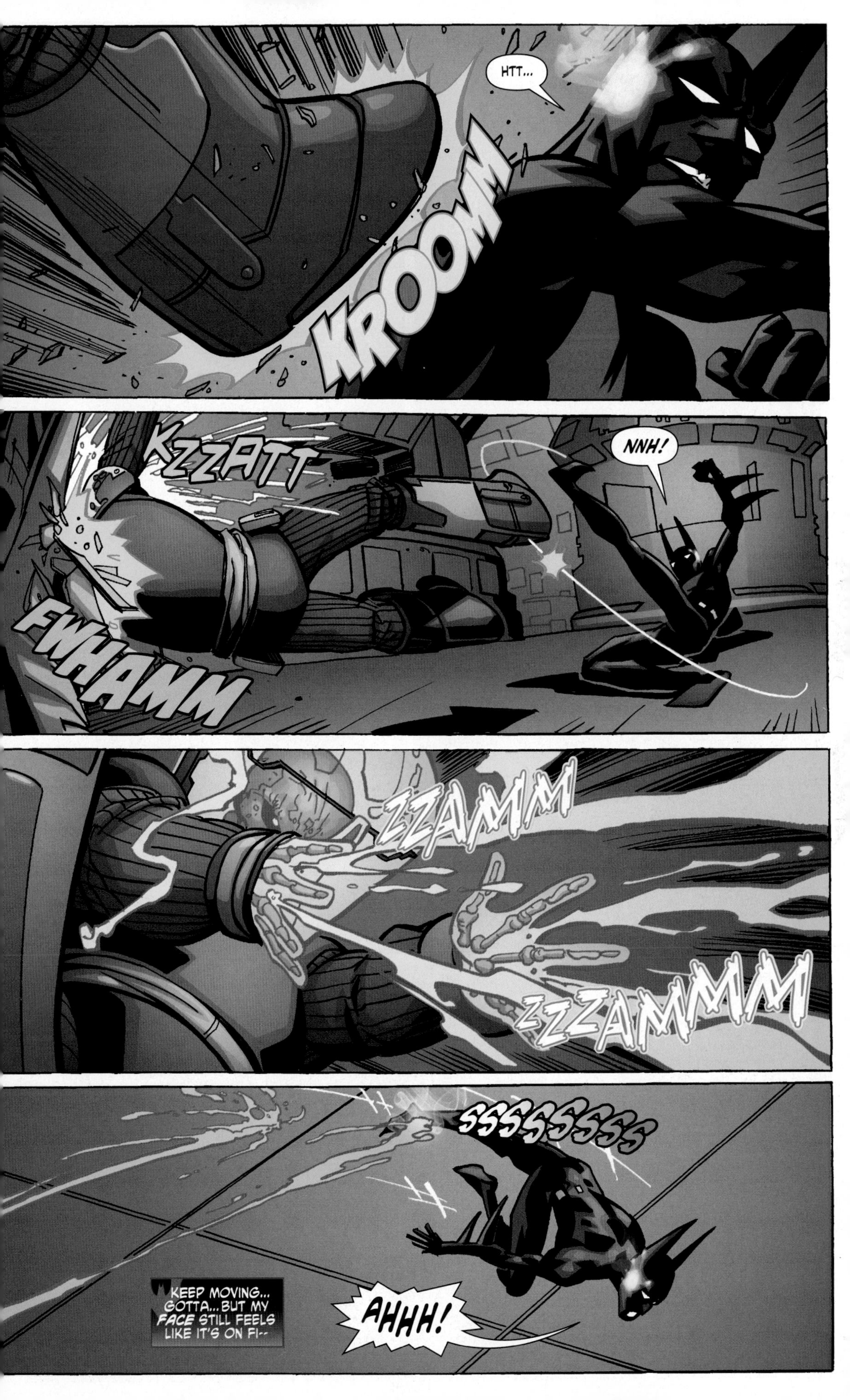
HTT...
KROOMM
KZZATT
NNH!
FWHAMM
ZZAMMM
ZZZAMMMM
SSSSSSSS
KEEP MOVING... GOTTA... BUT MY FACE STILL FEELS LIKE IT'S ON FI--
AHHH!

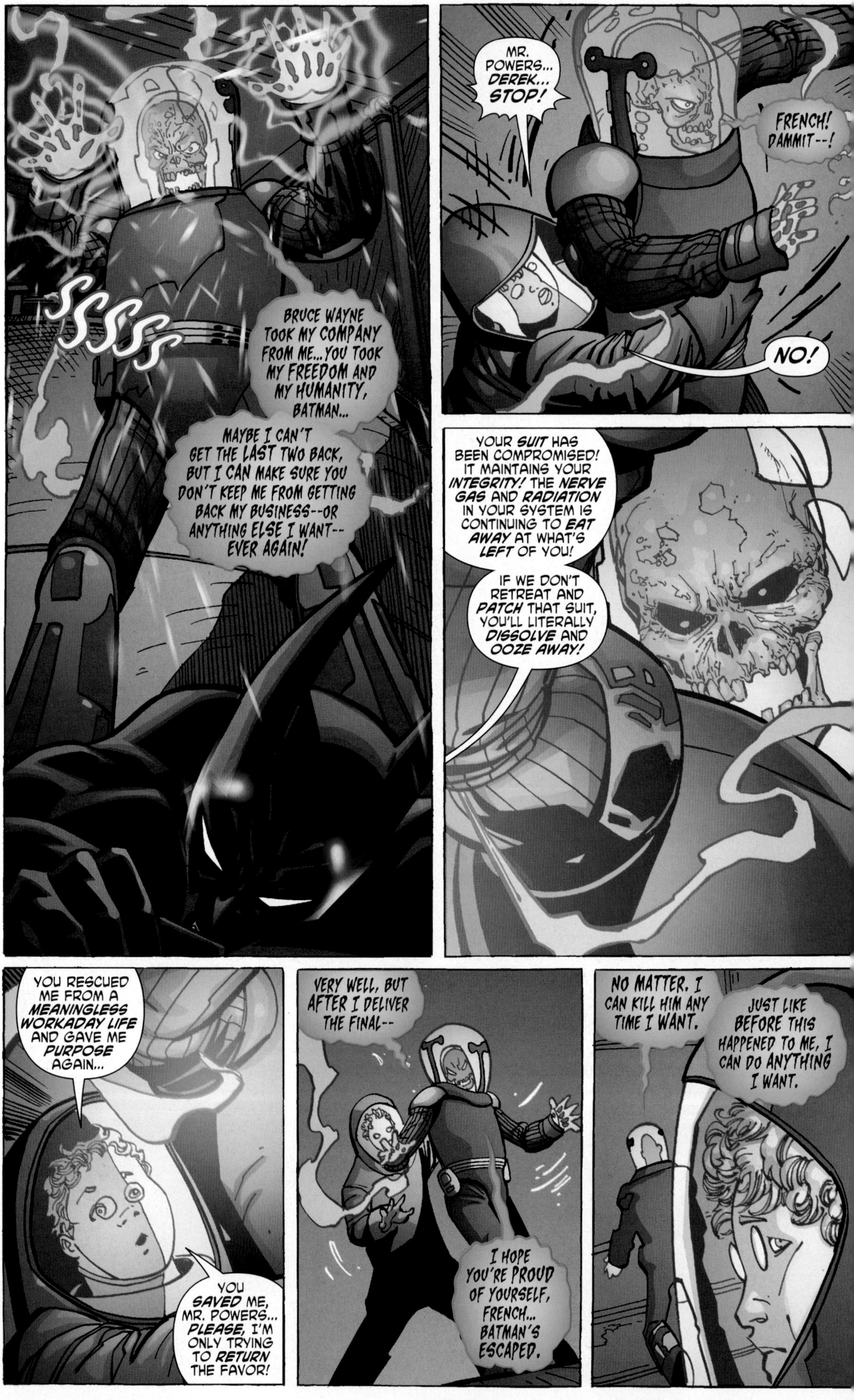
SSSSS
BRUCE WAYNE TOOK MY COMPANY FROM ME...YOU TOOK MY FREEDOM AND MY HUMANITY, BATMAN...
MAYBE I CAN'T GET THE LAST TWO BACK, BUT I CAN MAKE SURE YOU DON'T KEEP ME FROM GETTING BACK MY BUSINESS--OR ANYTHING ELSE I WANT--EVER AGAIN!
MR. POWERS... DEREK... STOP!
FRENCH! DAMMIT--!
NO!
YOUR SUIT HAS BEEN COMPROMISED! IT MAINTAINS YOUR INTEGRITY! THE NERVE GAS AND RADIATION IN YOUR SYSTEM IS CONTINUING TO EAT AWAY AT WHAT'S LEFT OF YOU!
IF WE DON'T RETREAT AND PATCH THAT SUIT, YOU'LL LITERALLY DISSOLVE AND OOZE AWAY!
YOU RESCUED ME FROM A MEANINGLESS WORKADAY LIFE AND GAVE ME PURPOSE AGAIN...
YOU SAVED ME, MR. POWERS... PLEASE, I'M ONLY TRYING TO RETURN THE FAVOR!
VERY WELL, BUT AFTER I DELIVER THE FINAL--
I HOPE YOU'RE PROUD OF YOURSELF, FRENCH... BATMAN'S ESCAPED.
NO MATTER. I CAN KILL HIM ANY TIME I WANT.
JUST LIKE BEFORE THIS HAPPENED TO ME, I CAN DO ANYTHING I WANT.

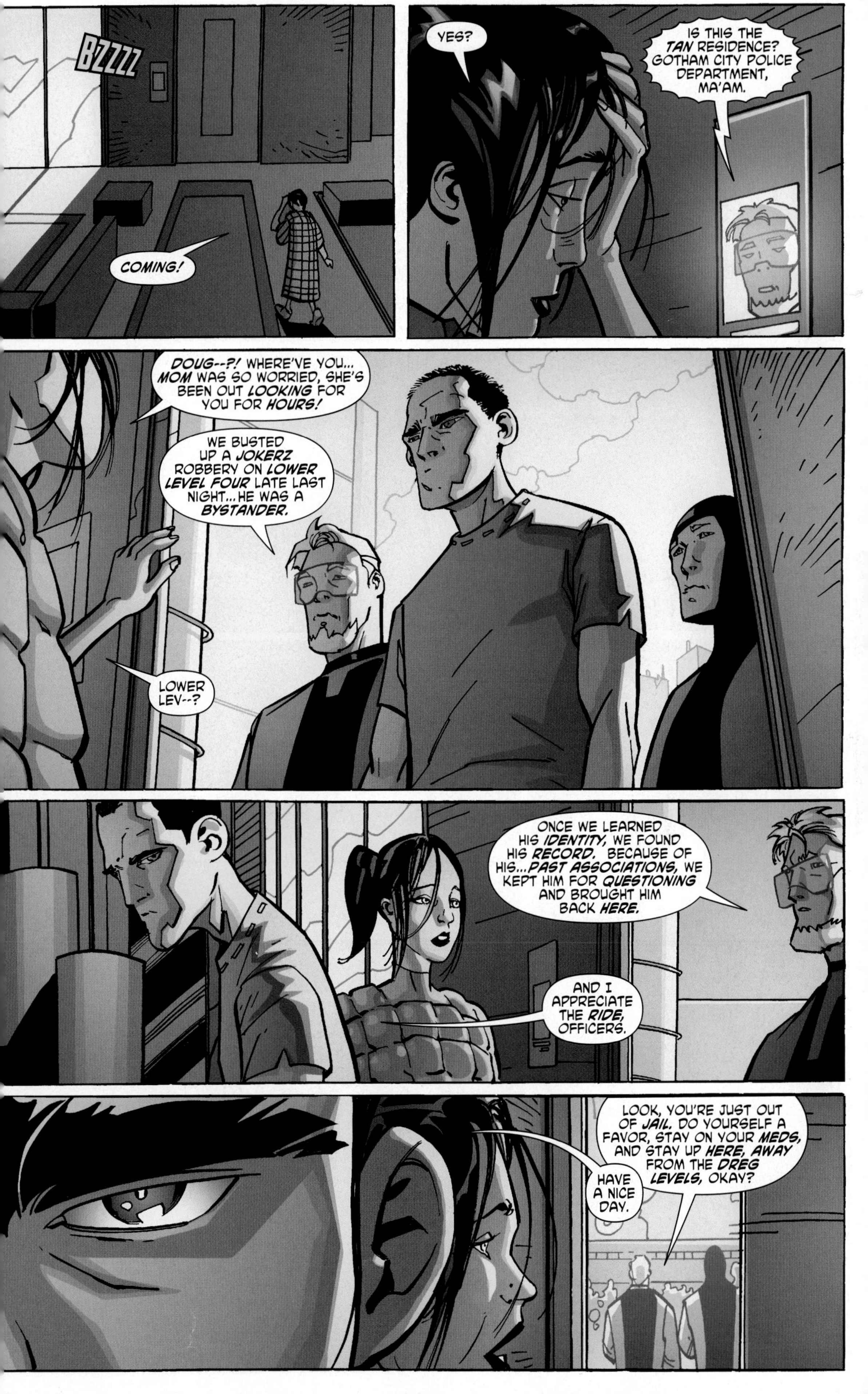
BZZZZ
COMING!
YES?
IS THIS THE TAN RESIDENCE? GOTHAM CITY POLICE DEPARTMENT, MA'AM.
DOUG--?! WHERE'VE YOU... MOM WAS SO WORRIED, SHE'S BEEN OUT LOOKING FOR YOU FOR HOURS!
WE BUSTED UP A JOKERZ ROBBERY ON LOWER LEVEL FOUR LATE LAST NIGHT... HE WAS A BYSTANDER.
LOWER LEV--?
ONCE WE LEARNED HIS IDENTITY, WE FOUND HIS RECORD. BECAUSE OF HIS...PAST ASSOCIATIONS, WE KEPT HIM FOR QUESTIONING AND BROUGHT HIM BACK HERE.
AND I APPRECIATE THE RIDE, OFFICERS.
LOOK, YOU'RE JUST OUT OF JAIL. DO YOURSELF A FAVOR, STAY ON YOUR MEDS, AND STAY UP HERE, AWAY FROM THE DREG LEVELS, OKAY?
HAVE A NICE DAY.

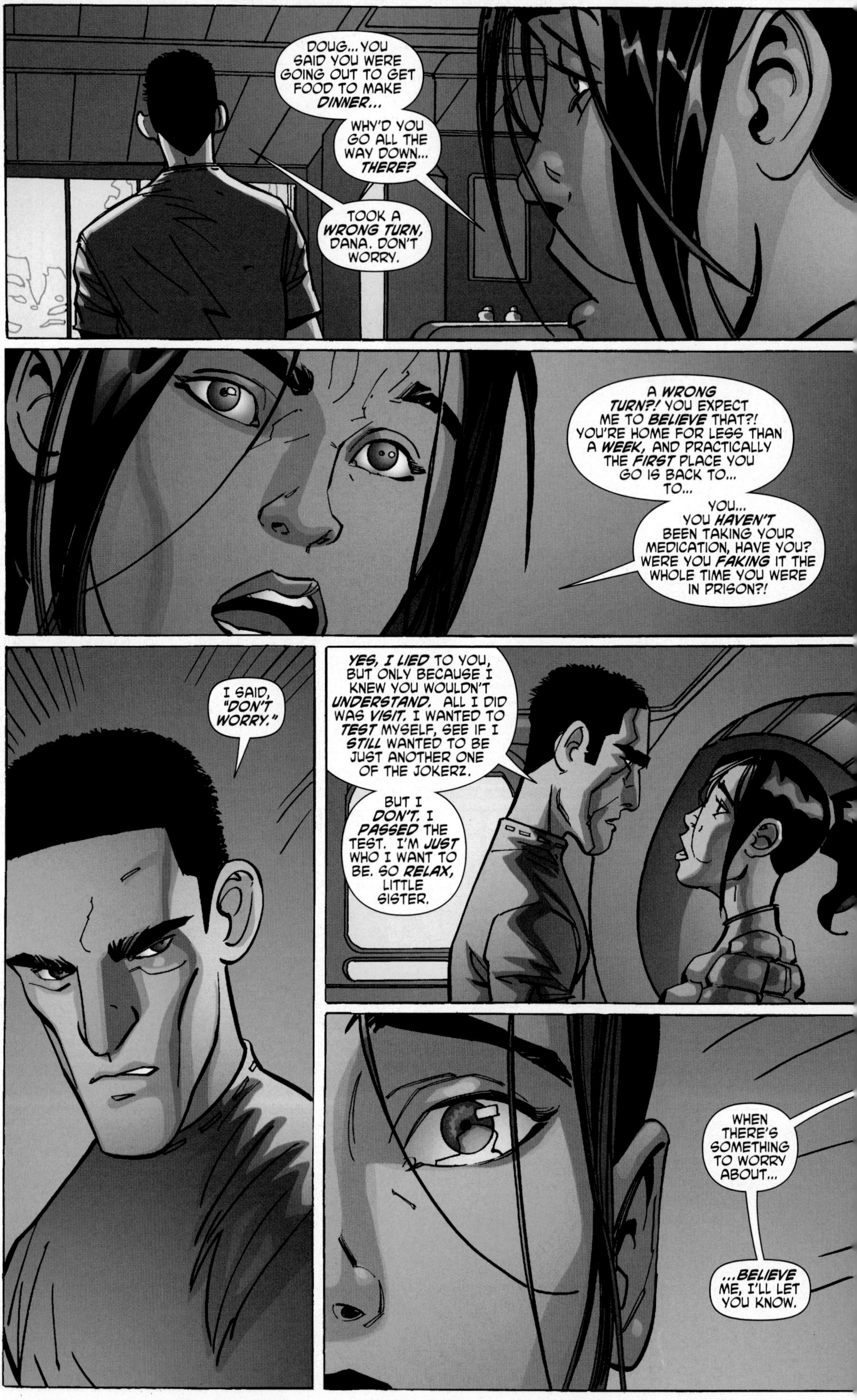
DOUG... YOU SAID YOU WERE GOING OUT TO GET FOOD TO MAKE DINNER...
WHY'D YOU GO ALL THE WAY DOWN... THERE?
TOOK A WRONG TURN, DANA. DON'T WORRY.
A WRONG TURN?! YOU EXPECT ME TO BELIEVE THAT?! YOU'RE HOME FOR LESS THAN A WEEK, AND PRACTICALLY THE FIRST PLACE YOU GO IS BACK TO... TO...
YOU... YOU HAVEN'T BEEN TAKING YOUR MEDICATION, HAVE YOU? WERE YOU FAKING IT THE WHOLE TIME YOU WERE IN PRISON?!
I SAID, "DON'T WORRY."
YES, I LIED TO YOU, BUT ONLY BECAUSE I KNEW YOU WOULDN'T UNDERSTAND. ALL I DID WAS VISIT. I WANTED TO TEST MYSELF, SEE IF I STILL WANTED TO BE JUST ANOTHER ONE OF THE JOKERZ.
BUT I DON'T. I PASSED THE TEST. I'M JUST WHO I WANT TO BE. SO RELAX, LITTLE SISTER.
WHEN THERE'S SOMETHING TO WORRY ABOUT...
...BELIEVE ME, I'LL LET YOU KNOW.

BRUCE?

BRUCE? ACE?

HELLO?

MCGINNIS.

BRUCE, I *BARELY* GOT AWAY... IT'S *BLIGHT* BEHIND ALL OF THIS, AND--

I KNOW.

WAIT, WHERE *ARE* YOU?

AT THE *OTHER* OFFICE. CHECK THE *NEWS.*

"OTHER...?" OH.

WAYNE BUYS OVERWHELMING MAJORITY OF WAYNE-POWERS STOCK.

Ending Labor Unrest "First P

YOU WENT AHEAD AND BOUGHT BACK THE COMPANY *ANYWAY.* SCHWAY.

WHAT'S THE--OW!--*SCENE* DOWN THERE?

UGLY. G. GLEN GODFREY HAS MY EMPLOYEES RILED UP AGAIN ON BLIGHT'S BEHALF, READY TO *RIOT.*

BUT I'M ABOUT TO PUT AN *END* TO IT.

YOU-- OW!-- WANT *ME* THERE?

NO. BECAUSE DEREK POWERS WILL BE IN A *RAGE* WHEN HE GETS THIS NEWS, AND HE *DOESN'T KNOW* I'M *DOWNTOWN.*

HE'LL BE COMING *THERE,* TO KILL ME.

UNDERSTOOD. THAT'LL GIVE ME TIME TO FIX MY *MASK* AFTER BLIGHT *BARBECUED* IT. TELL *ACE* HE OWES ME FOR PLAYING *WATCHDOG.*

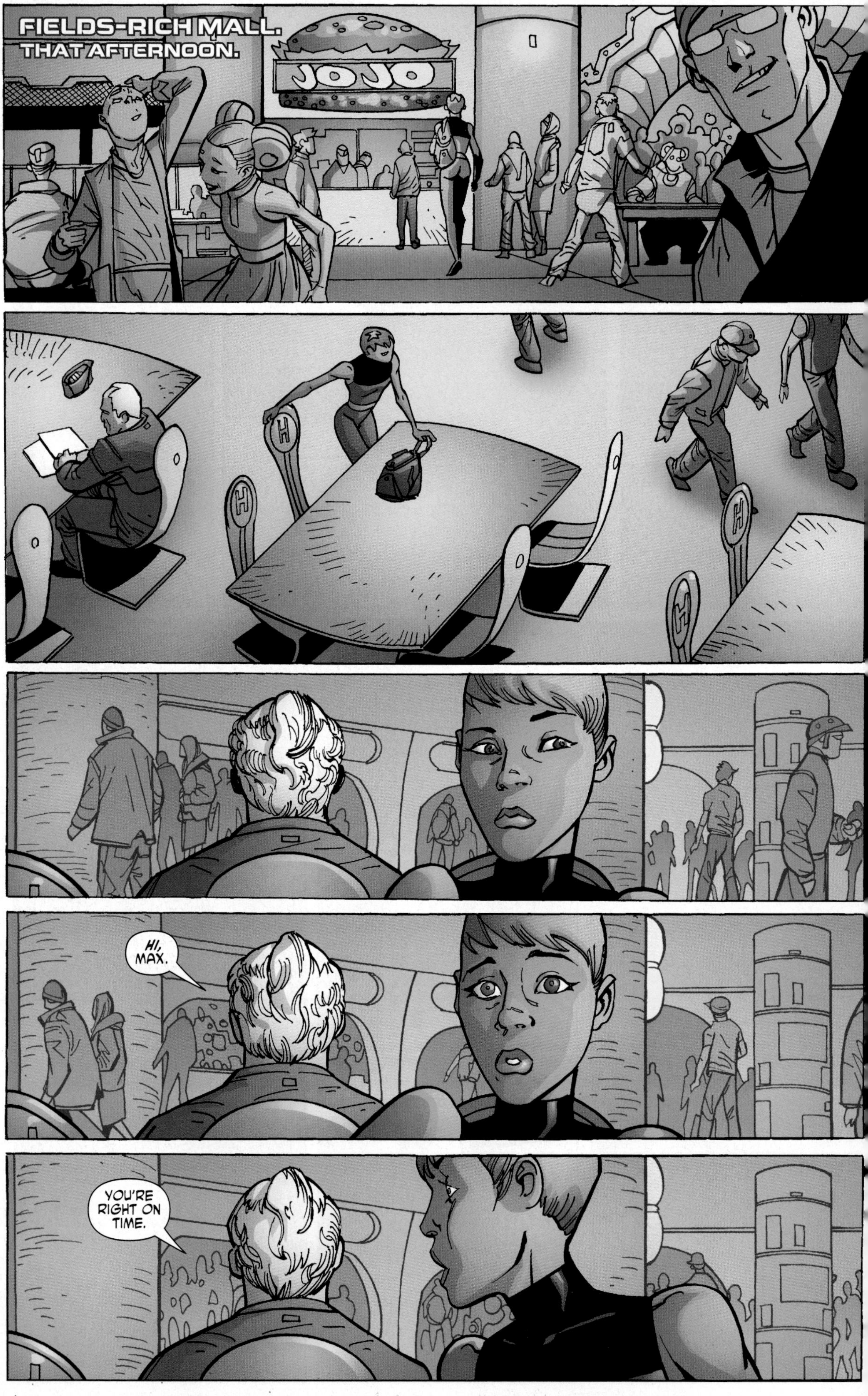
FIELDS-RICH MALL.
THAT AFTERNOON.
JOJO
HI, MAX.
YOU'RE RIGHT ON TIME.

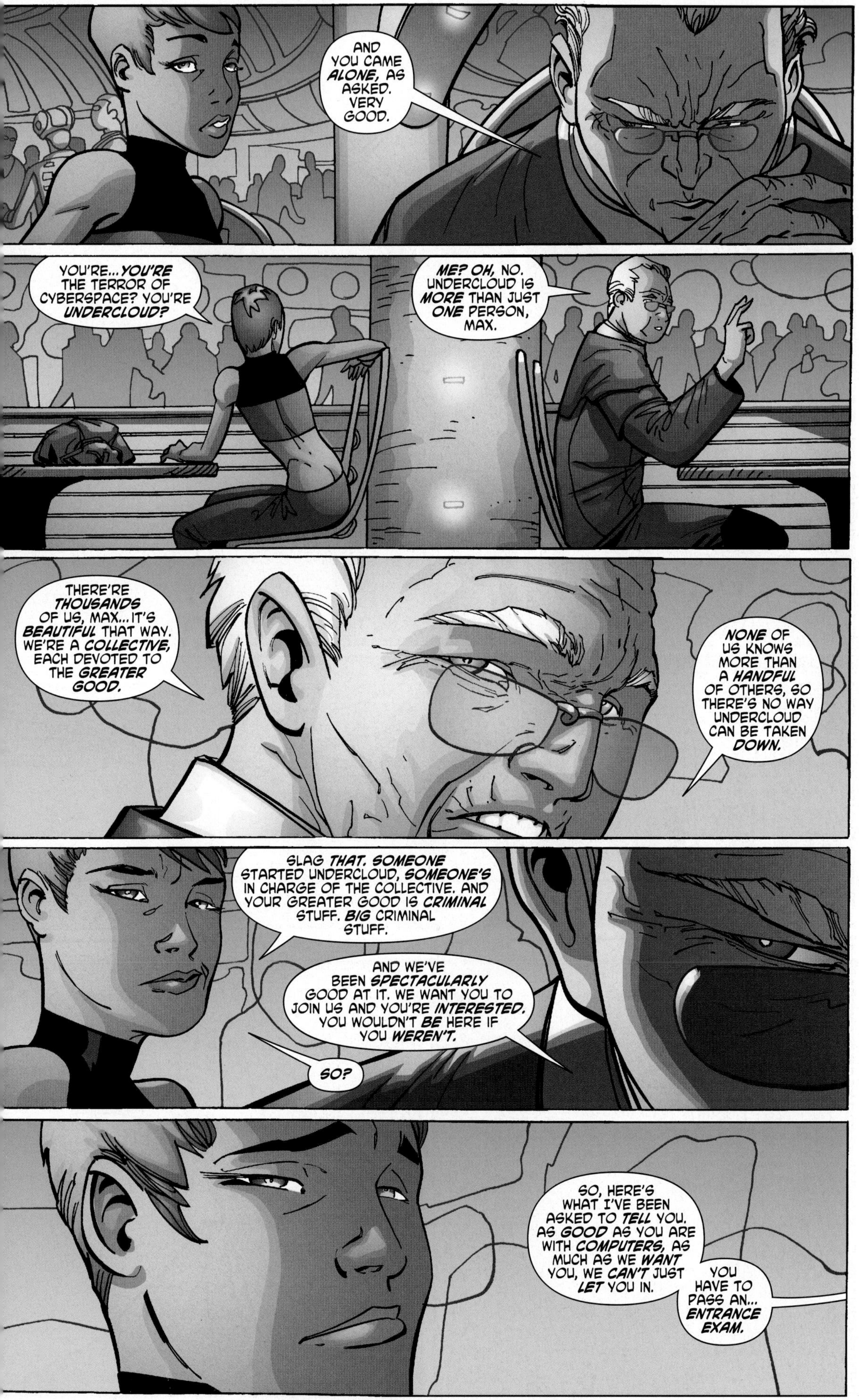
AND YOU CAME ALONE, AS ASKED. VERY GOOD.
YOU'RE... YOU'RE THE TERROR OF CYBERSPACE? YOU'RE UNDERCLOUD?
ME? OH, NO. UNDERCLOUD IS MORE THAN JUST ONE PERSON, MAX.
THERE'RE THOUSANDS OF US, MAX... IT'S BEAUTIFUL THAT WAY. WE'RE A COLLECTIVE, EACH DEVOTED TO THE GREATER GOOD.
NONE OF US KNOWS MORE THAN A HANDFUL OF OTHERS, SO THERE'S NO WAY UNDERCLOUD CAN BE TAKEN DOWN.
SLAG THAT. SOMEONE STARTED UNDERCLOUD, SOMEONE'S IN CHARGE OF THE COLLECTIVE. AND YOUR GREATER GOOD IS CRIMINAL STUFF. BIG CRIMINAL STUFF.
AND WE'VE BEEN SPECTACULARLY GOOD AT IT. WE WANT YOU TO JOIN US AND YOU'RE INTERESTED. YOU WOULDN'T BE HERE IF YOU WEREN'T.
SO?
SO, HERE'S WHAT I'VE BEEN ASKED TO TELL YOU. AS GOOD AS YOU ARE WITH COMPUTERS, AS MUCH AS WE WANT YOU, WE CAN'T JUST LET YOU IN.
YOU HAVE TO PASS AN... ENTRANCE EXAM.

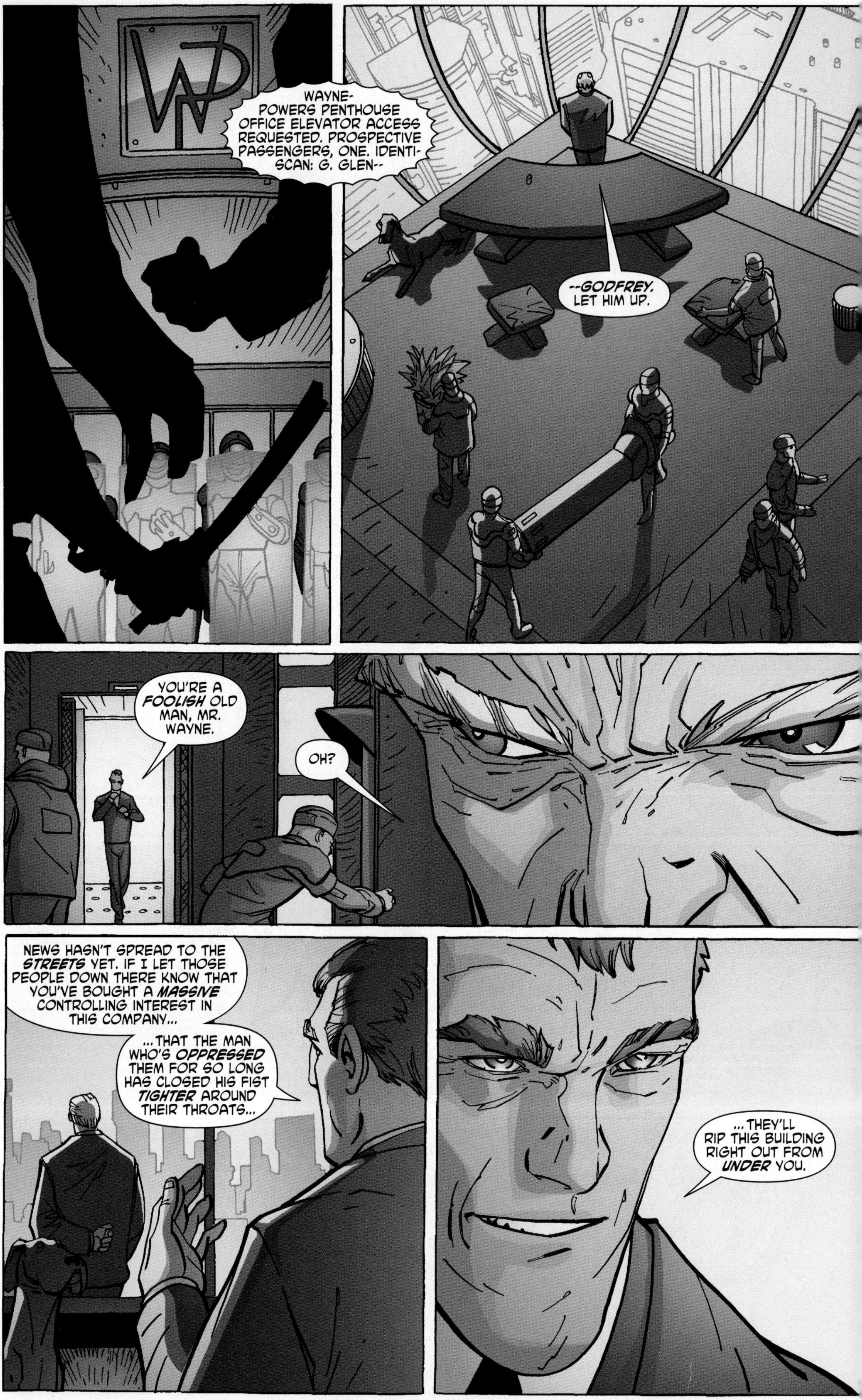
WAYNE-POWERS PENTHOUSE OFFICE ELEVATOR ACCESS REQUESTED. PROSPECTIVE PASSENGERS, ONE. IDENTI-SCAN: G. GLEN--
--GODFREY. LET HIM UP.
YOU'RE A FOOLISH OLD MAN, MR. WAYNE.
OH?
NEWS HASN'T SPREAD TO THE STREETS YET. IF I LET THOSE PEOPLE DOWN THERE KNOW THAT YOU'VE BOUGHT A MASSIVE CONTROLLING INTEREST IN THIS COMPANY...
...THAT THE MAN WHO'S OPPRESSED THEM FOR SO LONG HAS CLOSED HIS FIST TIGHTER AROUND THEIR THROATS...
...THEY'LL RIP THIS BUILDING RIGHT OUT FROM UNDER YOU.

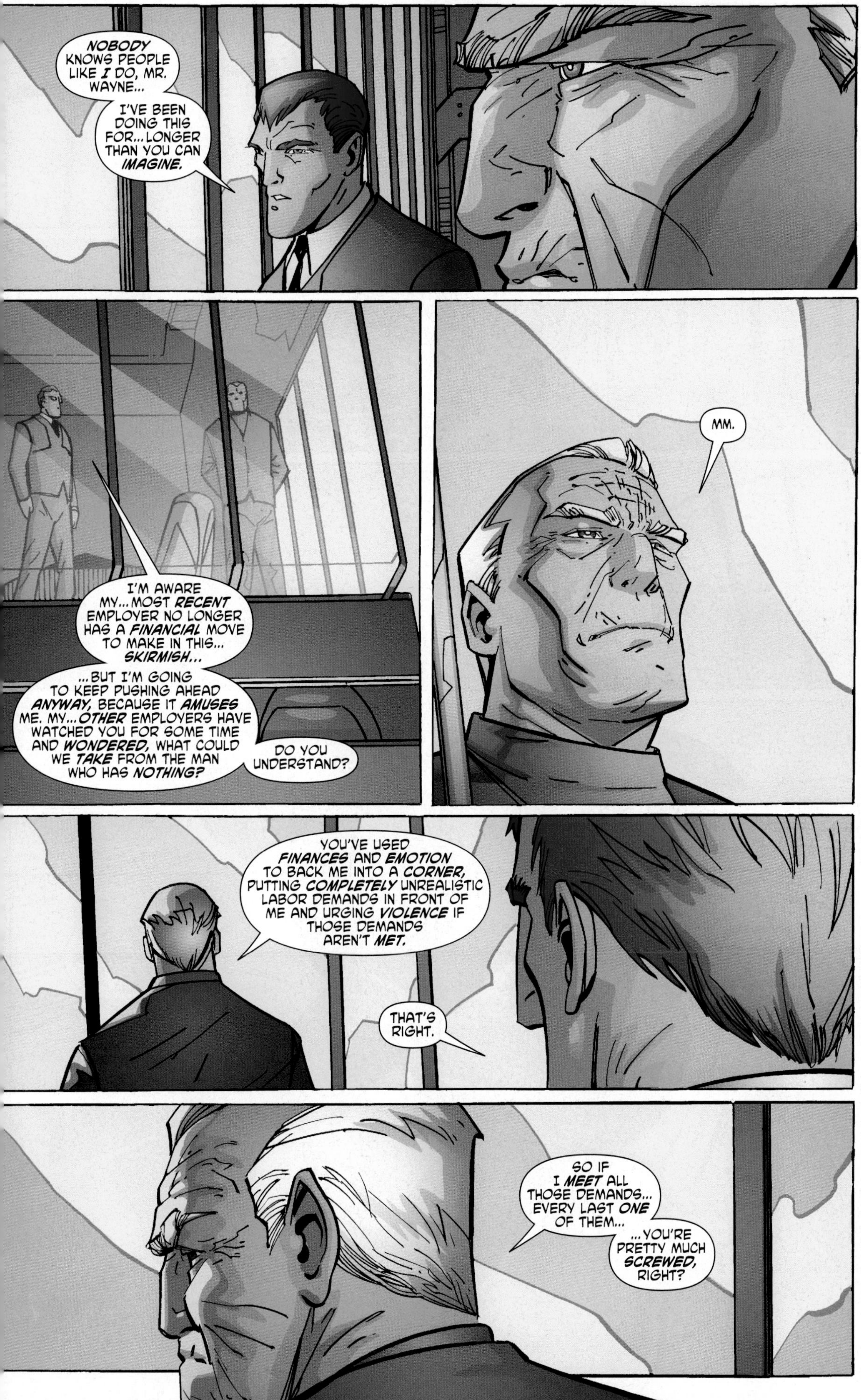
NOBODY KNOWS PEOPLE LIKE I DO, MR. WAYNE...
I'VE BEEN DOING THIS FOR...LONGER THAN YOU CAN IMAGINE.
I'M AWARE MY...MOST RECENT EMPLOYER NO LONGER HAS A FINANCIAL MOVE TO MAKE IN THIS... SKIRMISH...
...BUT I'M GOING TO KEEP PUSHING AHEAD ANYWAY, BECAUSE IT AMUSES ME. MY...OTHER EMPLOYERS HAVE WATCHED YOU FOR SOME TIME AND WONDERED, WHAT COULD WE TAKE FROM THE MAN WHO HAS NOTHING?
DO YOU UNDERSTAND?
MM.
YOU'VE USED FINANCES AND EMOTION TO BACK ME INTO A CORNER, PUTTING COMPLETELY UNREALISTIC LABOR DEMANDS IN FRONT OF ME AND URGING VIOLENCE IF THOSE DEMANDS AREN'T MET.
THAT'S RIGHT.
SO IF I MEET ALL THOSE DEMANDS... EVERY LAST ONE OF THEM...
...YOU'RE PRETTY MUCH SCREWED, RIGHT?

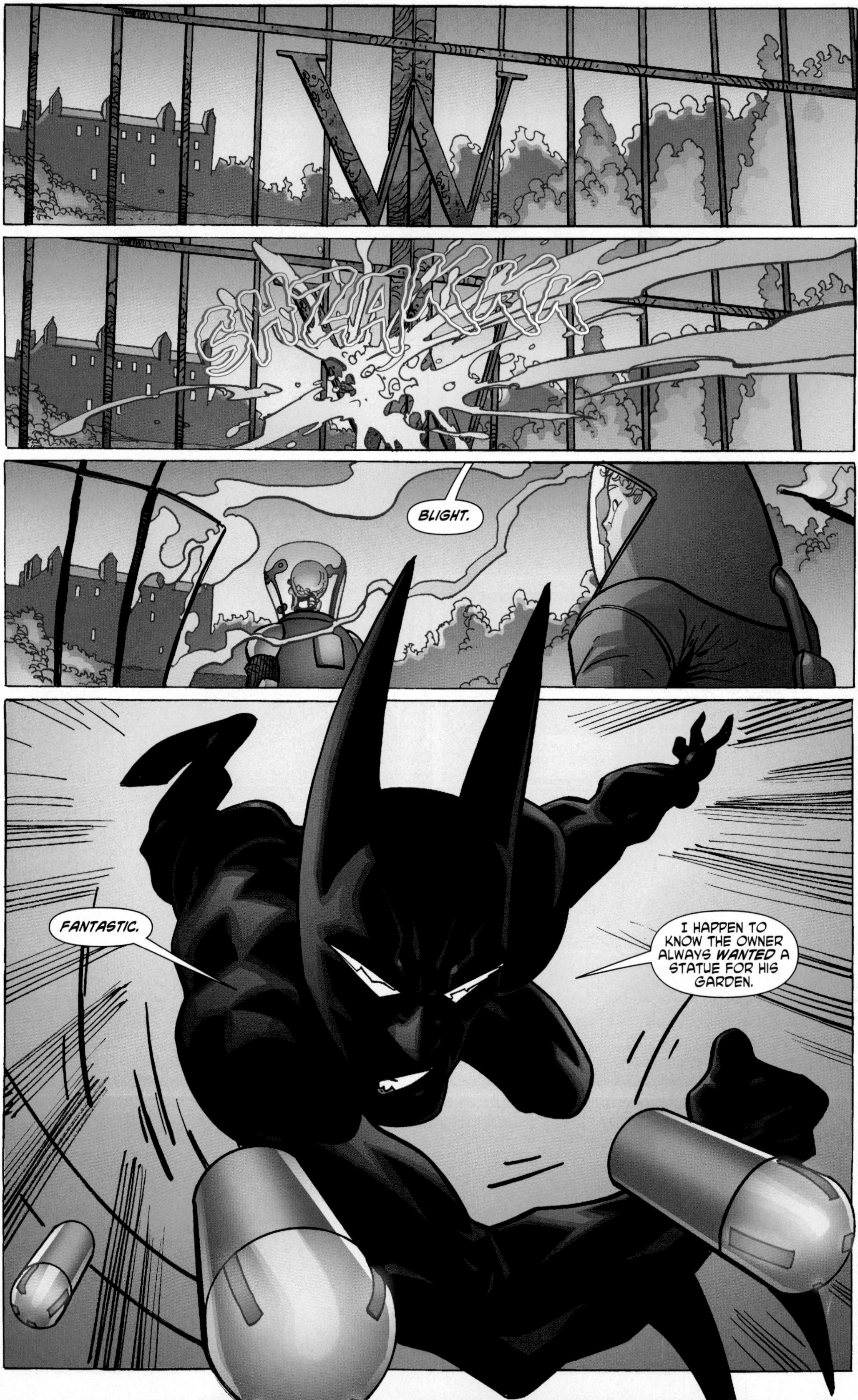
SHZAKKKK
BLIGHT.
FANTASTIC.
I HAPPEN TO KNOW THE OWNER ALWAYS WANTED A STATUE FOR HIS GARDEN.

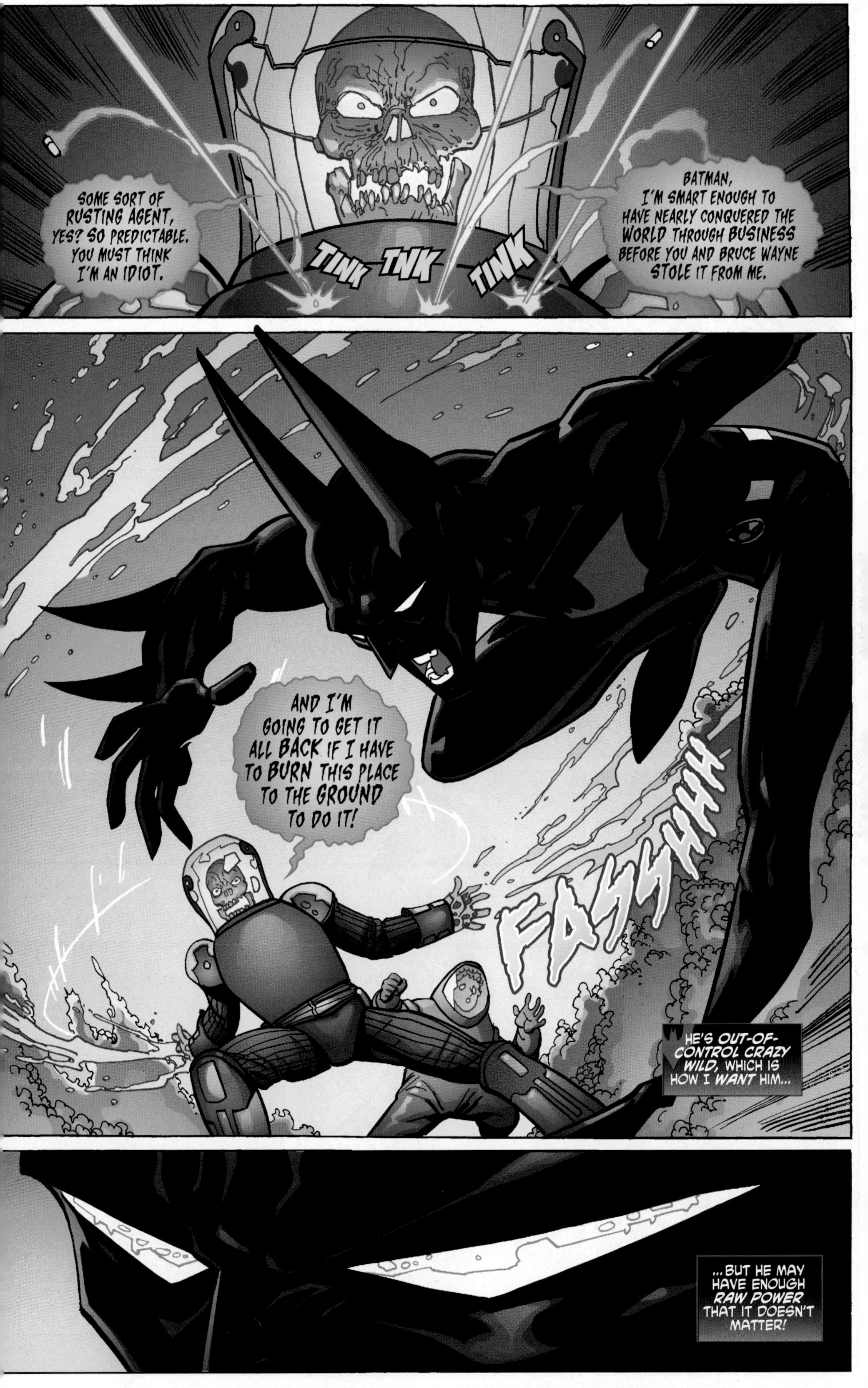
SOME SORT OF RUSTING AGENT, YES? SO PREDICTABLE. YOU MUST THINK I'M AN IDIOT.
TINK
TNK
TINK
BATMAN, I'M SMART ENOUGH TO HAVE NEARLY CONQUERED THE WORLD THROUGH BUSINESS BEFORE YOU AND BRUCE WAYNE STOLE IT FROM ME.
AND I'M GOING TO GET IT ALL BACK IF I HAVE TO BURN THIS PLACE TO THE GROUND TO DO IT!
FASSHHH
HE'S OUT-OF-CONTROL CRAZY WILD, WHICH IS HOW I WANT HIM...
...BUT HE MAY HAVE ENOUGH RAW POWER THAT IT DOESN'T MATTER!

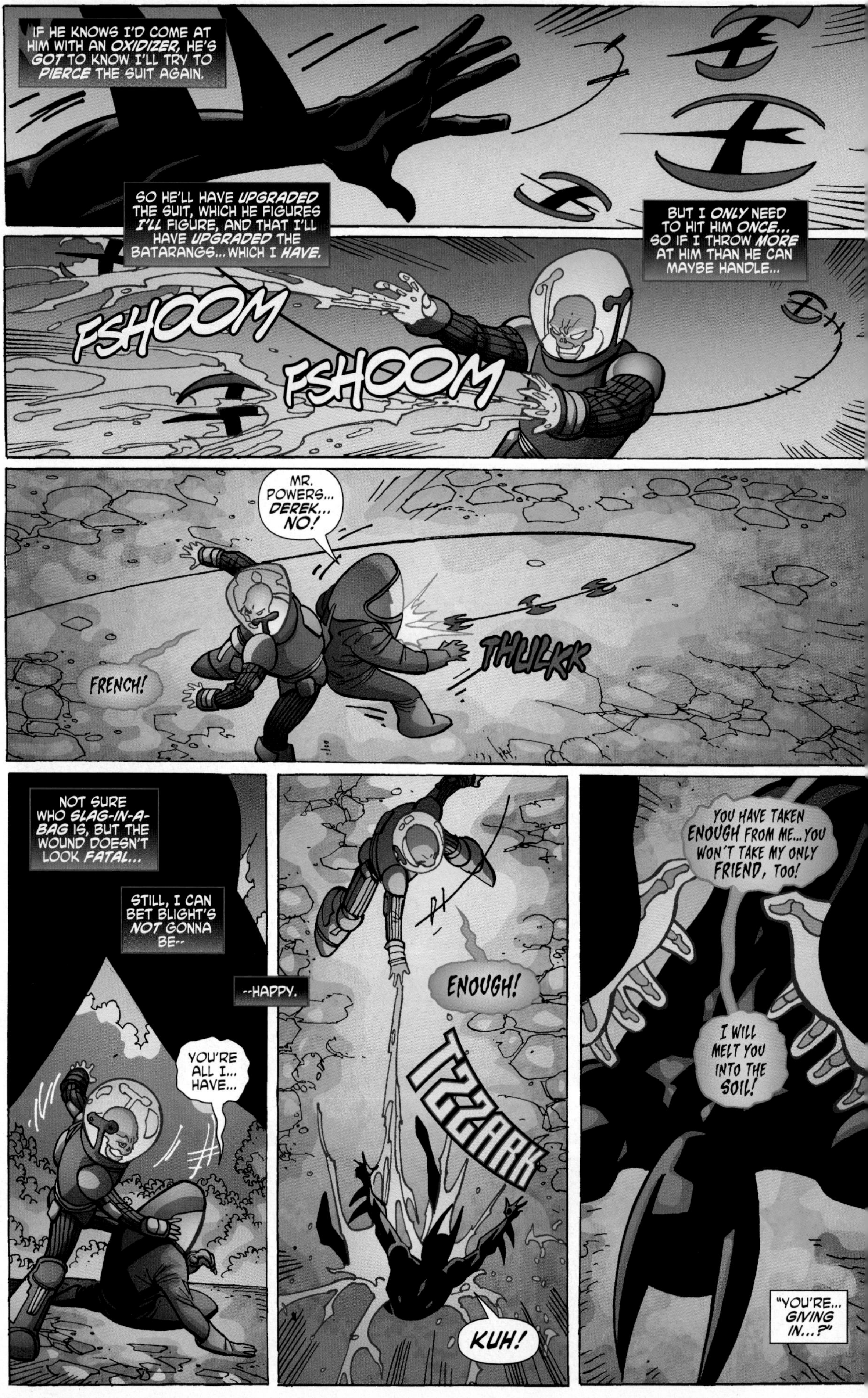

IF HE KNOWS I'D COME AT HIM WITH AN OXIDIZER, HE'S GOT TO KNOW I'LL TRY TO PIERCE THE SUIT AGAIN.
SO HE'LL HAVE UPGRADED THE SUIT, WHICH HE FIGURES I'LL FIGURE, AND THAT I'LL HAVE UPGRADED THE BATARANGS...WHICH I HAVE.
BUT I ONLY NEED TO HIT HIM ONCE... SO IF I THROW MORE AT HIM THAN HE CAN MAYBE HANDLE...
FSHOOM
FSHOOM
MR. POWERS... DEREK... NO!
THULKK
FRENCH!
NOT SURE WHO SLAG-IN-A-BAG IS, BUT THE WOUND DOESN'T LOOK FATAL...
STILL, I CAN BET BLIGHT'S NOT GONNA BE--
--HAPPY.
YOU'RE ALL I... HAVE...
ENOUGH!
TZZARK
KUH!
YOU HAVE TAKEN ENOUGH FROM ME...YOU WON'T TAKE MY ONLY FRIEND, TOO!
I WILL MELT YOU INTO THE SOIL!
"YOU'RE... GIVING IN...?"

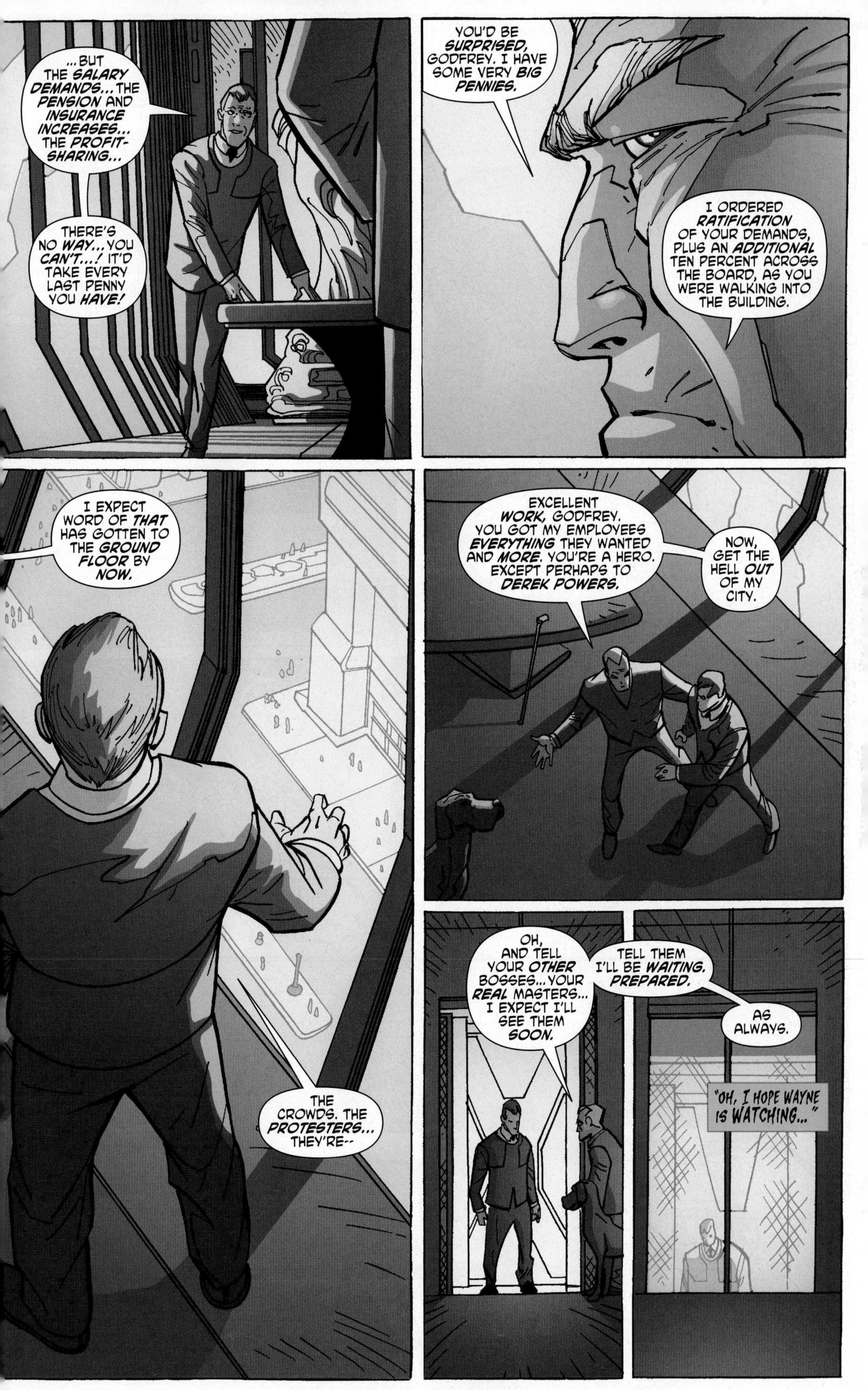
...BUT THE *SALARY DEMANDS*... THE *PENSION* AND *INSURANCE INCREASES*... THE *PROFIT-SHARING*...
THERE'S NO *WAY*... YOU *CAN'T*...! IT'D TAKE EVERY LAST PENNY YOU *HAVE!*
YOU'D BE *SURPRISED*, GODFREY. I HAVE SOME VERY *BIG PENNIES.*
I ORDERED *RATIFICATION* OF YOUR DEMANDS, PLUS AN *ADDITIONAL* TEN PERCENT ACROSS THE BOARD, AS YOU WERE WALKING INTO THE BUILDING.
I EXPECT WORD OF *THAT* HAS GOTTEN TO THE *GROUND FLOOR* BY *NOW.*
THE CROWDS. THE *PROTESTERS*... THEY'RE--
EXCELLENT *WORK*, GODFREY. YOU GOT MY EMPLOYEES *EVERYTHING* THEY WANTED AND *MORE*. YOU'RE A HERO. EXCEPT PERHAPS TO *DEREK POWERS.*
NOW, GET THE HELL *OUT* OF MY CITY.
OH, AND TELL YOUR *OTHER* BOSSES... YOUR *REAL* MASTERS... I EXPECT I'LL SEE THEM *SOON.*
TELL THEM I'LL BE *WAITING. PREPARED.*
AS ALWAYS.
"OH, I HOPE WAYNE IS WATCHING..."

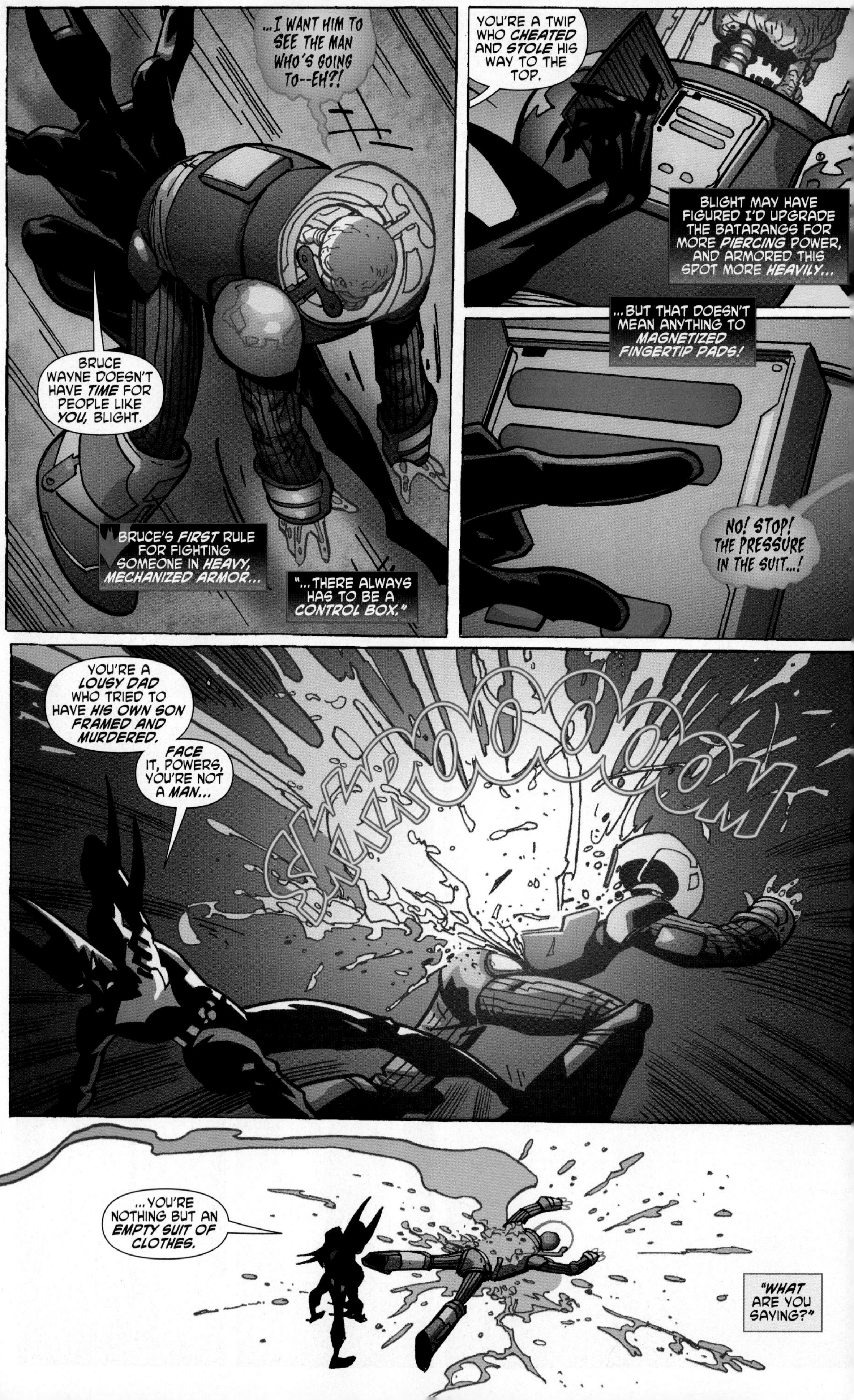
...I WANT HIM TO SEE THE MAN WHO'S GOING TO--EH?!
BRUCE WAYNE DOESN'T HAVE TIME FOR PEOPLE LIKE YOU, BLIGHT.
BRUCE'S FIRST RULE FOR FIGHTING SOMEONE IN HEAVY, MECHANIZED ARMOR...
"...THERE ALWAYS HAS TO BE A CONTROL BOX."
YOU'RE A TWIP WHO CHEATED AND STOLE HIS WAY TO THE TOP.
BLIGHT MAY HAVE FIGURED I'D UPGRADE THE BATARANGS FOR MORE PIERCING POWER, AND ARMORED THIS SPOT MORE HEAVILY...
...BUT THAT DOESN'T MEAN ANYTHING TO MAGNETIZED FINGERTIP PADS!
NO! STOP! THE PRESSURE IN THE SUIT...!
YOU'RE A LOUSY DAD WHO TRIED TO HAVE HIS OWN SON FRAMED AND MURDERED.
FACE IT, POWERS, YOU'RE NOT A MAN...
SKWOOOOOOM
...YOU'RE NOTHING BUT AN EMPTY SUIT OF CLOTHES.
"WHAT ARE YOU SAYING?"

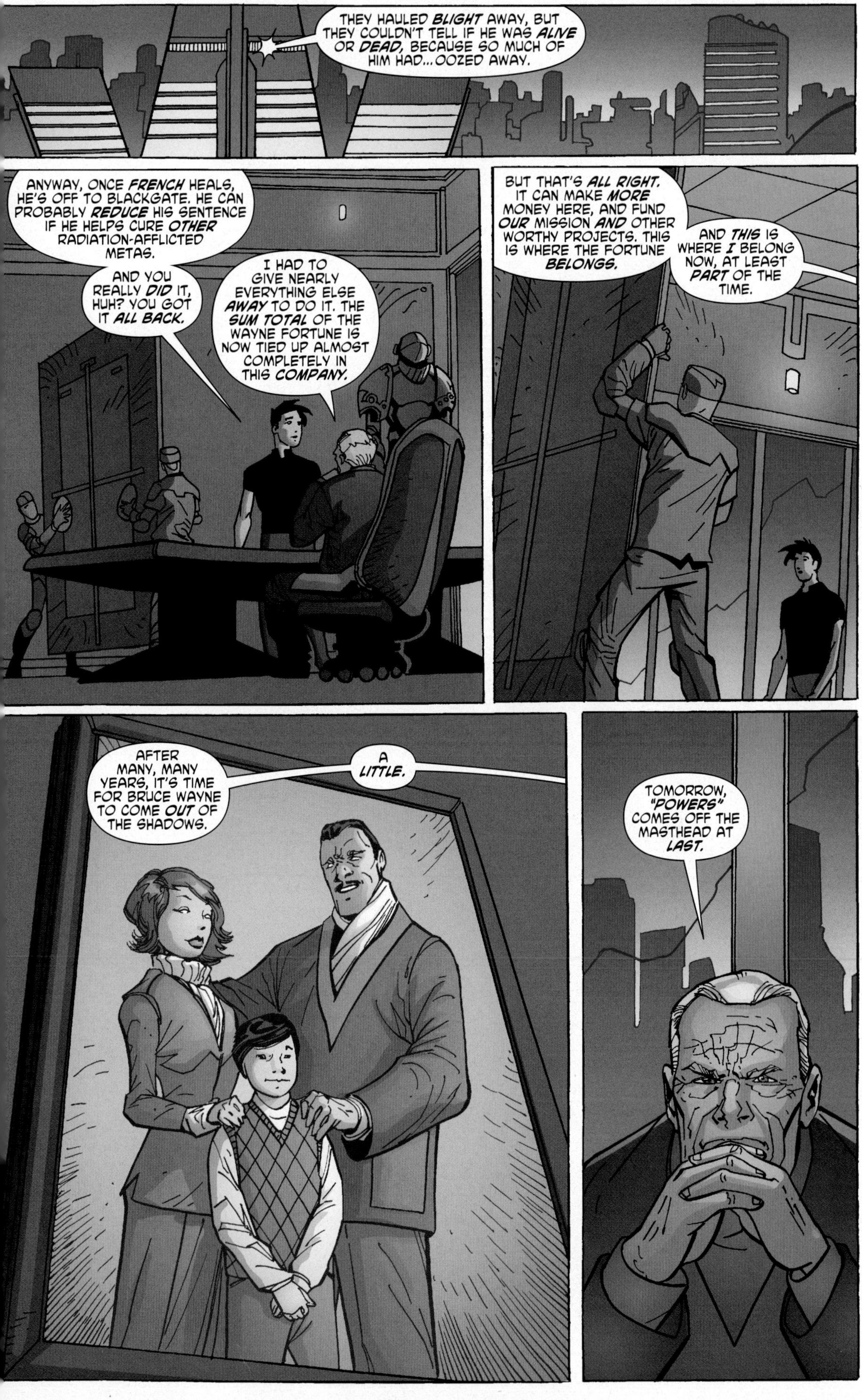
THEY HAULED BLIGHT AWAY, BUT THEY COULDN'T TELL IF HE WAS ALIVE OR DEAD, BECAUSE SO MUCH OF HIM HAD...OOZED AWAY.
ANYWAY, ONCE FRENCH HEALS, HE'S OFF TO BLACKGATE. HE CAN PROBABLY REDUCE HIS SENTENCE IF HE HELPS CURE OTHER RADIATION-AFFLICTED METAS.
AND YOU REALLY DID IT, HUH? YOU GOT IT ALL BACK.
I HAD TO GIVE NEARLY EVERYTHING ELSE AWAY TO DO IT. THE SUM TOTAL OF THE WAYNE FORTUNE IS NOW TIED UP ALMOST COMPLETELY IN THIS COMPANY.
BUT THAT'S ALL RIGHT. IT CAN MAKE MORE MONEY HERE, AND FUND OUR MISSION AND OTHER WORTHY PROJECTS. THIS IS WHERE THE FORTUNE BELONGS.
AND THIS IS WHERE I BELONG NOW, AT LEAST PART OF THE TIME.
AFTER MANY, MANY YEARS, IT'S TIME FOR BRUCE WAYNE TO COME OUT OF THE SHADOWS.
A LITTLE.
TOMORROW, "POWERS" COMES OFF THE MASTHEAD AT LAST.

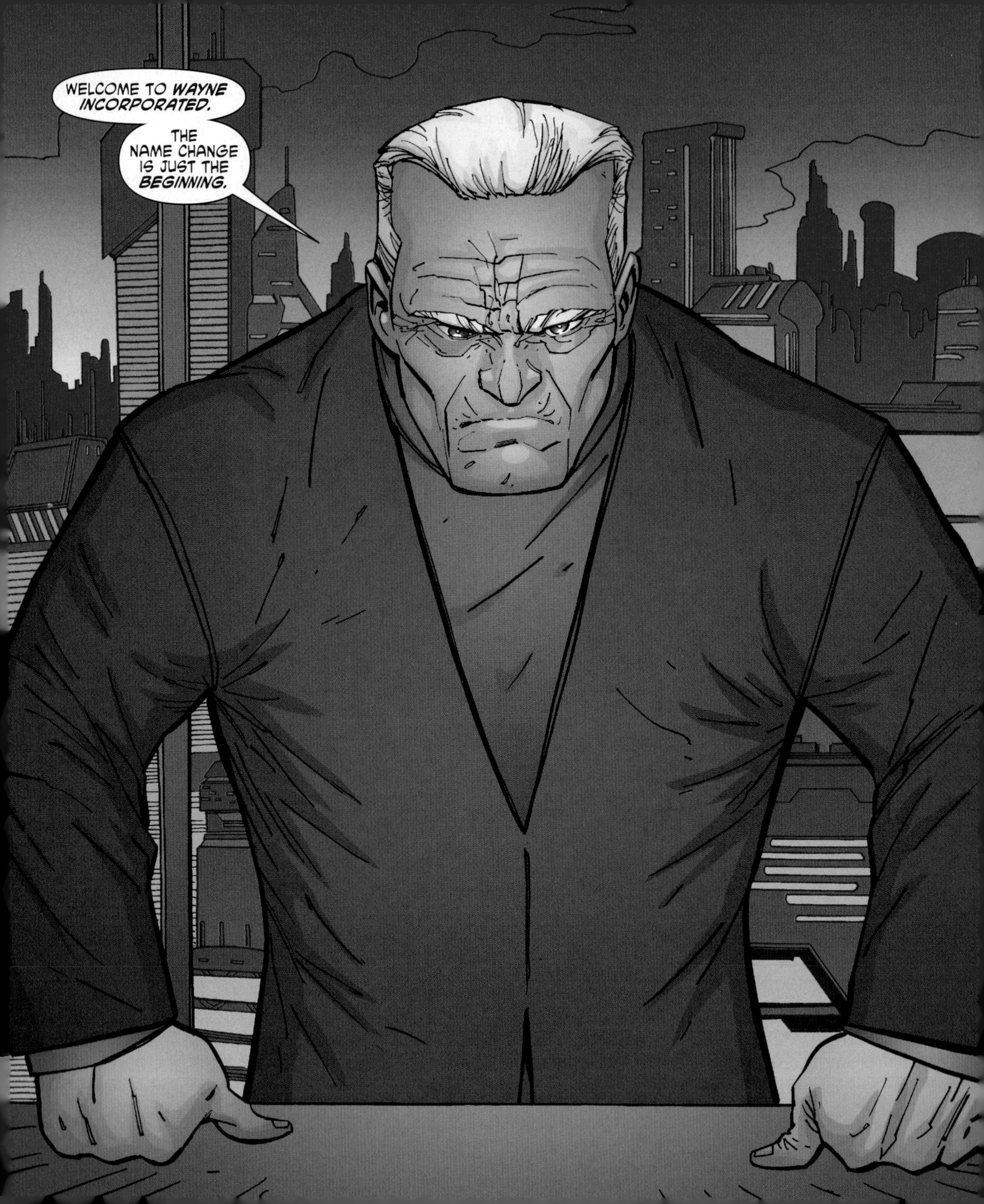
WELCOME TO *WAYNE INCORPORATED.*
THE NAME CHANGE IS JUST THE *BEGINNING.*

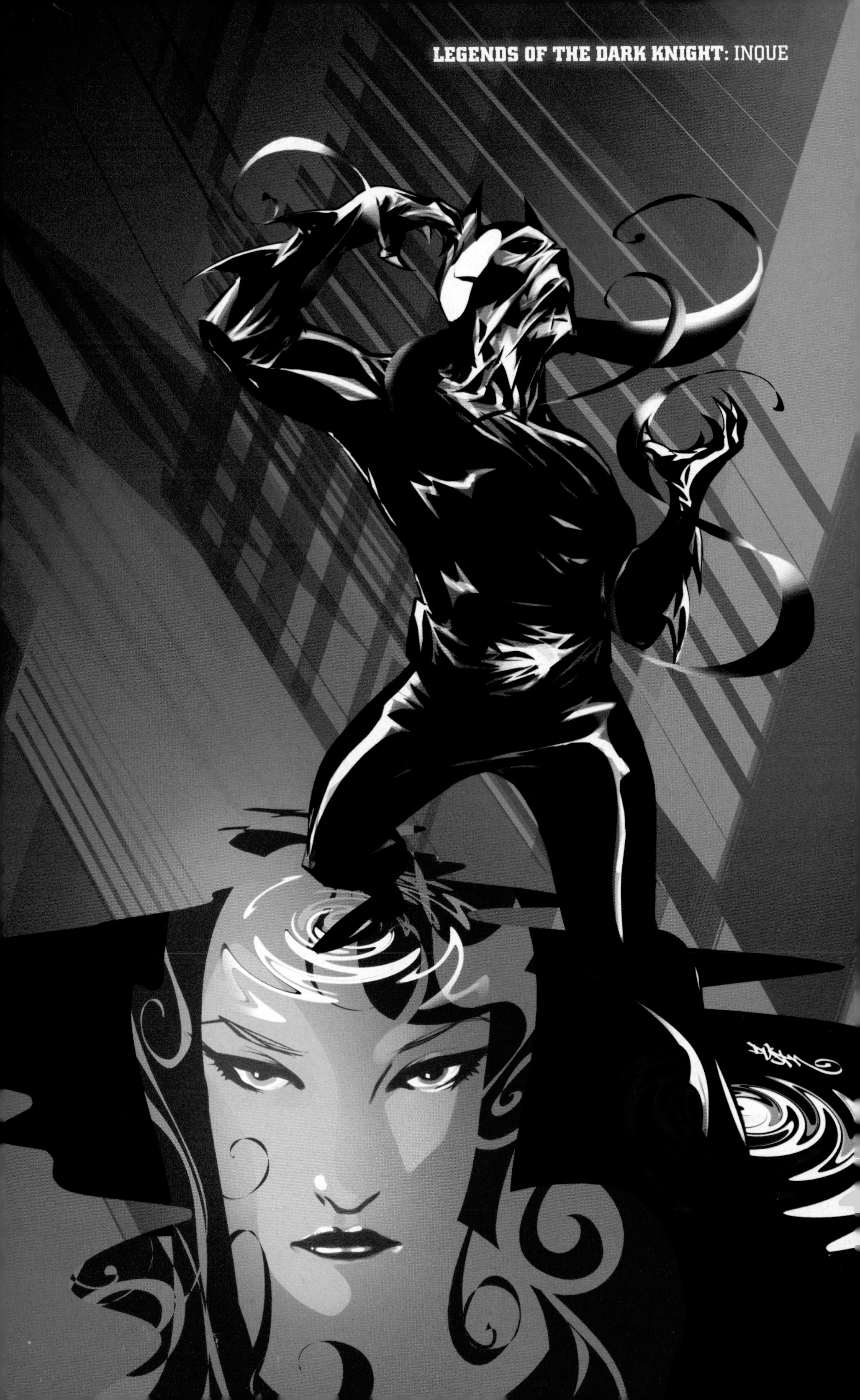

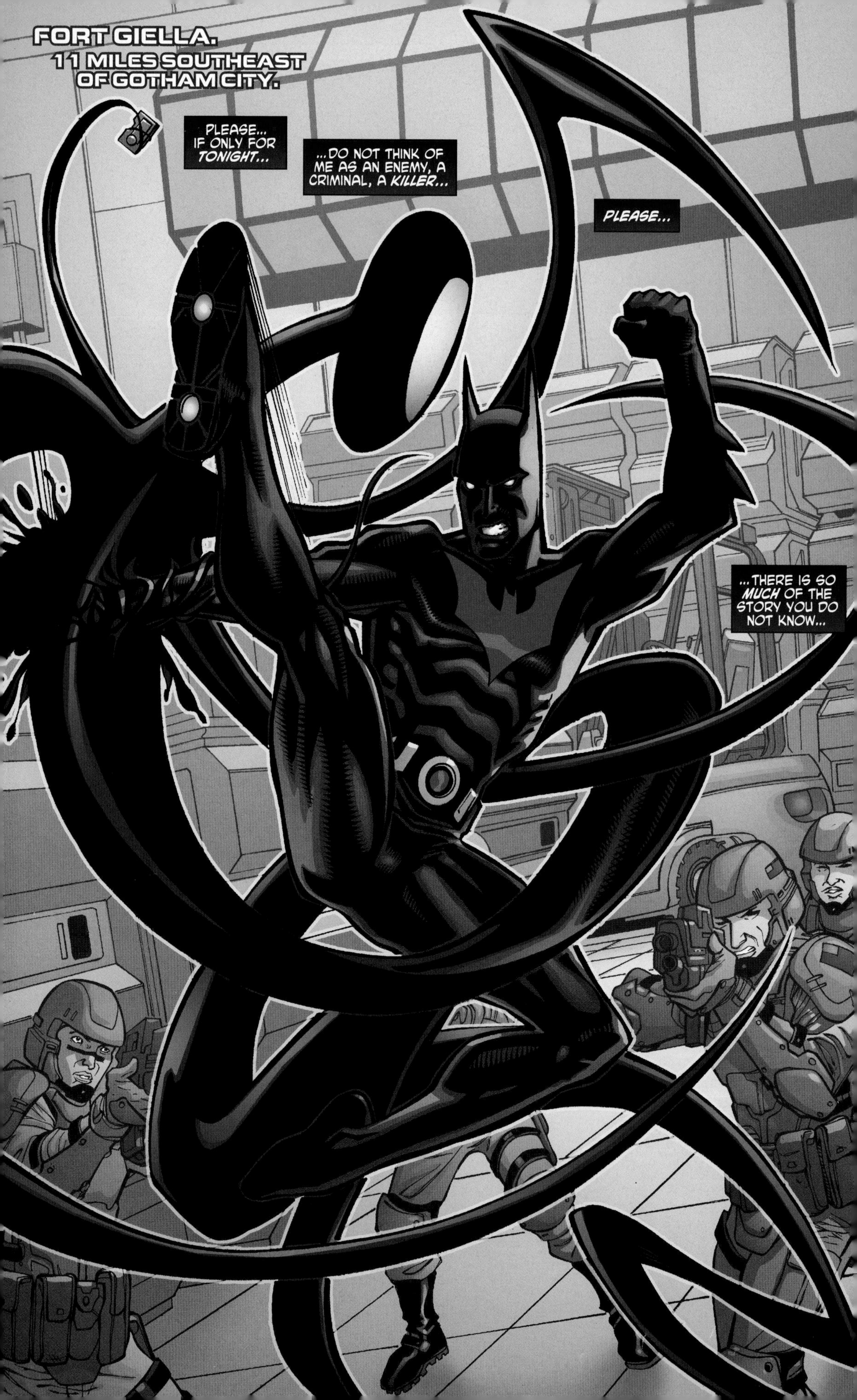
FORT GIELLA.
11 MILES SOUTHEAST OF GOTHAM CITY.
PLEASE... IF ONLY FOR TONIGHT...
...DO NOT THINK OF ME AS AN ENEMY, A CRIMINAL, A KILLER...
PLEASE...
...THERE IS SO MUCH OF THE STORY YOU DO NOT KNOW...

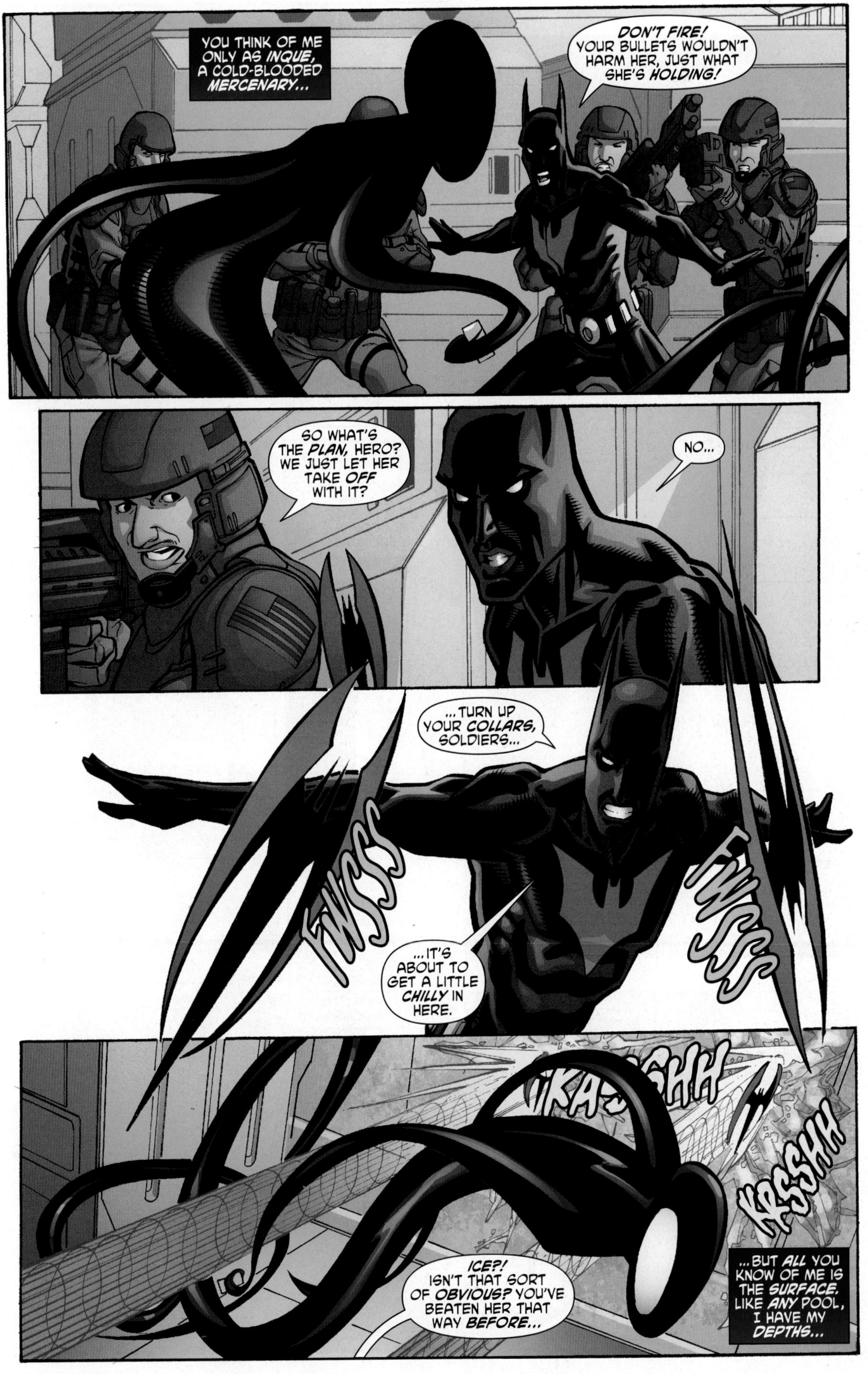
YOU THINK OF ME ONLY AS INQUE, A COLD-BLOODED MERCENARY...
DON'T FIRE! YOUR BULLETS WOULDN'T HARM HER, JUST WHAT SHE'S HOLDING!
SO WHAT'S THE PLAN, HERO? WE JUST LET HER TAKE OFF WITH IT?
NO...
...TURN UP YOUR COLLARS, SOLDIERS...
FWSSS
FWSSS
...IT'S ABOUT TO GET A LITTLE CHILLY IN HERE.
KRSSHH
ICE?! ISN'T THAT SORT OF OBVIOUS? YOU'VE BEATEN HER THAT WAY BEFORE...
...BUT ALL YOU KNOW OF ME IS THE SURFACE. LIKE ANY POOL, I HAVE MY DEPTHS...

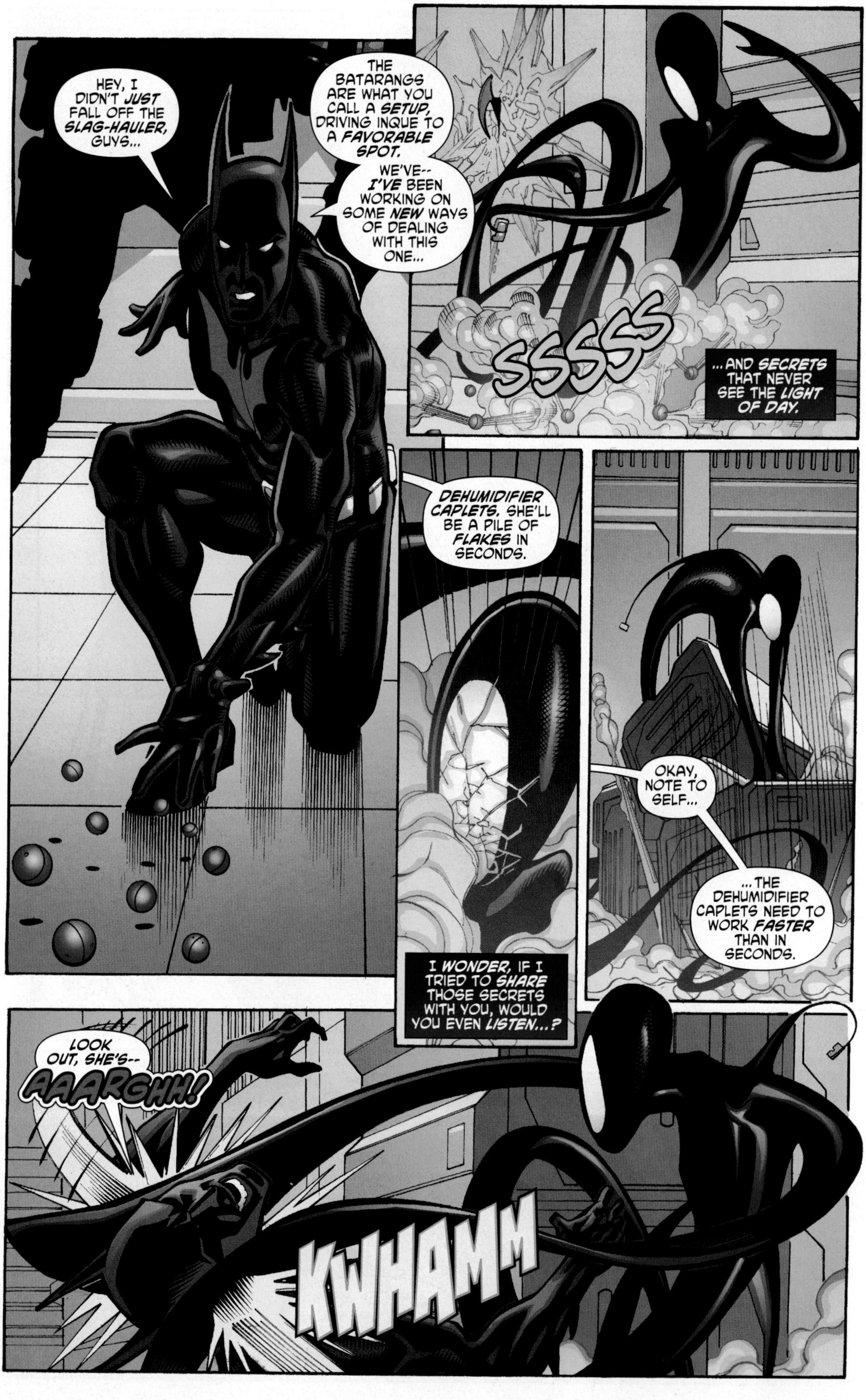
HEY, I DIDN'T JUST FALL OFF THE SLAG-HAULER, GUYS...
THE BATARANGS ARE WHAT YOU CALL A SETUP, DRIVING INQUE TO A FAVORABLE SPOT.
WE'VE-- I'VE BEEN WORKING ON SOME NEW WAYS OF DEALING WITH THIS ONE...
SSSSS
...AND SECRETS THAT NEVER SEE THE LIGHT OF DAY.
DEHUMIDIFIER CAPLETS. SHE'LL BE A PILE OF FLAKES IN SECONDS.
OKAY, NOTE TO SELF...
...THE DEHUMIDIFIER CAPLETS NEED TO WORK FASTER THAN IN SECONDS.
I WONDER, IF I TRIED TO SHARE THOSE SECRETS WITH YOU, WOULD YOU EVEN LISTEN...?
LOOK OUT, SHE'S--
AAARGHH!
KWHAMM

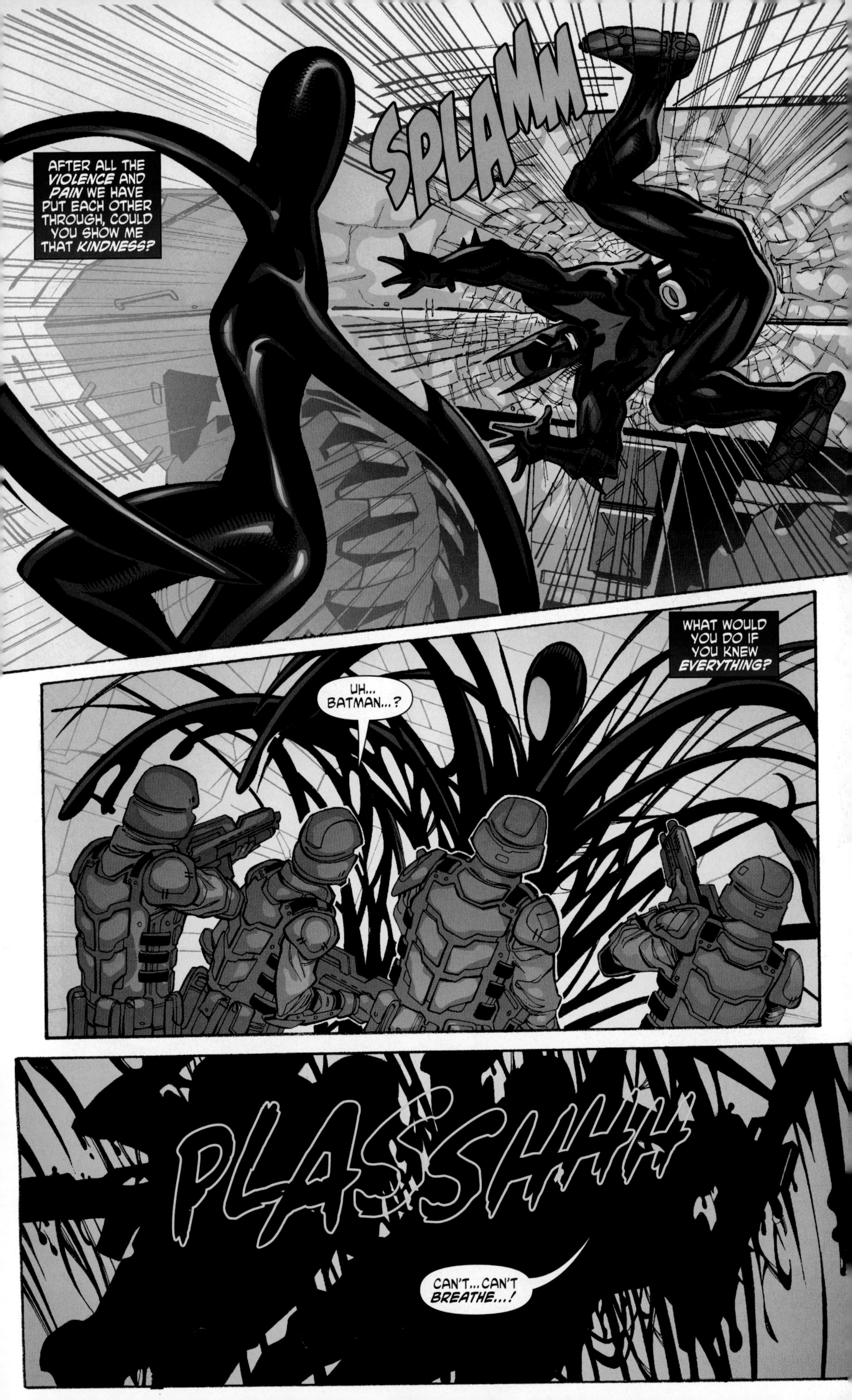
AFTER ALL THE VIOLENCE AND PAIN WE HAVE PUT EACH OTHER THROUGH, COULD YOU SHOW ME THAT KINDNESS?
SPLAMM
WHAT WOULD YOU DO IF YOU KNEW EVERYTHING?
UH... BATMAN...?
PLASHHH
CAN'T... CAN'T BREATHE...!

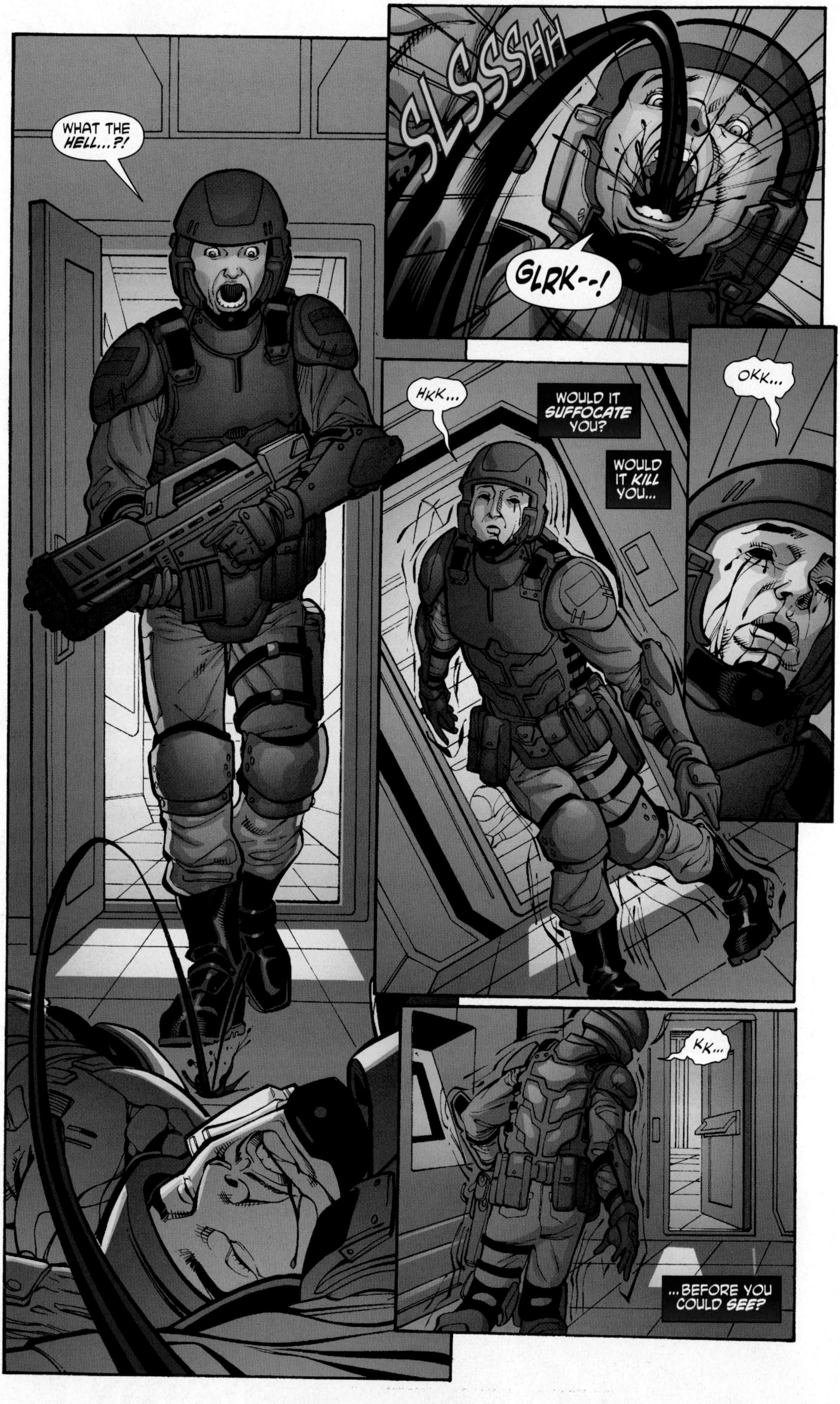
WHAT THE HELL...?!
SLSSSHH
GLRK--!
HKK...
WOULD IT SUFFOCATE YOU?
WOULD IT KILL YOU...
OKK...
KK...
...BEFORE YOU COULD SEE?

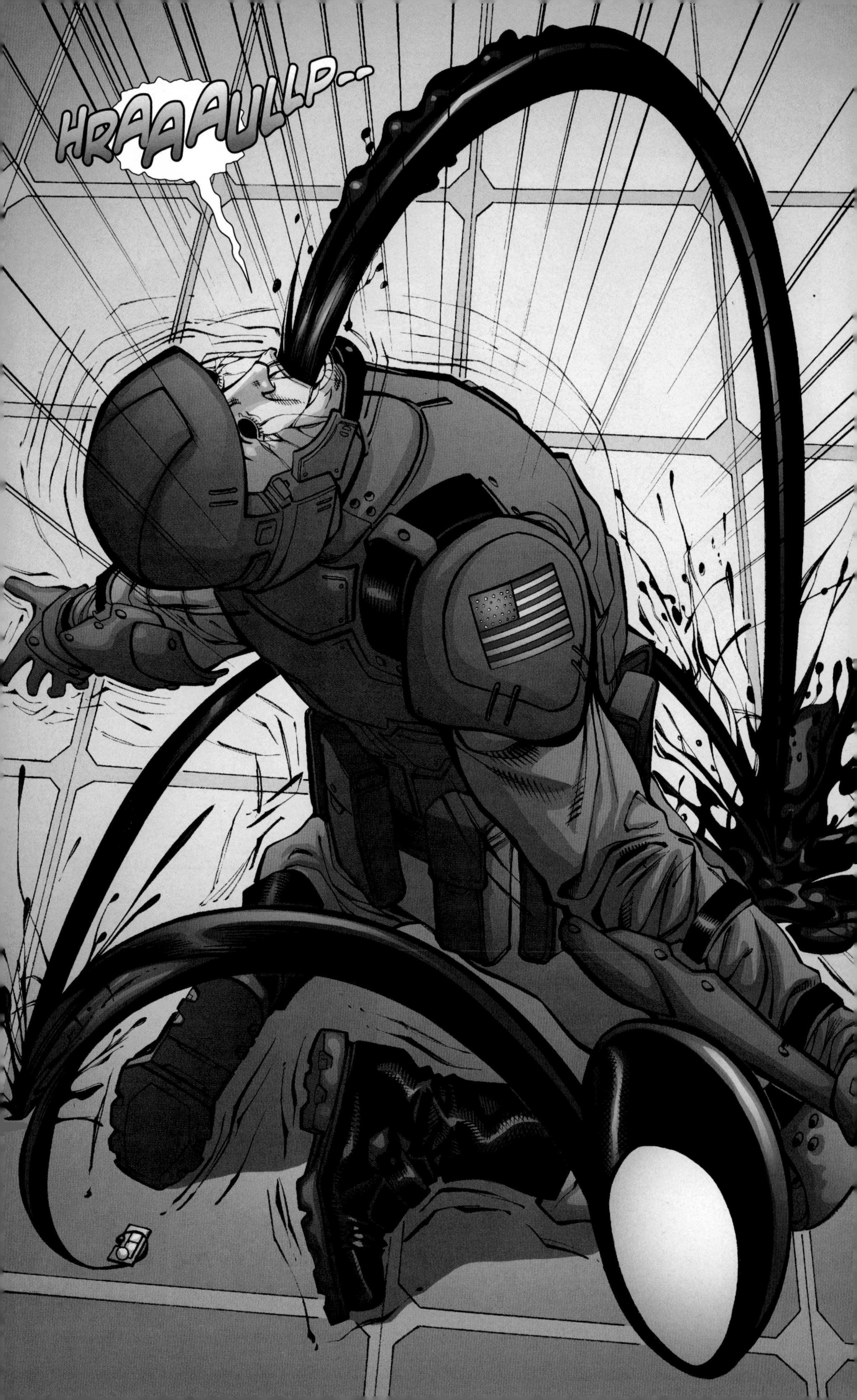
HRAAAAULLP--

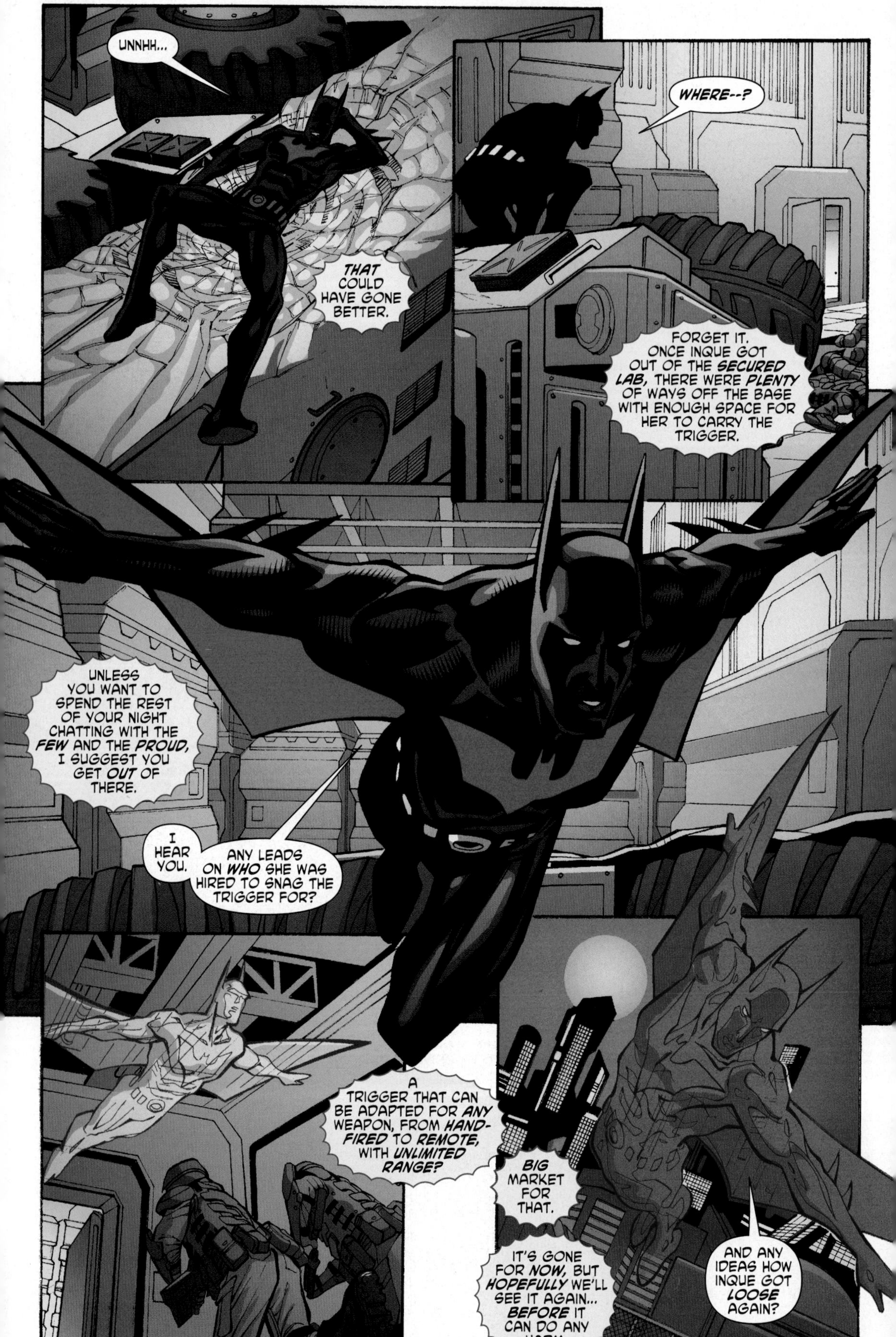
UNNHH...
THAT COULD HAVE GONE BETTER.
WHERE--?
FORGET IT. ONCE INQUE GOT OUT OF THE SECURED LAB, THERE WERE PLENTY OF WAYS OFF THE BASE WITH ENOUGH SPACE FOR HER TO CARRY THE TRIGGER.
UNLESS YOU WANT TO SPEND THE REST OF YOUR NIGHT CHATTING WITH THE FEW AND THE PROUD, I SUGGEST YOU GET OUT OF THERE.
I HEAR YOU.
ANY LEADS ON WHO SHE WAS HIRED TO SNAG THE TRIGGER FOR?
A TRIGGER THAT CAN BE ADAPTED FOR ANY WEAPON, FROM HAND-FIRED TO REMOTE, WITH UNLIMITED RANGE?
BIG MARKET FOR THAT.
IT'S GONE FOR NOW, BUT HOPEFULLY WE'LL SEE IT AGAIN... BEFORE IT CAN DO ANY HARM.
AND ANY IDEAS HOW INQUE GOT LOOSE AGAIN?

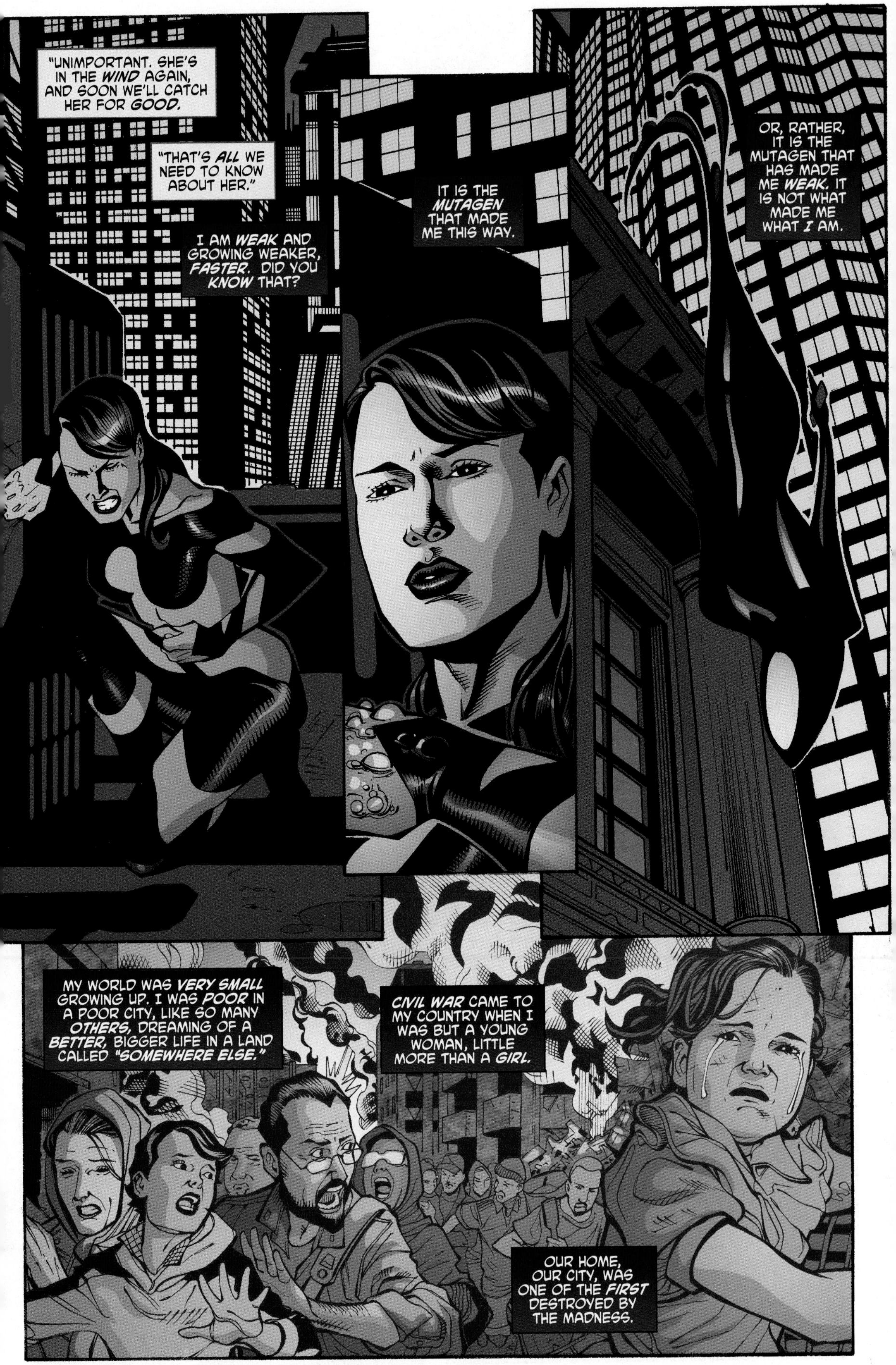
"UNIMPORTANT. SHE'S IN THE *WIND* AGAIN, AND SOON WE'LL CATCH HER FOR *GOOD*.
"THAT'S *ALL* WE NEED TO KNOW ABOUT HER."
I AM *WEAK* AND GROWING WEAKER, *FASTER*. DID YOU *KNOW* THAT?
IT IS THE *MUTAGEN* THAT MADE ME THIS WAY.
OR, RATHER, IT IS THE MUTAGEN THAT HAS MADE ME *WEAK*. IT IS NOT WHAT MADE ME WHAT *I* AM.
MY WORLD WAS *VERY SMALL* GROWING UP. I WAS *POOR* IN A POOR CITY, LIKE SO MANY *OTHERS*, DREAMING OF A *BETTER*, BIGGER LIFE IN A LAND CALLED *"SOMEWHERE ELSE."*
CIVIL WAR CAME TO MY COUNTRY WHEN I WAS BUT A YOUNG WOMAN, LITTLE MORE THAN A *GIRL*.
OUR HOME, OUR CITY, WAS ONE OF THE *FIRST* DESTROYED BY THE MADNESS.

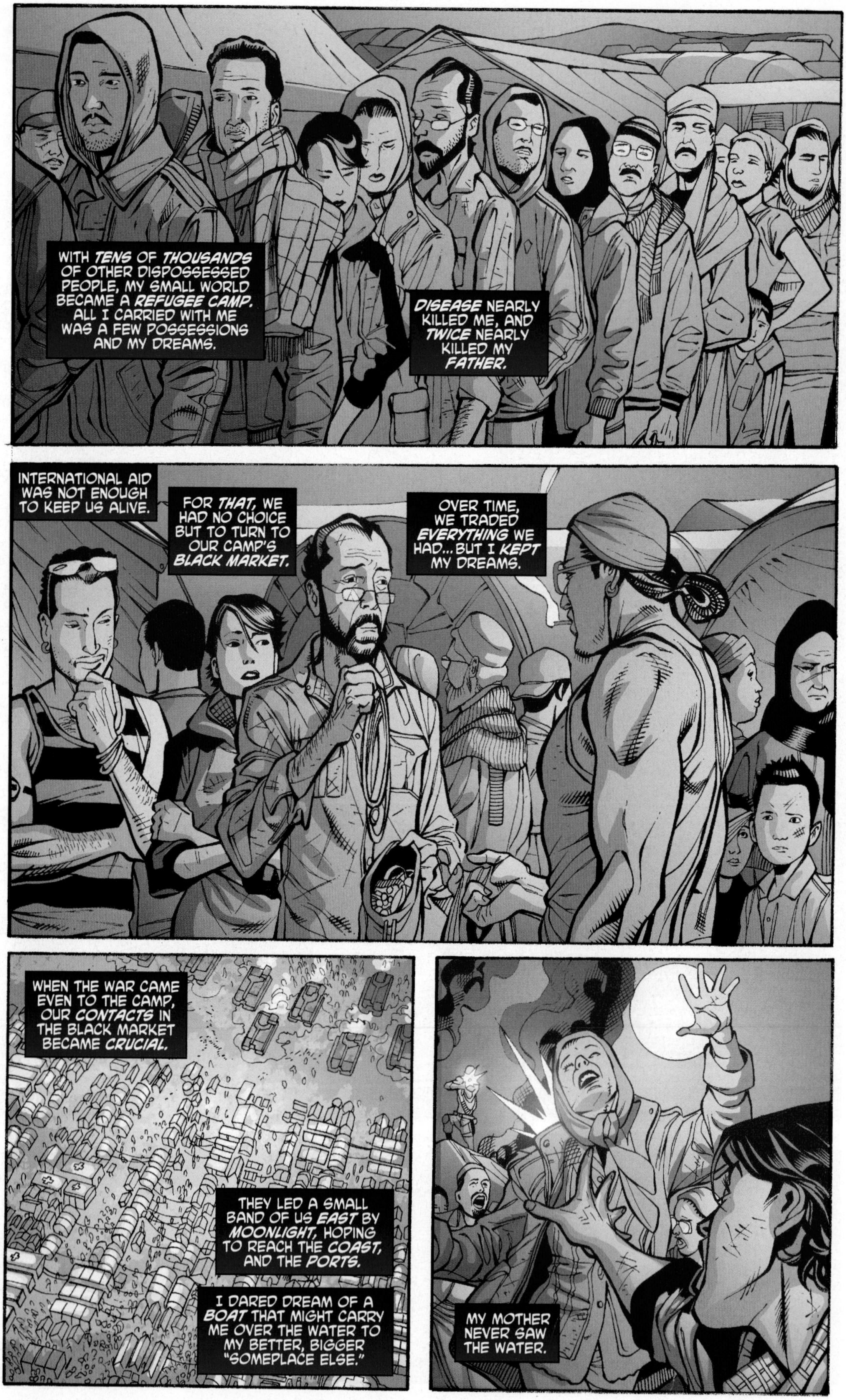
WITH TENS OF THOUSANDS OF OTHER DISPOSSESSED PEOPLE, MY SMALL WORLD BECAME A REFUGEE CAMP. ALL I CARRIED WITH ME WAS A FEW POSSESSIONS AND MY DREAMS.
DISEASE NEARLY KILLED ME, AND TWICE NEARLY KILLED MY FATHER.
INTERNATIONAL AID WAS NOT ENOUGH TO KEEP US ALIVE.
FOR THAT, WE HAD NO CHOICE BUT TO TURN TO OUR CAMP'S BLACK MARKET.
OVER TIME, WE TRADED EVERYTHING WE HAD... BUT I KEPT MY DREAMS.
WHEN THE WAR CAME EVEN TO THE CAMP, OUR CONTACTS IN THE BLACK MARKET BECAME CRUCIAL.
THEY LED A SMALL BAND OF US EAST BY MOONLIGHT, HOPING TO REACH THE COAST, AND THE PORTS.
I DARED DREAM OF A BOAT THAT MIGHT CARRY ME OVER THE WATER TO MY BETTER, BIGGER "SOMEPLACE ELSE."
MY MOTHER NEVER SAW THE WATER.

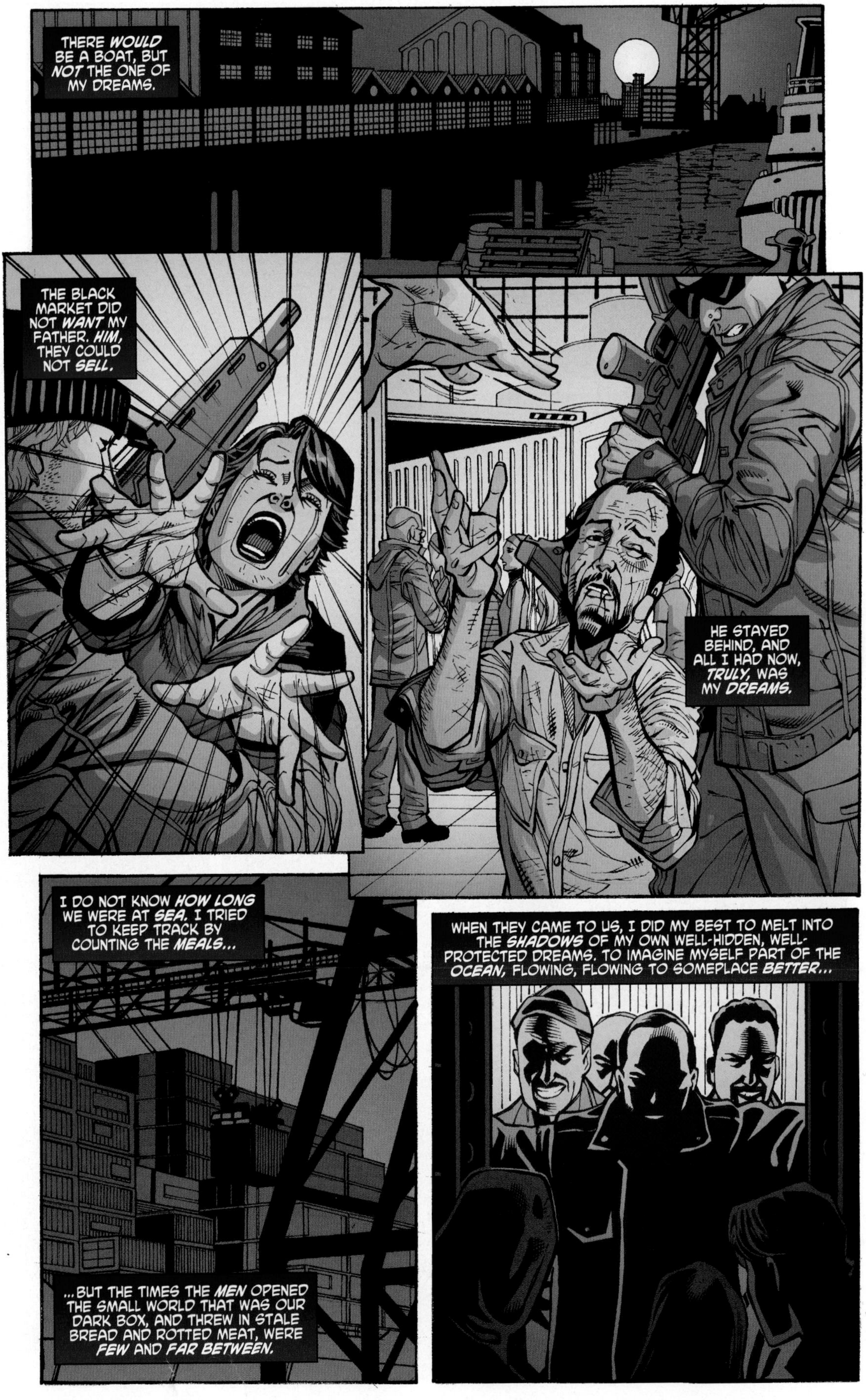
THERE WOULD BE A BOAT, BUT NOT THE ONE OF MY DREAMS.
THE BLACK MARKET DID NOT WANT MY FATHER. HIM, THEY COULD NOT SELL.
HE STAYED BEHIND, AND ALL I HAD NOW, TRULY, WAS MY DREAMS.
I DO NOT KNOW HOW LONG WE WERE AT SEA. I TRIED TO KEEP TRACK BY COUNTING THE MEALS...
...BUT THE TIMES THE MEN OPENED THE SMALL WORLD THAT WAS OUR DARK BOX, AND THREW IN STALE BREAD AND ROTTED MEAT, WERE FEW AND FAR BETWEEN.
WHEN THEY CAME TO US, I DID MY BEST TO MELT INTO THE SHADOWS OF MY OWN WELL-HIDDEN, WELL-PROTECTED DREAMS. TO IMAGINE MYSELF PART OF THE OCEAN, FLOWING, FLOWING TO SOMEPLACE BETTER...

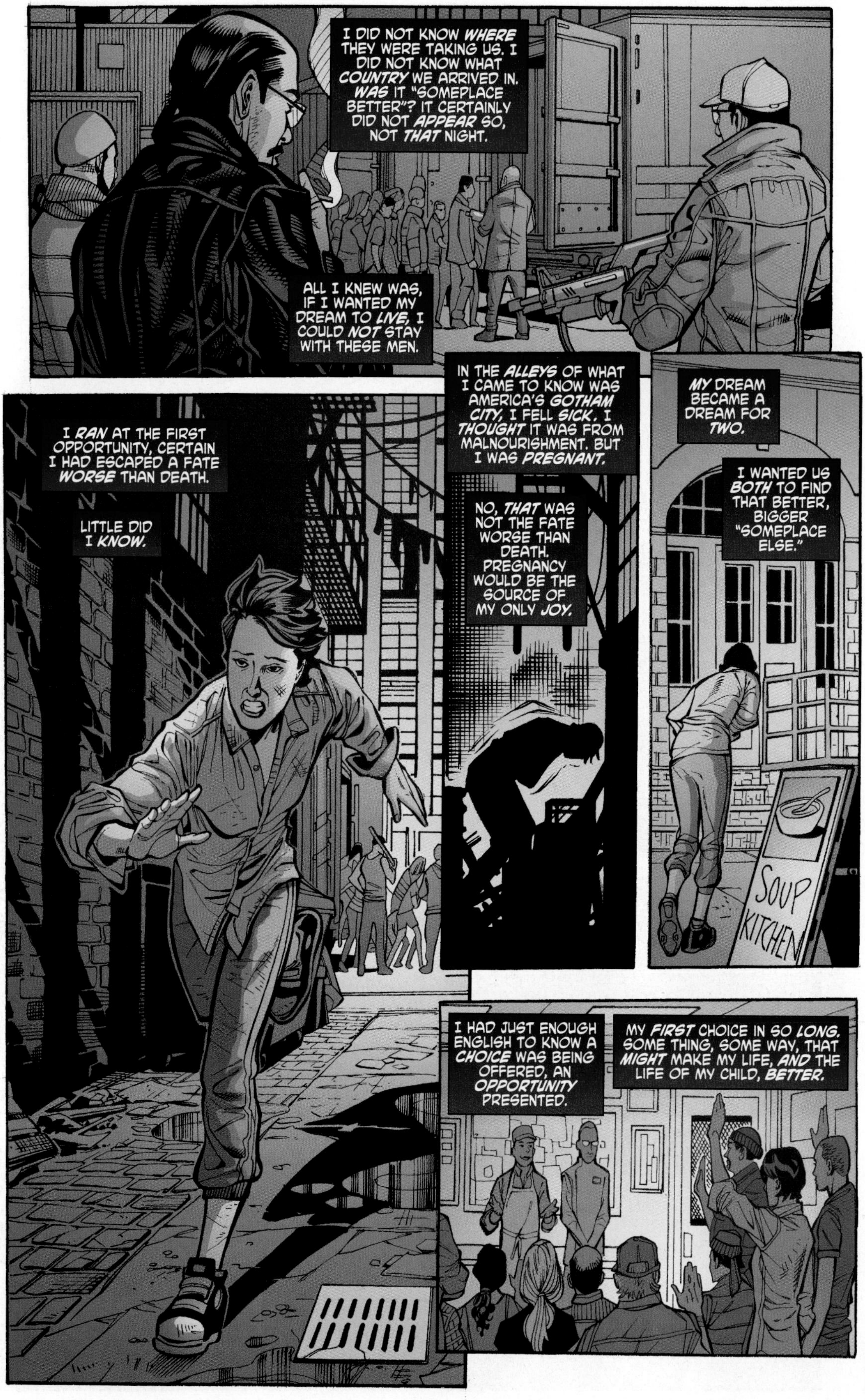
I DID NOT KNOW WHERE THEY WERE TAKING US. I DID NOT KNOW WHAT COUNTRY WE ARRIVED IN. WAS IT "SOMEPLACE BETTER"? IT CERTAINLY DID NOT APPEAR SO, NOT THAT NIGHT.
ALL I KNEW WAS, IF I WANTED MY DREAM TO LIVE, I COULD NOT STAY WITH THESE MEN.
I RAN AT THE FIRST OPPORTUNITY, CERTAIN I HAD ESCAPED A FATE WORSE THAN DEATH.
LITTLE DID I KNOW.
IN THE ALLEYS OF WHAT I CAME TO KNOW WAS AMERICA'S GOTHAM CITY, I FELL SICK. I THOUGHT IT WAS FROM MALNOURISHMENT. BUT I WAS PREGNANT.
NO, THAT WAS NOT THE FATE WORSE THAN DEATH. PREGNANCY WOULD BE THE SOURCE OF MY ONLY JOY.
MY DREAM BECAME A DREAM FOR TWO.
I WANTED US BOTH TO FIND THAT BETTER, BIGGER "SOMEPLACE ELSE."
SOUP KITCHEN
I HAD JUST ENOUGH ENGLISH TO KNOW A CHOICE WAS BEING OFFERED, AN OPPORTUNITY PRESENTED.
MY FIRST CHOICE IN SO LONG. SOME THING, SOME WAY, THAT MIGHT MAKE MY LIFE, AND THE LIFE OF MY CHILD, BETTER.

I WAS PUT INTO *ANOTHER* CONTAINER, *ANOTHER* SMALL WORLD...

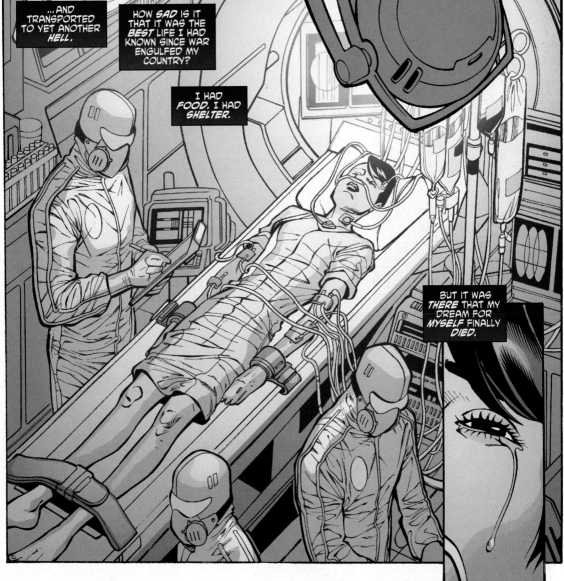

...AND TRANSPORTED TO YET ANOTHER *HELL.*

HOW *SAD* IS IT THAT IT WAS THE *BEST* LIFE I HAD KNOWN SINCE WAR ENGULFED MY COUNTRY?

I HAD *FOOD.* I HAD SHELTER.

BUT IT WAS *THERE* THAT MY DREAM FOR *MYSELF* FINALLY *DIED.*

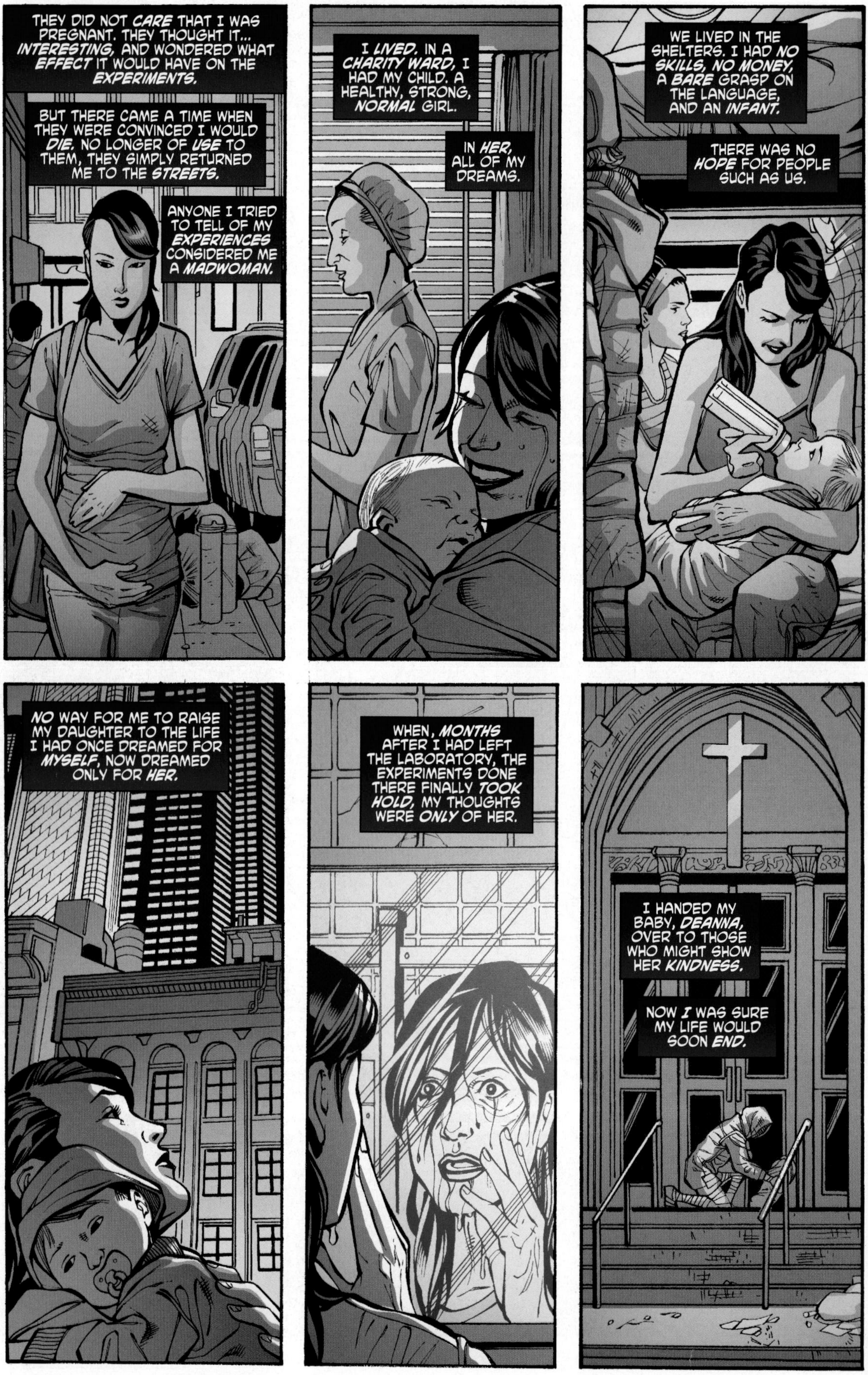
THEY DID NOT CARE THAT I WAS PREGNANT. THEY THOUGHT IT... INTERESTING, AND WONDERED WHAT EFFECT IT WOULD HAVE ON THE EXPERIMENTS.
BUT THERE CAME A TIME WHEN THEY WERE CONVINCED I WOULD DIE. NO LONGER OF USE TO THEM, THEY SIMPLY RETURNED ME TO THE STREETS.
ANYONE I TRIED TO TELL OF MY EXPERIENCES CONSIDERED ME A MADWOMAN.
I LIVED. IN A CHARITY WARD, I HAD MY CHILD. A HEALTHY, STRONG, NORMAL GIRL.
IN HER, ALL OF MY DREAMS.
WE LIVED IN THE SHELTERS. I HAD NO SKILLS, NO MONEY, A BARE GRASP ON THE LANGUAGE, AND AN INFANT.
THERE WAS NO HOPE FOR PEOPLE SUCH AS US.
NO WAY FOR ME TO RAISE MY DAUGHTER TO THE LIFE I HAD ONCE DREAMED FOR MYSELF, NOW DREAMED ONLY FOR HER.
WHEN, MONTHS AFTER I HAD LEFT THE LABORATORY, THE EXPERIMENTS DONE THERE FINALLY TOOK HOLD, MY THOUGHTS WERE ONLY OF HER.
I HANDED MY BABY, DEANNA, OVER TO THOSE WHO MIGHT SHOW HER KINDNESS.
NOW I WAS SURE MY LIFE WOULD SOON END.

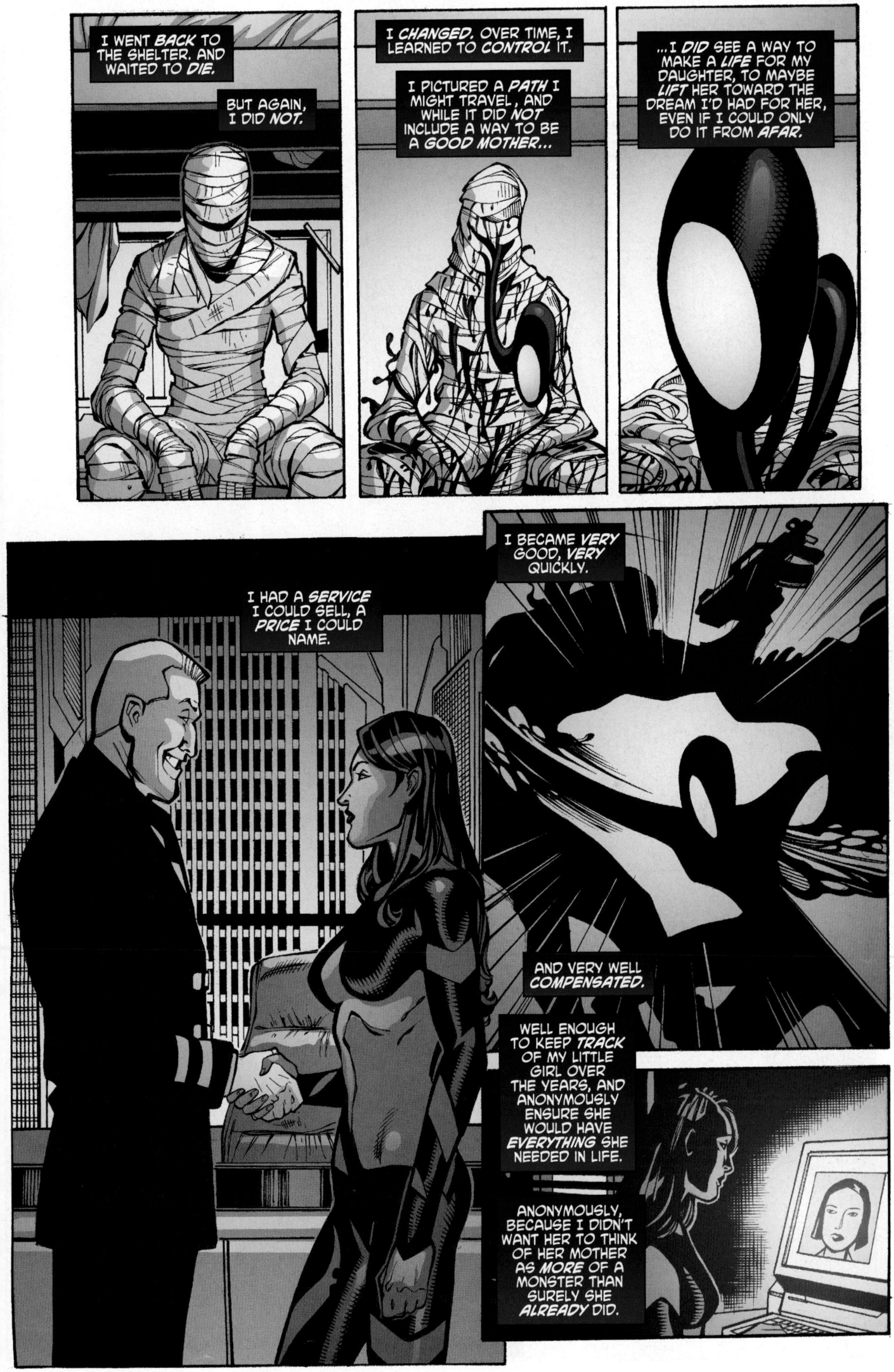
I WENT BACK TO THE SHELTER. AND WAITED TO DIE.
BUT AGAIN, I DID NOT.
I CHANGED. OVER TIME, I LEARNED TO CONTROL IT.
I PICTURED A PATH I MIGHT TRAVEL, AND WHILE IT DID NOT INCLUDE A WAY TO BE A GOOD MOTHER...
...I DID SEE A WAY TO MAKE A LIFE FOR MY DAUGHTER, TO MAYBE LIFT HER TOWARD THE DREAM I'D HAD FOR HER, EVEN IF I COULD ONLY DO IT FROM AFAR.
I HAD A SERVICE I COULD SELL, A PRICE I COULD NAME.
I BECAME VERY GOOD, VERY QUICKLY.
AND VERY WELL COMPENSATED.
WELL ENOUGH TO KEEP TRACK OF MY LITTLE GIRL OVER THE YEARS, AND ANONYMOUSLY ENSURE SHE WOULD HAVE EVERYTHING SHE NEEDED IN LIFE.
ANONYMOUSLY, BECAUSE I DIDN'T WANT HER TO THINK OF HER MOTHER AS MORE OF A MONSTER THAN SURELY SHE ALREADY DID.

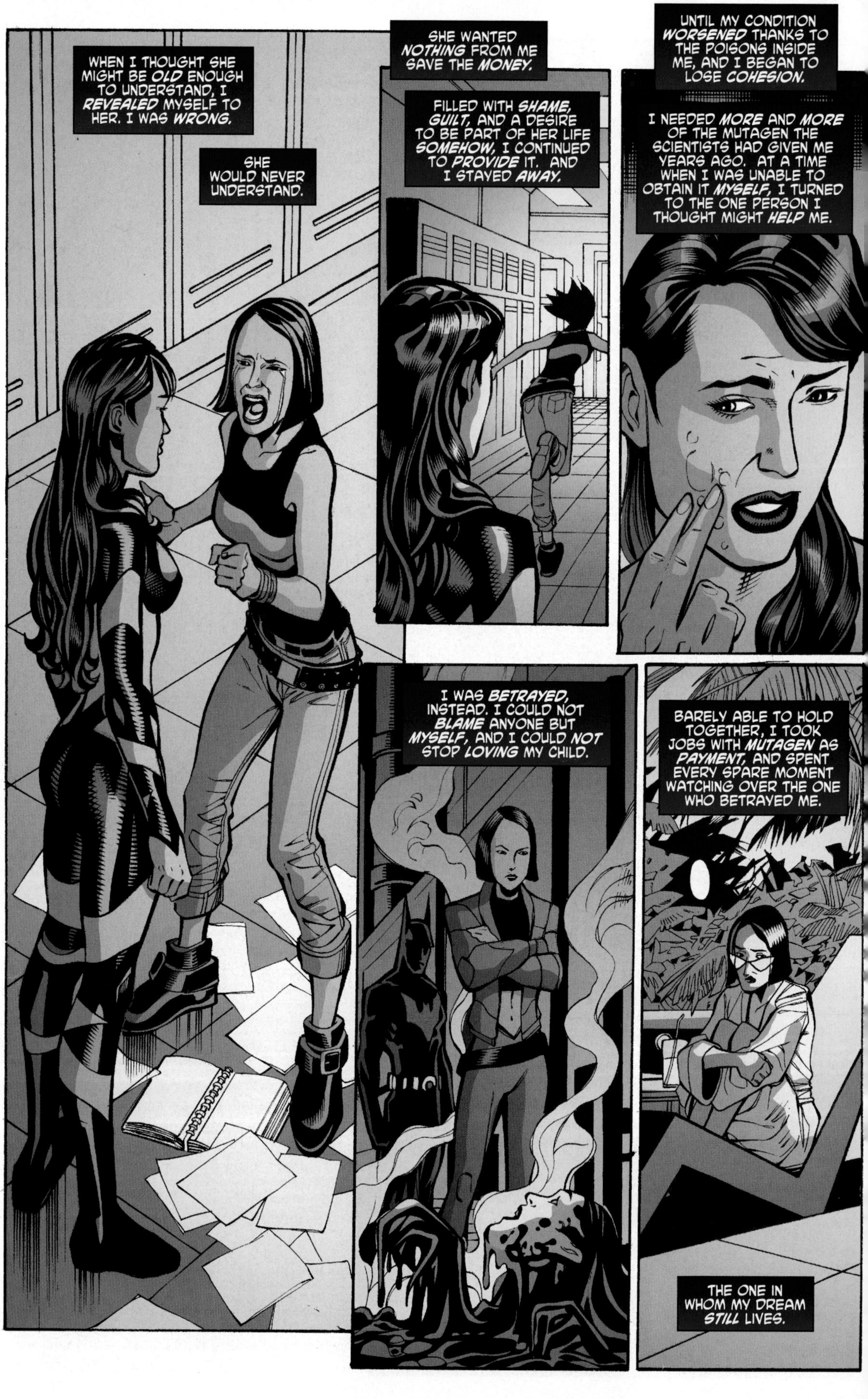
WHEN I THOUGHT SHE MIGHT BE OLD ENOUGH TO UNDERSTAND, I REVEALED MYSELF TO HER. I WAS WRONG.
SHE WOULD NEVER UNDERSTAND.
SHE WANTED NOTHING FROM ME SAVE THE MONEY.
FILLED WITH SHAME, GUILT, AND A DESIRE TO BE PART OF HER LIFE SOMEHOW, I CONTINUED TO PROVIDE IT. AND I STAYED AWAY.
UNTIL MY CONDITION WORSENED THANKS TO THE POISONS INSIDE ME, AND I BEGAN TO LOSE COHESION.
I NEEDED MORE AND MORE OF THE MUTAGEN THE SCIENTISTS HAD GIVEN ME YEARS AGO. AT A TIME WHEN I WAS UNABLE TO OBTAIN IT MYSELF, I TURNED TO THE ONE PERSON I THOUGHT MIGHT HELP ME.
I WAS BETRAYED, INSTEAD. I COULD NOT BLAME ANYONE BUT MYSELF, AND I COULD NOT STOP LOVING MY CHILD.
BARELY ABLE TO HOLD TOGETHER, I TOOK JOBS WITH MUTAGEN AS PAYMENT, AND SPENT EVERY SPARE MOMENT WATCHING OVER THE ONE WHO BETRAYED ME.
THE ONE IN WHOM MY DREAM STILL LIVES.

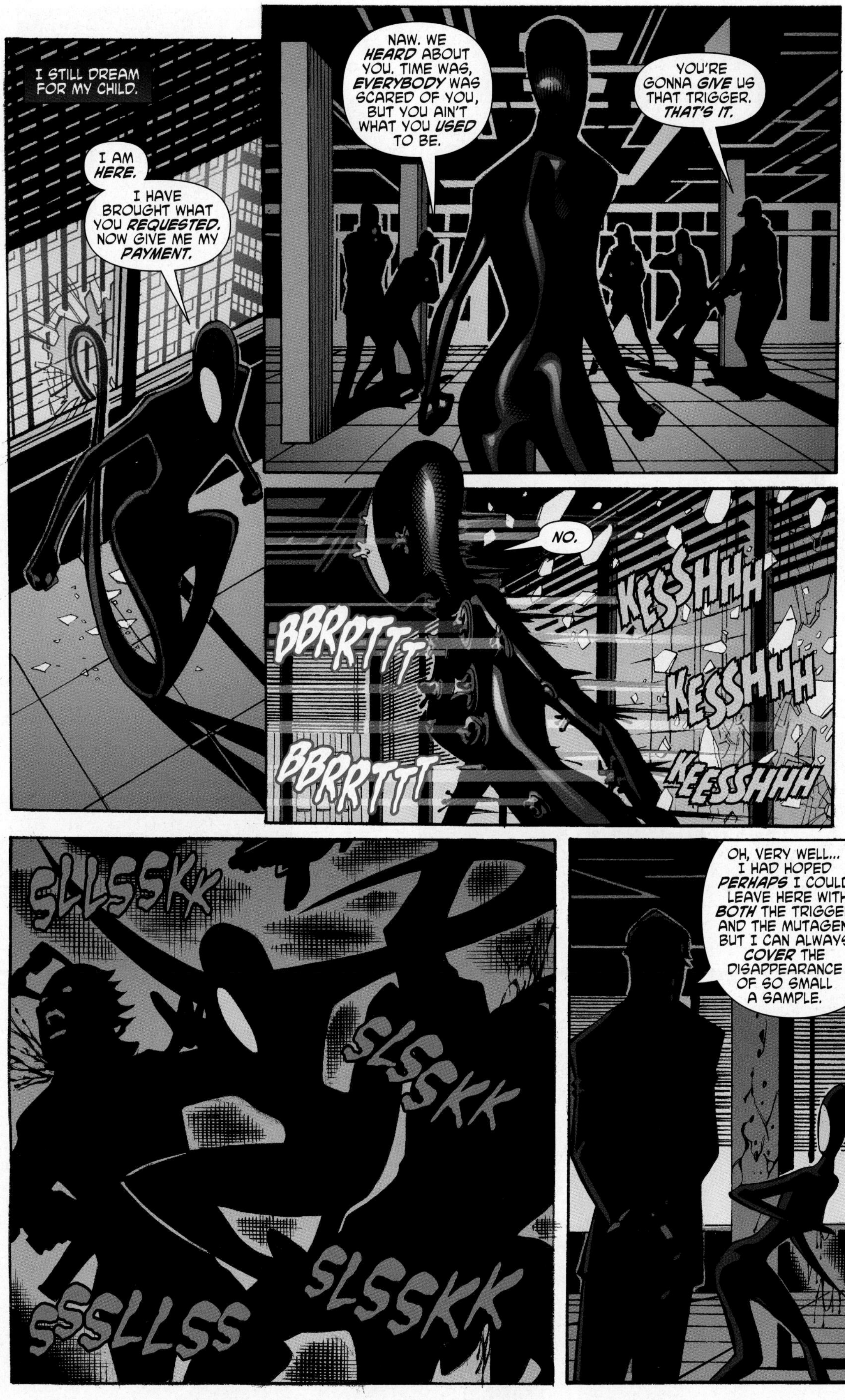
I STILL DREAM FOR MY CHILD.
I AM HERE.
I HAVE BROUGHT WHAT YOU REQUESTED. NOW GIVE ME MY PAYMENT.
NAW. WE HEARD ABOUT YOU. TIME WAS, EVERYBODY WAS SCARED OF YOU, BUT YOU AIN'T WHAT YOU USED TO BE.
YOU'RE GONNA GIVE US THAT TRIGGER. THAT'S IT.
NO.
KESSHHH
KESSHHH
KEESSHHH
BBRRTTT
BBRRTTT
SLLSSKK
SLSSKK
SLSSKK
SSSLLSS
OH, VERY WELL... I HAD HOPED PERHAPS I COULD LEAVE HERE WITH BOTH THE TRIGGER AND THE MUTAGEN, BUT I CAN ALWAYS COVER THE DISAPPEARANCE OF SO SMALL A SAMPLE.

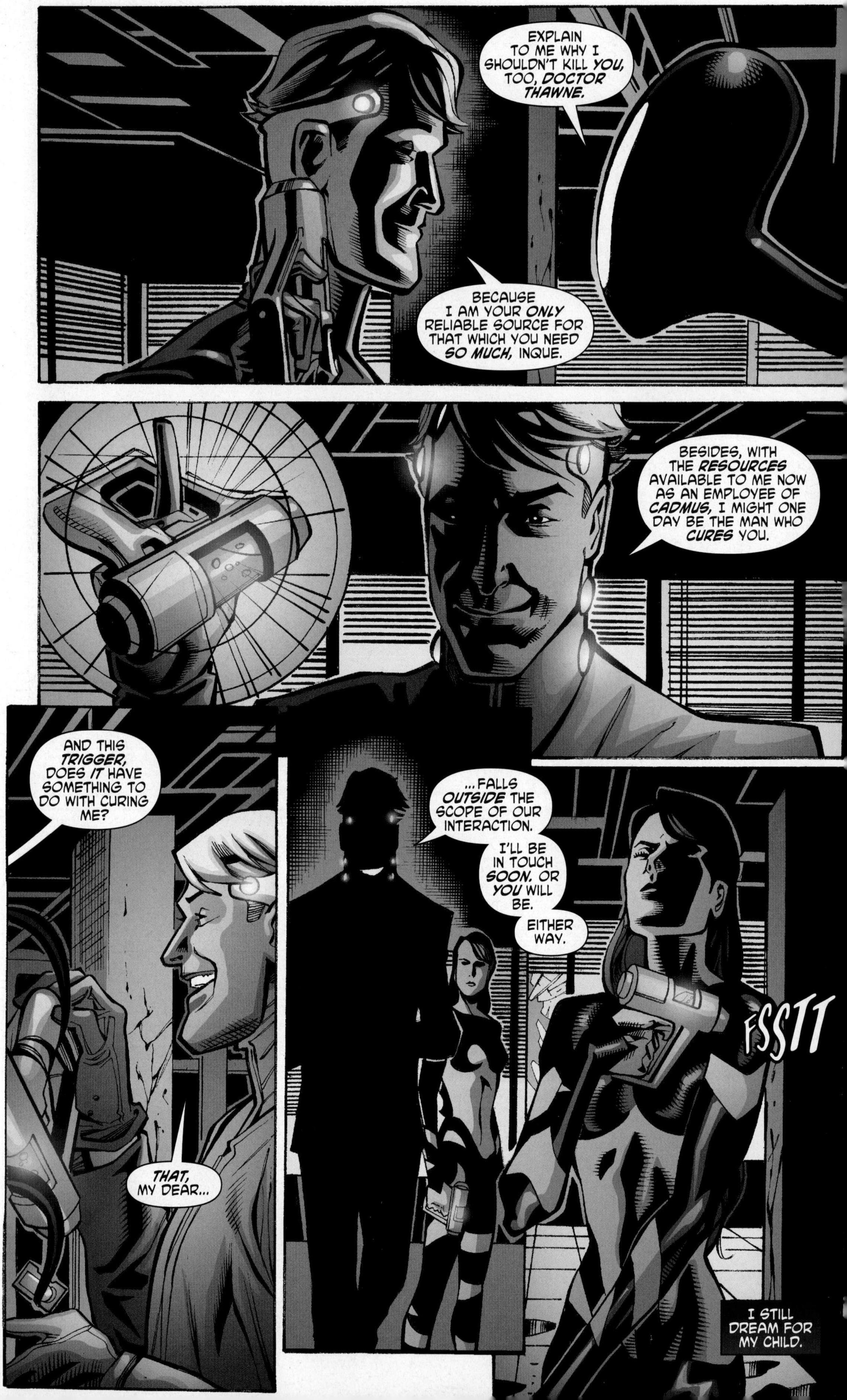
EXPLAIN TO ME WHY I SHOULDN'T KILL *YOU,* TOO, *DOCTOR THAWNE.*
BECAUSE I AM YOUR *ONLY* RELIABLE SOURCE FOR THAT WHICH YOU NEED *SO MUCH,* INQUE.
BESIDES, WITH THE *RESOURCES* AVAILABLE TO ME NOW AS AN EMPLOYEE OF *CADMUS,* I MIGHT ONE DAY BE THE MAN WHO *CURES* YOU.
AND THIS *TRIGGER,* DOES *IT* HAVE SOMETHING TO DO WITH CURING ME?
THAT, MY DEAR...
...FALLS *OUTSIDE* THE SCOPE OF OUR INTERACTION.
I'LL BE IN TOUCH *SOON.* OR *YOU* WILL BE.
EITHER WAY.
FSSTT
I STILL DREAM FOR MY CHILD.

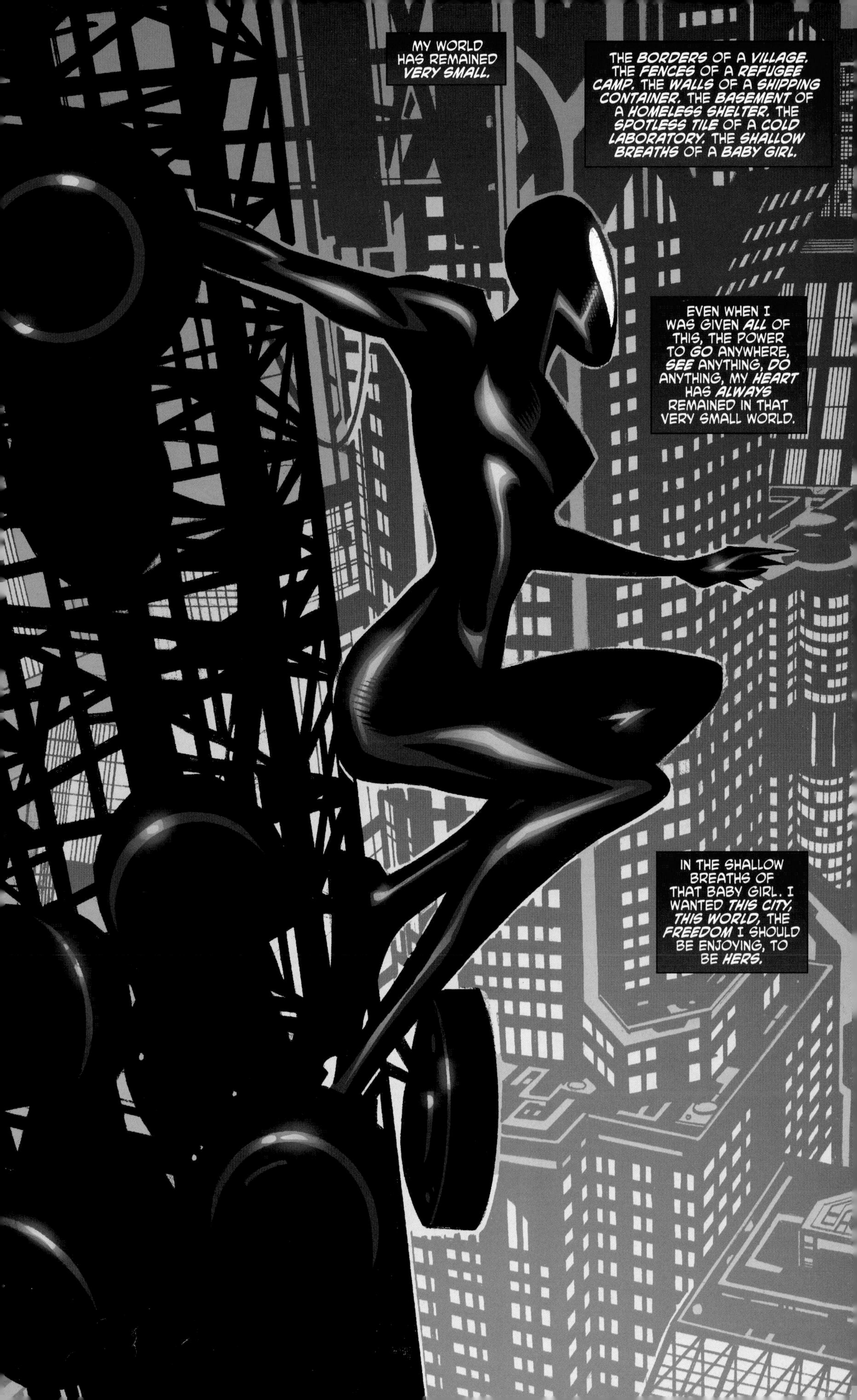
MY WORLD HAS REMAINED *VERY SMALL.*
THE *BORDERS* OF A *VILLAGE.* THE *FENCES* OF A *REFUGEE CAMP.* THE *WALLS* OF A *SHIPPING CONTAINER.* THE *BASEMENT* OF A *HOMELESS SHELTER.* THE *SPOTLESS TILE* OF A *COLD LABORATORY.* THE *SHALLOW BREATHS* OF A *BABY GIRL.*
EVEN WHEN I WAS GIVEN *ALL* OF THIS, THE POWER TO *GO* ANYWHERE, *SEE* ANYTHING, *DO* ANYTHING, MY *HEART* HAS *ALWAYS* REMAINED IN THAT VERY SMALL WORLD.
IN THE SHALLOW BREATHS OF THAT BABY GIRL. I WANTED *THIS CITY, THIS WORLD,* THE *FREEDOM* I SHOULD BE ENJOYING, TO BE *HERS.*

WITH MY DREAM, I PASSED ON MY *SICKNESS.*

IT ROSE TO THE SURFACE ONLY IN *RECENT MONTHS.*

MY DAUGHTER, *DESPITE* ALL HER JUSTIFIABLE ANGER AND HATRED, *STILL* NEEDS HER *MOTHER.*

A MOTHER WHO, DESPITE ALL THE *INJUSTICES* AND *BETRAYALS,* STILL DREAMS FOR HER *DAUGHTER.*

OH, DEANNA, MY BEAUTIFUL BABY GIRL...

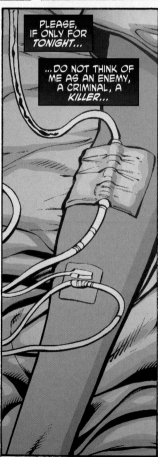

PLEASE, IF ONLY FOR *TONIGHT...*

...DO NOT THINK OF ME AS AN ENEMY, A CRIMINAL, A *KILLER...*

PLEASE, NOW THAT YOU KNOW THE *WHOLE* STORY, THE *HIDDEN DEPTHS* OF THE POOL...

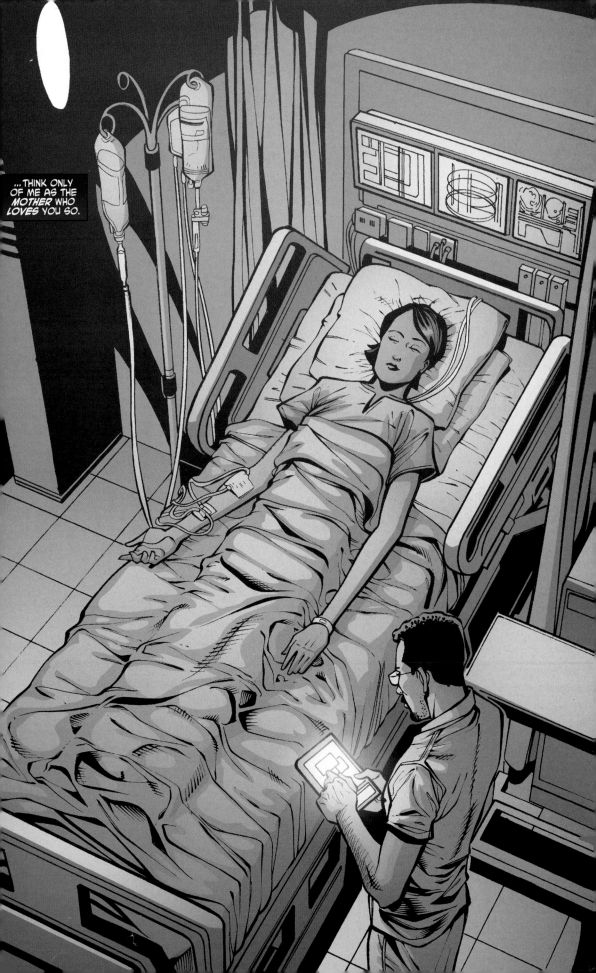

...THINK ONLY OF ME AS THE *MOTHER* WHO *LOVES* YOU SO.

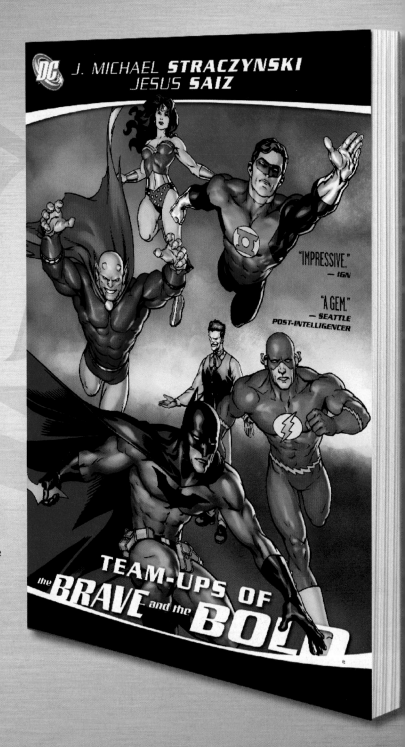

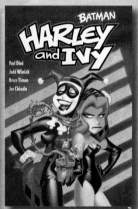

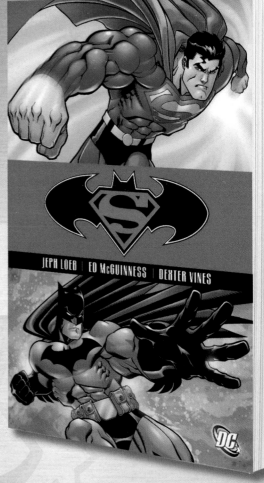